PSYCHOLOGY

✻✻✻✻✻

Development of the Human Soul

ANTONIO ROSMINI

PSYCHOLOGY

Volume 2

Development of the Human Soul

Translated by
DENIS CLEARY
and
TERENCE WATSON

ROSMINI HOUSE
DURHAM

Translated from
Psicologia
Critical edition, vols. 9a & 10, Stresa, 1989

Typeset by Rosmini House, Durham
Printed by Bell & Bain Limited, Glasgow

ISBN 1 899093 30 3

Note

Square brackets [ ] indicate notes or additions by the translators.

References to this and other works of Rosmini are given by paragraph number unless otherwise stated.

Abbreviations used for Rosmini's quoted works are:

AMS: *Anthropology as an Aid to Moral Science*
CS: *Conscience*
ER: *The Essence of Right*, vol. 1 of *The Philosophy of Right*
NE: *A New Essay concerning the Origin of Ideas*
PE: *Principles of Ethics*

Contents

Part Two
Development of the Human Soul

Book 2
(analytical)
Activities of the human soul —
how the soul's potencies differ

Book 3
(synthetical)
Laws governing the activity of the soul.
How the different laws governing the activity of the soul take their origin from the nature of the soul

Book 4
(synthetical)
Laws governing the activity of the soul — laws according to which the rational principle operates

Contents   xiii

Part Two

DEVELOPMENT

OF THE

HUMAN SOUL

Development of the Human Soul

κοσμοῦ κόσμος
Const. Ap., 7: 35

[INTRODUCTION]

731. The first part of *Psychology*, which deals with the essence of the soul, pertains to antiquity; the second, which deals with the development of the soul, is more accentuated today. To this extent, our modern age is a continuation of antiquity, just as the development of our faculties and the constant, ever more distinct growth of their powers (which under new forms add variety to the same humanity) is a continuation of the essence of the soul. Just as the soul's activity progresses naturally so in meditating upon ourselves, we first ask about the nature of the soul, and then about its modifications, that is, about its activities and how they are carried out. The history of philosophy shows this quite clearly.

There is, however, a very notable difference between the soul's progress in the spontaneous development of human life, and the progress of psychological knowledge during various ages of mankind's life. The soul, while attaining its final acts, never abandons itself; its ultimate acts are necessarily joined to the root which produces them. Philosophical considerations and attention are different. Often, philosophy departs from its first argument and finally, through natural limitation and weariness, forgets its original aim. Forgetfulness of this kind means decadence in philosophy, which first abandons the essence of things for which it searched so avidly and generously in the beginning, and then devotes its entire attention to what things do and produce. But such results, separated from their first, substantial cause, are nothing more than empty phenomena and inexplicable appearances.

[731]

This explains what at first looks impossible. Flourishing periods of profound philosophy are followed by totally superficial, material thought, deprived of life and without a spark of genius to warm it despite the heritage of truth to which it has succeeded. Noble, venturesome, sublime minds, enraptured by divine enthusiasm in their contemplation of truth, give way to philosophy which ignores its predecessors. This was the base, foolish but proud banner which the 18th century flaunted before our eyes.

Although many causes contributed to this deplorable state, the first and deepest, it seems to me, is found in the psychological cause on which the rest, as effects and second causes, depend. We are not dealing with lack of natural talent, which is given even-handedly by nature in every age — we only have to look at what has been achieved through great, social changes, or in natural sciences, arts and commerce to see how abundantly talent has been available. Rather, we need to look for an explanation of the mental progress which we mentioned. From generation to generation, humanity passes from one aspect of thought to another in an ordered series in which the first link is concerned with the nature of things while the others deal gradually with the operations and acts proper to different natures. The final links, which are very remote from the first, totally occupy our minds and distract our attention from previous links. Above all, we forget the first link from which all others have arisen. The result is a broken chain of scientific truths and a realisation that in some mysterious fashion human knowledge has become superficial and base. Because we do not see how this has happened, the final truths and conclusions, once detached from the unchanging principle, that is, from the nature and essence of things, have no value, no stability, no reason.

Lack of such a firm foundation in the philosophy of the last century is clear even from its own shameful, proud admission. Philosophers of the time gloried 'in not wanting to consider or discuss the essence of things'. Their presumptuous, overbearing modesty maintained that 'the essence of things is unknowable'. This maxim is the true principle and fount of all superficial knowledge.[1]

[1] *Teodicea*, 138.

But, thanks be to God, this period of philosophical superficiality, of materialism and sensism has now passed, or is certainly about to pass. Everyone feels the need to repair the broken chain and ensure that all its links are firmly connected, from the last to the first. I have done what I could to aid this extremely useful and necessary work. This explains why I studied the ancient part of psychology first, and examined the essence of the soul, which is almost entirely forgotten in normal treatises, before dealing with the modern part, the development of the soul. However, I did try to take care that ancient philosophy was revived and restored in such a way that it would not offend modern tastes.

732. The advantage from the point of view of knowledge and its perfection will become apparent as we go on. For the moment I want to show readers the principal division of this second part of the philosophical investigations we have undertaken.

If we are to describe the development of the human soul accurately and expound it clearly, two equally broad and necessary questions have to be faced:

1. What acts, potencies, functions and habits are produced by the human soul?

2. What laws does the soul follow in its continual activity and operations?

733. The first question has to be considered *analytically* because it aims at breaking up (if I may use the word) the essence of the soul into all the various activities of which it is capable. The second has to be considered *synthetically* because it aims at uniting under certain universal laws the different ways in which the soul acts and continually expands. The second question aims at reducing the infinite multitude of the soul's acts to the simplicity of the norms prescribed by nature. The soul's acts never deviate from these norms.

It is clear from this that all the material we have at hand is distributed of itself into two sections. The first, beginning from the essence of the soul, moves on to its extraordinarily various operations; the second moves from the operations, which are eventually drawn back to the unity of the essence from which they emerged and in which they finally come to rest.

734. Let us begin our first investigation into the activities of

the human soul. The intention is not simply to list these activities historically, but in addition to deduce them and make them originate from the essence of the subject to which they belong. Our work, therefore, is divided into two questions: 1. How are these different activities contained in the essence of the soul? and 2. What are these activities, and how can they be numbered and classified?

Book 1
(analytical)

Activities of the human soul — how the different activities are distinguished from the essence of the soul

CHAPTER 1

Different human activities cannot be deduced without some understanding of the essence of the soul

735. According to the ancients, for whom the powers of the soul can be known only through its acts,[2] an even more general opinion would be this: 'Only the actuality of entia is directly knowable; only through actuality do we understand the potency present within entia.'[3] This explains the mistake we have noticed in philosophers who, in discussing the soul, begin with its powers, as something known, instead of starting from observation of its acts.[4] — Why, then, did I decide to speak of the essence of the soul before everything else?

736. While it is true that acts come to our attention before powers, they are not known prior to essence, which is known along with acts because it remains undivided in them. Indeed, although act and essence are known simultaneously, information about them follows a logical order in which essence is known first, and then, in and through essence, accidental acts (cf. 115). It is indeed an illusion to imagine that an act can be known without some knowledge of the ens of which it is an act, that is, without reference to its subject. We cannot perceive or know any act except as an entity, and must, therefore, either take it as an ens, a substance, or think of something in which and through which it is (as I explained elsewhere[5]). I have, therefore, used the acts emanating from the essence of the soul as an occasion for acquiring knowledge of the essence itself, although I had to speak of the essence as the first and natural foundation of every other psychological knowledge. This illustrates further the defect of psychological treatises which either omit all discussion on the essence of the soul, or deal with this essence

[2] *A New Essay concerning the Origin of Ideas*, vol. 2, 528.

[3] Aristotle, *Metaph.*, 9. — St. Thomas, *In L. de Causis*, lect. 6.

[4] *NE*, vol. 1, 47–64; *Anthropology as an Aid to Moral Science*, 567.

[5] *NE*, vol. 2, 410–412; 615–624; *Sistema filosofico*, 90–93.

superficially as though it were of little or no importance, or assert that it is nothing more than a word.

737. Authors of works like this also lack any principle which makes rational deduction of human potencies and faculties possible. Consequently such writers can offer only a kind of empirical, arbitrary, causal list of these potencies. No deduction is possible. Nexus and unity between the potencies as a result of their common origin, justification of their number, or indication of their intimate relationships is impossible. In a word, there is no science of the soul. Moreover, such writers lack any possibility of resolving the apparent contradiction between the simplicity of the soul and its innumerable potencies and operations.

738. On the other hand, the problem can easily be solved if we know that the essence of the soul lies solely in its being the *first principle* of the soul's operations (cf. 127–129), and that a real principle can have a single activity suitable for producing several effects (cf. 140–183).

But we also know that an ens, an entity or several entities can in-exist in another ens if the latter is of a spiritual nature. This is the opposite of what occurs in reciprocal relationships between bodies, whose nature is to be impenetrable. The discovery of this extremely important ontological truth is the result of direct consideration of fact through intellective observation which alone provides the first data of systematic knowledge. This also gives rise to teaching about individuality because a principle is individuated in virtue of the active, passive and receptive relationships it maintains with what is foreign in itself and, more generally, with its term (cf. 560–584). These true discoveries led me to examine the terms and foreign entities in-existing in the soul and constituting it in great part by individuating it. Having found what these entities were, and accurately described and listed them, I was in a position to explain how a single power of the soul could be multiplied by reference to the multiplicity of these entities, and thus appear multiple in its acts and effects without ceasing to be single in itself, that is, in the principle forming the essence of the soul.

739. As a result of all this, I found in the essence of the soul all the elements which occasion and divide its activities, all the germs of its potencies. I saw that the following entities, which

differ from the soul but are intimately connected with it in varying intimate relationships, have their permanent seat within it: 1. *ideal being*, which is united to the soul through intuition; and 2. *animality*, which is joined to the soul through a fundamental, immanent perception. In animality itself, I distinguished several elements: 1. a *sensitive principle*, which itself contains foreign elements to which it is bound with its own relationships; 2. the *extended, corporeal element* which, with its immanent relationship of sensility, is contained in the same principle; 3. *matter*, that is, a power not acting directly on the sensitive principle, but on the extended, corporeal element which it changes violently and in doing so makes itself felt indirectly by the sensitive principle. Here, then, in the depth of the essence of the soul lie all the roots of human activity, and the explanation of the various potencies and faculties, which are distinguished through their roots on which they depend for their quantity and quality. This is how the human powers are deduced from the very essence of the soul. This essence, when examined thoroughly, furnishes us with the principle that permits their legitimate deduction.

740. Before going further, however, it seems necessary and useful to clarify the very notions of *potency* and *act* and, even before that, the notions of *matter* and *form*, granted that development of the soul is a kind of movement drawing it from one state to another as potency latent in the soul is activated. Another reason for dealing with potency/act and matter/form is to ensure that the imperfection of philosophical language does not, like dead branches on a path, hold us back or prevent those who accompany me in these laborious but delightful researches from going forward on the right path without losing themselves in inextricable ambiguities.

CHAPTER 2

The origin of the ontological notions of matter and form, of potency and act

741. The word *act* means every entity, and from this point of

view cannot be defined. It must be taken as understood.[6] However, its meaning, which is not restricted to mere entity, also bears a mental relationship to *potency*. The mind is led to this distinction between act and potency by its experience of the contingent things with which it finds itself in communication. It draws this distinction from the finite realities which fall under its feelings; the distinction is found in feeling itself, which is reality. This shows that we could never deduce it *a priori* from 'ideal being', which we intuit through nature without assistance from anything else. Ideal being intuited by us makes us know *pure being*, not the *mode* of being *per se* nor the *order* that being holds within itself. This order pertains entirely to the *reality* we experience in feeling.[7]

742. This explains why the interior order of being is never revealed to us. Human beings are something real, but limited; they communicate with a part of reality only, and in a limited manner.[8] This essential limitation of human knowledge imposes modesty befitting our human limitation on philosophers who intend to propound ontological teaching resulting from their meditation. In other words, we should not 'claim to describe being or the order of being in its totality, but acknowledge that our thought takes in only a tiny fraction of this immense order, the little our human intelligence has been given to know.' This modesty is a religious duty for human beings as such, and is even more incumbent on the individual. However intellectually gifted the individual may be, he has to believe that his research is very far from reaching what is attainable by the understanding of the whole human species. To do otherwise would be very foolish.

743. We are conscious, therefore, that we can reach out only to those elements of the order of being which are presented to our knowledge in the limited portion of *reality* we are given to perceive and experience, and that even here we are dependent on the strength of our individual, limited intelligence. With these elements or fragments of doctrine as it were, we have to

[6] *AMS*, 10–13.
[7] *NE*, vol. 3, 1438–1460.
[8] *Teodicea*, 397–410.

make up the imperfect *ontology* which is conceded to mankind and to us in particular.

744. The reality communicated to us is comprised in our feeling where the mind, as we said elsewhere,[9] can indeed take in real beings but only to the extent that feeling represents them. The mind cannot in any way perceive or recognise HOW other realities, outside feeling, are made. We have to ask ourselves, therefore: 'What are the realities communicated to us in our reality?'

745. We have already seen that they are reduced to three: 1. bodies, 2. the soul in so far as it is sensitive in a bodily way, and 3. the same soul in so far as it is intellective. These are the only realities *perceptible* by us. Besides them, we have, however, intuitible *ideality*, the means with which we know these realities through perception.

746. Hence, all the ontological notions concerning the *order of being*, and all the notions of *matter* and *form* as well as those of *potency* and *act*, have to be drawn from the experience we have of matter, animal feeling and intellective feeling. But these realities, which are all finite and contingent, can furnish us only with notions pertaining to the order of finite, contingent being. Consequently, they are not equivalent to being except through some kind of analogy, about which we shall speak more at length elsewhere.

CHAPTER 3

Origin of the notion of first matter

Article 1
Reasoning teaches us to distinguish between *body* and *corporeal principle*

747. Let me begin by examining the conditions of the ens called 'body'. We shall do this principally by reminding readers

[9] *Teodicea*, 86–87, 153.

of what has been said in *Anthropology*, where the subject is dealt with in detail.

First, however, we should note that body has to be considered as it is directly presented to us. This alone is the source of the meaning of *body*. If, then, we want to argue that what we perceive presupposes some preceding power or entity as its cause, we must remember that we have reserved the phrase *corporeal principle* for the immediate principle of body, which is not present in perception but seems to hide itself behind the scene.[10] The ontological notions we are seeking have to be drawn from the body which we can perceive, not from this hidden being.

Article 2
The perception of body furnishes three different entities:
the *felt*, the *sensiferous* and the *foreign force*

748. In *Anthropology*, I distinguished the *sensiferous* entity, the proximate cause of corporeal sense-experiences, from what is *felt*, that is, the sensible element (cf. 61), which is the extended, proper term of feeling. I also included under the word *sensiferous* both the power directly producing the felt element in the fundamental feeling, and the power which, operating in the fundamental feeling and causing it to change, occasions sensation. Now, however, we have to take our analysis further and distinguish these two powers (which are reduced to the same activity working in two ways, as we shall see). For one, I shall retain the word *sensiferous*; the other I shall call *external force*. The former is the power underlying the felt element in the fundamental feeling; the latter is the power altering the fundamental feeling itself by occasioning in it a passing sensation.

749. Having stated how I shall use these words in the future, let me say that perception of body furnishes three strictly connected entities: 1. something felt as extended; 2. an activity, which I call 'sensiferous', directly sharing in the soul with the production of the felt, extended element; and 3. a foreign force which violently changes what is felt as extended.

[10] *NE*, vol. 2, 855–857.

750. The concept of 'felt, extended element' united with the concept of sensiferous is properly speaking the concept of *corporeity*; the concept of agent that changes what is felt is the concept of *materiality*.

751. The felt, extended element is perceived as a kind of property of what is sensiferous, with which it forms our very own body. However, we do not call it 'body' until we know it as solid. This does not occur until we add to the *subjective experience* of what is felt as extended the data of *extrasubjective experience* through which we perceive the limits of our own body by means of *surface* sensations.[11] But in every *extrasubjective* experience, we perceive (in addition to our body) some foreign force, that is, matter. In other words, we perceive an impulse which changes our bodily feeling in such a way that we perceive an agent extraneous to our feeling in the very place where the new sensation arises. The only known property, however, of this extraneous agent is found in its power of changing *what is felt*.

752. Again, we soon notice that the sensiferous element, the direct cause of *the felt element* in us, has the power to change violently some other part of the sensiferous element and thus some other part of what is felt by us. We conclude from this that our very own body is *material*, that is, it has the same property of acting violently as the foreign force.

753. However, even this does not seem a rigorous demonstration of the identity of the foreign force and the sensiferous element. We could in fact conceive two different entities (the sensiferous and the foreign force) in the same place, and still grant to the first the production of what is felt and to the second the violent change in the sensiferous. Creative wisdom would, in this hypothesis, have posited a wonderful harmony of operation as both entities reveal themselves simultaneously in the same place according to certain laws. However, although the sensiferous entity in producing what is felt reveals itself as acting on the sentient principle, which is the soul, its action is considerably different from that exercised on itself as agent which makes it act on the soul in a different way. It would seem, therefore, that we have here a series of four terms: the *soul*,

[11] *AMS*, 103–228.

which in its own way is passive; *the felt element*, which is produced in the soul; the *sensiferous element*, which produces the felt element; a *foreign force* which changes the sensiferous. This foreign force reveals itself sometimes in a place common both to what is felt and to the sensiferous element, and sometimes in a different place. From these four elements, we certainly draw every concept of body and matter that human beings have.

Let us see, therefore, if there is some identity of substance between the sensiferous element and the foreign force. The identity of the place they occupy would seem to give us a positive answer; the difference in their effects a negative one.

Article 3
The difference between the soul, the sensiferous element and the foreign force

754. We begin by noting carefully the difference between soul and sensiferous element. This will enable us to proceed in an orderly fashion and eliminate difficulties that could confuse the argument or distract the attention of the reader.

First, the action of the soul moving its own body must be direct, at least on some part of its body. There has to be some place in our body where the first movement is communicated. In fact, even if we suppose that we move our hand as a result of movements in the nerves which stretch throughout it, and that the movement impressed on these nerves is communicated longitudinally, we still have to call upon one or more nerve extremities to which motion is first communicated by the soul itself.

755. Second, keep in mind that the soul's action on the body does not have *what is felt* as its direct term, but the *sensiferous element*, that is, the force which produces what is felt. What is felt remains itself unchanged if the power or force directly producing it does not change or move. *What is felt* is passive, and supposes a sensiferous element which produces the felt element with an immanent or passing action.

756. But the *sensiferous element* is perceived in three ways:

1. As the direct cause of what is felt. As such, it acts directly on the soul without any violence. Violence is present only when the action on the soul is in opposition to the spontaneous action of the soul itself. The soul concurs in what is felt with the initial spontaneity which I called *life instinct.*[12]

2. As the recipient changed by the action of the soul. — In fact, when the soul uses the imagination to produce some internal sense-experience or image for itself, it operates on and modifies the sensiferous element so that it will either produce the image or cease to produce one image and produce another in its place. Moreover, in all those actions with which the soul produces new corporeal feelings for itself, or changes them (through the movement of its own body) the soul by changing the sensiferous element, also changes the felt element directly produced in it by the sensiferous element.[13] All this takes place without violence relative to the soul's direct action because the change occurring in the sensiferous element is in conformity with the spontaneous action of the soul, not opposed to it. Now, it is clear that the sensiferous element changed by the soul's direct action is identical with the first sensiferous element because it is precisely that which directly produces the *things felt* by the soul.

3. As the recipient of an impulse of an external force which changes the soul violently without any initial co-operation from the spontaneity of the soul. The soul, as ceaselessly active, is opposed to whatever does not concur with its action.[14]

757. In these last two cases, we can already see the difference between *soul* and *sensiferous element.* The former is active, the latter passive. We can also see the difference between *soul* and *foreign force.* Although both have the power to change the sensiferous element, the action of the soul is *spontaneous,* that of the foreign force *violent.* This means that in the first case the human soul is conscious of its own operation; in the second, it is conscious of being passive relative to an agent altogether different from itself.

[12] *Ibid.,* 370–384.
[13] *Ibid.,* 350–366.
[14] *Ibid.,* 392–400.

[757]

Article 4
Body is an extended agent; the corporeal principle can be an unextended agent

758. If we consider that the sensiferous element, which produces directly what is felt, is changed by two agents (by the soul, and by a force totally foreign to the soul), we come to understand that it is not repugnant for a foreign force to have a spiritual principle. The soul itself is a spiritual principle, but has power to operate in and change the sensiferous element which produces what is felt. The extension of what is felt, which of its nature exists in what is simple,[15] furnishes no obstacle here. However, our knowledge of the soul's operation reaches out not only to the term we see as *extended*, but also to the principle which we recognise as *simple*. We know a foreign force only in its term, but do not perceive its principle because we perceive the foreign force only in *what is felt*, that is, in what is changed by the foreign force. Perceiving this force in its effect, that is, in the change of the sensiferous element, which is the immediate cause of what is felt, we cannot determine the nature of its principle by adhering solely to the perception we have of it. In other words, we cannot affirm that it is spiritual, although we can affirm that such a possibility is not repugnant.

Article 5
Identity of substance between the sensiferous element and the foreign force

759. For the moment we shall leave aside the problem about the internal constitution of the principle of the force which changes the sensiferous element, the direct cause of what is felt. We shall deal instead with the following question: 'Can we prove the identity between this foreign force and the directly sensiferous force?'

We have already observed that the directly sensiferous element (considered as such and not relative to what it may be

---

[15] *AMS*, 94–97.

in itself) offers exactly the same measure of extension as that of the felt element which it produces in the soul.[16] This proves once more that the sensiferous element, precisely as sensiferous, is not the soul, which is simple. The same argument also proves that any external force which changes what is directly sensiferous must have extension, and an extension identical to that of the direct sensiferous element. It also proves that the external force, precisely as external force, is not spirit. Nevertheless, the identity of the extension is not properly speaking the identity of the force because the identity of the force can be deduced only from the identity of the effect. Here, however, the effect is different. The effect of the direct, sensiferous element is to produce what is felt; the effect of the external force is to change the sensiferous element. We need, therefore, to show that the external force also has the power to produce directly what is felt. Only then can we affirm the identity we are seeking. This path, however, will not take us much further forward.

760. It is indeed true that the sensation which arises when one part of my own body acts on another part is exactly similar to that which is produced when I am acted upon by an external body or foreign force. It is clear that what I call my own body is that where I feel, where there is continuous production of something felt (the fundamental feeling). Consequently there is, in the same place as the (fundamental) felt element, a force which produces the same effect as the external force, whose effect is to change what is directly sensiferous. We can conclude, therefore, for the moment that this force is of the same nature as the external force. As I said, the identical nature of such forces is deduced from the identity of the effects. There is another identical effect in these two forces: both my body and an external body produce equal effects upon a third body. Nevertheless, the doubt already expressed about the identity of the sensiferous element and this foreign, violent force remains. If two different forces, one sensiferous and the other changing what is sensiferous, are simultaneously present in the same place as what is felt, could not the one changing the sensiferous element be identical with the external force and the other not? We have to take some other way, therefore, of showing that the

[16] *NE*, vol. 2, 841–844.

sensiferous force and the force changing the sensiferous element are identical. The only suitable proof is the identity of the space they occupy and the in-existence of the foreign force in what is felt. Let us see if this will help us.

761. The whole action of the sensitive soul, which has the felt element as its formal principle, begins, therefore, in what is felt. The spontaneity with which it collaborates in feeling is spontaneity capable of changing the sensiferous element.[17] Granted that the sensitive soul's action cannot exceed the sensiferous element (because it cannot exceed what is felt, to which the sensiferous element adheres as proximate or formal cause), we have to see if the soul can also change directly the external or *foreign force*. If the soul, in changing the sensiferous element, also changes the foreign force, we have to say that the sensiferous element and the foreign force are identical, that is, are activities of the same subject. This is precisely what happens: the soul never changes what is felt by it except through movement produced in parts of the body. Movement, however, is a phenomenon pertaining to the foreign force. If, therefore, the effect produced by the soul cannot exceed the sensiferous element, but does nevertheless change the foreign force, we have to say that the *foreign force* and the *sensiferous element* are identical. In other words, they pertain to the same substantial subject. This proof is founded on the following principle: 'If the effect of a determined action, limited to one entity, appears also in another entity, we have to say that the two entities are identical in substance.'[18]

762. Another argument based on the same principle can be drawn from this consideration. Although we understand how the external force, in which neither what is felt nor what is sensiferous is found, can produce movement which is only a change of position of the same external force, we do not understand how it can act on the sensiferous element without supposing that what is sensiferous forms one substance with it. In

---

[17] *AMS*, 380–400.

[18] Nevertheless, this argument does not exclude the possibility of some harmony, pre-established by God, between the change of the sensiferous element and that of the external force. This mere possibility seems to have no real value, however, in the light of the law of economy according to which the Creator works.

fact, imagining that the foreign force could produce two actions as different as 1. moving another external force (motion) and 2. changing the sensiferous element, would mean confusing in a single concept two concepts of very different forces. In other words, we would change the concept of merely foreign force by making it into two forces, which however must also be excluded according to the principle that forbids unnecessary multiplication of entia. We have to say, therefore, that the external force in these two, very different effects acts upon a single substance, and that the sensiferous element and the external force are consequently identical in nature.

763. A third argument arises from the life of the primal elements for which, I think, I have provided sufficient proof (cf. 500–553). Granted the existence of this life, the root of the difficulty is removed because there is no longer a merely foreign force; every foreign force has become sensiferous. This consequence appears to offer a new proof of our opinion. Even if we suppose the contrary (that a part of matter is not animated), the simple fact of animation, which brute matter receives in the event of our hypothesis, is still sufficient to prove the identity of the sensiferous element and the foreign force. In this case, the same foreign force, which previously furnished no phenomena other than those of relocation of another portion of similar force, now becomes sensiferous itself. That it is the foreign force which becomes sensiferous can be deduced as follows. When, by means of contact, the brute force changes and alters the sensiferous element, the felt element is very quickly extended towards that force. But wherever the felt element is present, there also is the sensiferous element. Hence the phenomena of the sensiferous element also appear where brute force is present. It is true that *hoc post hoc, ergo propter hoc* [one thing coming after another depends on the other] is not a valid argument, but the demonstration becomes rigorous when this argument is united to the first and we consider that brute force comes under the control of the soul.

764. A fourth argument can be drawn from the nature of *contact*. If two forces were from the point of view of position simply contiguous, they could not be said to be in contact. The concept of contact presupposes reciprocal action between two forces which, in the case of brute forces, is shown by the

phenomenon of cohesion. But if we apply brute force to a nerve, the effect of this cohesion or even impulse is *sensation*. It is true that the sensation may arise through an intestine movement of the sensory organ. But this in turn could not arise if the movement of brute force had not passed into the sensiferous element which thus produces alteration in what is felt. If the sensiferous element communicates with brute force by way of motion and receives its action, we have to say that the sensiferous element, too, is extended and capable of motion and impulse. But this is precisely the concept of brute or foreign force.

Article 6
How the sensiferous element and brute force clothe themselves in what is felt

765. These arguments prove the identity of substance between the foreign force (matter), which offers only a concept of inanimate body, and the sensiferous element, whose concept is that of animate body. We have already seen the relationship of identity between what is directly sensiferous and what in the first instance is presented to our experience as pure *foreign* or brute *force*. Now we have to see how both the *sensiferous element* and *brute force* clothe themselves, as it were, in *the felt element* which, mingling with the sensiferous element provides the concept of body, and with brute force provides that of *matter*.

766. Relative to the sensiferous element, it is clear that it appears clothed in sensation because it is the direct, proximate cause of what is felt. It is, therefore, present where the felt is present. The sensiferous element is not divided from what is felt; it is the term of the act of the agent which produces it.

767. It is rather more difficult to understand how this intimate, individual union arises between what is felt and the foreign or brute force. The nexus is never sufficiently considered.

The union comes about first because the soul, in changing the sensiferous element, does so precisely where the sensiferous element is, that is, in the same place as that occupied by what is felt.[19] This identity of place makes the sensiferous element necessarily appear clothed with extension itself and with the qualities of what is felt. For the same reason, the foreign, brute force which produces sensations is individually united with what is felt, and clothes itself with what is felt. When the change in what is felt comes from a principle foreign to the soul, this force is felt only at the same place occupied by the felt element, which it changes. It is through the place itself where the force acts that what is felt unites itself with the force. This is why we attributed colour, taste and all second qualities to external matter. These are, in fact, our own sensations, or better, they are our felt element. When the foreign force reveals itself in this felt element, we make a single thing of it and of what is felt because we perceive the two entities with the same act and in an identical extension.

When exterior bodies cease to act on our bodies, we can imagine them only in the way they have appeared when we perceived them. Our perception of them is our one, original and direct way of knowing them. As a result, even when they are separated from our senses, we furnish them with the sensible qualities with which we have clothed them in our act of perception. Our memory of them is only the memory of our perception.

Article 7
How philosophers are right to deny second qualities to bodies, and how common sense is right in attributing them to bodies

768. When external bodies have been cut off and separated from our felt element and are no longer in act in it, we consider them as agents *in potency*. But how do we imagine them as separate from us? What is the meaning of the phrase, 'separated from what is felt'?

---

[19] The activity of the soul arises from *what is felt*, as I have explained in *Anthropology*.

It means 'existing in a place different from that in which our felt element exists'. This happens as a result of movement, as I have shown in *Ideology* and *Anthropology*. Nevertheless, although we think of external bodies as existing in a space other than that of our *felt element*, we imagine that they have taken our felt element with them. As I said, when we first perceive them, they occupy the same place as the felt element, and we have perceived their force and the felt element in a single act of perception.

It is, however, contradictory to consider them *in potency* to acting upon us, yet clothed and accompanied by *what is felt*. This explains why philosophers, by reasoning, rightly strip material-bodies of sensible qualities in act, and grant them only sensible qualities in potency. In other words, philosophers conceive bodies as agents suitable for modifying our feeling and producing sensations, but not as possessing any yellow or green colour, any sweet or sharp taste, any acute or dull sound, and so on. It is, nevertheless, extremely difficult to carry out this separation mentally. Potency is not determined or known except in the act which it produces. Consequently if we want to form some determined concept of material potency, we always have to refer it to sensation, or to what is felt. But we cannot make this reference unless we think of potency as joined to what is felt in the act of modifying it. We think of it in the same way as we first perceived and knew it. This, however, requires potency to be in act, individually united to what is felt through identity of place. In this way, bodies are always clothed or accompanied by colours, sounds, tastes and other ways of being felt, even when, for example, we imagine them closed in a dark cupboard and giving us no sensation. It is difficult even for philosophers to free themselves from an image of this kind.

Later, reflection makes us realise that these qualities cannot be joined to bodies which are separated from what we feel. At this point, our reason conceives them as divided from what is felt and we finally form the concept of inanimate, brute-matter, devoid of what is felt.[20]

769. We can go further. The felt element, although the opposite

---

[20] This concept is not found in babies, who consider all things as animate. I hope to show this clearly in *Pedagogia*.

of what is sentient, is found in the sentient principle; otherwise it would not be felt. But the external, corporeal force, which modifies what is felt, is neither felt nor sentient when separated from what is felt and merely in potency to act. It remains a mere *potency*. Now, if we observe people carefully when they reason about bodies, we can easily see that they use two concepts of bodies alternatively without realising that they do so. Sometimes they speak of matter as inanimate — totally separate from sensation; sometimes they attribute sensible qualities to body as though it were felt in act, without realising that the felt element is in the sentient, and that if we attribute what is felt to an ens, we also have to posit in the ens a sentient principle.

Article 8
Origin of the concept of material substance

770. Mere *potency* is a concept that includes relationship only with the act or effect that it produces; this is a relationship external to potency which does not, therefore, include of itself the act of its own *subsistence*. At the same time, according to the *principle of cognition* nothing can be conceived by the intellect except through the act by which it subsists. On the one hand, therefore, the understanding has to conceive a potency capable of modifying what is felt; on the other, it cannot attribute to potency either the act according to which the felt element subsists (because potency is separate from this act) or the act according to which the sentient element subsists (because potency is totally foreign to sentient activity). The understanding has, therefore, to suppose in the potency for modifying what is felt, an act proper to the potency. Otherwise this potency could not be conceived by the understanding. This act, however, is unknown and is not the term of any perception. If it were, we would have a concept not of potency, but of some act. In other words, the act is merely supposed in virtue of the law of the intellect, although this supposition is not without reason nor merely subjective. Indeed, it comes about by logical

necessity, that is, through the *principle of cognition*, as I said.[21] This act of subsistence remains totally unknown except for the fact that it exists. The act thus conceived through supposition is *material substance*, whose existence is certainly posited by logical necessity although nature hides it from us. At the same time, we determine it through its relationship in such a way that it cannot be confused with any other entity. We know that such a substance, or act of subsistence, is the *subject* of the potency which, as sensiferous, changes what is felt, and which, as a foreign force, changes the sensiferous element. The sensiferous element and the foreign force are potencies which converge in the same substance, as I have shown.

771. We can express the *principle of substance* in a way more helpful to our present discussion by saying: 'A transient act occurring in an ens cannot be conceived without another, physically anterior, stable act. This stable act is the substance through which the transient act exists.' The stable act in an ens is also called first act; it is the act through which the whole ens (the full essence) subsists. The transient act is called second act. We know the transient act by perceiving the passive effect it produces in us. Thus what we experience as felt in us is some passivity of our own, some mode of our own which is imposed on us. What is felt, therefore, presupposes the act which produces or imposes this passivity, this mode. An act of this kind is the sensiferous element. But the sensiferous, as such, expresses a transient act. At the same time, the act of the foreign force changing the sensiferous element, and the act changing the foreign force, are also transient. These three acts cannot be conceived, therefore, unless we presuppose a first act as substance. Our previous arguments have, however, shown that all three of these acts pertain to one and the same substance, the substance of bodies.

772. Let me add one comment here. We must not believe that the mind passes from what is felt to the sensiferous element, from the sensiferous to the foreign force, and from this to another foreign force until it finally discovers the substance through reasoning. It embraces contemporaneously all these terms with a totally simple act of *perception*, and begins to

[21] *NE*, vol. 2, 559–866.

know them and to know body only when it has embraced them all, not before, as I have shown in *A New Essay* and elsewhere.[22]

773. Material substance, or first act, is therefore something unknown. We know only its second acts (what is felt, the sensiferous element and the foreign force).

774. But because the first act, the material act correctly supposed by the mind, is determined for us only by its second acts, it is thought by us as individually united to these acts. Moreover, because the effect of these second acts are felt elements, whose mode is extension, we unite each of these effects produced in another ens (in the sentient principle or soul) to the second acts and therefore to the material substance which, as a result, is seen by us as extended and furnished with all its sensible qualities.

Article 9
How extension pertains to the primary qualities of body

775. At this point we have to consider carefully the difference between *extension* and *sensations*. I have defined extension as 'the mode of bodily feeling'.[23] Observation presents it to us in this way and, as we know, observation allows us to capture the concept at its origin: 'The true nature of the objects of our thought is found only by returning to the first formation of their concepts.' Measured extension, therefore, pertains to feeling, from which it is divided only through abstraction. But what has led us to place such extension amongst the primary qualities of body, that is, amongst those qualities which furnish the essential concept of body?[24]

I have to admit that if we were to strip the concept of body of every felt element, we would necessarily strip it of its extension, which is thought of only as a mode of what is felt, and therefore as felt. But in this case, the concept of body and of matter, as formed by mankind and expressed in the two words, would no

[22] *Sistema filosofico*, 90–98.
[23] *NE*, vol. 2, 749–753.
[24] *Ibid.*, 882–900.

longer be available to us despite our intention of always 'speaking about things as they are perceived and expressed by mankind in general.' We *must* use ordinary words to express things conceived by human common sense founded on perception. Granted this, we cannot use these words to mean something else without falsifying their meaning; we would be introducing endless equivocation and asking unintelligible questions. This is why I have defined body as 'the proximate cause of sensations and the subject of sensible qualities.'[25]

According to this definition, body is sensiferous and, as we have seen, identical with foreign force. But we are forced to attribute extension to the sensiferous element (as the proximate cause of sensations) even if we strip what is sensiferous of its sensible qualities. In fact, we consider the sensiferous as present wherever what is felt is present. What is felt, however, is extended. Consequently, its proximate cause must be 'a power which, relative to its act, is diffused in the same extension as that which is felt (because the active element is present in the same place as the passive element).' This is, in fact, how we have demonstrated the extension of body.[26]

It may be objected that the attribute which pertains to the term of the sensiferous action of body cannot be predicated of body (substance) because 1. the sensiferous element is not properly speaking substance itself but an act of substance which is known as a result of its term, and 2. *body* is a substantive, that is, a word expressing substance.

We have to consider, however, that if we are to conceive the sensiferous element mentally, we have to take it as substance, although this does not give us licence to add to or subtract from the sensiferous element. What we add is and must be simply the means by which we know what the sensiferous element is; it must be what is sufficient and no more for us to perceive what is sensiferous as *ens*. We are left, therefore, with the concept of body given to us by *perception* and named as 'body', that is, entirely enclosed in what is sensiferous. And to the sensiferous element, as we saw, pertains the concept of 'force operating in extension, and therefore extended.'

[25] *Ibid.*, 662–669.
[26] *Ibid.*

After this, we may want to ascend higher through *reflection*. If so, we shall undoubtedly find that the subject-ens of the sensiferous power, considered in itself and not as we perceive it, could be an unextended ens. In this case, we come to see that extension pertains originally to what is felt and to what is sentient, and consequently to what is unextended.[27] Now, however, we are no longer thinking the concept of body, but the concept of something else, which I call *corporeal principle*.

Article 10
Origin of the concept of first matter

776. So far, we have provided sufficient explanation of *body*, given through perception, as sensiferous and as foreign force. We saw that this force, which manifests itself either as sensiferous or as foreign, is perceived by us as extended in the term of its operation. We also saw how, through this extension, it is called *body* (sensiferous) or *brute matter* (foreign force). Again, we saw how this extended force comes to be clothed with sensible qualities, and properly speaking with what is felt. Finally, we saw how philosophical meditation may rise from body to *corporeal principle*, the unknown thing which produces the body we perceive. We can now move on to show the origin of the opposite concepts of *form* and *matter*, which are not foreign to common sense and which the most ancient philosophers used so extensively and in such general terms in their philosophies.

To do this aptly, we first have to observe the different way in which we clothe body with *extension* and with *what is felt* (according to the concept given to us by perception).

777. As we said, measured extension is the mode of what is felt. This mode is always present, although with varying limits of shape and size. Feeling itself, however, varies specifically in another totally different way because colour, for example, is specifically different from taste. Moreover, in the same kind of sensation (in sight, for example), what is felt can frequently vary

[27] *AMS*, 94–96.

without any variation in the mode of extension;[28] the same surface can present successively different colours and gradations of colour *ad infinitum*. If then, we consider measured extension in general, we find something invariable in corporeal sensation. In other words, every corporeal sensation always has some extension. This constancy of extension amid all the variables provided by the other properties or characteristics of what is felt makes us consider extension as something permanent, as a permanent extended element. Since, however, we consider the act according to which anything subsists (that is, substance) as something permanent relative to its accidents, we attribute extension to body as an essential quality preceding all the variable qualities in body.

When we speak about this force, or bodily force — either as the sensiferous element or as foreign force which, as we have seen, are identical — we say that 'an extended force' is permanent and substantial in bodies. At the same time, we must always remember that in calling the extended force the substance of bodies, our mind presupposes the first act necessary to the subsistence of 'this extended force', a subsistence which it identifies with the extended force. The mind has no aim except to perceive this extended force; it does not want to search for what perhaps lies beyond it. The *corporeal principle*, therefore, is not the corporeal substance spoken about by mankind when it uses the noun *body*; it is an unknown principle lying beyond this substance.

778. But, before we go further, we have to consider carefully how we form the concept of the various substances we *perceive*. Because *perception* is an *action* exercised in us as beings capable of receiving it, that is, of feeling or understanding it, this *action*

---

[28] This led certain Scholastics to exclude the concept of matter from the definition of extension. 'Since, therefore, all dimensions are of the same species in any matter whatsoever, matter does not form part of their definition, etc' (St. Thomas Aquinas, *In IV Sent.*, d. 12, q. 1, art. 1). As far as I can see, the concept of matter does not form part in any way of the concept of *unmeasured extension*. In the concept of *measured extension*, however, it is necessary to find something which determines limits. This can only be either real matter or imaginary matter (which forms mathematical bodies). The concept of measured and determined extension does not, however, form part of the concept of matter.

is *what* we *first* know about the agent. We fix our mind on this action because prior to it nothing else is perceived. This perceived action thus becomes the base, the first act, of the substance which we think. This in turn means that we elevate this action to an ens by supposing in it the mere act of subsistence, which is substance (the act is certainly not lacking because this action actually subsists). The human concept of substance[29] is, therefore, the *first action*, the action thought as subsistent and perceived in the sense. This concept, although limited, is true because we do not rise with it to the absolutely first act, which we cannot perceive. We reach first act only relative to ourselves. This first act, which undoubtedly subsists, is what we perceive, and perceive as first act. We describe it, therefore, with a noun, a substantive. In other words, what we perceive is the *agent in act*. This act can be second act relative to the agent in potency, but relative to ourselves it is first act, and therefore the agent itself to us.

Investigation about acts anterior to perceived substances pertains to transcendental philosophy, that is, to *theosophy*.

Article 11
The concept of first matter

779. We come now to the concept of first matter. The sensiferous element and the foreign force appear to us clothed 1. with limited extension; 2. with limits to this extension, that is, shape; and 3. with what we have called secondary sensible qualities. These qualities are never perceived except in a shape; shape is always perceived in extension; limited extension presents itself to us as so indivisible from the sensiferous element and from the foreign force that apart from some kind of extension we cannot in any way perceive or think of them. Extension, therefore, is always and invariably present in direct perception, although shape and other sensible qualities can vary. Consequently, because limited extension (in general) pertains invariably to what we first think and perceive, and substantial essence is

---

[29] *NE*, vol. 3, 1213–1244.

precisely 'that which we first think' (cf. 52), I said that the sensiferous element and the extended force are a substantial essence and can conclude that shape and other sensible qualities are accidents. I call the substantial essence 'body'.

Although these accidents are variable, some of them always accompany body. The substantial essence of body never exists on its own. If we want to think it on its own, we have to make it a mental object from which we separate such accidents. The substantial essence of body is separate only in our idea; it is an abstract that can be realised only on condition that it is clothed with certain accidents. We say, therefore, that 'the substantial essence of body possesses its accidents in potency'. This means that 'such an idea, when realised, can and must be clothed with some, not all, of its possible accidents.'

780. However, if body is 'an extended force', its nature cannot be known as it should be unless we know the nature of extension which, through the imagination, can be divided into parts so that the force in one part of an extension is altogether separate from the force in some other part, whether contiguous or not. This means that bodily forces do not act in one another; they act in their own extension without exceeding it in any way. 'The substantial essence of body', therefore, possesses the property of being divisible into parts in such a way that it has no unity *per se*. Its acting principle is not seen, it is not body and, if it exists, pertains to transcendental philosophy, as we said. Rather, it is action perceived by us in its term, and as such is essentially divisible. This entity, which presents its activity in a single part, in one limited extension, is not identical in number (but only in quality) with the entity which presents its activity in some other part, in some other extension. This is the sum total of all the data from which we can draw our concept of first matter.

781. Bodily force stripped of every extension is annihilated because it no longer operates in any place.[30] It cannot, therefore, be first matter because first matter is not nothing.[31]

---

[30] St. Thomas says: 'First matter *per se* is in a place, or is part of what is in a place' (*In I Sent.*, d. 37, q. 3, art. 1, ad 2).

[31] Hence St. Thomas' statement: 'Although matter, in its potentiality, does not offer any likeness of God, it does retain some likeness to the divine in so far as it has being' (*S. T.*, I, q. 14, art. 11, ad 4).

[780–781]

782. Moreover, first matter cannot be mere extension, which is not *per se* divided. Extension is divided only in the imagination (cf. 563–565); matter is subject to real division.

783. Third, first matter, created by God and really existent, cannot be infinite. This is another proof that it is not extension, which is naturally perceived as immeasurable and thus as infinite. It is also conceived as immobile and without potency to any shape. It is only the mind which designs shapes in pure extension through imaginary signs which are not extension itself.

784. Fourth, first matter has no determined confines. If it did, it would have shape. Nevertheless, it is a real ens conceived by the mind, although stripped through abstraction of its confines. It has limits and shapes in potency.

785. Fifth, first matter has real, substantial parts in potency. In other words, it *can* be divided into indefinite parts, each of which is equally matter in concept, but different in reality. This is the result of the extended quality which is its mode of being. This mode is in potency to any dimension,[32] shape, form and multiplicity[33] whatsoever.

786. We can conclude, therefore:

1. The concept of *first matter*, although abstract, presents the mind with a first, indeterminate element of bodies which pertains to their reality but cannot subsist except through the addition of determinations.

787. Note here that abstraction has two functions: *a*) it makes us think some realisable element, but without its determinations (*thetical abstraction*); *b*) it also makes us think some non-realisable *quid* when it separates things which cannot be totally separated without rendering them inconceivable — like the centre of a circle without its circumference, corporeal force without any generic extension, and so on (*hypothetical abstraction*).

---

[32] Determinate dimension is not an element in the definition of matter, although dimension in general is, because matter is not infinite.

[33] 'Matter is not suitably divided into parts unless it is understood as quantity. If quantity is removed, an indivisible substance remains, as *II Phys* (text 15) says' (*S.T.*, I, q. 50, art. 2). But we have to note that material things are necessarily annihilated if quantity in general is removed from them.

788. We can, if we wish, reduce the second kind of abstracts to a general formula and define them as: 'Abstracts in which abstraction has removed even the *potency* of receiving the determinations necessary to become real.' The concept of *first matter* is not given through the use of the second, but the first abstraction. Hence

789. 2. *First matter* is an extended force which is in potency,

    a) to having a determinate quantity of extension;

    b) to having a determinate shape;

    c) to being divided into parts, each of which has its own determined quantity and its own shape;

    d) to having a determined, sensible element.

790. 3. Again, first matter is the *substance of bodies*. In this sense, Aristotle was correct to call first matter 'substance'. The determinations of quantity, such as shape, quantitative numerability and sensibility are conditions according to which first matter can possess the *act* of subsistence. Taken together, these conditions constitute the *form* of body.

791. These determinations can vary, but some or other of them are necessary and as such form the *substantial form* of body together with the act of substance. In other words, determined extension or quantity, shape and sensible element are said to be the *substantial form of body* in so far as they terminate and perfect the act which makes them subsist, that is, the act of material substance from which they receive unity.[34]

---

[34]'Modern and ancient writers, when speaking about corporeal matters, posit the form of physical bodies in mechanical principles, namely, in shape, size, texture, the movement of parts. To these, Buffon (*Observ. et Expér. sur la product. des animaux*, t. 1, c. 3) adds impenetrability, divisibility, communication of movement. These concur in constituting matter, but not its form, that is, they do not make it one rather than another matter' (Baldinotti, *Metaph. Gen.*, n. 850). None of this is exact because it does not distinguish what pertains 1. to the realisation of matter; 2. to matter itself; 3. to substantial form; and 4. to accidental forms. Quantity, divisibility, situation in space and consequently texture pertain to *realisation*, not properly speaking to the matter or form of bodies. Impenetrability, extension in general and certain *dispositions*, that is, an aptitude for receiving substantial and accidental forms, pertain to *matter*. Determined shape, but not one shape rather than another, and a determined felt element, but not one rather than another, to which the shape refers, pertain to *substantial form*. The choice of these forms and determined felt elements pertains to the *accidental forms*.

792. As variables, however, they constitute *accidental forms* or accidents. As such, they are not considered in the unity of the substance which makes them subsist, but as separated from one another by abstraction [*App.*, no. 1].

793. 4. The different elements of corporeal nature possess an order, as follows:

1. force, whose essential mode is extensive quantity. Force cannot be considered separate from extensive quantity except through second-level abstraction. Otherwise, it is an absurdity: it is force on the one hand, but on the other lacks its essential constitutive element. As such it is force in potency. But what we conceive is force in act;

2. extensive quantity, which has confines determining a *shape*. Shape, therefore, is to extension what limits are to what is limited;

3. shape is not presented to us without some felt element. Although we can indeed prescind through abstraction from every felt element, we cannot prescind from what is felt in general. An abstract shape is not a shape with a felt element, but a shape which 'is thought as possible to be felt, without any determination relative to the felt element included in it; shape can in fact include different felt elements.'

794. In thinking of abstract force, therefore, we think of extension, but leave it indeterminate. This is the concept proper to *first matter* of bodies.

795. In thinking of abstract force, but at a lower level of abstraction where some extension or determined, extensive quantity is present, we think of its shape, but without determining it. This is *matter* with some dimension (not first matter).

796. Again, in thinking of matter at an even lower level of abstraction, with a determined quantity and shape, we think of what is felt, but leave its quality or sensible qualities without determination.

797. Finally, in thinking of matter together with quantity, shape and determined felt element, we think of formed body, that is, matter together with form, the *full species*, the universal, but not abstract, idea of body [*App.*, no. 2].

798. The *real* body is then perceived intellectively when the sensitive perception is united to its corresponding idea, that is, to the full species.

799. That which is thought prior to its determinations is called the *subject of the determinations*. *First matter*, therefore, is the first subject of all the corporeal determinations; *extensive quantity* is taken as the dialectic subject of shape; and *shape* is taken as the dialectic subject of the sensible qualities.

800. Note, however, that human reasoning runs along two opposed paths, or better, runs along the same path in two directions, going and coming. In going, it follows its natural, common order by moving analytically from the whole to the parts; in coming, it follows a scientific or learned order by moving synthetically from the parts to the whole. This 'return' of the mind presupposes its prior 'departure'; learned synthesis presupposes normal analysis.

801. When we descend from first matter to real body, we return from the parts to the whole. The spirit, however, before moving in this direction, had to move in the opposite direction (from the whole to the parts). During this process, the order of predicates and subjects is changed. First, we have what is felt, then its shape, then its quantity. Here, we predicate shape of the felt element, and quantity of shape. In other words, we say that shape is a mode of what is felt, and extensive quantity a mode of shape. Matter, however, being the actual proximate cause of what is felt, cannot be predicated. Instead, we have to predicate of it all that has been predicated of the felt element, which is the term of its act, in which it is perceived. Thus, it is always of matter that we predicate shape, quantity and felt element as its effect. Whichever direction is taken by the mind, therefore, matter is always considered as first subject, that is, as substance; it can never be predicated, but only considered as subject.

CHAPTER 4

The concept of form

802. It is clear from what we have said that matter is the act in which and through which bodies exist,[35] that is, the act through

---

[35] The word 'act' expresses every entity. The nature of act is taken, in our case, from the nature of bodies to which it refers, and which we have described.

[799–802]

which and in which corporeal qualities subsist. Matter is what our thought first understands when we mentally conceive bodies.

803. This act cannot be realised, however, in isolation from all the corporeal qualities conceived as potentially present in it. What perfects it are the corporeal determined qualities which we call 'form'.

804. Some of these qualities are variable. If they are altogether necessary for us to be able to think of realised matter, they are called *substantial form* of body and as such they have a part to play in constituting the act through which body can be conceived as suitable for realisation. In this sense, we say that *form*, too, is substance. In other words, it comes to be part of substance.

805. But simply as variables, these corporeal qualities are called *accidental forms* because what is necessary to the subsistence of a body remains indeterminate. Nothing more is needed than the presence of one or other of these qualities.

806. However, while it is possible on the one hand to conceive of bodies furnished with all the substantial and accidental qualities necessary for their realisation, they can be realised in different sizes. The same size can even be repeated any number of times. We say, therefore, that the *continuous or discrete quantity of matter* is not determined by either the concept of *matter* or that of *form*, but by that of *realisation*, which depends upon the will of the Creator who realises bodies.

807. Matter, therefore, is the first reason for conceiving everything present in a body as subsistent. Consequently, matter is the first element to be called 'substance' and 'first subject'. It follows that matter is also the subject of the substantial form, as the substantial form is the subject of accidents. Finally, *realisation* has its explanation not in body, but in the creating cause; it is not the subject of body, but that which makes the subject subsist.

CHAPTER 5

How the words 'matter' and 'first matter' were used equivocally by the greatest philosophers

808. Having unfolded the concept of *first matter* and seen that it is found in bodies where its perfection and final acts are called *form*, we can show (although this follows also from what has been said in the first part) that such matter is not found in the soul. However, in order to avoid arguments over words, and at the same time to offer a key to the proper understanding of the greatest philosophers, it will help if we first note the occasional imprecision of these philosophers when they deal with *first matter* or try to fix its concept accurately (I have tried to be precise myself by using the words *matter* or *first matter* to indicate different things). This imprecision has led them into apparent contradictions, and given rise to heated and useless questions.

Article 1
Some philosophers confused *reality* with *first matter*

809. First, almost all confused *first matter* with *subsistent reality* (for me, they are distinct). This was the case with Plato who made *the quantitative element* something dependent or consequent on matter, although it is not in fact included in the concept of matter, but posited through the *realisation* of matter and determined by the decision of the one who causes it to be realised.

810. Aristotle made matter the principle of individuation. As I have shown, however, this principle must be posited rather in subsistent *reality*,[36] which is always fully determined.

[36] *AMS*, 782–788 [*App.*, no. 3].

Article 2
By using the second method of abstraction (hypothetical abstraction), some philosophers made matter an immaterial ens

811. We have seen that the concept of matter expresses nothing whatsoever if we mentally remove from it all thought of extension in general. In this case, we no longer consider such force with thetical, but with hypothetical abstraction. This explains why St. Thomas teaches that by abstracting from all extension we inevitably abstract from all matter. He says:

> Mathematical species can be abstracted intellectually from *sensible matter* whether *individual* (reality) or *common* (essence of matter). These species however cannot be abstracted from common, intelligible matter but only from individual, intelligible matter. Sensible matter is called corporeal matter in so far as it underlies the sensible qualities, such as hot and cold, hard and soft, ansd so on. Intelligible matter is substance in so far as it underlies (continuous) quantity. It is clear, then, that quantity in-exists in substance prior to the sensible quantities. These quantities, like numbers (I mean numbers of continuous quantities), and like dimensions and shapes which are the terms of quantities, can be considered without sensible qualities, that is, they can be abstracted from sensible qualities. They cannot be considered, however, without reference to some substance which underlies quantity. This would mean abstracting them from common, intelligible matter. They can, nevertheless, be considered without reference to any particular substance. This means abstracting them from individual, intelligible matter.[37]

Let us pause here.
812. We saw that *first matter* is 'a force that operates in extension'. This force is in potency to: 1. determined extension or quantity (which may be more or less, and hence still numerable); 2. shape; 3. sensible qualities.
Mathematical species are shapes and their terms, that is, surface, line, point. These species are not, therefore, *first matter*,

[37] *S.T.*, I, q. 85, art. 1.

but matter already reduced to the act of quantity and shape and therefore, partly informed. We simply prescind from consideration of the sensible qualities to which it is in potency. Precisely because it is in potency, it is still called *matter*. This is what the Scholastics call 'mathematical matter'. When they say, therefore, that in the concept of mathematical matter abstraction is made from both individual and common sensible matter, they mean that the sensible qualities, considered as real and as ideal, are abstracted from the potency. When they say that abstraction is made from *individual, intelligible matter*, they mean from determinate quantity and realised shape (and whatever appertains to shape). This, however, is an improper way of speaking. As the Scholastics themselves said, *individual* is not conceived by the intellect. They were, therefore, out of harmony with their own teaching when they posited matter which was both *intelligible* and *individual*.

They called this matter, *intelligible*, however, because quantity and shape, abstracted from what is sensible, is simply an object of the intellect. They did not see that as such it is never individual unless arbitrarily fixed in some place in space. Nevertheless, because it is possible to encounter in reality that which is in the intellect, the word they used is not completely without meaning. When they go on to say that the concept of mathematical matter does not abstract from common-intelligible matter, they mean that quantity and shape are considered by mathematicians not only in abstraction from sensible qualities, but also without referring them to a real body as something possible to be realised. St. Thomas goes on:

> Certain things, such as ens, one in potency, act (and other things which can exist without matter of any kind) are abstracted from common, intelligible matter, as we see in separate substances.[38]

Clearly, these words already take us outside all matter if we prescind from extension and all continuous quantity; the concept of matter slips away from us completely. We are left only with some final, abstract elements that can be realised both in matter and outside it. There is, therefore, something anterior to

[38] *S.T.*, I, q. 85, art. 1.

matter, something proper to act and to active potency.[39] The concept of matter begins in our mind only when we think of 'a sensiferous potency in extension'.

813. However, this concept was not always adhered to, as we said. Consequently, some Scholastics, when speaking about matter, say that 'such potency is not referred to action, but to being'[40] (instead of saying 'to form'). The concept of matter is thus broadened and is now able to be applied to every creature. In fact, every creature, even spiritual creatures, have potency *ad esse* before they exist, that is, they have the potency to receive subsistence. If the Scholastics' principle is understood literally, matter is converted into 'that which is possible', in other words, into idea. This is incorrect. As we said above, we can have ideas of forms as well as of matter.

814. As a result of this, some Scholastics asserted that all things, visible and invisible, movable and immovable, corporeal and incorporeal, are composed of matter and form. But, as St. Thomas observed, this is to take the word 'matter' in two meanings, not in its true, proper meaning.[41]

815. Those who take matter as a synonym for 'that which is in potency' exclude from its concept every relationship with extension. As a result, they necessarily make it an ens from which matter itself has already been abstracted. This ens, as St. Thomas observes, remains as something indivisible:

> It is right to divide matter into parts only to the extent that

[39] This proof of the thesis that there is some other principle prior to matter, is drawn from the order of ideas, from the very notion of matter, which cannot be conceived without our thinking some preceding actuality. St. Thomas comes to the same conclusion from another argument, that is, from the necessity of an active principle which can draw matter, which is in potency, to its act. 'The material principle, which in our experience is imperfect, cannot simply be first, but must be preceded by something perfect. Semen, for example, although the principle of animals generated from seed, is preceded by an animal or plant from which it comes forth. There must, therefore, be something in act prior to that which is in potency. Ens in potency is not reduced to act except through some ens in act, (*S. T.*, I, q. 4, art. 1, ad 2).

[40] St. Thomas Aquinas, *Quodl.*, 10, q. 3, ad 5.

[41] 'Matter is used equivocally (in two senses) of movable and immovable things' (*In II Sent.*, d. 2, q. 2, art. 2, ad 4. Cf. also, *Quodl.*, III, q. 8, art. 1).

it is understood as a subject of quantity. Remove quantity, and we are left with an indivisible substance, as we see in *Physics*,[42]

where *quantity* has to be understood about any kind of quantity, not about a particular, determined quantity.

Article 3
Is first matter inert?

816. The philosophers we have mentioned were unaware that the concept of matter reveals to the intellect something related to extension. Relying too much on abstraction, they eliminated this relationship and destroyed the concept of matter. All that remained for them was the concept of something immaterial and indivisible preceding the concept of matter.

But there were other philosophers who did not entirely abolish the relationship with extension. They granted that matter could be moved in space, but nevertheless stripped it of its faculty for motion and declared it inert. Were they correct?

817. The logical cause leading them to this conclusion was the attention they gave to the phenomena of *material mass* which presents itself to us as something mobile, as an entity very different from the sensiferous element. Because this mass is sometimes in motion, sometimes at rest, they correctly deduced that motion is not essential to it, that motion does not form part of the concept of this mass, and that *matter* receives motion from some other active principle different from itself. It is indubitable that no body moves itself, and that the principle of motion must be sought elsewhere.

818. Nevertheless, the extrasubjective phenomena of motion are not the first to present themselves to us in the concept of body. As we saw, the first phenomenon is the felt element in which we have the intellective perception of the sensiferous element whose concept is that of an activity on our soul — an activity which extends throughout the extension of the felt element. We can have no doubt, therefore, about such activity

[42] *S.T.*, I, q. 50, art. 2.

which produces the felt element and, as *first* in the concept of body, constitutes the knowable and nameable essence of body. The same activity is also the subject of motion, which is simply 'the manifestation of the sensiferous element in a felt entity which successively occupies different extension.' From this point of view, it is therefore true that the sensiferous element is passive, that is, apt to receive and transmit motion, but not to give it.

819. Where, then, shall we find this principle of motion? First, in the soul, which changes the place of the sensiferous element.

We also understand that outside the soul there must be some other principle which produces motion. This is shown by the phenomenon of attraction. Third, we understand that this principle of motion outside the human soul can be neither the mass nor the foreign force which, if it has not received motion, cannot transmit it to another force. It must, therefore, receive motion. It does not produce it; it is not its principle.

820. Is the principle of motion the same as that which we have called corporeal principle? We cannot answer this question without examining the concept of corporeal principle. We deduced this concept from our realisation that the *felt element*, and the sensiferous force, too, that we have perceived in this element, is simply the term of an action done in our soul. The agent is unknown in itself, that is, in its principle, because we know it only from its living action in its term. It is our ignorance of the principle of this action which led us to call it *corporeal principle*. According to this concept, we know that the corporeal principle is the principle of the action we call *sensiferous*. The action has to be given a name as an ens because of our need to conceive it intellectually. However, this action on the soul is still not motion, whose nature consists in relocating the sensiferous element. We cannot, therefore, affirm that it is the *corporeal principle*.

821. I do not want to speak here of the faculty of transmitting motion which, properly speaking, constitutes *foreign force* and *mass*. This faculty must undoubtedly be attributed to the corporeal principle, which serves as its subject. My aim here is simply to discover the principle of movement.

822. In the first part of this work, I explained how every material element is the term of a feeling principle. This opinion

posits a principle of movement in nature. It explains the natural movements of bodies without need to call on the Almighty as some kind of second cause. It also reconciles the great, everlasting question about the inertia and activity of matter.

Some philosophers, in considering the concept of matter, thought that matter as the cause of motion was repugnant. As far as I can see, they are entirely correct. Others saw that everything in nature moves, and that the phenomena of attraction, expansion, elasticity, and so on, together with the phenomena of the mechanical clash of bodies, are visible in nature. These philosophers, who were unwilling to turn to God's immediate action to explain these phenomena, but were unable to posit some other cause, made matter active. They did not notice that the attribution of such activity clashes with the concept of matter given to us through perception. Nevertheless, they were correct in so far as they recognised a principle of spontaneous motion dispersed through the whole of nature. This confirms the opinion I have offered about the animation of matter as a very easy and logically coherent explanation of all natural phenomena.[43]

CHAPTER 6

The intimate union of spirit and matter

823. The reason why the concept of matter (and indeed that of form of body) does not provide us with the principle of motion is that the concept of matter and of body comes to us from perception, which shows us the act in its term, not in its principle. This term (the felt element) is extended. When this felt extension is relocated, motion is present, but the displacement is not in the term itself which is perceived when already constituted, not before. Prior to perception, it is not term, it is not felt. On the contrary, the action relocating the term by transporting it from one place to another is an action anterior to the constitution of the term (the felt element), and consequently does not fall under perception.

---

[43] Cf. Cudworth, c. 1, §1.

824. We should also consider that the term (the felt element) from which alone we derive the concept of mass, body, matter and even of foreign force (the sole concept of which we have experience) is something that we feel in our spirit, in the sentient principle. This allows us to conclude without doubt that the spirit itself concurs with the sensiferous element to produce this term. In fact, the sentient principle receives the action in its own way, that is, as an active principle. But how does the sentient principle collaborate in this? We have to say that it concurs in everything, that is, in 1. the sensible element and 2. the mode of the sensible element, which is extension. The sentient principle collaborates in producing the sensible element because without a sentient principle there can be no feeling; the sentient principle collaborates in producing the mode of the sensible element, extension (continuum), because extension or continuum can be present only in what is simple.

825. The sensiferous element can only arouse the spirit to produce the felt element with its mode, with extension. This, however, is the transcendent concept of the sensiferous entity, the concept that shows the sensiferous element in its principle, in the corporeal principle. This does indeed help to explain how matter and its concept are generated, but it is not the concept of matter.

826. Note that matter, as given to us by perception (the common or popular concept), is highly involved with what is subjective. We should be careful not to reason about the concept of matter as though it had some truth even outside perception; it is true, but in perception. If we want to know what matter is outside perception, we find that it slips away from us. We are no longer speaking about that which holds the attention of the whole world — the world always speaking of matter as it is perceived. So too, the senses do not delude us if reason recognises in them what they give us and nothing more. If, however, we claim that the senses furnish us with something they were not destined to give us, we immediately fall into error — although it is not the senses, but reason which errs by judging beyond the limits conferred by sensible data.

827. Second, it is very helpful to consider carefully the transcendent concept of matter, or better, the transcendent concept of the entity which corresponds to the common

concept of matter. This concept enables us to understand the connection between things in nature and, in our case, between spirit and the corporeal principle. It also helps us to see how several entities[44] are produced from their connection and interaction.

We rightly conceive these entities in isolation, and hence as *entia* or substances. We say nothing about their nature, but simply affirm that they are 'the first act which we perceive, in which and through which many second acts subsist.' Substance, as we know, is 'the first act that makes other acts subsist.'

828. The word 'substance' does indeed have two meanings. Its transcendent meaning expresses the absolutely first act which makes everything subsist. In this meaning, substance is proper to God alone. Its common meaning expresses 'the first act (in our perception) of the entity we perceive.' In this meaning, relative to us, we distinguish several substances which we can suitably call *relative*, not absolute, *substances*. In this sense, matter is substance.

829. Finally, the distinction between the two concepts of matter (the transcendent and relative concepts) is extremely helpful in explaining the origins of the different opinions of philosophers about matter, and reconciling them.

CHAPTER 7
The human soul is devoid of all matter

Article 1
Demonstration

830. Having clarified the concept of matter and of first matter, it is now easy to show that the human soul is entirely devoid of

---

[44] This is another example of the *synthesism* in nature of which I have written on several occasions. — *Principles of Ethics* (*PE*, ch. 2); *Storia comparativa*, c. 8, a. 3, §7; *AMS*, 258–268.

all matter. In fact, the concept of matter, summarised briefly, is made up of several elements. It provides us with:

1. an activity in act in its *term*, not in its principle;
2. some extension, some mass, as the mode of this activity in act in its term;
3. mobility, that is, an aptitude for receiving and transmitting motion, not for producing it (receiving and transmitting motion pertains to the term; producing it to the principle of activity). But all these things are inherently contradictory to 'soul'.

831. Soul, as we have defined it, is indeed 'the sentient, rational and active principle, according to feeling and rationality'. This definition posits not only a difference, but true opposition between the concept of soul and that of matter. Soul is the *principle* of an act; matter is thought of simply as *term*.

Soul as principle is unextended; matter has extension, mass, as its very own essential condition.

The soul as principle is mover, but is not mobile. It is the principle of motion, but is itself immobile.

The soul, therefore, is exclusive of all those elements which constitute the concept of matter.

832. It may not seem easy at first sight to understand how the soul is *immobile*. The difficulty is overcome by considering carefully that everything moved is thought of as *term* because movement is the term of the mover-action.

833. Second, motion takes place only in extension. The soul, however, is not in extension either as a continual solid, nor as lines and points, which are only the abstract limits of what is solid and therefore pertain to the solid. In fact, what is solid, and hence its limits, exists only in what is simple. This explains why the best philosophers call the soul *that which contains* the solid, not that which is *contained* by it.[45] The continuous solid is, therefore, in the soul without its being soul. Rather, it is in

---

[45] Another proof that soul contains body is found in the nature of the action exercised by the soul: '(The soul) TAKES HOLD of the body which is always in flux and prone to corruption and TIGHTENS ITS GRIP on what in the body is insecure and mortal. It bears up what falls, and allows changing, corruptible nourishment to reach fruition. It is not right, therefore, for it to lose its force when separated from the BODY which it CONTAINS and PRESERVES' (St. Isidore of Pelusium, *Ep.* bk. 3, 235).

opposition to soul as term is in opposition to principle, and object to subject (this is a result of the connection and communication of substances that constitute the synthesism of nature). In the same way, it can rightly be said that motion occurs in the continuum which is in the soul, but never in the soul itself which has its term, the continuum, in itself.

834. It may be objected that the soul, too, is transported when we take the body from one place to another. This is not true. The soul does not move. All that arises is a new relationship on the part of the soul between its body and the place occupied by the body. It is the body which changes, not the soul. When the body belonging to the soul finds itself in relationship with other exterior objects and with different space, it seems that the soul is transported together with its body. In fact, all that has moved is the felt element of the soul, not the sentient principle. All that is felt in the soul through movement is in the soul as something once felt but now passed. Note carefully that the felt element here is understood as the place of one's own body; the soul, on the other hand, is present to space as a whole (cf. 554–559).[46]

Article 2
The soul is a principle-ens and matter a term-ens

835. The notion of matter implies, therefore, some activity

[46] St. Thomas offers two arguments to prove that the soul is not composed of *matter* and *form*. According to the first argument, the soul is *form*. But if it had some matter in it, this material part would not be the soul. This argument harmonises with our own proof based on the soul as principle of acts, and matter solely as term. The other argument (which is valid only for the intellective soul) depends on the fact that the intellect understands only by abstracting from *matter*. In this argument, *matter*, taken as synonymous with *reality*, has another meaning (*S.T.*, I, q. 57, art. 5; *Quodl.*, 3, art. 20). Moreover, St. Thomas begins from the definition of matter as 'that which is in potency ONLY', a definition which would be suitable only to things considered in their possibility or idea. He would be coherent in doing this because matter would once more be taken as synonymous with reality, which in the idea is only in potency. But amongst possible things soul, as well as matter, is found. This explains why the argument starting from this definition, although basically true, does not convince me.

considered in the term of its action. But because the *term* of an action is that which *is done* and not that which *does*, matter has in itself the concept of *passive potency*, not of active potency.[47]

836. However, the concept of matter does not solely imply the activity lying in its term; it is the term considered as ens, as a term-ens. The understanding, through the principle of cognition, conceives something only as an ens, and ens is joined to that which we first perceive of an entity. If we perceive a term-entity, and nothing prior to it, our concept has as its object a term-ens. In this term-ens, the first thing conceived (the first co-act of the ens which holds everything else that can be distinguished in the ens) is called act or substance or subject.

837. We perceive entia, therefore, in two ways: as principle and as term.

We perceive entia as term when we are passive and receive their activity in our feeling. At that moment, we perceive activity in us as in the term of action, and take the nature of the perceived ens from the nature of the term of its action, the only thing we perceive. This takes place when we perceive bodies.

838. The ens that we perceive as principle of activity is simply ourselves, the soul, which is perceived as our own feeling. In this feeling what we think as first act is distinguished from everything else subsisting in the soul. This first act is, therefore, substance, subject; it is a principle-ens.

839. It is true that the soul also perceives itself as term. Precisely because it perceives itself as feeling (which involves passivity), it realises that its very own existence must have a cause. Its thought is raised to the Creator. Nevertheless, it also perceives itself as active principle. Under this aspect, its concept is opposed to the concept of body which it perceives solely as term-ens, and not as principle-ens.

---

[47] Matter, because it is a term-ens, retains its name even in the order of cognitions. Consequently, we say that the felt element is the *matter* of knowledge. But when we say that every object is matter of cognition, we use matter with another, relative meaning. We say that the object is *matter* of cognition because it is its term. *Ideal being* considered not as object, but as means of knowledge in which we know everything that we know, is essentially *form*, and cannot in any way be called matter. This is strengthened by the fact that it is not passive in any sense.

CHAPTER 8

The intrinsic order of being in corporeal entity — The concept of act — Substantial and accidental acts

840. So far, we have considered matter under the guidance of experience, that is, of perception, through which our understanding is placed in communication with matter and hence with its concept. Our consideration has shown us the nature of the *intrinsic order of being* in a corporeal entity.

What we see is this. In this entity, which is called 'body' and 'matter', there is an act prior to all others, on which all others are founded, and without which they cannot be thought. We can think this prior act perfectly well without thinking of the other acts, although we have to understand that this act, when realised, is accompanied by the other acts which are in part variable. This first act that we conceive is substance. The other acts, which have the first for their subject, are thought by us after the first and are called *substantial* in so far as they are altogether necessary to the subsistence of the first act. They are not necessary, however, to its concept (in their unity, they are called 'substantial form'). But in so far as they are not necessary, that is, in so far as they can in part vary without weakening substance or substantial acts, they are called *accidental*. They are accidental acts, or accidents. Added to these accidents are certain extrinsic determinations coming from *reality*, not from the *idea* of this ens.

841. The following, therefore, is the intrinsic order found in material ens by the understanding:

1. a first act, substance, without which the other acts are not understood, and to which is given the name *ens*;

2. acts, or substantial forms, which have for their subject the substance which dominates them, but which are necessary for the complete concept of this ens;

3. acts or accidental forms, which have for their subject substantial forms;

4. determinations not included in the full-specific idea of the ens, but coming from its *reality*.

CHAPTER 9

Substance-principle, substance-term and mixed substance

842. Hence, the first act perceived in the object of perception is substance. But this *first act* is sometimes *understood as principle*, sometimes *as term*. Moreover, this *first act* ('first' must always be understood relative to the intrinsic order of the perceived or conceived entity) sometimes presents itself as essentially and solely principle; sometimes as essentially and solely term of the very act whose principle remains hidden from us; sometimes as containing in itself the twofold relationship of term of one act and principle of another.

843. There are, therefore, three species of substance. One is first act (in the conceived object) which has and never loses the nature of principle. Another is first act (in the conceived object) which has and never loses the nature of term. The third is first act (in the conceived object) which is understood as term relative to an act preceding it (a different substance, therefore, from itself), and as principle relative to its own and subsequent acts of which alone it is first act and act-principle.

844. To be essentially and solely act-principle pertains to God alone; to be essentially and solely act-term pertains to material substance; to be first act but term relative to some preceding activity, and principle relative to the act of one's own subsistence and to second acts, pertains to spiritual creatures, and therefore to the human soul.

845. We need to note carefully that this is the classification of substances, or first acts (where we understand 'first' in the sense of what we conceive of an ens, according to the logical order, prior to other things in it). It is not a classification of acts in general. If we forget this, we may object that bodies, too, are principles of their operations. This is not the case. In all extrasubjective operations of bodies, it is always the *term* that is under consideration. Hence our previous proof of the inertia of matter. Changes in bodies are not, therefore, *operations* of corporeal substance, but *modifications* of it. This activity is always perceived in its term, never in its principle.

CHAPTER 10

The sense in which the soul can be considered as a mixed substance, comprising principle and term

846. We said that the soul can be considered as term of some preceding action (of the Creator). This needs some explanation.

To say that the soul is term of some action prior to itself is one thing; it is another to say that this action situated and acting in its term is the soul. The second affirmation is obviously mistaken. First, it is absurd because it would follow that the soul would be the creative action; second, its absurdity can be proved directly (as it should be philosophically) by comparing our perception of soul with that of matter.

Bodies are perceived as direct effects of a foreign action in the soul. Because the concept of bodies results from their action in some other perceived ens, they are perceived in so far as their activity is in its term, in the passivities proper to the soul. But this activity of bodies in the soul as in their term is not the principle, unperceived by us, that makes them subsist as entia in themselves. The soul, on the contrary, is never perceived as acting in another ens different from itself, but as existing in itself. It is perceived, therefore, whole and entire even in the principle of its activity. The action of which it is term is something foreign to the principle called soul, and anterior to it. That which is principle of an act cannot be term of the same act, but of some preceding act.

The concept of the soul is that of principle. It is not term relative to its first (substantial) act, but term relative to another act different from itself which is not perceived.

CHAPTER 11

Is 'substance' distinguished from 'substantial form' in the soul?

847. We have examined the nature of the *intrinsic order* of the

ens called body. In this order, we distinguished: 1. matter, the first subject of the other qualities, or substance; 2. substantial form, and so on. Matter, however, is not present in the human soul. Is there no distinction, therefore, between substance and substantial form of the soul?

Every question requires a prior understanding of the value of the words in which it is expressed, and this one is no exception. In other words, we have to define our language accurately, and then go forward in accordance with the definition given. So, what do I understand by the phrase 'substantial form'?

848. By 'substantial form' I mean 'an act perfecting another act in such a way that a substantive used to name the new act expresses the perfection which the new act receives' (cf. 52). Thus, matter is not called *body* unless it is conceived with those determinations, a given size, shape, and so on, which are necessarily conceived in bodies.

849. Granted this, we have to note that 'the act which perfects another act' can be conceived in two ways. 1. 'the perfecting act gives perfection and completion to an act in which and through which the perfecting act itself exists.' This occurs even in matter, in which (as in a subject) and through which its determination (its size, its shape) completes and perfects it. Or 2. the perfecting act can be understood in such a way that it gives perfection to another act through which and in which it does not exist, an act, that is, different from that in which and through which it exists. So the soul is conceived as the form of the extrasubjective body in so far as the animated body offers to external observation life-phenomena which are considered as its perfection (relative to ourselves).

The body, when considered subjectively, results from 1. an action of an agent in the soul; and 2. from the nature of the effect that this produces in the soul (the effect is the felt element and its mode, that is, its extension). But because these effects take place in the soul and through the essentially feeling nature of the soul, it is the soul again which is modified in such a way that it presents such feelings in itself. When human thought takes these feelings and unites them to the agent, that is, to the sensiferous element, the latter receives from the soul the sensible qualities together with their extension. Again, it is still the soul and its act that clothes the body (the term of the agent) and what is called 'substantial body'. The soul, therefore, even from this point of view, gives matter its substantial form. I say that it *gives* matter its substantial form because in this operation the substantial form of the body is more an effect of the soul, and the internal term of its operation. Here, it is not the soul itself which is the substantial form of the body.

If we consider the soul as perfecting and informing the body, it is the substantial form not of itself, but of some other ens, that is, of the body. Considered in itself, the soul must simply be called *substance* rather than substantial form.[48]

850. But isn't it of the essence of the soul that it should be the form or entelechy of the body? — I have already shown in the first part how this is to be understood, but something can be added here to resolve the objection. If by 'body' we understand an ens different from the soul, we cannot say that the essence of the soul consists in being form of the body because the action or relationship between the two entia never constitutes the essence or the substance of either of them. This relationship can indeed follow necessarily on the substance of one or other of these entia, but that which follows on substance is not substance. I say 'which follows on substance' because substances are so united amongst themselves and, as it were, inexorably joined in the nature of the universe that one sustains and produces the other. In other words, they are reciprocal conditions of their existence. I call these consequences *synthetical consequences of substances*.

851. However, if we consider the substance of the soul *in se*, and not in its *synthetical consequences*, we first have to distinguish between the merely sensitive soul of brutes, and the human soul. The sensitive soul must certainly have, besides the principle, the term (felt-extended) of its act. Its substance, however, does not reside in this term, but in the principle; this term is only the condition of its existence and the reason for its individuation. But if we want to call this term the form of the soul in

---

[48] St. Thomas says that there is no distinction between *form* and *nature* in simple things; the distinction is present only in things composed of matter and form. 'Form is the very nature of things, as in simple things, or it is a constituent of the nature of things, as in things which are composed of matter and form' (*S. T.*, III, q. 13, art. 1).

so far as it perfects the act through which the soul is, and individuates this act, it does not follow that the informing element is matter. What informs is conceived as principle and act; but the essence of matter is to be term. On the other hand, matter understood as sensiferous is the occasion when *form* is aroused. This form is the *fundamental felt* element; it individuates the soul and is where the sentient principle resides and unfolds itself. The felt element, therefore, but not matter, can be called the substantial form of the soul. What is felt does not receive its perfection from the principle, but rather gives it to the principle. This is the contrary of what is achieved by matter, the most imperfect, highly indeterminate[49] element that can be thought in bodies. Whichever way we think about it, therefore, the notion of matter cannot be harmonised with that of soul. This will be understood more clearly if we consider that the very term of the soul is in the soul as in its principle, as I shall explain shortly. In the soul of brutes, therefore, we find sentient and felt, substance and substantial form, both of which are united in such a way that one cannot be thought without the other. But there is no matter in the soul.

852. Speaking about the soul which is both sensitive and intellective, we saw that its essence consists in being a rational principle, and that the sensitive principle itself receives the nature of term of such a principle in so far as it is united to the rational principle by natural, continuous perception (cf. 264–273). Relative to the rational soul, therefore, we can exclude matter by using the same reflections that were employed with respect to the merely sensitive soul and, in addition, the particular arguments that prove the intellect to be immune from all matter as a result of the logical opposition existing between the essential characteristics of soul and matter.

853. Consequently, we have to say that while we distinguish between substance and substantial form in the soul, the substance of the soul does not include the concept of matter, but of act-principle — although in this act-principle we can distinguish something that perfects and individuates it, and is

---

[49] It is what is thought as extremely imperfect and indeterminate in bodies, provided that the nature of *matter* is preserved. In other words, it is something imperfect, something indeterminate, relative to bodies.

included in the notion of term. Nevertheless, it remains that the soul is essentially principle even in this its term. This perfection and term can be called 'substantial form'.

CHAPTER 12
Act and potency

Article 1
The nature of act

854. By 'act' I understand any *entity* whatsoever. However, 'act' also expresses entity in its relationship to *potency*. Consequently, we have to turn to the concept of *potency* in order to determine fully the notion of act.

855. At the same time, we must note that the notion of act involves sometimes a positive, sometimes a negative relationship with the notion of potency. The involvement is *positive* if *potency* is opposed to *act* as though potency were not itself an act. The involvement is *negative* if potency is excluded from the act as, for instance, when we speak about an act for which there is no corresponding potency.

Article 2
The nature of potency

856. As we said, the intrinsic order of ens cannot be deduced *a priori*, but has to be gained through experience of those *entia* which come within our feeling. These are bodies, and our soul. We considered these *entia* carefully, therefore, to know their intrinsic order, that is, how they are internally constructed and, as it were, organated. We concluded that every ens presents us with an entity, but that we mentally discern several elements in this single entity. These elements are ordered in such a way that one is conceived prior to another. In other words, the second

element cannot be thought to exist except with the element that precedes it in the logical order. The second is said to exist in and through the first. The first element of all, which can be conceived by itself before all the others, is said to contain and sustain the others, and make them exist. We call this element *substance*.

However, amongst all these elements (which I also call 'entities') not all are equally necessary to think an ens and to name it substantively. The elements or entities which can vary without our losing the concept of an ens and without our having to change the noun with which we name it, are called *accidental forms* or *accidents*. Accidents, therefore, are certain actualities or entities which are not necessary for the concept of an ens. However, they either perfect it, or are *privations* of these actualities, or are entities subject to variation. But even these accidental actualities cannot be conceived without the substantial form of an ens. They are said, therefore, to exist in and through substance.

857. It follows that an ens can be conceived either furnished with or lacking these actualities. When we conceive an ens without them, we also see that it *can* have them and, having them, remain the same ens. In this case, we consider the ens as a *potency*. We also say that these actualities exist in the ens in potency, not in act. This means that the ens is susceptive of such actualities even though it does not possess them. Potency, therefore, is the relationship that the mind conceives between an ens and its accidental actualities in their variation or absence.

858. Several consequences flow from this concept.

First, we realise that it is not possible to have a mere potency without any act. The potentiality of an ens always supposes the ens and the act by which the ens is as substance, and as substantial form.

Second, we see that absolutely speaking act precedes potency. Substance is a first act, of which substantial form is the perfection necessary for its constitution. As we said, potency is only the relationship that the mind conceives between first act and accidental acts, their variations and their privations.

859. Third, it is clear that every potency is joined to an act without forming an ens different from that to which it adheres. On the other hand, acts can depend on and receive their existence from other, previous acts in such a way that the previous

acts constitute different entia. This explains St. Thomas' very acute teaching:

> Acts can be reduced to a first act as to their first cause; potencies cannot be reduced to one another in such a way that we come to some first potency, which does not exist.[50]

Article 3
Receptive, active and passive potencies

860. We can go on now to consider the internal construction of entia that fall within our experience. Here, we easily recognise

[50] *S.T.*, I, q. 75, art. 5, ad 1. Cardinal Cajetan explains this teaching of Aquinas with his usual extraordinary perspicacity: 'Note the beautiful teaching: in the order of acts, which is the order of efficient cause, we can reduce things to one in number, from which all other acts are. But in the order of potency, which is the order of material cause (*that is, material cause pertains to the order of potency, although the order of potency does not always pertain to* material cause, *properly speaking*), there is no reduction of the universal order to one potency in number, but to one by analogy. The reduction is to many potencies ordered to different acts and harmonising amongst themselves in a certain proportion. In other words, each potency is related to its own act as other potencies are related to their acts. The order between potencies depends on the acts of which they are capable. Hence, reduction in the genus of material cause can be understood in a threefold way. First, reduction is appropriate to all potencies of the same genus, and so to one potency in number (*This would not seem completely correct. They are not always reduced to one in number, but sometimes to one in essence. This happens in the case of matter, one part of which, although of the same essence as the other, differs through its different reality. This is why acts pertain to different parts of matter*). Second, we have reduction of all potencies to one through analogy. Third, we have reduction of the potencies themselves. In this case, one is not reduced to another universally speaking because the potency of the intellect cannot be reduced to the potency of matter, nor vice versa, although one — first matter, for example — is the lowest in the order of imperfection. St. Thomas offers an extremely subtle explanation of this: even the first potency, IS INTRINSIC TO THE THING TO WHICH IT PERTAINS, and must therefore be different for different things. The FIRST EFFICIENT CAUSE, however, IS TOTALLY INDEPENDENT OF THINGS and, as such, stands as the one on which all are dependent. MATERIAL CAUSE (*and, more generally,* potential *cause*) IS INTRINSIC (*or, as we say,* 'connected with act'); EFFECTIVE CAUSE IS EXTRINSIC.'

that the potentialities of which we are speaking possess three modes. This explains the division of potencies into three classes. Sometimes, we see that one ens can receive another in itself without being confused with that which it receives. For example, known objects are in the soul which knows them. Such potentiality gives rise to a class which I call *receptive potencies*.[51] Sometimes one ens, in receiving the action of another, is modified by the other in some way. This passivity gives rise to another class, that of *passive potencies*. Finally, the ens itself can posit acts accidental to itself. In this case, we attribute to it the relationship I call *active potencies*.[52]

861. Note carefully that everything said about acts in potency is also said, but in a contrary sense, of their privation. Being able to be deprived of such actualities, etc., takes the form of *negative potencies*.

---

[51] *Receivable forms* correspond to *receptive* potencies. *Being* is a *receivable* form; it is essentially objective. But it is in three modes: ideal, real and moral. — If received in its ideal mode, it informs the soul by rendering it intelligent, and becomes the soul's substantial form. In this case, the sentient soul is the *receptive potency*. Cajetan, although maintaining that phantasms receive nothing positive from the light of the intellect, again comments very acutely: 'The acting intellect is turned OBJECTIVELY, not formally on the phantasms, just as colours are illuminated.' He explains specific abstraction as follows: 'Abstraction consists simply in producing species by use of phantasms as REPRESENTATIVE OF NATURE, not as they are individually' (*In S.T.*, I, 85, q. 1). But what is this *nature* represented by phantasms? Not the phantasms. Where is it found then? This nature is ens, seen by the mind as object, and clothed with phantasms as a result of *primal synthesis*, whose theory we have outlined in *A New Essay* (vol. 2). — If ens is received as real being, real things are posited in being. St. Thomas says that being 'is not compared with other things in the way that what receives is compared with what is received, but rather as what is received is compared to what receives' (*S.T.*, I, q. 4, art. 1, ad 3). — Finally, if being is taken in its moral mode, the result is moral virtue, holiness, the supernatural order.

[52] Philosophers did not always distinguish *receptivity* from *passivity*, as we see in St. Thomas. Consequently, they considered understanding as *passivity* when, in fact, it is properly speaking *receptivity*. 'All receiving is called "experiencing" and "being moved", as the Philosopher says in his *De Anima* (bk. 3, t. 7): understanding is a kind of experiencing' (*In I Sent.*, d. 8, q. 3, art. 2).

Article 4
Principle-entia and term-entia considered as potencies

862. Wherever a substance is united to an idea, an ens is present. Substance is the first act that we conceive. This first act makes other acts subsist in a given mode.

I have distinguished substances, and consequently entia, into two classes, which I called *principle-entia* and *term-entia* (cf. 842–845).

Term-entia are those not conceived as sentient. Matter is of this kind.

Principle-entia are those conceived as sentient. The soul, and all intelligences, are of this kind.

Both principle-entia and term-entia are substances because a first act is conceived in them through which all other acts exist, active and passive, which are mentally discernible in them.

Some of these (active and passive) acts distinct from substance are necessary (substantial forms), others are accidental (accidental forms).

863. Because accidental acts are present both in principle-entia and in term-entia, *potency* must be distinguished from *act* in them. Again, receptive, active and passive potencies are found in entia that pertain to the classes of both principle-entia and term-entia, which can therefore undergo development. In other words, both classes are subject to modifications and actualities that can perfect them, and to privations or negative potencies that can cause them to deteriorate.

864. We must note, however, that both principle-ens and term-ens retain their nature as principle and term in all their development. Principle and term pertain to their essence, which cannot change without ceasing to be the ens it was previously and becoming something else.

CHAPTER 13

Act and potency are present in the human soul

865. From what I have said, it is clear that *potency* as well as

act is present in the human soul. Indeed, the many accidental acts found in the soul must depend upon potencies which are related to them. These potencies, I said, have to be found and carefully described, but to do this we first have to investigate how acts and potencies can be contained in the soul.

CHAPTER 14

How accidental acts are contained in the essence of the human soul

866. The question: 'How are accidental acts contained potentially in an ens?' is extremely serious and difficult, like all questions which consider the internal construction of an ens. Here, too, we have to start from a long way back.

Article 1
Preliminary remarks

867. First, we must remember that in speaking of an ens whose nature and internal constitution we want to discover, we are dealing with an ens existing before our mind, not about some other ens. Unless we had mentally conceived this ens, we could neither reflect on it nor talk about it. The existence of a mentally non-conceived being is different from that of a conceived being which, in addition to what is in the former, contains our conception, the work of our spirit (cf. 57–70).

Second, we must also remember that we know an ens in a different way from that in which we know its mode, its intrinsic order. As we said, we know it through a natural intuition; we gather its intrinsic order *a posteriori*, from experience, when we perceive the reality.

868. Third, we need to note carefully the following rule, which can never be sufficiently repeated: 'All that regards an ens and is supplied by intuition, is essentially objective; all that regards the intrinsic order of an ens, and comes from our experience, is subjective.' This rule enables us to distinguish

[866–868]

what is objective from what is subjective in being, as we perceive it.

This principle could be misunderstood if we wished to infer from it that everything subjective in our knowledge were false. In this case, nothing true would be known about the subject. On the contrary, everything we know of the subject and its appurtenances is true provided we do not claim that the subject and its appurtenances are object. In this way, what we know subjectively is true if we affirm it subjectively, just as it would be false if we affirmed to ourselves that we knew it objectively.

Nevertheless, what is true always arises from the object as from its formal cause in the same way that every cognition arises from the object. This is so true that the subject alone, and everything subjective, would be unknown as subject and subjective without the light of the object. For example, when I say: 'I (subject) exist, I affirm the existence of MYSELF, as subject.' Existence is objective, although that to which it is referred is subject. This is applicable whether we are speaking about possible or real existence. If I did not annex either possible or real existence to the subject, the latter would remain totally unknown and would not exist in any way for me, an intelligent being.

869. It follows that for human beings, and for every other intelligence, reality exists only in so far as it is known. The very act of knowledge adds objective being, called existence, to the real subjective thing. It is also the act of knowledge, therefore, which adds truth to the real, subjective thing because truth is simply that which is.[53]

Article 2
Cohesion amongst the substances which make up the universe — their classification from this point of view

870. Granted all this, we ask: 'How are accidental acts contained virtually in the essence of the soul?'

It is clear that this is a question concerned with the intrinsic order of an ens, and cannot therefore be solved without

[53] *Sistema filosofico*, 56–70.

recourse to some fact. Everything more that we can say is reduced to demonstrating lack of contradiction or absurdity in the fact. Sometimes, however, the fact itself seems at first sight to be loaded with contradictory elements.

871. In our case, there is no lack of apparent contradiction. On the one hand, the soul is a single, simple ens; on the other, it presents itself with a plurality of acts and potencies. We now have to add other considerations to what we have already affirmed about this in the first part.

872. Light comes to us in such an arduous argument from the ontological principle which I have already explained (cf. 34–44): 'The substances which make up the universe are so cohesive and packed together that one sustains another, and informing it, as it were, makes it be. This takes place without any of these substances losing what makes it distinctive, and without its being confused with another.' Hence, a law of continuity arises between substances which, however, does not destroy their specific distinction.

Another consequence is what I have called *synthesism* of nature. For example, the nature of the sensitive soul cannot be conceived without our positing some extended element, that is, the felt and sensiferous element which provides our concept of body. Nevertheless, the soul is a substance altogether different from the extended element and the body. In its turn, the extended, felt element can neither be understood nor conceived unless we suppose that it exists in what is simple, from which it receives unity. Here again, though, the extended, corporeal element is a substance altogether different from the soul. We have two substances, therefore, one of which sustains the other and makes it exist, but neither of which can be conceived without the other. Yet there is still an immense difference between the two.

The same law is noticeable if we speak about the rational soul. It is impossible to conceive an intelligence without a primal object.[54] But the essential object of intelligence is being in general, which cannot be called substance because it is more than substance. Hence, between the substance of the rational soul and the object which informs it, there is an infinite distance in

[54] *NE* , vol. 2, 1005–1019.

nature which makes one totally unconfoundable with the other. Yet the rational soul is what it is only in virtue of this other thing, which is not the rational soul, but dwells in it in its own way. The same is true of being in general which, although it can be understood without the human soul or any other contingent intelligence, is essentially intelligible (intelligibility itself) and can be conceived only in so far as its very own essence is understood. This explains our *a priori* deduction of the existence of God, that is, of an intelligent reality whose nature is not different from that of intelligible being itself, even though the intelligent reality is distinguished from intelligible being through intimate relationship.[55]

873. More light will be thrown on what I have said if we consider the ontological cohesion of the substances from which creation results. We can classify things in the following way:

1. Sometimes two substances sustain and actuate one another in such a way that one of them is thought of as principle (substance-principle) and the other only as term (substance-term). It is clear that these are two species of substance because the first idea we have of each is not only different from but even opposite to the first idea we have of the other, with which it is in synthetical relationship. We see this in the two substances of soul and body.

874. 2. Sometimes a substance is sustained and actuated by a term which, as I said, is not properly speaking a substance. This occurs with the intellective soul, whose term is ideal being, essentially object. In the conception of being, we find no act different from being. In fact, we understand clearly that the act with which it is can only be being itself. At this elevated level, the communication of different substances ceases; substances no longer buttress one another, as it were, nor sustain one another. All that we have is being, which is superior to all substances. The intellective soul leans as it were on this being and, in doing so, exists.

875. Our examination of the interior of contingent substances, which we undertook for the sake of discovering the order of their constitution, provides another classification which forms part of the first, but is worth considering separately.

[55] *NE*, vol. 3, 1456–1460.

1. Some substances are extrasubjective. Their existence is only relative to other finite substances. We recognise the truth of this if we remember that we have to speak of substance according to the concept given us by perception. The words we use are imposed on things as a result of perception. But every sensitive principle is excluded in the concept of corporeal or material substance, substance-term. Consequently, the act of any subjective, proper existence is also excluded. Such a substance is left with existence relative to a sensitive principle only, precisely because it is not perceived except as felt. It is only our understanding which adds the act of existence in an absolute way. We noted, however, that the understanding does this because otherwise it would not be able to conceive such a substance; the understanding does not intend to change the nature of the substance nor add anything foreign to it. The act of subjective existence, which must certainly be present, is not something additional that pertains to the corporeal reality we have perceived, but is supposed virtually by thought. It springs from the necessity of knowledge; it is neither a specified nor specifying act about which we can, through reflection, induce that it pertains to some other ens outside the body, that is, to something we have called corporeal principle.

876. 2. Some substances are subjects because they are principles. A principle, although it may have a synthetical relationship with its term, is nevertheless conceived prior to its term. Hence its real existence is physically relative not to things which precede it but only to things which follow on it. Sensitive souls are substances of this kind.

Nevertheless, these substances still do not have any selfness. 'Self' is not proper to them, nor properly speaking are the words 'his' or 'hers', nor any personal pronoun. We speak of them, however, as if they had some existence in se, and we apply personal pronouns to them. We do this, as I said, not to transnature them, but to conceive them mentally. By acting like this, we do not intend to attribute our own selfness to them, but the objective and subjective mode of being without which we cannot mentally conceive them. This mode supposes that 'a being has its own proper act, that it is something in itself, and therefore has an ITSELF, has some personship'. In fact, being which is not person is incomplete; person is the ontological condition of being. Merely sensitive souls, therefore, are subjects, but incomplete subjects, and do not have that reality necessary for their constitution as real entia.

877. 3. Finally, some subjects are perfect because they possess a SELF, and hence can rightly be said to have existence *in SE*. These are intellective substances. They are principle-entia and do not depend upon any other contingent, consequent or antecedent substance, but solely on eternal, divine being. These substances alone possess selfness and can say: MYSELF, as I have explained (cf. 71–80). But granted the existence of MYSELF, a true cause exists. Such causes are true agents, endowed with freedom. The act with which these substances exists is independent of every created substance. They can, therefore, stand above all others and act in such a way that they are not necessitated by the action of any creature. This has to be understood, of course, in so far as they are pure intelligences, not bound to sensitive or corporeal being as human beings are. In our own human case, we have a mixture of corporeal sensitivity and intelligence.

Article 3
Explanation of the origin of the accidental acts of substances

878. Having classified substances according to their intrinsic order of construction, we can finally turn to the question we have in hand: 'How are accidental acts contained in the essence of the human soul?' This question depends upon a more general question: 'How are accidental acts contained in the essence of substances?'

The general answer to this question arises from what has been said. It can be stated as follows: 'Different contingent substances are reciprocally united in such a way that one sustains the other and makes it exist. It is sufficient therefore to conceive some *change* in the ontological union in order to conceive how substances must be modified in different ways. These modifications are the accidental acts of substances.'

879. The accidental acts of substances depend therefore upon the *ontological connections* which substances have amongst themselves. Such acts can be called 'extrinsic'.

880. The unity of substance is thus maintained in the multiplicity and variety of its acts, and one of the most difficult

problems of ontology is resolved. The nature of the act called contingent substance is such that it is joined to another substance, and through this nexus subsists. Consequently, although no change is posited in the very act itself of substance, the substance acquires another mode and comes to be actuated differently when there is some change in the ontological contact between itself and something different from itself. The change does not lie in the substances, therefore, but in their different ontological connection, although there is some change in the substance in so far as its actuality depends on the mode of that connection.

881. In how many ways can we conceive variation in such a connection?

1. First, we can conceive the total destruction of connection. In this supposition, the synthesising substances are themselves annihilated. Thus, if we separate the sentient principle from what is felt, the sensitive soul is annihilated. It no longer exists where all feeling and every possibility of feeling have been extinguished.

If we separate what is felt from the sentient principle, we annihilate corporeal, material substance. In this case, we no longer find extension, nor sensiferous force, nor external force which changes the sensiferous force, nor sensible qualities — all of which are the constituent elements of the concept of body.

If we separate the intellective soul from ideal being, the former no longer exists because that which understands nothing is not in any way an intellective soul. But if we separate ideal being from the soul, we realise that of its essence it must be understood. It is not, therefore, annihilated because it is independent of the soul and of every substance in this world, although it presupposes some real thing that has an identical existence with it.

882. 2. Second, we can conceive that one substance joined to another, to which it gives actuality, is changed, either through substitution by some other substance, or by being joined either by another substance or by another substantial part (as in the case of matter, whose parts are numerically separate substances, although of the same nature).

883. The first case is impossible. If the substance giving actuality to another were entirely changed, the substance receiving

actuality would no longer be because it receives its nature and formal existence from its connection with the first substance. Thus, if the soul no longer had as its term the felt, corporeal element, but some intelligent being, it would no longer be a soul (cf. 184–199).

884. The second case, in which we are dealing with one substance uniting itself to another of the same species, is possible in different ways. We are dealing with corporeal, material substance, and therefore of different portions of the same substance.

Consider, for example, the different species of brute animals. Properly speaking, all non-intelligent animals constitute a single species. They are specifically equal substances; an equal, first act of existence is conceived in all of them. This consists in the union of a sentient principle with a harmoniously stimulated, felt entity. Animals appear different because of the variety of quantity of the felt element, of the stimulus, and of the harmony with which the sentient principle is stimulated. These are the three elements which make up animal substantiality.

This variation in the connection between the two substances (soul and body) does not properly speaking change substance, but places it more or less in act with the result that animals are more or less perfect. On the other hand, these varieties cannot be called transient accidents because the felt element has been changed substantially and stably. So, common sense considers these varieties as different species. If we wished to call them varieties, we would have to distinguish two species of variation. The first would be *constitutive varieties*, the second *consecutive* or transient varieties, which are accidents relative to the first kind of variety.

If a new sense were added to an animal (this can be conceived as possible relative to imperfect animals, although I do not think it possible for perfect animals if we are speaking about corporeal senses), a constitutive, stable change would take place because of the union of a new felt element. This would differ from the preceding felt elements not only from the point of view of quantity, but also because of the quality of the connection.

885. The concept of what I have called *integral parts* of a whole also arises from possible variations of quantity and quality in substances ontologically joined to other substances. A

man whose leg has been amputated suffers a constitutive, stable change in so far as a part of the substance which should have adhered to him according to his ideal type does so no longer. Nevertheless, the essence of that man remains intact. Nothing of the first idea of that man is changed. What changes is the ontological union through which human beings subsist.

886. 3. Finally, change in the ontological union does not always entail stable change in one of the two substances. In this case, the only change is that one substance is united to a different degree or in a different way to its companion, and in a transient, variable manner. This gives rise to the accidental, common changes to which created substances are subject.

Article 4
Application to the acts of the soul

887. Applying all that we have said to the human soul, we see that it is informed by two elements: the corporeal felt element (corporeal substance) in so far as the soul is sensitive, and ideal being in so far as it is intellective.

As we have seen (cf. 672–675), perfect sensitivity in the human soul resulting from the human organism seems a necessary predisposition for intelligence. But granted a given conformation of the human organism, that is, of the felt element, it does not follow, if the soul is to be sensitive in a human manner (suitable for receiving intelligence), that the conformation is so determined as to make variation impossible. Hence, differences in sex, age, temperament, states of health and degrees of perfection in the organism, and so on. These differences are:

1. partly stable. As such they pertain to the varieties or *constitutive accidents* according to nature, such as sex;

2. partly changes of *integral* parts. This occurs in monsters who either lack some part or have had some part added to them. This is another class of varieties or *constitutive accidents against nature*;

3. partly of quality alone. Examples are: different degrees of health, black or white skin.

[886–887]

888. As we said, animal constitution is a necessary predisposition for rationality. Humans, therefore, receive the *matter of cognition*, and the *signs* according to which they reason, from animality and, consequently, their aptitude for reasoning at different levels of perfection. Such an aptitude depends on the facility with which they possess, recall, maintain or mix at will different sensible *signs* of things. The result is multiple variety in the reasoning and affective faculty corresponding to the varieties we have indicated in human animality.

889. Moreover, if the being intuited by humans were to acquire reality, their intellective state would change substantially. This would entail a passage from the natural to the supernatural state (an argument pertaining to theology). This change to the supersubstantial form of human beings would be followed by a relative change in their reasoning faculty, and even in their body as a result of the activity exercised by the intellective part on the animal part (cf. 288–389).

890. These varieties, which may be according to or against nature, and integral or qualificative, are called accidental in the sense that they are not contained in the idea of the human being. They are relevant, however, to all the varieties of *state*. They are not *transient acts*, about which we still have to speak.

891. Corporeal matter, because thought of as term, is necessarily inert (cf. 816–822); it does not include any passage from potency to act. All its mutations happen from outside. It is merely passive. Its acts, therefore, are passive, or rather are not acts properly speaking, but passions. These passions of corporeal entia are always related to quantity and thus cause change in plurality, forms, localities of bodies, and so on.

It would seem that sensitive beings have accidental acts, which can indeed receive that name. But if we consider carefully how the sensitive being is constituted, we notice that these acts have their sufficient reason not in the sensitive being itself, but in the substance sustaining and actuating it, that is, in corporeal substance. The different ways in which the sensitive being is sustained and actuated cause the accidental mode of its activity. As we saw, it is an activity because it is a principle-ens.

But this activity is sustained, informed and actuated by its term, that is, by the felt element. When the latter changes, the activity of the sensitive being increases or diminishes, and reveals itself in different ways without, however, any change in the law or in its own theme. For example, if we view a surface over which different coloured, arranged shapes pass, the reason for the successive change lies altogether outside the eye, whose activity remains the same as long as the eye looks, although what is presented to it changes. The eye always sees with the same power, with the same act, although the visual act seems to change. The change, however, takes place in the term, not in the eye. Nevertheless, this term of our act of vision is necessary for sight; the term seen by the eye actuates vision. Thus as the surface which is seen changes, the eye's act changes, although its theme (the seeing principle and the law by which surfaces are seen) remains the same. Now, there is no doubt that if the number of the shapes on the surface seen by the eye were to diminish, and the shapes were to grow smaller, the eye would begin to see fewer things. If the images were to cease altogether, the eye would see only a uniform surface. But if this visible surface were to decrease, the act of sight would also decrease. If the visible surface vanished altogether, the act of sight would also cease; there would simply be no vision. This is because the act of sight does not depend solely upon itself, but is conditioned to its term, In other words, visual activity does not increase, diminish or cease through any deficiency of its own, but through some deficiency in the term actuating and informing it.

In the same way, every sensitive principle resulting from this kind of duplication of substances ceases with the cessation of the substance that serves as its form and term, and changes as this substance changes. The sensitive principle itself ceases or changes through its own deficiency or through spontaneous increase or diminution of activity.

But if this were so, surely the sentient principle would be only passive, to the detriment of any explanation of the animal phenomena in which the sensitive principle is seen to act on the body, as for example the circulation of the blood?

The objection is not valid, precisely because all these movements are explained by the primal activity of the sentient principle. This activity is always acting on its term, according to the same law and the same theme. So if, for example, some irritation, some sharp pain causes an increase of circulation, this would mean, according to me, increase of action in the sentient principle. The increase does not arise because the sentient principle has of itself augmented its own activity, but simply because the activity it already possessed has found another term to actuate and inform it at a higher level, and thus enable it to develop. If, for example, I place an opaque body in the rays of the sun, and then substitute a diaphanous body, the sun's rays fall in both cases according to the same law, and with the same speed and incision, upon the body placed under them. In the first case, however, they are blocked and reflected; in the second, they pass through, not because they have modified their own activity, but because their activity, in unfolding, is conditioned by the bodies of varying nature which lie in the path of the rays.

892. Human accidental acts are *sensitive* and *intellective*. As sensitive, they develop in the way I have described. As intellective, they cannot develop unless they have recourse to their own term, that is, to the idea (object, being in general) which actuates intellective activity. Being in general, however, is extremely simple, and *per se* unchangeable. Consequently, the intellect, as such, is also unchangeable in the order of nature. It is only susceptible of a supernatural change when ideal being is realised before it. This happens only in the order of grace and glory, something which is superior to human philosophy. We can however doubt whether ideal being itself shines with the same light on all human intellects. For myself, I would be inclined to deduce the primal difference in intelligence from the rational order rather than from the intellective order alone.

893. The rational order begins with a fundamental perception (cf. 254–271). Its development starts as soon as the human being perceives exterior realities in the order of ideality. *Acts of perception* depend, therefore, on the realities which fall within our feeling. They develop by having recourse to the variety present in the term of perception and to the primal rational activity through which the soul is always inclined and as it were directed towards the perceptible term present to it in feeling. The soul has no need to posit any spontaneous change beginning in this primal activity. Reflection in human beings is then determined according to human needs. These *reflective acts* are unfolded in the same way because needs immediately make

themselves felt in the animal nature of human beings. Only when we acquire the use of individual freedom[56] does a very different kind of act become clear in us. The explanation of this fact seems, however, to require that the agent move himself in such a way that the passage from potency to act does not depend on the term but on the operating principle.

894. Here lies our greatest difficulty. We have to explain how these accidental acts do not eliminate the unity of the acting principle. The matter is indeed so difficult that even when a person succeeds in understanding how to solve this kind of philosophical mystery, he still has immense difficulty in putting his thought into words that have some real meaning for others. But I shall try.

First, we have to remember that freedom (I am speaking of bilateral freedom) is the faculty for choosing between two volitions.[57]

Next, consider how bilateral freedom resides only in the moral order where we are dealing with a choice between a volition harmonising with law, and its opposite. Outside this case, there is no reason for inducing human beings to put subjective evil before good, or lesser subjective good before greater good.[58] When, however, we are dealing with a comparison between the subjective order and the moral-objective order, it is possible to understand how we can put the smallest moral-objective good before the greatest subjective good, or do the opposite by placing subjective good before any great moral-objective good.

The explanation lies in the fact that the subjective order and the moral-objective order do not pertain to the same category; moreover, their various levels cannot be compared or measured. They have nothing in common, neither species nor genus, and consequently no true similarity nor even any true analogy. If we consider moral good purely as such (as it appears in moral obligation), we find that it has no force to detach us from the subjective good with which it comes in collision, unless we add

[56] *AMS*, 543–559.
[57] *Ibid.*, 606–611.
[58] *Ibid.*, 560–566.

to it our own energy and determine ourselves in its favour. It is precisely here that freedom lies.

The moral order, that is, the ideal-moral order (the law) is, therefore, the term of moral activity just as subjective good is the term of real activity. Because these two terms are categorically distinct, the two activities which they sustain and actuate are also categorically distinct. Each activity varies its accidental acts according to change in its own term. The soul, because it has a double term, has a double, categorically distinct activity, whose terms have no common measure. When these terms come into collision, therefore, they cannot determine the soul to develop through one activity rather than another. The soul itself has to enter the field, as it were, and decide for itself. This is where the soul's freedom lies, as I have said before. The whole difficulty, therefore, consists in explaining how the soul, which is one, can have two such distinct activities and adhere to one rather than another without its being determined by either.

It is not absurd that the soul should have two terms. The twofoldness is in the terms, not in the principle (cf. 161–173). The soul's two activities arise from the twofold term because, as I have said already, the adhering term actuates the principle to which it adheres. Granted two categorically different terms, two categorically different activities are aroused in the soul. The greatest difficulty lies in explaining how these two activities, being categorically different, can have a single principle, that is, the soul.

895. In offering an explanation, we must first consider that these categories are a consequence of the forms of being. We said that identical being is in three forms or modes, that is, *real*, *ideal* and *moral mode*.

These three incommunicable categories, although far more distinct among themselves than differing genera, come together in being, that is, in the unity of being. Granted this nexus — in other words a single seat of the categories where an extremely simple unity resides with an extremely distinct trinity — we can understand how being, which communicates with the soul under the real and moral categories, can maintain, not destroy, unity in the soul provided that we conceive in the soul, prior to its real and moral activity, an activity contemporaneous with the soul and connected with the unity of being. The presence of this activity in the soul is proved simply by considering intelligence, which has being as its term. It is true that this faculty has being under its ideal form for its term, but even prior to this it has for object *pure being* because it cannot communicate with the ideal form of being without communicating with being itself, which is manifested in this form. Hence we also find in the soul effective unity and trinity, an obvious trace of the divine Trinity. The soul has a single activity in so far as it communicates with being. All the other activities, even those as categorically distinct as the real and moral activities of which we have spoken, are unified in this single activity. But because being, which although one and extremely simple has three forms, it is not absurd that the soul, to which being is communicated, should be both extremely simple and possess three categorically distinct activities in its unity.

896. We still have to explain how this single activity (which corresponds to being and in which reside the two real and moral activities corresponding to the two categories of being) can determine itself when some collision prevents contemporaneous acceptance of both.

If we are to reach some solution (and this is our aim), we have to consider that in entire, complete and absolute being[59] the forms of being can never come into collision. The real form is conceived as principle, the ideal form as means and the moral form as end. Thus the order of being is such that the moral form is compared to the other forms as their complement and perfection. In the same way, even where being is participated in a limited fashion, the moral form can never properly speaking lose the element of end and perfection which forms its concept. If, therefore, it were put after the others and made to serve as means, or set aside altogether, some disorder would be present. In other words, the intrinsic, natural order of being would be destroyed. A visceral combat, present in being itself, would tend to destroy being, which can only exist with its proper order. Hence the soul, or any intelligence having being with its categories as its term, must in its first act observe the order furnished by being which, by communicating itself, sustains and actuates the soul. It follows that the still undefiled soul, when acting

[59] *Teodicea*, 384–397.

[896]

according to its well-ordered first activity, would retain in its operations an order wholly analogous and corresponding to the order of being itself; the soul would be determined to act with moral perfection by the order of being. We have to suppose, therefore, the existence in the soul of some spontaneity for acting morally, that is, of clinging always to moral good without ever sacrificing it to real good. This limits our question. We simply have to explain how the soul can abandon the moral order to pursue purely real, or subjective good. In other words, how is sin possible? If we can explain this, we shall also have explained freedom and its accidental acts.

Consider, then, that the soul, in so far as it possesses real activity, is extremely mobile. Any good or evil whatsoever, however small, is sufficient to determine it to act.[60] Moreover, as long as this operation is not opposed to the moral order, the soul acts according to the spontaneity proper to its real activity. When, however, the operation is opposed to the moral order, the two activities are seen to clash and determine the soul in contrary directions. Each of these activities, taken singly, would be sufficient to make the soul act, but granted the collision, which of them will conquer?

Moral activity is superior because of the excellence and breadth of the term which produces it. This term is being in its completion and final perfection which embraces everything. If this moral order were to act in the soul with the efficacy of which it is capable it should produce consistently prevalent spontaneity. But this order, although the term of the soul, does not act upon the soul with total efficacy. The soul does indeed understand the dignity of the moral order and the absolute necessity for preferring it, but does not derive from this understanding the force necessary to repress the spontaneity of real activity.

It can, however, succeed in repressing this spontaneity provided that of itself it unites itself more closely to the moral term that informs and actuates it. This increases the salutary force that the term has over the soul, and morally invigorates it. The soul sees the necessity for doing this, as we said. Knowledge of this necessity certainly does not determine but simply

---

[60] *AMS,* 623–627.

counsels the soul that it can, if it wishes, determine itself in that direction. I say 'if it wishes', that is, if it increases the vigour of its moral spontaneity by adhering more intimately to the moral term and thus receiving an increase of force.[61] Hence, *its vision of moral necessity*, this special term of its intelligence, is the fount of its freedom. Through it, the soul knows what it can and must do, although it is not determined in its will.

Intelligence, therefore, is the fount of freedom because intelligence presents to the soul the moral order and its supreme necessity. It shows the soul that the force it is lacking, and for which it depends on the moral order, can come to it from this order. As we have seen, the other activities of the soul are determined to their acts by determined objects or terms which actuate and sustain the activities. In the same way, freedom is determined by its object which, however, is that of intelligence. The object of intelligence for its part embraces two opposite elements, real and moral, without determining the soul to one or the other. The soul, however, finds in this object the possibility for making the moral element prevail because the object reveals to the soul the supreme excellence of morality, together with its necessity and finally its power of being actuated in an unlimited way. Thus the soul is left capable of determining itself towards what is better, or of giving in to what is wrong.

I conclude: every real substance which, through ontological nexus, sustains and actuates another, gives it some determined activity. But ideal being, when joined ontologically with another substance (the soul) gives it only a potency for determination, not a determined activity.

[61] I do not mean that the soul can really do everything in the moral order. Its forces are limited. It can also be determined to sin, even before it acquires the use of its freedom, as we see from the dogma of original sin. I am speaking here in theory (as Aquinas often does, although some people misunderstand him). I am considering the soul in itself, prescinding from its particular circumstances; I am supposing that the conditions for its action are present.

CHAPTER 15
How potencies are contained in the soul

897. After considering the acts of the soul, we must consider its potencies. But first, a summary of what I have said.

Second acts of the soul can be reduced to two kinds: necessary and free (bilateral freedom). Necessary acts are made known through the changes that arise in substances adhering ontologically to the soul; strictly speaking they are revealed through their reality, which has the power (when unopposed) to determine the actuality of the soul. Free acts manifest themselves in accord with the nature of ideal being which, adhering ontologically to the soul, actuates the soul not to a determinate action but in such a way that it acquires the faculty to determine itself, as I explained. Ideal being must present all, not some realities, and also reveal their value. Thus, through ideal being, the soul knows different realities and their value, but is not determined by these realities. Although it knows them, they are not all connected to it ontologically. The soul has the faculty to choose between them and also to join itself ontologically to the full, moral good to which it is not connected. This good imparts to the soul the determinate activity which enables it to rise above the impulse of every other reality pulling it in another direction.

898. These *realities*, joined ontologically to the soul and arousing its activities, are variable and therefore the origin of the soul's potencies which necessarily act.

899. On the other hand, *ideality*, joined ontologically to the soul, is universal. By means of this universality, it reveals all realities, even those not yet actually operating in the soul; it reveals the supreme Being, the order of being, the necessity of this order, and moral good. Ideality therefore is the origin of the potency of freedom.

900. The soul can by itself use this potency of freedom to change the terms to which it is ontologically united and on which it rests. But in the case of its other potencies, we still need to show how the realities change which maintain and actuate the soul.

901. Experience tells us that bodies are in continual movement. Their movements alter the soul's felt element, that is, they alter one of the substances and realities that maintain and actuate the soul. But how do we explain the movement of bodies?

902. We have seen that the concept of bodies does not contain the explanation of their movement; matter, as we saw, is inert (cf. 816–822). Influenced by this fact, some of the greatest philosophers thought that the principle of movement could be explained only by direct recourse to God's action. Others, including nearly all modern thinkers, saw no necessity for making God intervene in nature. They took the view that matter was not inert, and wrote books to show how it had an energy of its own. If however they had firmly grasped the concept of matter at its very origin in our soul, they would never have held this view. If we are to have pure, genuine concepts of things, we have to grasp concepts at the moment they are born in our spirit. Otherwise, they are quickly changed by the activity of our spirit, and even become composed of and mixed with other concepts. This explains the error of attributing to one entity the properties of another; two concepts become a single concept, which although composed, is seen as simple.

I certainly grant God all his creative and maintaining activity, but I do not think he intervenes by imparting movement to bodies, any more than he does in any other fact of nature. In keeping with good philosophy, I think there must be a second cause of motion, which must not be referred directly to divine action. I have discussed this second cause in the first part, beginning from a definite datum of experience which tells us that properly speaking the sensitive principle is a motor activity. Consequently, I tended to the opinion that all atoms are joined to a sentient principle (cf. 500–553) which never alters the law or implementation of its own activity, as I explained in the previous chapter. Granted therefore a particular distribution of matter at the beginning (a first, all-wise distribution that must be attributed solely to the Creator, because no other explanation exists),[62] there is no contradiction in supposing that in virtue of sentient activity this distribution continually and

---

[62] *Teodicea*, 238–242.

ceaselessly changes to another in a certain order. This supposition may not explain the laws of communication of movement (which must be attributed to the *corporeal principle*), but it does explain all movements in the universe. An example in miniature is found in the animal body. As I said (and will demonstrate later at greater length), all animal movements, which follow a cycle whose complex process I call the 'zoic course', are most fittingly explained by the supposition that their sole cause is sensitive activity, an activity that never changes in law or implementation. By means of this sensitive activity, given to it at the beginning, the animal passes through all stages of life and modifies its own organisation, until it dissolves in death.

Experience also supplies us with another indubitable cause of motion: intelligence. It is not impossible for intelligences unknown to us to intervene and produce mondial movements. There is more philosophical foundation for such an opinion than for the absurdity of denying the inertia of matter or for the unbalanced attribution of such movements to God as proximate cause.

All these changes take place in the terms of the soul. We must therefore grant to the soul potentiality, which in the last analysis is only activity susceptible of being differently modified by its term.

CHAPTER 16

The distinction between the potentiality and the essence of the soul

903. Are the potencies of the soul distinct from its essence? We must first distinguish between the soul's *general potentiality* and its *special potencies*. I will speak about its potentiality in general and see how this differs from the essence of the soul. In the succeeding books I will discuss the various powers.

Philosophers conceive the potentiality of the soul in two ways: 1. as the soul's principle separated from its term, and 2. as the principle of the soul informed by its term.

The first way presents to our mind a non-informed principle which is neither the soul nor anything belonging to the soul. It lacks any act proper to the soul, even its act as principle, which ceases to be when separated from its term. If however we consider this potentiality in relationship with, but not isolated from its term, it ceases to be potentiality because it is a first act, that is, the soul.[63]

904. In the second way, the term is *variable*, as I said. This variability, which is the cause of the potentialities, pertains to the soul's term, not the principle, which is the soul itself actuated in different ways by its term. This is true potentiality that remains distinct from the soul's essence, because the essence could be conceived even if the term never varied. For example, while a sensitive soul cannot be conceived without a *felt element*, the felt element can vary in numerous ways and change from one way to another. Hence, in order to conceive the soul, that is, think its essence, an extended felt element is necessary whose quality need not be determined.

905. The soul, in so far as it has any kind of extended felt element, is conceived in its *essence*, but in so far as it has a particular felt element, is conceived in its *potentiality*. Thus, its *potentiality* differs from its *essence*.

The same reasoning can be applied to the object which is term of the intellective soul, except that the intellective soul has a determinate object, universal being. Here, strictly speaking, the variability does not concern the object (this is immutable) but the realities known in and through it.[64]

---

[63] St Thomas says: 'The potency of matter is its essence.' Here he starts from the concept of unformed matter whose act is substantial form (*S. T.*, I. q. 77, art. 1, ad 2). But we have seen that totally unformed matter is not an ens; properly speaking, it is that nothing conceived by the mind as the *term from which* springs the existence of contingent things which are drawn from nothing. It is a hypothetical abstraction.

[64] This explains what St. Thomas says when he proves the difference between *essence* and the *powers* of the soul. He poses the following objection: 'Is the sensible element essential to the sensitive soul, and the rational element to the rational soul? If so, the powers of sense and of intellect do not differ from the essence of the soul.' He replies that 'the rational and the sensible elements, in so far as different, are not received by the powers of sense and of reason but by the sensitive, rational soul' (*S. T.*, 1, q. 77, art. 1, ad 7). This means that 'there is a sensible and a rational element which both pertain to the essence of the soul, because without them the soul cannot be conceived. Moreover, there is a sensible and a rational element which do not

906. But why are the terms of the soul variable? Because they are limited. In anything limited we can conceive variation and degrees of quantity.

If however there were an ens whose term were all being and therefore the whole order of being, it would be pure act without any kind of potentiality. All being together with its whole order is perfectly one and immutable. This is proved, as mathematicians say, by the absurdity that would result from the contrary supposition. In fact, let us suppose that some variation arises in the whole. Every variation pertains to the order of being. The term of the ens, contrary to the supposition, was not therefore all being with all its order; the order lacked the variation which has now come about.

It is impossible therefore for God to have any potentiality; he is pure act. His term is all being with all its order, because it is himself. Furthermore, what we conceive in God as potency cannot be distinguished from his essence without error.

907. There is another consequence. If we conceive a potency as the essence of being, the acts we attribute to this potency must be identified with the essence of being, that is, it must be a single act whose term is all being in its perfect unity and simplicity.[65]

Nevertheless, the essence of the soul is the source of its potencies and consists in the nature of a *principle* actuated by its term. Clearly then, this *principle*, that is, the *soul*, when actuated differently by different terms, performs all the different kinds of acts to which the potencies are referred. This explains why St. Thomas makes the soul the remote principle of acts, and potencies the proximate principle.[66]

pertain to the essence of the soul. These vary, or vary in different degrees; they are the objects of the potentiality.'

[65] St. Thomas shows that potency cannot be identified with the essence of an ens unless the acts also are identified with its essence: 'Because potency and act divide ens and every kind of ens, both act and potency must be referred to the same kind. Thus, if the act is not in the genus of substance, the potency itself predicated of that act cannot be in the genus of substance.' From this he deduces that the potencies of the soul are not the essence of the soul because 'the action of the soul is not in the genus of substance, but in God alone is action his substance' (*S.T.*, 1, q. 77, art. 1).

[66] *S.T.*, I, q. 77, art. 1.

CHAPTER 17

The nature of habits, and how they are contained in the essence of the soul

908. I turn now to habits. I want to show how their multiplicity does not prejudice the unity of the soul, just as I showed that this unity is not prejudiced by the multiplicity of acts and potencies. What has been said will help us to do this. But to proceed more clearly, I will begin by defining what is meant by habit, and I will determine its nature.

Article 1
The nature of habit

909. Generally speaking, habit is some acquired, accidental disposition of the soul which places the soul in a better or worse state, and makes it more apt to act in a given way.[67]

Article 2
Double meaning of 'habit'

910. 'Habit' has therefore two principal meanings, 1. relative to the essence of the soul and 2. relative to its potencies.

911. Relative to the soul's essence, habit is that which adds something better or worse to the soul's natural state, placing the soul in a better or worse state than it would have had without the habit.

912. Relative to the soul's potencies, habit is a disposition which gives the potencies greater facility to act in a given ordered or disordered, good or bad way.

[67] It has been said that there are habits inherent to human nature or even essential to it. I do not wish to discuss this question here. I am speaking only about acquired habits.

913. An example of the first meaning is the state of a soul made better morally by an act of virtue or the acquisition of merit, or made worse by a sin or fault.

An example of the second meaning are all skills, which are acquired dispositions for acting without difficulty to produce what skills should produce.

914. Careful consideration reveals that strictly speaking both meanings of habit are applicable to the intellective, moral soul. The second meaning is applicable to the merely sensitive soul, which totally lacks personship. Because the sensitive soul is not the cause of its own actions and possesses no ideal norm to follow, it is susceptible of natural perfection only one step at a time. One sensitive soul can be perfected in its nature to a greater or lesser degree than another; the same soul can even flourish or wane, although what it gains or loses pertains to nature, not to any habit which makes it better or worse. For example, a sensitive soul (an animal) with a term that is greater, more manifold, stimulating and better organated for the preservation of life is much more actuated. But this greater actuation is of the same nature as natural actuation. All we can say is that its nature has increased or diminished; it has not been made better or worse. 'Better or worse' can be used only in a kind of transferred sense, in so far as we apply what is human to the archetypal idea of that animal. Thus, a larger body is not necessarily a better body, nor does it possess habit; it simply has a greater quantity of matter.

On the other hand the potencies of a sensitive soul can have habits understood in the second sense, that is, as a disposition of the potency to act in a given way.

The rational soul, however, because it has an ideal norm to follow, is susceptible not only of greater or lesser natural activity but of being better or worse, according to its degree of conformity to its norm. This conformity endows it with dignity, merit and the right to eudaimonological good, which properly speaking does not pertain to its nature. It is a relationship with something other than the soul. This is precisely why we speak of 'habit'. In virtue of this relationship the soul acquires a better or worse state. The relationship itself is better or worse, and this explains why the goodness or evil of the relationship is reflected in the soul.

[913–914]

915. This also explains how the soul can have supernatural habits, if God is joined to it. God is not a natural object and therefore does not pertain to the nature of the soul; he comes to it from outside. However, in some way this kind of habit adds to the essence of the soul a kind of new nature, something which no other habit adds.

We must now consider habits in the second sense, that is, as dispositions of the potencies to act in a given way. In doing so, we will note several things about their nature.

Article 3
Habits of potencies have primarily the same division as potencies

916. First of all, we must note that the classification of the habits of potencies must follow the classification of potencies themselves.

Potencies are of two kinds: some have only one purpose, others, the higher potencies, are ordered to directing and commanding the lower potencies. Hence, habits either perfect a potency in its own purpose or perfect the order of the potencies by carefully disposing and evaluating those which must direct others.

917. Although habits by their nature perfect potencies, they sometimes indirectly cause harm, and disorder in the subject. This happens when a habit perfects potencies that have to be directed and subordinated and gives them greater force and promptness of action than that given by the commanding potency. In this case the potency perfected by a habit is disturbed and causes disorder in the ens, which it sometimes destroys.

Article 4
The origin of habits

918. We must now see how habits are produced. We have already been helped in this by seeing how potencies and their accidental acts are produced and constituted.

[915–918]

919. I said that accidental acts arise through the accidental change of the term informing an ens. These second acts presuppose a first act, that is, the informed ens itself, in which there is principle and term. The term, when accidentally changed and made able to arouse a second, accidental act, arouses the activity of the principle. Although this accidental act is transient, its cessation leaves a residue of actuality in the principle. Consequently, a principle that has more actuation is more prepared for, and responds more energetically to a new stimulation which it receives from the term. The term thus changes for a second time, just as it did the first time when it aroused the accidental act. This law shows that a greater frequency of acts must produce greater habit, although habit begins with the first, accidental act.

920. Because the cessation of the act involves the removal of the term that aroused it, we may perhaps find it difficult to understand how the principle of an ens must remain more actuated when the accidental act ceases. We could object that, even if this were the case, it would no longer be true that an actuality in the principle of an ens depends (as is supposed) on the action and the inherence of the term. We should instead be looking for some other cause of the greater or lesser actuation of the principle. If the principle remains more actuated when the term has ceased, such a cause will be independent of the actuation arising from the term.

I reply. When the transient act ceases, the inherence of the term does not entirely cease. We see this in the acts of both sensitive and rational faculties.

921. Indeed, when sensitive faculties have had an external perception or have experienced a passive or active feeling, some trace of what it has experienced remains in the sense. It is certain that the sensitive principle preserves in its felt element a modification produced by the action of external bodies on the body it is vivifying, even when these bodies have ceased to act. It is also certain that some kind of passion or an instinctive inclination remains, even after the cessation of an action in our felt element. These permanent modifications are the cause of habits, or rather are the habitual activity of the sensitive principle.

922. This can be understood better if we bear in mind that the activity of the sensitive principle is greater and more extensive

than it seems; it does not terminate simply in a sensation, in the felt element alone, but acts on the sensiferous element. With every change of the felt element, the activity acts on the sensiferous element in order to adapt it to itself. By doing this the activity can enjoy the best possible state; this is the origin of its organising power (cf. 474–489). Its state improves in corresponding proportion after it has experienced certain sensations and, by means of the activity these have aroused in it, has adapted the sensiferous element to itself in the best possible manner.

This will be more clearly seen if we bear in mind the law of *sensuous instinct*, which is part of the principle's activity. Before finding a pleasant sensation, the sentient principle is unable by its activity to produce the sensation for itself. However, after experiencing such a sensation, the sentient principle exerts all its energy to maintain it. If it cannot do this fully (because the external stimulus that aroused the sensation has been removed), it maintains some part of the sensation, to which it adapts its sensiferous element, which has not been removed, as much as possible. It now has a tendency to reproduce the sensation as soon as possible. Whenever the occasion returns through the renewed application of the external stimulus, the principle is already prepared and keen to co-operate promptly with the stimulus so as to enjoy the same pleasure. As I said, the sensiferous element, which the principle has kept in the attitude necessary for this kind of actuation or prepared for the effect, helps it to maintain this greater activity. Indeed, the sole action of the external stimulus does not arouse the pleasant sensation; a principal role in the arousal is played by the movements of the sensiferous element. These movements depend on the disposition of the soul at the time of the accidental act which, although it ceases, does not do so entirely. The sensiferous element remains on the alert, although the external stimulus has ceased.

This is confirmed by the fact that sensitive habits cease whenever the human body (and therefore the sensiferous element), is incorrectly disposed, just as sensitive activity itself ceases if the body becomes disorganised and destroyed. We are thus able to explain the habits of the sensitive faculties and the total development of the sensuous instinct, which pertains principally to habitual activity.

923. Habits of the rational faculties also can be explained in a

similar way, by means of the term which remains fixed as it were in the soul, even after the cessation of the bodily feelings which occasion reasoning.

In fact, in the order of rationality, we have:

1. A constant, immutable term, that is, indeterminate being in its ideal form.

2. Perceptions, that is, transient acts. As we saw, these acts leave some traces in sense, some instincts which arouse images, and some active and passive feelings. The traces and residue contain the stimulus for acts of intelligence which are used to arouse the activity of concepts, etc. Language also pertains to the sensible order because it is composed of sounds and other sensations, which themselves leave traces in internal sensitivity. Habits of the sensitive faculties therefore and instinctive movements explain how rational potency is aroused and drawn to its many acts by what is sensible, even when no external stimulus acts in sensitivity.

3. Finally, what happens in sensitive activity happens in rational activity which, after an act, retains an inclination to repeat the act because something of the object remains in the intelligence. We can understand this if we consider that the object of reason is a sensible element considered as an *ens* which, because it pertains solely to intelligence, is retained by the intelligence in an (ideal) concept even after it has ceased to be perceived.

924. But two things still need investigation:

1. Can the ideal concept remain without any sensible trace to which to refer it?

2. Can the perception of the real existence of a mentally conceived ens remain?

Relative to the first question, I maintain that the determinate concept of an ens cannot be actually thought without reference to some trace of its reality. Nevertheless, while the trace lasts, intellective activity certainly acquires habits in relationship to the trace. The fact of *abstracts*, which seem not to refer to any trace of reality, does not invalidate the first part of my position. Careful consideration reveals that these abstracts depend on and refer to some element of the trace, not to the whole of it. It seems that the mind can think of abstracts only when aided by some trace of their reality.

925. On the other hand, persuasion of their subsistence, experienced in the past, requires proof which involves some perception of reality that the same ens still subsists. Similarly, the help of some sensible trace seems indispensable if we are to be persuaded that we have perceived something subsistent in the past (that is, we remember it). The sensible element is sometimes the matter proper to rational cognition and sometimes the stimulus to its act of rational cognition, as I will later explain.

926. The habits of each rational potency would therefore cease totally if every corporeal felt element were removed from the soul without being replaced by another bearing some relationship to the previous elements.

927. It does not follow however that remote habits of the rational principle cease altogether. As I said (cf. 701–711), the separated soul preserves the principle of space, which is the remote principle of the body. This principle can be a subject of remote habits, that is, vestiges of acts of the living subject.

Article 5
Multiple habits do not prejudice the unity of the soul

928. We now know something of the nature of habits and are aware that as activities they are maintained by terms which arouse the acts and potencies of the soul. If follows that even multiple habits do not prejudice the unity of the soul. Their multiplicity depends not on the soul but on its terms. The soul's different activities are reduced to an identical principle which can be abstractly conceived as a kind of *per se* indeterminate activity, actuating itself in different ways according to the variation of its terms.

929. This principle, united to its terms, has its own activity because it is a substance distinct from its terms. Thus its activity and inclination increase. But completely divided from its terms it is no longer conceivable, and so no longer possible.

CHAPTER 18

Is the soul the subject of all its potencies?

930. Everybody agrees that the soul is the *principle* of every action and potency. But some say that the *subject* of the potencies which need a corporeal organ is not the soul but the whole composite.[68] This is true from one point of view: the soul, in order to have a special sensation, must have an organic body. Consequently, its own activity does not arouse any special sensations within it — the same is true about every act needing corporeal organs.

931. Nevertheless I have shown that acts, potencies and habits depend on the same law, that is, 'they are activities aroused in the soul by entities different from the soul, but ontologically united to it as form and term.' Hence, the composite cannot be a subject of potencies, acts or habits. That which in the composite is not soul, is thought of as term, not principle. The subject, which is always understood as principle,[69] is the soul alone precisely because the soul is the one principle of all its activities. Some activities however need one term, others another. Thus, the intellective potency needs ideal being as its term, the sensitive potencies the body with its changes, and the rational potencies both ideal being and the body.

---

[68] *S. T.*, 1, q. 77, art. 5.

[69] This teaching seems to harmonise better with another thesis of St. Thomas that 'the potencies of the soul flow from its essence,' which he proves by the following principle: 'An accident proper [to the soul] is caused by the subject in so far as the subject is in act and received in the subject in so far as the subject is in potency.' St. Thomas is saying that potencies are *accidents proper* to the soul. They are therefore produced by the soul as by their subject, and received in the soul as in their subject. Cajetan explains St. Thomas' thought by saying that the potencies in the composite 'are from the soul because a composite is in act only BY REASON OF THE SOUL' (*S. T.*, 1, q. 77, art. 6).

Book 2
(analytical)

Activities of the human soul — how the soul's potencies differ

[Introduction]

932. Philosophy, according to the ancients, was happy to be judged by the few;[70] the masses were kept at a distance as the greatest sages confided the finest fruits of their meditation to tested disciples. I cannot do that. My love for people makes me want to speak to the whole of mankind. What I think I can say to one person, I am glad to say to all.

On the other hand, judgment is the right of the few hearers or readers who have sufficient knowledge. The majority do not possess enough knowledge to make me happy with their judgment, and would do better, for the sake of their own dignity and for the advancement of science, if they paid quiet attention. This applies to intelligent people as well. Often, they have neither the time nor will to devote to fundamental questions. Sometimes they are distracted by the turmoil of life or by other studies; sometimes they see no need for careful meditation (a very common prejudice!), and never manage to attain clear, intimate persuasion of the truth. These people, too, would do more for themselves and philosophy by remaining quiet.

Perhaps I should qualify that last sentence. Intelligent people could help philosophy considerably if over-confident, curious writers were criticised severely, and a flourishing new form of education enlivened national morality (this will happen soon, I think). The dignity proper to authors would then increase, and they would be ashamed of writing about subjects to which they had given little thought. But this is not the case today. Conscience seems to play no part in writing. Very few authors think they have a moral duty to think carefully before communicating their opinions to the public. Clarity and certainty (the fruit of patient, careful study) are not seen as moral pre-requisites for publication; there is no harm, it would seem, in causing confusion in the minds of others.

[70] Cicero, *Tusc*, bk. 2: 1.

[932]

933. I would not be surprised to find that the questions I have dealt with in the previous book are considered useless and difficult, and thus finicky, by some at least of my fellow-citizens (not all, though, thank heaven!). People imagine that problems about humanity and other matters can be made easy or difficult at will. They prefer to be satisfied with superficial, lying and presumptuous knowledge rather than work hard and lovingly to become disciples of nature, ready to follow her courageously with all the energy they have wherever she goes, even to her darkest recesses.

Well, if this is the case with some of my compatriots I am still quite content to go on. Let them lie back in their comfortable chairs, if they wish, and sing all day: 'You won't have much company.' They will be singing to themselves.

934. So far, I have explained the distinction between the essence of the soul and its potencies or activities. We have seen that while the essence is a single principle, its activities are multiple. My conclusion is justified by a very beautiful ontological law concerning the communication of beings. This law allows many, different beings to communicate with a single being and arouse in it different activities in keeping with the variety of the beings, but without affecting the unity of the principle. The principle always remains a first, single act, virtually embracing second, multiple acts. In this way the order of being is followed, because those entities which, considered in themselves, are multiple, are one considered in their common principle.

We must now distinguish the activities of the soul by deducing them from its essence, that is, by showing how they emerge gradually from that first, single, very extensive act which virtually contains them.

CHAPTER 1

Summary of the distinction between potencies and habits

935. The soul, we remember, cannot really be divided without being destroyed. Nevertheless we saw that, in order to exist, its constitution needs two entities, a *principle*, which is the soul itself, and a *term*, which is not the soul but arouses the soul's

activity, a condition necessary for the soul's existence. The principle, if separated from its term, vanishes into nothing; united to its term, it is very distinct from it and, although aroused by the term as by a quasi-cause of its form, has its own activity.

936. Consequently, the activity aroused by the term which posits the principle in being, is one thing; the activity of the principle already in being is another.

937. Potencies are determined by the term and vary as the term varies; habits proceed, as from their source, from the activity proper to an already constituted principle.

938. I said that the laws which increase, diminish and modify the activity proper to the principle independently of the term, cannot be deduced *a priori* but must be determined by attentive observation.

Observation also shows us that the principle has a power by which it strives 1. to keep its term united to itself. 2. to maintain the term in the attitude and disposition which most satisfies the principle, or 3. to modify the term itself sufficiently to provide this attitude, and even 4. to bind the term to itself with a stronger bond. In these four different ways the principle, that is, the essence of the soul, unfolds its activity.

939. These four ways are the origin of habits through which potencies act more *easily*, more *promptly*, more *effectively* and more *pleasantly*. When the soul exercises one or more of its activities, it feels pleasure; each of the activities, as activity, is essentially sensible and pleasant. The exercise of an activity is itself an activity, and therefore pleasant. When the accidental act ceases, a trace of the experienced feeling remains in the soul which, retaining the pleasant feeling and increasing its activity, tends to reproduce it by renewing the accidental act. Habit is precisely this active tendency.

The trace of feeling experienced in the exercise of an activity endures in the soul by means of the activity proper to the soul itself. As I said, the soul does all it can to keep united and bound to itself the term which aroused the pleasant act in it. It maintains the term in an attitude suitable for reproducing the pleasant act. It also helps the term to place itself in the kind of attitude formed by the four above-mentioned ways in which the principle, that is, the essence of the soul, is active.

940. In the case of the sensitive soul, nothing of this is prevented by the cessation of the external stimulus which arouses the actual sensation. The constant term of the soul is the living body, not the external stimulus directly aroused by the sensation. True, the actual sensation ceases when the external stimulus ceases, but the disposition of the animate body does not cease. The body is maintained by the soul in that attitude and mobility through which the body can promptly and vividly re-acquire the sensation at the approach of the external stimulus.

Moreover, traces remain in the phantasy. The soul, aided by casual, internal movements that take place in a living body where everything is movement, easily re-awakens the images in the phantasy. The images pertain to the accidental acts of sensitivity and give to the rational soul a new or changed term, as sensations do.

941. Even when accidental acts have ceased, the soul itself retains those traces of its acts which constitute memory. Thus the sensible and intelligible traces remaining in the soul after accidental acts are a development of its term and increase its habitual activity.

When the rational soul has come to the point of actually having an end before it, it becomes arbiter of many sensitive and intelligible acts and uses them as means to the end. Thus it can move by itself, draw nearer to its term, bind itself more tightly to it, and apply to itself external stimuli.

CHAPTER 2

Summary of the distinction between potencies and their acts

942. The soul's term can undergo change or modification from two sources: from the principle which is the essence of the soul, and from a cause different from the soul. This change can be conceived in different ways: 1. the term is completely divided from its principle, in which case it is no longer term; 2. one term is removed and another, specifically different term substituted;

here, the essence of the soul is changed; the soul ceases to be what it was; 3. the term is specifically increased, in which case the essence of the soul, although increased, remains the same (cf. 184–199).

I will pass over these conceivable changes to speak about those which can not only be conceived but, as experience attests, occur every day.

943. The following can be said about these changes:

1. The soul's term is partly constant and invariable; it specifies the human soul and determines its nature. The invariable part is twofold, being *a*) an extended felt element that contains a continual change of parts causing the feeling of stimulation and a determinate organism; and *b*) indeterminate, ideal being.

2. The soul's term is partly variable. Relative to the body, this variability consists in extension and intestine movement, which is the cause of the stimulation and the organism, and of perpetuity of life. Relative to ideal being (not subject to change), variability is only in the soul in so far as the soul sees in being the real things perceived in sense, and extracts from them the doctrine of reality. Thus its object is enriched without change to itself, because the soul sees in its object that which it did not see previously.

All these changes give rise to accidental acts which, when they cease, leave habits in the soul.

944. Accidental acts arise therefore through the changes which take place in the terms of the soul, without the terms changing specifically. The changes take place either in virtue of the activity proper to the soul, in which case they are *active acts*, or in virtue of a cause foreign to the soul, in which case they are *passive acts*.

Habits arise from the traces of activity remaining in the soul when accidental acts cease.

Finally, *potencies* arise from the specific diversity of the terms joined to activity of the soul.

CHAPTER 3
Activity and passivity of potencies

945. Granted that the soul's activity arises in virtue of the action of the term, *passivity* and *receptivity* must, in the logical order, be conceived before *activity*.

946. I say 'in the logical order' because in the chronological order activity does not always come after passivity. Accidental, second acts must be distinguished from the first act which posits the soul in being.

Observation reveals that in the case of second acts passivity precedes activity in the soul in both logical and chronological orders; the soul first feels and receives, then moves and acts. But this is impossible relative to the first act, because the soul exists through this act and cannot be passive before existing. Hence, in the first act, passivity and activity must be contemporaneous.

On the other hand, as soon as we see that the relationship between passivity and activity in the first act is considered similar to that of cause and effect (because the first act arises in virtue of the term's action), passivity is said to precede activity in the logical order, although no ens exists as long as there is no activity.

947. Granted that activity arises from passivity, we need to know whether passive potencies are specifically distinct from active potencies.

I said that potencies are distinguished according to the specific distinction of the terms. Consequently, passivity and activity do not properly speaking constitute different potencies, but rather different faculties or functions of the same potency; activity is the continuation of the movement that begins in passivities, just as a line is the continuation of a point.[71]

In fact, the term is in the principle as agent, causing the principle to appear passive. At the same time, the principle has come into act and operation, and thus become active, that is, an individuated principle. Once posited in being, it can be first passive

---

[71] *AMS*, 367–370.

in its own way and then active. Hence, in the series of second acts, we can easily conceive a kind of passivity that precedes activity both logically and chronologically.

Because the soul's *activity* begins in *passivity*, which gives rise to the spontaneous or free movement of the active principle constituting the soul, the passive and the active faculty corresponding to this activity constitute a single potency. Although this single potency has a single term, it is distinguished into two faculties according to the different mode of its exercise.

948. We must note that in the intellect *receptivity* takes the place of *passivity*. The term is produced neither partly nor totally by the principle's activity; it is by nature utterly immutable, so that between it and the soul there is properly speaking no relationship of action and passion but only of presence and intuition. Such is ideal being. The felt element on the contrary receives its nature as felt from the sentient principle itself, as I said. The felt element is posited and constituted as such, that is, as felt, by the principle itself.

CHAPTER 4

We begin to explain how the terms which give rise to the potencies of the human soul are distinguished

949. The potencies of the human soul are distinguished in the same way as its terms. Note however that the terms first inform the soul, that is, they give it its first act and then, when modified, arouse and occasion second acts without losing their specific nature. This activity of the soul considered relative to second acts is called 'potency'.

950. In the soul therefore, as I said elsewhere, there is a sensible and an intelligible element pertaining 1. to its nature, because they posit its essence in act, and 2. to its potencies, that is, potencies of feeling and understanding.

951. Because the diversity of the terms is fundamental to the diversity of the potencies, we cannot classify the potencies with philosophical rigour without investigating how the terms differ specifically from each other. Let us do this now.

[948–951]

The terms are entities acting in the soul. How they differ from each other concerns the intrinsic order of being. I said that the order of being cannot be found or discovered *a priori*; only attentive observation can present it to us as it is, and our knowledge of it will extend only as far as our observation. We have to be content with what observation gives us, unless we wish to create a philosophy of vain illusions.

All that we learn from observation about the primal order of being can be reduced to this: every thinkable entity whatsoever belongs ultimately to one of the following three categories: it is 1. a *feeling* or something that happens in our feeling, for example, the energy that changes our feeling, or 2. an *idea*, or 3. an *order* between feeling and idea. In each of these categories we find the same being. I call it *real being* relative to feeling; *ideal being* relative to idea, and *moral being* relative to the complete *order* between real and ideal being.

If we reduce all possible entities to these three categories, the terms of the soul, which are entities, must themselves first be reduced to these three modes of being. We would then be able to see that the trinity of the soul must be present in its *essence* and in its *potencies*. This presence would not prejudice the soul's unity, because in all three modes, being is one and the same, not divided but complete.

952. Note however that moral being, which results from the union of the first two, seems posterior to them in the logical order. We must however distinguish between finite and absolute ens. In the latter, *moral being* cannot be posterior because completion and perfection are essential to this ens. On the other hand, finite, intelligent ens, although constituted by being under the forms of reality and ideality, does not necessarily require being under the form of morality.

953. Nevertheless, wherever the two forms of reality and ideality are found united, they exhibit some tendency to order, because being necessarily tends to complete and be united with itself. This results in the third form, that is, the moral form in act. Consequently, while there may be no need in finite, intelligent beings for moral order in act (also called *moral good*), the *potency* to obtain it cannot be lacking, nor the *tendency*, and ultimately the *necessity*, if moral order is to be perfect.

The potency cannot be lacking because it is joined to the

simultaneous presence of both real and ideal being. Real and ideal being, as term of the soul, arouse two potencies in the soul. These two potencies, joined in the unity of the soul, give rise first to a third potency, *reason*, which in turn gives rise to moral potency. Reason, perceiving what is real in the light of what is ideal, unites these two and sees the order of being. If the soul adheres to this order with all its rational activity, it becomes morally good; wicked, if it opposes the order.

At its beginning however the soul possesses this potency only virtually. Naturally speaking, it possesses not the order of being, but only being in its ideal form and partly in its real form. Hence, in the soul, moral potency is posterior and solely virtual.

954. We also need to consider how both ideal and real being concur in constituting the soul, because they do not do so in the same way. The difference is this: real being is both principle and term of the soul, and as principle, constitutes the essence of the soul. Ideal being on the contrary is only term, not principle. It does not constitute the essence of the soul but as formal cause or, if preferred, cause of the form, contributes to the production of the soul by arousing within it the act of intelligence.

955. Knowing that real being relative to the soul is of two kinds, that is, principle and term, makes it easier to see how the act of moral being is generated. Moral being is rooted in real being in so far as the latter is principle, not term. Strictly speaking, we understand morality as principle, not term, because it consists in the pleasure an intelligent subject takes in being known as such. This pleasure comprises the complete order between what is real and what is ideal. Reason however must first present this order to human beings as the object of their rational activity, that is, of their will, and thus constitute the term of moral potency.

Moral order therefore arises as follows: intelligent, real being knows being under all its forms in what is ideal, and takes pleasure in it proportionately. Why this pleasure? Because it knows being or, and this is the same, finds it in ideal being. By means of ideal being, intelligent, real being takes pleasure in being, that is, in being under all its forms. This taking pleasure is moral order in the soul, is good itself.

956. Summarising this chapter, we can easily understand that the presence of two actuated terms in the soul necessarily

implies two primal potencies, that is, sensitivity and intelligence. Furthermore, the presence of a third term which is only virtually understood in the first two, gives rise necessarily to a third virtual potency, that is, morality.

957. If we add to this what was discussed in the chapter before the last, namely, that every potency begins by being passive or receptive, and then moves to be active, the two potencies of sensitivity and intelligence will each have two faculties, a passive and an active faculty.

958. Finally, moral potency does not have a term in act but only a virtual term necessarily produced by the act of the other two potencies, or better, of the rational soul itself which directs the potencies. Consequently, moral potency cannot have any passive characteristic; it remains a purely active potency, because the passivity related to it is simply that of the potencies producing it.

CHAPTER 5

The distinction between the actual and virtual potencies of the soul

959. Two kinds of potency must be distinguished in the soul: *actual* and *virtual*. Actual potencies are those whose term is supplied by the nature of the soul; virtual potencies, those whose term is not supplied by the soul but produced by the soul's action.

It is true that even the potencies we call actual are in fact not distinguishable, as long as they remain immersed in the essence of the soul. They are joined in the unity of the principle, where they lie quiescent, so to speak. At least they cannot be distinguished as potencies, whose concept involves a *relationship* with different kinds of accidental acts. But when *accidental acts* arise and the soul's term alters without changing its specific nature, the potencies we call actual appear.

960. Now, just as the terms of the human soul are two (the *felt* element and the *understood* element), so the actual, primitive potencies are two: *sense* and *intellect.* Each is endowed with a

passive and an active faculty: sense with the active faculty of instinct, intellect with the active faculty of will.

961. Granted that the soul has felt and understood elements, where the two potencies of sense and intellect terminate, the term of a new potency arises. This term is the coupling of the felt and understood elements. By means of this coupling, 'the felt element is known in the understood element', that is, in the idea, and as known can be willed and loved. This derived potency is *reason* whose task is to apprehend the unity of an ens; in other words, it apprehends the identity of an ens in the felt and understood elements, that is, in reality and in the idea, as well as in its order. The potency, although a consequence of the first two (this is why it can be called *derived*), is not only in human nature virtually, but actually. As we have seen, we have in our soul a first, fundamental perception of our animality. This consists in the union of the intellective soul with the body, which gives rise to the human composite. This perception is the first act by which *reason* exists (cf. 254–285).

962. If, however, *moral potency* is to be posited in act, the soul needs more than the real and ideal elements, the terms of sense and intellect, and more than their logical union, the term of reason. The existence of moral potency requires at least the perception of an intellective being to whom we can give all the affection it merits. In other words, we can esteem and love this being for itself. It is not, as in the case of brute beings, a mere means for ourselves. This just measure of our esteem is where morality begins.

963. Furthermore, the nature of morality, which is the act completing and perfecting being, includes a certain relationship with the whole of being. Hence its object can only be intelligent being, understood as end, and understood as such because intelligent being touches upon the infinite.[72] Thus, although we feel, we do not naturally perceive or know any intelligent being, not even *ourselves*. *Our animality*, which we naturally perceive, is not ourself, which explains why we lack the term of moral potency and must obtain it through use of our reason. Hence moral potency is correctly called *virtual* as well as consequent and *derived*, because the only thing we find in human nature is a

[72] *PE*, 101–113.

power for producing the term of the potency and positing it in being. The same must be said about bilateral freedom which follows moral order, as we have said, and about *reflection* which presupposes perception and is a function of reason.

964. From all this, we can see that potencies, faculties and functions originate from each other whenever they accompany their accidental acts and produce a product which itself becomes a term, a variable term, of the soul's activity. Consequently, this activity, when related to its variation, is understood as potency, faculty or function.

965. Before we discuss special potencies, it would be helpful to present a synoptic schema [p. 104] of actual, derived and virtual potencies, so that the complex of potencies can be readily identified and our investigation proceed more easily.

SYNOPTIC SCHEMA 1

POTENCIES OF THE HUMAN SOUL

*A schematic presentation of the intrinsic order
of the primal potencies
in the essence of the soul*

ESSENCE OF THE HUMAN SOUL

which gives rise to the

PRIMAL ACTUAL POTENCIES

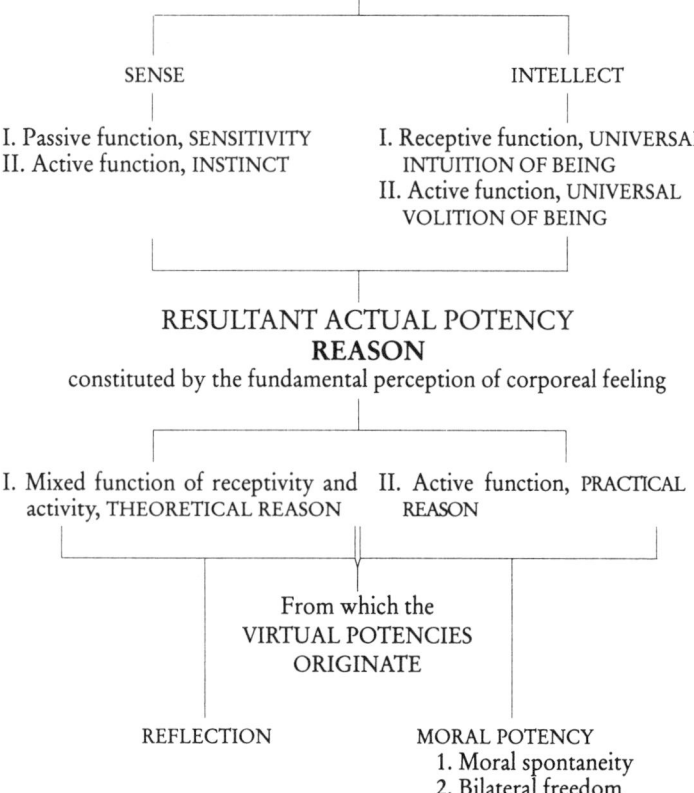

SENSE

I. Passive function, SENSITIVITY
II. Active function, INSTINCT

INTELLECT

I. Receptive function, UNIVERSAL
   INTUITION OF BEING
II. Active function, UNIVERSAL
   VOLITION OF BEING

RESULTANT ACTUAL POTENCY
REASON
constituted by the fundamental perception of corporeal feeling

I. Mixed function of receptivity and
activity, THEORETICAL REASON

II. Active function, PRACTICAL
REASON

From which the
VIRTUAL POTENCIES
ORIGINATE

REFLECTION

MORAL POTENCY
1. Moral spontaneity
2. Bilateral freedom

CHAPTER 6
Sense as 'primal potency'

Article 1
The potency of sense in general — Psychical sensitivity

966. I said that the extended felt element is one of the terms of the human soul. Corporeal sensitivity, although related to this term, must not be thought to comprise the whole of the sensitivity of human nature; it is simply a special sensitivity.

967. We recall that the soul has the nature of principle. This principle cannot be conceived without its correlative term because a principle without a term is an absurdity and nothing.

If however we conceive the principle joined to its term, we immediately have the concept of something whose existence is essentially distinct from the term united to it, and endowed with own activity.

The nature of this activity is feeling. This explains why I defined the human soul as a substantial feeling (cf. 81).

A feeling however cannot be conceived without the two poles, so to speak, which I have called *sentient* and *felt*. Thus, if on the one hand the human soul is essentially feeling, and on the other is by nature a principle, not a term, we must say that essentially it is felt as principle, not as something whose nature is term. But because the felt element, as such, is by nature term, principle and term are identified in the felt principle. This means that the soul which feels is that which is felt in its term, with the result that the principle in the felt term becomes felt itself; in other words, it is individuated.

968. Two kinds of feeling must therefore be distinguished: that which pertains to the principle of feeling and that which pertains to the term. The principle is sensible in a way different from that of the term. What is felt is properly speaking term, but the principle is present in the term, so that it is felt only because it adheres to, and is situated in the term, whose essence is to be felt. Hence the soul, that is, the principle, does not have its own sensibility but sensibility drawn from its term. Nevertheless the

soul's term, which is proper not extraneous to the soul, is produced by the soul itself precisely because the soul is the principle of the term. But if the soul is considered at the moment when it has not yet produced its term, it is totally insensible and not soul. Moreover, although this moment can and must be conceived by the mind because it pertains in fact to the order of being, it would be an error to think of it as an instant different from the moment when the soul becomes a nature and an individual through the production of its term. The soul becomes a nature in a single instant in such a way that the soul which produces the term is not divided by a moment's delay from the soul that has produced the term; in the very instant that the term is produced the soul is producer. Consequently, the principle of the productive act and the completion of the act itself take place at the same instant without any delay whatsoever. Nevertheless, these are two ontological moments distinguishable by the mind. The mind sees an intrinsic action in the entia, an order in the action, and in the order a before and after which is very different indeed from the before and after of time. In other words, we have here not chronological but ontological succession.

969. Let us return to our argument. The soul, when already formed, feels the principle and term, but the way in which the sentient principle is sensible differs considerably from the way in which the felt term is sensible, as follows:

1. The sentient principle is not sensible in itself simply as producer, but through and in the felt element it produces. The felt element, however, is felt and therefore sensible through its own essence.

2. The sentient element is equally sensible in every felt element and can be called *universal sense*. But the felt elements which exclude one another vary. This sensibility can be called *special sense*.

3. The sentient element as such is always identical; the felt element varies. Because the sentient element is principle by nature, it is one and simple like the vertex of an angle, although the two lines forming the angle are divergent and of different lengths. Nevertheless the sentient element is felt together with its connections to different felt elements. The soul therefore feels its potencies, functions, faculties, acts, etc.

[969]

970. The way, in which the soul feels itself and all that it does, I call *psychical* sensitivity.

Article 2
Special sensitivities

971. I must now say something about special sensitivities. At least four can be conceived as possible in the human soul. I call them *corporeal, pneumatic, ideological*, and *theoric*. Corporeal and ideological are certain; pneumatic and theoric are not so evident.

972. The nature of special sensitivity requires the felt element to be a different entity from the feeling element. Hence, in every special sensitivity there is some *otherness*; the soul feels something different from itself. This *otherness* is a characteristic common to all possible special sensitivities.

973. Otherness reveals itself in two ways, as *passivity* and as mere *receptivity*. Passivity is present in *corporeal* and *pneumatic* sensitivity; receptivity, in *ideological* and *theoric* sensitivity.

974. *Passivity* must be carefully distinguished from *receptivity*. These are two ways by which the soul feels and perceives otherness, that is, some entity different from its own entity. The double characteristic distinguishes them as follows:

1. In *receptivity*, the thing received is not modified by the soul receiving it, because the thing is immutable. For example, the nature of a gold coin is not changed by being placed in a purse, nor does the coin cease to be what it was simply because it is placed in the purse. In the same way, *ideal being* is in the human soul.[73] In the case of *passivity*, the entity acting in the soul takes something from the nature and activity of the receiver, that is, of the soul, which responds by giving being to the entity. Thus the *extended felt element* receives extension from the soul.[74] The foreign force, although acting in opposition to the tendency of the soul, changes the extended felt element with the help of the soul which is aroused to terminate its act spontaneously in another extension.

---

[73] *Rinnovamento*, bk. 3, cc. 39–47.
[74] *AMS*, 92–134.

2. In *receptivity*, the soul is not properly speaking modified but simply acquires what it had previously lacked. Although the purse in which the coin was placed does not change nature, it is worth more full than empty; although a shaft of wood is not changed or modified when a metal arrowhead is added to it, it becomes a new instrument, is given a new name and has a new capacity. In the same way, when ideal being is added to a sentient principle, the principle properly speaking is not modified; it has simply acquired what it previously lacked. From being a sensitive soul, it has become a rational soul. On the other hand, *passivity* properly speaking modifies the soul, as in corporeal sense. If the felt element is posited in act by the soul itself, the soul does more than receive. It acts, and its action is reduced to the general concept of modification. Moreover, when its felt element is changed, the soul again needs to concur with the change, although it may resist for a short time. Resistance followed by inducement to action is already a modification of the acting subject.

The soul, which cannot offer any resistance to ideal being, nor co-operate in forming it, must simply receive. The soul, which cannot act before it exists, does not exist prior to its contact with ideal being. It cannot therefore oppose ideal being. Consequently modification of the soul is out of the question. What happens is this: on the one hand, the soul simply acquires something; on the other hand, the power which posits ideal being in the soul acts creatively.

Action therefore corresponds to *passion*; *giving* to *reception*. The Scholastics, who sometimes confused the two, introduced a tendency to *sensism* in their teachings. They spoke about the intellect as if it were a fully passive, not receptive potency, and thus made it too much like sense.

Article 3
Corporeal sensitivity

§1. *Different kinds of corporeal sensitivity*

975. The term of corporeal sensitivity is the *extended element* with its passions and modifications, that is, the *intestine*

movement of the extended felt element. The term is also the organisation, that is, a given arrangement of the parts, and hence the *harmony* of the sensible movements.

The extended felt element supposes the *continuum*, and only one continuum;[75] if there were two continua, the two felt elements would have no relationship or communication with each other. Moreover, because the sentient and felt elements are always together, there would be two sentient elements just as there are two continua, without any relationship or communication between them.

But if the parts of the continuum move according to some law, without ceasing to be continuous, stimulation of the sentient element takes place. Together with stimulation there is vivid sensation corresponding to the intestine movement of the felt parts. These movements and corresponding sense-experiences can be simultaneously multiple and in different localities because they are joined by a felt continuum in which they arise, and by the oneness and simplicity of the sentient principle.

Our actual, reflective attention is drawn much more easily to stimulated sense-experiences corresponding to local, intestine movements, than to a general, uniform feeling. We think we feel simultaneously in many separate places. In fact, we feel a single, continuous extended element which is not felt uniformly but more vividly and variedly in certain parts where the tiny movements are aroused, as I said.

976. Although the fundamental, extended felt element is *limited*, it is not in itself *shaped*. Shape is perceived only when we distinguish the lines and surfaces surrounding and forming it. These lines and surfaces, which are not distinct in the fundamental feeling, are distinguishable only by the perception of something outside their boundaries.[76] But the fundamental feeling does not distinguish the boundaries, outside of which feeling ceases, because it does not exceed the confines of its extended element. If we take sight as an example, we will be able to understand the difference between boundaries marked by a *perceived* line or surface and those determined by the cessation of feeling. When I look at the table where I am writing, I

---

[75] *NE*, vol. 2, 823.
[76] *AMS*, 134–180.

distinguish lines which terminate the table, and I distinguish them because my eye also encompasses what is outside them, that is, the rest of the room. But I cannot see or determine the boundaries of my field of vision, much less compare the field of vision with another larger area, even if I wished to do so. My vision does not extend but ceases beyond the field. Consequently, if I determine the shape of my field by my vision alone and not by reasoning, I cannot say whether the area enclosed by my vision is round rather than square, or any other shape.

977. I explained elsewhere how special sense-experiences are caused by stimulation of the fundamental feeling (cf. 315–317, 420–428). But it has to be admitted that philosophy still cannot explain all the very extraordinary varieties of feeling-experiences, nor classify and list them fully.

I distinguished sense-experiences into *shaped* and *nonshaped*. I called the former 'surface shapes' because they constitute the surface or part of the surface of our body and of bodies exterior to our own, for example, sense-experiences of touch, sight, etc. Non-shaped sense-experiences, although dealt with more attentively by physiologists, have been practically ignored by psychologists.

978. A shaped felt element, we must note, is not felt in us. In other words, we do not feel it by referring it to ourselves. It is felt in itself as a surface, which is certainly not in us in the way that a small surface is in a large surface. In fact, it has no place or, if we prefer, is itself its own place. For example, the field of vision is not in another space larger than itself, but is exactly the total space seen. The place where sense-experiences are located therefore is formed either when we consider a part of the surface sensation relative to the whole felt surface, or when our imagination joins many felt surfaces together to form a single surface which, as I explained,[77] is, if not felt, at least imagined or understood in the way we form the concept of unlimited space by means of movement. But I discussed the locality of sense-experiences in the *Anthropology* (cf. 205–229).

979. Here, I simply wish to point out that because shaped, surface sense-experiences have as such no other space than themselves, we can understand how the internal sense of

[77] *NE*, vol. 2, 821.

phantasy is able to reproduce them. These feeling-experiences have no relationship of place with our body, that is, they do not appear to us as located on the surface of our body or within it, but in themselves, as I said. It is fully possible therefore that the image of a bell-tower or church, for example, corresponds to the movements of that part of the brain which is the organ of phantasy. The *felt element* is that which appears to us; it is not the brain as anatomically known, nor what appears in the brain, which is not seen. Indeed, its only locality is that which appears in the image or in the vision.

980. How then do we perceive the surface of our body? How do we know that the surface of the human body which we see is the surface of our body and not of someone else's?

Surface sensation alone does not tell us, but surface sensation in relationship with other sense-experiences does. For example, if I am touched by a foreign body, I have a single sense-experience, but if I touch myself, I have two sense-experiences, which I refer to the same place. I conclude that I am both toucher and what is touched. Thus, if I see a body and experience a tactile sensation when this body is touched by any other body at a point I can see, I conclude that the touched body I see is mine. This also was discussed at great length in the *Anthropology* (cf. 205–228).

981. As I said, no one has yet managed to explain the different kinds of sense-experiences. The general principle for their explanation however can be deduced from my whole theory of corporeal feelings and stated as follows:

'Intestine movement which takes place in the continuous felt element is at least the co-relative, extrasubjective phenomenon of sense-experiences, if not their cause. Variety of movement must therefore correspond to a variety of sense-experiences. Hence, this variety of movement can be, even if in fact it is not, the explanation of the variety of sense-experiences.'

In order to apply the principle, we first have to list all the varieties of the continuous felt element and of the different organs that can be conceived in the intestine movement. We would also have to establish, with the aid of experience, what kind of sense-experience corresponds to each of those varieties. This task pertains to the future progress of philosophy. I am quite unable to undertake it, and must be satisfied with some suggestions which may perhaps open the way to the great study necessary for the application of the principle.

982. 1. Intestine movement is as varied as organisation. Indeed, diversity of organisation not only causes diversity of intestine movements but even prior to this causes some diversity in fundamental feeling, and in a variety of ways. For example, the concentration of the fundamental feeling is greater in those parts of the sensible body where texture is more delicate and compact than in another equally sized space where texture is porous, less dense and less compact.

983. 2. The total size of the sensible animal body determines the extension of the fundamental feeling, which therefore varies as size varies.

984. 3. The intestine movement which produces acquired sense-experiences varies in keeping with the variation of the fundamental intestine movement in different parts of the animal body. The fundamental intestine movement itself is produced by the life and sensuous instincts whose very action receives its law from organisation.

985. Apart from this, we can say that the intestine movement which corresponds to acquired sense-experiences is explained in all its varieties by the following three causes: 1. the varying organisation of the body and of its individual parts; 2. the varying activity of the animal instinct, and 3. the variety of stimuli that initiate the movements.

986. But is the intestine movement under discussion a subjective or purely extrasubjective phenomenon? The answer is provided by factual description.

sense-experiences of colours and sounds result from vibration or oscillation of the optic and acoustic nerves. This vibration or oscillation is the intestine movement under discussion; the colours and sounds are the sense-experiences. Hence, the intestine movement we are speaking about is outside sense-experience, that is, it is not the felt element and must therefore be extrasubjective

But how do we know that the optic and acoustic nerves oscillate? Reason tells us, although it is not absurd to imagine that the oscillation can be externally observed. When we imagine vibration or oscillation, we are certainly speaking about something we know by external observation; if we had never seen or experienced vibration, we could not imagine vibration of the nerves of sight and hearing. Vibration is therefore a phenomenon whose nature is the same as that of phenomena which fall under our sight and external senses.

For example, if we look at the oscillatory movements of a spring, we have another visual sense-experience in which the spring and its movement are the felt element. A similar movement is found precisely in the intestine movement of the optic nerve to which the first sensation of colour corresponds. Relative to this first sense-experience, the intestine movement is extrasubjective, as we saw, but relative to the second, it becomes subjective because it forms the felt element of this sense-experience. Every intestine movement therefore to which a sense-experience corresponds is extrasubjective relative to the sense-experience, but can stimulate a second sense-experience which takes the stimulus as its term.

Here, we must bear in mind that the reasoning we make about the first sense-experience can be applied to the second. If the second sense-experience had as its term the intestine movement of the first, it certainly did not have as its term its own intestine movement, which could become the term of a third sense-experience. A person who saw the frequent movement of the spring as it expanded and retracted, or even saw the oscillation of the other person's optic nerve, would not therefore see the oscillation aroused in his own optic nerve to which his own sense-experience corresponds.

We could go on to infinity with a series of sense-experiences, but it would always remain generally true that 'the intestine movement of each sense-experience is not the felt element of the sense-experience. Nevertheless it can have the nature of a felt element for the next sense-experience, and therefore be something extrasubjective relative to the first, and subjective relative to the second'.

987. We must next consider carefully how movement can pertain to the felt element. Movement in the felt element is not a single, simple sense-experience but a succession of sense-experiences aroused in the extended felt element. If we perceive a movement with an organ — for example, our eye catches sight of a shooting star — we have to suppose that our organ is organised with a complex of parts, each of which can

be freely moved independently of the others. The organ is thus a kind of complex of distinct organs. This is how I described the structure of the optic nerve, that is, it is not a single nerve but a bundle of filaments, like little tubes. Each of these can oscillate internally and externally with varying frequency. This causes a different colour and successive, different colours, according to the oscillations of the different filaments.[78] Here we see how varying organisation changes the manner of feeling. If the eye were so constructed that each of the tiniest filaments making up the cord were unable to move with its own movement, but all the filaments had to move as one with the same rhythm and at the same time, there would be no variety of colours nor sensation of movement.

988. Various colours and sounds correspond to the number of vibrations or oscillations of the nerves which control the vibrations. It is also clear that the greater power and rapidity with which some parts of our body move depends on 1. their special organisation which makes them more prompt and swift to move, and 2. the greater activity of their animal instinct. Once again therefore different organisation and the resulting different action of instinct explain the different human sensories.

989. There is then no relationship and similarity between the number of vibrations and the sensation of sound. As I said, vibrations relative to sound are an extrasubjective phenomena; sound itself is subjective and of a totally different nature. Nevertheless, if we accept that feeling is connected with the atoms of matter, we can easily conceive how intestine movement, which does not sever continuity, would alter but not displace the felt element, whose nature is to be continuous and without sensible parts. Intestine movement alters the felt element by producing in it stimulation, which I have described elsewhere. Stimulation depends on the primal laws of the life instinct, whose ultimate explanation is found in the depths of creation.

990. Relative to the different kinds of sense-experiences and their varying modes and degrees, attention is needed to the size of the sensible body, to its form and the form of the individual organs, to the diversity of textures and to the diversity

[78] *AMS*, 131–133.

of molecules contained one within another. In the case of molecules, we need to study their different, denser orders, their varying smallness of size, their shape and their points of contact, their special mobility, the different directions in which they move and the varying degree to which they communicate and propagate this movement, together with its rapidity and frequency. All these and other similar varieties found in animal bodies and in their parts are circumstances that need study. They offer an explanation of the various kinds of sense-experiences.

991. The second special sensitivity I distinguished was *pneumatic sensitivity*, as I call it. By this kind of sensitivity, I understand the faculty by which we feel the spirit of others, or receive from them a feeling which makes them present to us.

992. This faculty has scarcely been studied and may appear something new. However, I think that observation makes its existence probable.

It is true that because human beings are mixed beings, their sensitivity can never have a pure spirit as a direct term. Nevertheless, I think that one soul may feel another soul or spirit by means of the body and in the body.

In fact, an animate body gives sense-experiences which differ in character from those given by an inanimate body. I remember reading in a work of Count de Maistre a very acute and eloquent passage about that mysterious, profound communication present in a kiss and in the feelings it produces. In such communications there would seem to be something living and spiritual which cannot be attributed to matter alone. In love and friendship, two souls seem to feel each other and communicate with each other by affection and the union of their bodies.

993. Furthermore, it seems to me that this spiritual communication must not be restricted to beings of the same nature. Angels could also in some way make themselves sensible to human beings by acting on their bodies in an appropriate way.

This topic is highly promising and deserves careful study.

§2. *The phrenology and philosophical works of Gall and Spurzheim*

994. Leaving the above investigation to the philosophers who follow me, I will interrupt my argument to consider the merit of the works of Gall and Spurzheim in the light of what has been said so far.

The teaching of these two physiologists begins from the following principle: 'The brain is not a single organ where all the actions of understanding originate, but a complex of nerve systems or distinct organs, whose individual function is to produce a particular faculty.'

995. In this principle and in the teaching which the authors develop from it, we must distinguish what is true, the solid base of phrenology, from what is false. The erroneous element results from ignorance of the most important and evident psychological truths. The observations which the authors use as evidence support the truth of their claims, but the mistakes, far from being the result of accurate observations about the form of the brain and its parts, are simply a product of the imagination and arbitrary judgment. This is quite common in the works of physiologists.

996. The true part can be reduced to the following:

The soul, although a single principle, has several terms. One of these is the extended element which arouses general corporeal sensitivity in the soul. Various organs can be distinguished in this term. These cause corporeal sensitivity, when modified in different ways, to divide into different modes of feeling, which are then considered as separate faculties. Consequently, it is acceptable for the brain, although primarily considered as a single organ, to be seen as an aggregate of various organs. Each of these controls a branch of corporeal sensitivity, provided we do not think each is independent of the others, that is, a continuous extended element separate from the others. As we saw, the term of the soul is certainly a single continuum with differently organated parts which move with such harmony that all the others concur with the particular movement of each.

997. This, and this alone, can be the foundation of phrenology. The errors which Gall, Spurzheim and other phrenologists have introduced into it, are principally the following:

1. *First error.* They confuse the order of sensitivity with the order of intelligence. The functions of the different organs of which the brain is composed can indeed be regarded as faculties of sensitivity but never of intelligence. This confusion resulted from the following fact: sensitivity provides the matter for intelligence; the latter, in receiving new matter, develops in a new way for every new branch of sensitivity.

2. *Second error.* At least some phrenologists fail to realise that the potency of sensitivity considered in itself is not a production of the organ, which is only the term of the sentient principle called soul. The potency of feeling arises from the union of the principle with the term, of the soul with the organ, not from the latter alone. Indeed, the potency pertains to the principle, not to the term; it pertains to the soul, not to the organ. The principle is the subject of all the acts of the potency and therefore of the potency itself.

3. *Third error.* The second confusion, of the organ with the sentient principle, is tied up with the other confusion between the order of sensitivity and the order of intelligence, and gives rise to the false concept of human intelligence formed by some phrenologists. They claimed that as the brain is an aggregate of organs, so human understanding is the complex of a multitude of very different acts. Careful consideration would have shown that despite the many varied acts the person performs, it is always the same subject who understands. This would have led to the recognition of the unity and simplicity of intelligence as a faculty of a single, very simple subject. The understanding does indeed perform many, very different acts, but it is not the aggregate of its own acts; it is the author, cause or sole principle of its acts, to which it is logically, and in most cases, chronologically prior.

4. *Fourth error.* There is nothing more fatuous than the pride these physiologists take in having anatomised intelligence. They think that by simply applying the scalpel to the encephalic mass, they have actually inserted intelligence into it! Clearly, they confuse the most disparate things, and are incapable of forming a correct classification of the faculties of the human spirit. For example, Spurzheim, when dividing the faculties of the soul and spirit into *affective* and *intellective*, does not see that some affective faculties are intellective: the intelligent subject has affections arising from his intelligence.

[997]

Again, after dividing affective faculties into *inclinations* and *feelings*, he reduces inclinations to the precise number of nine. The names he gives them would make a cat laugh: *inhabitivity, affectionivity, combativity, destructivity, constructivity, eativity* and *secretivity*. By these he means the inclination to inhabit, to be affectionate, to fight, destroy, construct, feed and secrete fluids, but forgets all intellective and moral *inclinations*. Moreover, he does not include the *primal* inclinations of the soul, but only some *effects* produced in animals through the collaboration of many primal inclinations and faculties. For example, the inclination to have and build a dwelling-place is not a primal faculty but the result of various needs felt by animals which react instinctively to satisfy themselves. The same can be said about all the other inclinations.

The *feelings* of the soul, according to Spurzheim, are exactly twelve. Four of them, *self-love*, *approbation*, *circumspection* and *benevolence*, are common to humans and beasts. However, he fails to see that intelligence is present in all four feelings which, therefore, are appropriate only to human beings. On the other hand, the affections of beasts, although resembling these four, are in fact totally different. A wise philosopher will determine the recondite, essential distinction between one kind and another, and not allow himself to be deluded so grossly by their apparent phenomenal similarity.

Spurzheim claims that the eight feelings proper to humans are *veneration*, *hope*, *supernaturality* and *justice*, from which he derives the religious and moral notions of *perseverance*, *wit* or pleasantry, *ideality* and *imitation*. There are other feelings, totally different from primal feelings, which result mainly from the use of many primal faculties, their products and effects. Thus the humorous, witty person depends for his persiflage only on a certain temperament and a certain measure of various faculties. He adds that some of these feelings, like *imitation*, depend on an obviously animal instinct, which reveals its power in monkeys more than in any other being.[79]

The same imperfection is noticeable in Spurzheim's classification of intellective faculties, which he divides into three

[79] I showed how the imitative instinct pertains to animality in *AMS*, 487–490.

orders: 1. *functions of the external senses*; 2. *perceptive faculties*; 3. *reflective faculties*. The first, however, do not pertain to intelligence but to corporeal sensitivity, something totally different. The perceptive faculties are divided into two groups. In the first, he places those which concern *perception of individuals*, and in the second, those concerning *perception of the relationships of objects* and their phenomena. Thus in the first group he puts the faculties of *individuality, configuration, extension, weight* and *colour*. But these, when separated from each other, pertain to abstraction, not to perception, which refers always to the object endowed with all its perceptible properties, according to the nature of different perceptions. In the second group he places the faculties of *place, number, order, phenomena, time, melody* and *artificial language*. These things, far from pertaining to pure perception, are functions of abstraction and reasoning, effects of many primal and secondary faculties which act and co-operate to produce them. For example, the faculty of language is certainly not a primal faculty; it is an exceedingly complex effect of nearly all human faculties, and depends on the external senses, animal instinct, judgment, reasoning, etc. The third order of intellective faculties (that of reflection) is divided by Spurzheim into the two faculties of *comparison* and *causality*. Every philosopher who has meditated only a little on the human spirit can easily see the insufficiency of this classification. Furthermore, a primal faculty of causality does not exist. There is only an ontological law, obeyed by the intellect that seeks the cause of everything contingent.

998. Our conclusions therefore must be the following:

1. The brain is an aggregate of various organs which are harmoniously interconnected in a single continuum.

2. Each organ has particular functions, but only in the order of sensitivity.

3. In human beings, varying development of intelligence, which receives the matter of its operations from sensitivity, corresponds to different functions of corporeal sensitivity and to the development of these functions. Nothing like this happens in beasts, who have no intelligence at all but only sensitivity whose instinctive effects simulate intelligence.

4. The different functions of corporeal sensitivity corresponding to different organs of the brains are primal, direct

[998]

functions, functions of sight, hearing, taste, etc. They are succeeded by corresponding active faculties; for example, the function of hearing is succeeded by the faculty of vocal sounds (not by the faculty of speech, which pertains to intelligence). An accurate listing of these primal, direct functions of corporeal sensitivity relative to the organs of the brain still needs to be achieved by phrenology. Such a task has hardly begun: very few propositions have been accurately verified by observation. But I will cite a proposition of Gall which has great probability: 'The cerebellum is the organ of physical love'. Physical love is in fact a primal function of corporeal sensitivity.

5. When we say that an organ presides over a function or a branch of sensitivity, we must not think that it alone is sufficient for producing the corresponding sense-experiences. On the contrary, one organ separated from the others no longer has an effect. Phrenologists must also establish, by repeated observations and careful experiments, the necessary connection which each organ has with others in order to produce its effect. In general, they must identify not only the nature of the organ of a given function of sensitivity, but also 'the nature of the apparatus of organs which is ordered to produce the function'. Finally, after demonstrating these two things, they must investigate 'the nature of the connection between every apparatus, the whole nervous system and the entire structure of the animal'. This vast field, studied today by physiologists, has the potential to be a very rich source of solid knowledge.

Article 4
Ideological sensitivity

999. The third kind of sensitivity is ideological.

We are indeed conscious of intuiting ideas, but unless we felt ourselves as intuiting, we could not be conscious of our intuition. We must therefore have a feeling of ourselves as intuiting. It may seem that this way of feeling is one with that of *psychical sensitivity*. It certainly can be conceived as a branch of this sensitivity, because in both cases the soul feels as a principle. However in psychical sensitivity (as I have called it), the soul feels as principle in the *extended term*; in ideological sensitivity it feels in the *idea*; the two terms of the soul are the extended element and the idea and, as we know, a principle feels in its term. Because there are two terms which by nature are not connected in any way, the same principle has a double feeling. Note that the feeling which the soul has in so far as it terminates in the idea is an objectified feeling. The soul, a subject, feels itself objectively, almost losing its individuality in pure intuition. Here lies the mysterious point of union between the subjective and objective orders, between sense and intelligence, about which I intend to speak more fully in *Theosophy*.

The idea however is not the proper term of ideological sensitivity but of *intuition* alone. This difference between the term proper to *feeling* and the term proper to *intuition* is of the utmost importance. The term proper to feeling must pertain to the sentient element; the term of intuition is something intuited as different from the sentient element, something purely in itself. The soul which sees the idea feels itself in ideal being. This is the special ideological sensitivity under discussion. The soul, when it feels itself in possession of the idea, feels itself intelligent and enriched, and acquires an *intellectual* and *rational instinct*. This is the active part of ideological sensitivity.

Article 5
Theoric sesitivity

1000. Finally, what I call theoric sensitivity is that which God produces in the soul by giving himself to it to be perceived.

1001. God grants himself to the potency of the intellect alone, provided we understand the intellect in general as 'the potency of being', which alone has an infinite capacity because being is infinite.[80] As we saw, being is one, but in three forms. If the potency of intellect is considered relative to being, it is one, but

---

[80] 'There is nothing wrong in saying that an infinite, passive potency can be present in the creature. As we said, a potency implies relationship to what is possible. A passive potency of the creature is called infinite when it is related to an infinite potency, as the potency of first matter is related to infinite forms and shapes, and the continuum is endlessly sensible. In the same way the possible intellect is related to infinite, intelligible species. It does not follow from this however that something created is purely infinite, but only infinite in potency' (St. Thomas, *Opusc.* 9, q. 8). Here, the word *passive* is understood as *receptive*, a meaning commonly given by the Scholastics.

considered relative to the forms, it takes on three forms, that is, appears as three potencies.

Under the ideal form, intuited being is the light of the soul. The intellect natural to the human being (which I often call simply 'intellect') refers only to the soul.

Under the real form, contingent being is limited; it is not the realisation of infinite, ideal being. Separated from the light of ideal being, contingent being remains as it were, in the dark; it is no longer an object of any intellective potency. But united to light, that is, to ideal being, even real being becomes knowable and an object of the special potency, *reason*. Precisely because the contingent real is unknowable in itself but needs to have ideal being applied to it by an act of intelligent being, the apprehension of real contingent being is not attributed to the simple potency of intellect but to the potency of reason.

1002. But if infinite ideal being reveals itself as realised, the intellect apprehends infinite being as real and of its nature indivisible from ideal being. In this case the intellect has the perception of God, something impossible to nature (although ancient and modern Platonists imagine otherwise). Considered relative to reality, this is an intellectual-supernatural sense.

1003. But how, relative to God, can the two conditions necessary for sense come about. In other words, how are both agent and soul changed?

First, God is not changeable; in himself he experiences nothing from the soul to whom he communicates himself. But we need to note that the soul does not totally comprehend God. God in himself, unlimited and incomprehensible, is one thing; the qualitative extent or degree to which he communicates his reality to the soul is another. This qualitative degree is determined by the soul itself and formed by the soul's limitation, which itself is restricted to the measure in which God communicates himself. Thus we can say that God is limited by the soul of the receiver to the extent that he is perceived in a limited way by the soul. This measure or limit does not lie in God himself, but in the relationship of union between God and the soul, a relationship through which God makes himself the proximate, direct object of perception.

1004. The modification which the soul receives from the communication of God's reality arises from the action of God's reality in the soul with its consequent marvellous effects. The object of the intellect is the natural aim of rational affection which lies deep in human nature, and also of the primal will which tends to good in general. Consequently, because affection and will find such a great object, they must be strengthened, elevated and transnatured. In addition, the soul must receive a new potency as different from its other potencies as God is different from other objects, that is, infinitely. Theologians call this new potency the '*the light of grace*' and '*of glory*'. Just as every specifically different term arouses a new potency, so a new potency must be aroused by the object which differs from all others, not only in species, genus and category, but in being itself. The human intellect, therefore, through perception of the divine substance, maintains the same root but receives a new activity. The difference between this new activity and the soul's previous activity is greater than that between any of its potencies.

1005. Explaining how the soul comes to receive the action of the divine essence is difficult, but less difficult than explaining how the divine essence can act in the soul. For the moment, it is sufficient to say in general that God acts in creatures in the way that creatures are in him, for we read: 'In him we live, move and have our being'. Thus, in order to act in creatures, he does not need to act outside himself. It is not contradictory to say that the action which in God is his divine essence has a limited effect outside him. Contingent natures have an existence relative to themselves. When God creates and acts in them, he does not remove, but on the contrary forms their subjectivity and individuality. This act, which does not destroy subjects and individuals but, after creating them, gives them what it wishes, need not be limited in itself in the way that it is limited in its relative term. This discussion however pertains to theology and, God willing, I will deal with it in *Theosophy*.

Having spoken about the sense of the soul as a passive potency, I should now discuss it as an active potency, that is, as *instinct*. But in order to avoid continual repetition, it is better to treat the matter in the book dealing with the laws governing the soul's activity.

I will however summarise the various branches of feeling in the following synoptic schema [pp. 124–125].

SYNOPTIC SCHEMA 2
POTENCY OF SENSE

SENSITIVITY

Sensitivity, as a universal potency, is simply the soul itself, sensible through its own essence and considered as principle of its accidental acts. Sensitivity intermingles with and accompanies all the other potencies, faculties, functions and actions of the soul; its development is as extensive as the development of all the other potencies together. The soul is a substantial feeling in which there is *principle* and *term*. Feeling, when considered in the *principle*, which is the soul itself, is called universal PSYCHICAL SENSITIVITY, a sensitivity that is uniform because the principle itself is always the same, although it acquires different relationships with its terms in so far as they inform it. If however we consider the felt *terms*, there are many kinds of sensitivity. In this schema, I will indicate *sensitivity* relative to its *special terms*, which present four conceivable ways or kinds of sensitivity. Hence, the distribution of

SPECIAL SENSITIVITY
into

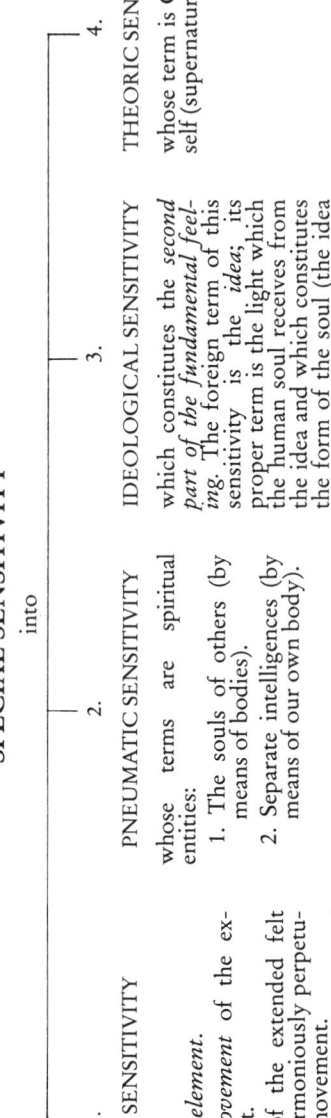

1.

CORPOREAL SENSITIVITY

whose terms are:
A. The *extended felt element.*
B. The *intestine movement* of the extended felt element.
C. The *organism* of the extended felt element, which harmoniously perpetuates the intestine movement.
This faculty is in part immanent, and the *first part of the fundamental feeling*. This feeling is limited but not shaped, and has transient acts which are MODIFICATIONS OF THE CORPOREAL FUNDAMENTAL FEELING.

2.

PNEUMATIC SENSITIVITY

whose terms are spiritual entities:
1. The souls of others (by means of bodies).
2. Separate intelligences (by means of our own body).

3.

IDEOLOGICAL SENSITIVITY

which constitutes the *second part of the fundamental feeling*. The foreign term of this sensitivity is the *idea*; its proper term is the light which the human soul receives from the idea and which constitutes the form of the soul (the idea informing the subject).

4.

THEORIC SENSITIVITY

whose term is God himself (supernatural).

The faculty of modifications of the corporeal-fundamental feeling has the two functions of:

1. Undergoing *feeling-expriences*;
2. retaining the *traces* of feeling-experiences (here habit begins and with it animal instinct).

These two functions are exercised relative to many kinds of sensations which constitute corresponding faculties and are:

a) *Shaped feeling-experiences*
   1. on the surface of the body, FACULTY OF EXTERNAL SENSITIVITY OR TOUCH, which includes
      i) *special touch*,
      ii) *taste*,
      iii) *smell*,
      iv) *sight*,
      v) *hearing*,
      vi) ...other particular kinds of feeling;
   2. inside the body, FACULTY OF INTERNAL SENSITIVITY, OR PHANTASY.
b) *Non-shaped feeling-experiences*, or feelings of different kinds.
c) *Physical affections*, which are the effect produced in the unity of the soul by many contemporaneous feeling-experiences fused together in such a way that they are the source of *passions*, specified in the Synoptic Schema of Instinct.

CHAPTER 7

The intellect as a primal potency

1006. The intellect in general is the potency of being as being, that is, of the essence of being.

No created intellect naturally apprehends the essence of being in its real form; only in its ideal form. Being, in its triune form, is naturally known only to itself.

Ideology deals sufficiently with the human intellect as formed by ideal being; *Supernatural Anthropology* deals with the intellect which has been given being in its real form and become a supernatural potency.

1007. In the intellect to which being is communicated in the real form, there must be perfect harmony and reciprocal suitability between ideal and real being. This harmony and suitability constitute moral being, and are understood as completion, perfection and good. Consequently, there is a third relationship under which the human intellect or any other intellect can be considered. This relationship is treated fully in *Agathology*.

1008. Let me deal here with an important question. I said somewhere that it is not absurd to conceive a subject which is purely intellective, but not affective and volitive. This is true when the matter is considered from the subject's point of view; the conclusion will be quite different when considered from the object's point of view. In fact, being is essentially good; it can be known therefore only as good. To know being as *good* requires some affection or inclination towards it. As light, being creates the intellect as formal cause of the soul (or if preferred, as cause of the formal cause, cause of the enlightenment of the soul). In the same way, being, as the essential condition of good, creates the primal will as final cause which actuates the first affection, that is, the first volition directed towards being in general. Thus intellect is the receptive potency; the will, the active potency corresponding to the intellect.

1009. The intellect is not susceptible of any development because its essential object is ideal being which in itself is immutable; it is therefore more an *immanent act* than a *potency*. It can of course be perfected, increased and elevated by the supernatural order in the way I have described, that is, by the revelation of essential being in its reality.

1010. It is true that ideal being is also intuited as variously determined and limited. The Scholastics attributed the intuition of these ideas, and consequent development, to the intellect. If this is first clarified, the word 'intellect' can obviously be used to mean generally 'the potency of intuiting ideas'. However, when we consider that the determination and limitation of ideal being cannot be attained without the perception of contingent realities and the traces of the perception which remain in the soul, we see that it is more exact to attribute to *reason* the intuition even of determinate ideas. Reason is not a simple intuition but contains deep within itself the application of ideal being to reality, which is precisely its task.

1011. In the same way we can say that the primal, universal will is not understood as potency but as immanent act, the principle and base of the potency. It would therefore seem better to call the primal will 'primal volition'. For these reasons, I will not give here the synoptic schema of the potency of intellect.

CHAPTER 8

Reason as a resultant potency

1012. The potency of reason arises in the soul, that is, in the common principle of sense and intellect, as a result of both felt and understood terms. The common principle unites these two terms in a *perceptive union*, and through the union apprehends real being in ideal being as in its essence. The potency of reason is therefore the acting subject itself rather than something subjective; the idea prescribes the law for this subject.

1013. Furthermore, in the logical order reason is a potency posterior to the two potencies of sense and intellect from which it results. In the chronological order the case is different, because *reason* exists as soon as the human being exists. I prove this in the following way.

The human being is a single subject composed of intellective soul and animal body. But the union of intellective soul with animal body comes about by means of a first, immanent perception (cf. 254–266). This perception is the *first act* of reason, the act through which reason exists. Hence the existence of the human being and of reason are contemporaneous. If reason exists as soon as the human being exists, but neither corporeal sense nor intelligence exist before the human being, these two primal faculties are not in the human being before the existence of reason, although reason results from them almost as a consequence from its principles.

It is true that feeling, or better the animal, can exist prior to the human being, but I am speaking of sense and intelligence as proper only to the human being.

1014. Priority in the logical order without necessary consequent priority in time is a problem that deserves the consideration of philosophers. There are many examples of it, and I think the one most worthy of attention is the syllogism. In a syllogism, the union of the first two terms, that is, the consequence, is not mentally posterior in time to the terms, although it results from them. In fact, as long as the mind has not seen the connection between the two terms, there is no syllogism; the first term cannot be called 'first', nor the second 'second', and there is no major or minor. But as soon as the mind has seen the consequence, it sees at once that one notion is a first term, and the other, a second term; it has therefore discovered the major and minor. A particular example is the perception of bodies: although it seems to involve some kind of reasoning, this perception is altogether immediate,[81] because it forms its own object.[82]

1015. This important truth, that 'in an ens there are elements which have a relationship of before and after without any temporal before and after', gives rise to the very beautiful, ontological principle that 'deep in an ens there is immanent, continuous action'. By applying this principle, we can reform and correct the popular concept of an ens. People in general always take the example of an ens from matter, and mentally conceive it

---

[81] *Sistema filosofico*, 89–93.

[82] *NE*, vol. 1, 121–129.

as something immobile and dead, because they cannot imagine any action other than local movement and transient acts.

1016. But our problem does not concern an action that passes and is done in sections, even though one section has passed and another must follow. In the depth of an ens there is a fully continuous action through which the ens is posited in being and made to persist. The action is such that if it were not done totally, the ens would not be, and if it were not continuous, the ens would not endure. Nevertheless, the action contains within itself its own order analogous to that of the succession of things in time. This succession could be called 'age', as the Scholastics called it.

1017. This helps us to explain memory which supposes that what is successive in itself becomes contemporaneous. The whole of succession, in which time consisted, now remains present. Memory is a faculty of reason because it could not exist unless some feelings signalled successive, particular entities in ideal being. However I will have to return to memory when I discuss the unity of the human being and how his multiple activities emerge from this unity (Bk. 3, c. 1, a. 3).

1018. The end therefore to which the potency of reason is ordered is that of placing the intelligent being in communication with the reality of things.

In fact, human beings, as intelligent, communicate through their nature only with ideality which constitutes the light of intelligence. But while reality is either infinite and necessary or finite and contingent, in pure ideality there is neither infinite nor finite reality. Hence the intelligent being, intuiting pure ideality, does not communicate through its nature with any reality. Reality, therefore, which is not essential to human intelligence, must be bestowed on it. But how? Infinite reality, that is, Almighty God, can come to intelligence only through a gracious communication of God himself. This reality, bestowed on human intelligence, is intelligible *per se* because it is the very essence of ideal-real being. In order to be understood, infinite reality needs no other potency than that of intellect which intuits ideality. But there is a difference: the intellect is now perfected, elevated and made to perceive absolute reality.

Finite, contingent reality is not *per se* intelligible because it lacks the essence of being. In order to be communicated to intelligence, it must be rendered intelligible by intelligence. This action constitutes a new potency which differs from intellect and is called 'reason'.

1019. In fact intuiting what is intelligible is one thing; making intelligible what is not intelligible is another. These are two specifically different acts with specifically different formal objects. Because potencies are distinguished (cf. 937–957) according to the distinction between their acts and formal terms, reason is a different potency from intellect.

1020. I have explained elsewhere how contingent reality, which is not the essence of being, can be made intelligible, but I will summarise the explanation here:

1. The first condition for making contingent reality intelligible is that reality must be accessible to intellective being.

2. The second condition is that intellective being must add ideality, that is, essence, to reality, and of these two make an ens as object of understanding.

But when and how can contingent reality become accessible to an intellective ens? — The reality accessible to an intellective ens is the reality of the intellective ens itself, because this is something real. It is clear that the reality of the intellective ens must become accessible to itself because the reality is itself, not something else. As a feeling, the reality is not dead but living. To say that an ens intuits ideal being is the same as saying that a feeling is joined to ideal being. Feeling and ideal being are therefore joined by nature and constitute a single, intelligent being. But because ideal being is the very intelligibility of all things, feeling is made intelligible through the intimate union that it has with intelligibility. This union, founded in nature, is such that a single ens, called 'intellective', results from feeling and its intelligibility.

1021. There is a great deal to be considered here.

First of all, I said that the reality of intellective being is feeling. But this does not mean that intellective being can perceive only its own reality. It is true that 'intellective perception does not extend outside its own feeling', but it must obviously include all the modifications of its feeling. Furthermore, we must not forget the ontological observation I have frequently made: the action of one ens manifests itself in another without confusing itself with the action of the ens in which it manifests itself (this is the origin of the distinction between the two concepts of activity and passivity). If therefore the action of another ens is manifested in our feeling, we must perceive this other feeling by perceiving its action, precisely because we perceive our own feeling and all that takes place in it. The objection that perceiving the action of an ens is not to perceive the ens is invalid, granted the immutable law of perception that 'actions of entia are not perceived without conception of the entia to which the action pertains.' Indeed, properly speaking, 'the only thing that is conceived and understood is an ens and what takes place in an ens', because only an ens is the object of intelligence. This is precisely the reason why contingent realities are not intelligible *per se*; they are not entia but actions of another ens, or if we prefer, terms of its actions. Hence our very own substantial feeling is not an ens *per se* but, strictly speaking, the term of the action of an ens which remains hidden from us. If we are to understand our feeling therefore as well as all the contingent realities that happen in it, we must supply the ens with an act of our intelligence. In this way we complete realities and render them intelligible. Similarly, the actions performed in us by entia different from us are understood when we add them to an ens, that is, we unite them to an ens of which they are actions.

1022. Secondly, we see how this principle is the origin of the authority which the testimony of our own *consciousness* provides. This is not the first intellective perception we have of our own feeling; it is a reflection on the first perception and on other reflections. On the one hand, this first, natural *perception* makes us know our animality; on the other, our perception of this perception, that is, our perception of the perceiver (which is our first reflection) makes us intelligible. Perceiving ourselves as intelligent, we finally form the concept *myself* in the way I have described (cf. 61–68). But if the first perception were not natural, nor the foundation of the other perceptions which we acquire successively of our modified self, the testimony provided by our awareness would not possess the universal authority it holds among human beings who are persuaded that its witness is infallible and clear. This persuasion arises because the first union between feeling and the idea is a fact of nature itself. In this fact we habitually perceive our own feeling without a shadow of doubt. This persuasion is indeed the natural completion of our perception. This is the witness given by our awareness, which is always a perception of a perception.

1023. In the third place, we can easily see that *reflection* and its nature have their origin in the activity of the *rational subject*. We noted that the rational subject is posited in being through the *fundamental, intellective perception* which unites intelligent ens individually to animal feeling. This union constitutes the human being, and without it the subject or rational principle would not exist. But granted its existence, it has its own activity which, relative to its mode, is independent of the term. As we saw, although the activity of every principle exists through its term, it acts in its own way, which must be deduced from observation (cf. 742–743, 929).

The activity of the rational principle can generically be called 'attention', although this word is not used in this general sense. It usually expresses 'free or chosen intellective activity, normally accompanied by awareness which is applied to and concentrated on a determinate object.' On the other hand, an intellective power that is freely applied to a chosen object does not differ from the power applied instinctively to the object when this is first presented to the spirit. I think it better therefore to use 'intellective attention' to mean generally 'the power of the spirit applied to any object whatsoever, without particular concentration, and even instinctively.'

1024. If the intuition of being is understood in this way, it becomes a first act of attention — perception also involves this act. But later attention is directed and concentrated sometimes according to different laws, sometimes by instinct guided by needs, sometimes by spontaneous choice, and sometimes even by free choice amongst the objects present to the spirit. The power proper to the principle is the ability to concentrate on many objects or on one or on an individual part of an object while withdrawing partly or even totally from the others. The law proper to the activity of the principle or rational subject is, we must remember, *to concentrate* itself in an object or part of an object among those present to our spirit.

How then is the spirit able to reflect upon its own actions?

Granted that all the passive or active actions of the spirit are feeling, and that every human feeling is the object of a natural perception, we immediately see the origin of reflection. It is, as I said, simply a perception of previous perceptions and acts. Perceptions themselves are feeling and therefore capable of being perceived.

1025. If this is the explanation of how we can reflect on acts of our spirit, we can explain even more easily how we can reflect on the objects of these acts. These objects are united to perceptions and constitute their term; the acts of the spirit are the principles of perceptions. Both term and principle of intellective acts (which do not exist without principle and term as their two extremes) are therefore perceivable, and by *force of concentration* the spirit can apply its attention to one or the other, to terms or principles exclusively.[83]

1026. In the fourth place, we can explain how the rational principle can act on reality and on matter itself. We say that the rational principle is itself something real, that is, a principle of feeling which makes itself intelligible, granted the natural union between it and ideal being, the intelligibility of all things. When the rational principle perceives itself, it perceives other real things that cause effects in it. Real being, that is, substantial feeling, has an active principle with which it can modify itself and also re-act on what acts in it. But if this real being perceives and consequently knows itself and its different states, it also learns through this condition to know how it must move and use its activity in order to be capable of modifying itself and other things united to it. If therefore the rational principle knows how it must act and is at the same time the operative power, clearly it will act on itself as it wills, and on the real things which by virtue of the action they exercise on it are in continuity with it and it with them.

1027. So far I have spoken of the origin and nature of *perception* and *reflection*, the two faculties of reason. It will be helpful to add a short analysis of both faculties.

Perception has three levels which I call 'apprehension', 'affirmation' and 'persuasion'.

1028. Affirmation and persuasion are virtually contained in

---

[83] Philosophy begins from reflection. It is not surprising therefore to see that Maine de Biran tried to base the classification of potencies on reflection alone. The *philosophical distinction* of potencies is in fact the task of reflection, but reflection uses previous data.

the (intellective) apprehension of reality. The fundamental perception of our animality comes to a halt at this first level. In fact our animality is expressly affirmed not in the first moments of our existence but only much later when we begin to speak. The doctrine of the fundamental perception is thus reconciled with the other opinion I have expressed, namely, that the human being first perceives external things and much later himself and what is his own. I said this in reference to *express affirmation*, which is the second level of perception, the level which completes perception and entails *distinct persuasion*.

1029. I must also say that affirmation alone forms the strongest part of the mind, the part which is present in apprehension in a kind of implicit, virtual mode.

1030. Persuasion is more a habit than an act of the spirit; it is distinct and actual when produced by affirmation. In this case it is affirmation itself habitually present in the spirit.

1031. Perception brings with it the faculty of 'universalisation', that is, of *full, specific ideas*. I have discussed this faculty sufficiently in *A New Essay.*[84]

1032. I have already laid down the principle relative to the analysis of reflection. The rational spirit has the power to direct its attention to perceived objects, by limiting its attention to a few or by extending it to many or to all of them or to a part which in reality is indivisible, or by concentrating attention on a single point, increasing its strength, as it were.

---

[84] *NE*, vol. 2, 487–504, 400–412. — I do not recall having ever found among philosophers an accurate description of *universalisation*. In the following passage of Leibniz we see that this great man, when reflecting on the application of names, noted that the smallest accidents could be common qualities. This was an indirect acknowledgement that in order to obtain *what is common* or *universal*, it was not necessary to abstract accidents or something else from a thing, but simply to prescind from individual subsistence: 'General terms which certainly help to perfect languages are also necessary to constitute them. If by particular things we mean individual things, it would be impossible to speak whenever there were only *proper* but not *common* names, that is, if there were only names of individuals. New individuals, accidents and actions, which we especially wish to indicate, are presented to us all the time. However if by particular things we meant *the lowest species* (*species infimas*), very often it would not only be difficult to determine them, but clearly they would already be universals founded on similitudes' (*Nouveaux Essais sur l'Entendement humain*, bk. 3, c. 1 §3).

But before undertaking this analysis, we need to recall that reflection, which is always a perception of a perception, must compare the object on which it is reflecting with universal being,[85] from which it draws transcendent principles. As a result, the faculty of reflection does not act as simple reflection. If it did, it would not increase the objects of knowledge but simply see and view them again. Merely looking at them again is not what I call *reflecting* philosophically; it is purely a renewal of the act of attention which has ceased and become habitual. This new act of attention, in the case of things known habitually, is not *reflection* but *reminiscence*. A prior, external perception which is repeated later is not reflection but simply *repetition* of the perception. Reflection therefore must be carefully distinguished from 1. *memory*, which is the deposit of habitual knowledge, 2. *reminiscence*, which is actual advertence to knowledge, and 3. *repeated perception*. The principal distinction is this: neither memory nor reminiscence nor repeated perception increases human knowledge; only reflection does this. As I said, reflection increases knowledge because it always relates and compares a perception already perceived with ideal being, discovering the relationships which are changed into principles.

1033. Reflection must therefore be divided into *partial* and *total*.

I call partial reflection that which uncovers relationships which divide or unite objects under reflection, but not relationships between objects and essential, universal being.

I call total reflection that which uncovers and enunciates relationships between its objects and essential, universal being.

Reflection in fact always has recourse to universal, essential, ideal being; otherwise, it could not discover anything new. But sometimes it compares its objects with being to find their mutual relationships (*partial* reflection); sometimes it compares them with being to find their relationships with being itself (*total* reflection). This nomenclature is not based on different *means* of knowledge, because reflection always uses the same means, that is, ideal being. It is based on different results, which are partial if they stop at the relationships between partial

[85] *Sistema filosofica*, 98–104.

objects; total if they ultimately establish the relationship between being itself, universal being, and objects, even if partial.

1034. Relationships of universal being are always universal, and therefore in some way encompass all that is knowable. Relationships between partial objects are partial and constitute only a part of what is knowable.

1035. The various levels of reflection are rooted in and have their explanation in the nature of partial reflection. After I have reflected on a perception, I can, by a second act of reflection, reflect on my reflection, and with a third reflection I can turn my thought to the second; I can do the same with a fourth reflection, and so on. Every time I raise myself to a higher level of reflection therefore, I always extract some new knowledge. The possibility of these different levels of reflection is founded in *partial* reflection. Clearly, if my first reflection exhausted what is knowable, I could not know anything new with the second and subsequent reflections; I would be limited to repeating the first reflection.

1036. The great importance of the study of the different levels of reflection is understood only by those who have noted that it is the source of the supreme principle of method,[86] of the principle which must govern the philosophical history of systematic knowledge, and of the principle for a history of humanity, as well as countless other consequences of supreme importance in the moral and political government of mankind.

1037. Multiple levels do not exist in total reflection which, having attained the supreme, most complex truths, cannot be the source of new discoveries. Thus, if my mind has attained the intuition of some supreme principle, I can certainly discover its applications (which means a return to reflection), but cannot proceed higher with total reflection; I can only repeat the act by which I contemplate the principle I have already discovered. This is *contemplation*.

1038. But whatever the level of reflection, reflection always acts in the same way. Its intention is to find *relationships*, which as differences, opposites, etc. sometimes divide things, and sometimes as equalities, similarities, co-relationships, analogies,

---

[86] Cf. The *Prefazione* to the *Catechismo* [*disposto secondo l'ordine delle idee*].

etc. unite and bind things together. The two ways in which partial reflection acts are above all *analysis* and *synthesis*.

1039. Analysis divides, synthesis unites, but in both cases the objects involved are known. Partial reflection sometimes finds not only the relationship between known objects but also simultaneously produces with its own activity one of the terms of the relationship. It does this by using and applying the idea of being, but in two different ways: it either deduces the term or invents it. This is what I call respectively 'rational faith' and 'rational creation'.

Analysis, synthesis, rational faith and creation are therefore the four ways in which reflection acts. I will say something about each.

1040. Analysis, which separates and divides known objects, is *material* or *formal*.

Material analysis is that in which the parts of the divided object have all the same nature and logical condition. Their similarity derives from the division to which matter (which is taken as uniform) is susceptible. Consequently, the parts do not differ in nature, only in size. Chemical analysis, numeric division, etc., are of this kind.

On the other hand, formal analysis is that in which the parts of the mentally severed object vary in nature. For example, when a genus is divided into many species, the genus has a logical nature different from that of the species, and each species has a nature different from the others. Thus the faculty of abstraction obviously pertains to formal analysis.

1041. Synthesis has a similar classification, because it also can be *material* or *formal*. It is material if parts of the same nature are united, as in addition or multiplication or in something whole formed by the adjacency of parts. It is formal if parts of different nature are united, as in a judgment, where the mind unites a predicate with a subject.

1042. The subject therefore of material analysis and synthesis is quantity; the subject of formal analysis and synthesis is quality, modality or relationship.

1043. Note however that formal synthesis, whose general form is *judgment*, undergoes marked modification when the levels of reflection proceed higher. Thus, if at the first level of reflection I make various judgments by a synthesis, and then raise my thought to another synthesis at a higher level and see the nexus between the two judgments, I soon have the form of a *syllogism*. We see in this form how reflection can produce new knowledge; I unite two judgments, but the resulting syllogism contains three. In other words, reflection has enabled me to gain an extra judgment, the conclusion itself of the syllogism. Clearly therefore, if by synthesis I proceed higher to other levels of reflection, I can, by comparing syllogisms with judgments, and syllogisms with each other, draw other conclusions. This is the origin of *reasoning*.

1044. Here, I must point out that some kind of synthesis is present in every analysis. In order to find differences and oppositions, which enable us to separate one thing from another, we must first collate and compare the things before going on to distinguish and separate them. This comparison is a kind of synthesis, a first degree of synthesis. Consequently, the distinction between analysis and synthesis lies in the *result* rather than in the *action of reflection*, whose proper form is always synthetical.

1045. This explains why I classified judgment and reasoning as synthesis rather than analysis, although the result can sometimes be analytical rather than synthetical. In fact, whenever judgments or the conclusion of a syllogism are negative, the *result* is normally analytical and divisive, but the *form* always synthetical. This will be clear to those who know that the human mind conceives what is negative under a positive form, conceives nothing as something, and that negation is, in its form, an affirmation. Thus a negative predicate is synthesised with a subject when we want to separate and distinguish. This law of thought led algebraists to add up positive and negative quantities by the same process, which they called precisely 'sum', equivalent to union or synthesis.

1046. Let us now consider the actions of reflection in which the faculty discovers or imagines one of the two terms of its analysis or synthesis. I said there were two such actions, *rational faith* and *rational creation*.

Sometimes the human mind reflects upon a perceived object, and by comparing it with the essence of being, finds that its existence is conditional on another ens which has never been perceived by the mind. In other words the notion that the

[1044–1046]

perceived object should exist by itself contradicts the essence of being. This gives rise to 'rational faith', that is, 'a reasonable persuasion that the other term exists, although the mind has never perceived or known in any way whatsoever its mode of being.' I call this function 'integration'.

For example, when Leibniz compares real created beings with the essence of being he finds that the *law of continuity* lies in the order of being itself. He then sees a link missing from the chain of natural things known at his time. But he believes in the existence of this unknown link and thus predicts the discovery of *zoophytes*, which were discovered later.

Le-Verrier discovered the existence of his planet in a similar way, *a priori*, we could say. As Arago fittingly commented, Le-Verrier did not see the planet in the lens of his telescope but on the point of his pen. The two principles of *cause* and *analogy*, which produced the discovery, were already known from the comparison of real entia with the essence of being. Le-Verrier argued that some irregularities in the movement of the known planets had to have a cause because of the principle of cause. He noted that other irregularities and disturbances could be explained by the mutual attraction of an unknown planet. He calculated its position and the planet was discovered in the indicated spot.

A similar argument moves from contingent to unperceived, necessary being; it is a contradiction to say that contingent being can exist alone without necessary being. The following syllogism expresses this truth: 'The contingent exists, that is, is an ens. But ens is never solely contingent. Therefore, for the contingent to be an ens, as it is, what is necessary must exist.' Thus the whole human race, by means of spontaneous integration, ascends to the reasonable belief that the supreme Ens exists.

1047. Positive faith in divine things is also reduced to rational faith, if rational faith in the existence of God already exists. The reasoning is as follows: 'If this man were not sent by God to announce the truth, he would not do things which presuppose the intervention of God. But this extraordinary individual does exist and proclaims these divine things which must therefore be true because their truth is a necessary condition for the existence and preaching of this man.' In other words: 'The truth of the divine things which this man is proclaiming is the necessary reason for explaining how and why he does these things.' What he proclaims remains unseen but the above-mentioned form of reasoning, which I call *integration*, makes us believe it simply because what is perceived could not be unless the unperceived proclamation existed. This kind of reasoning makes a blind person believe in the existence of colours. He says: 'These colours, which I do not perceive, exist because there is someone worthy of belief whom I do perceive. If the colours did not exist, this person worthy of faith could not exist. But such a person does exist, therefore the colours exist also.'

1048. These examples show that:

1. The argument for integration is founded in the *intrinsic, necessary order of being* which is normally expressed in forms proper to ontological principles. This order is found in the natural contemplation of being and means that a given, perceived part of being would not be what it is unless there were some other, unperceived part.

2. The rational faith under discussion concerns unperceived entities, that is, entities whose realisation was never communicated and whose nature is therefore positively unknown. This nature is made known to us solely by means of perception or of similarity with what is perceived [*App.*, no. 4].

1049. What is to be said about the *faith* we have in a person who asserts the existence of something whose realised essence we have perceived at other times? Does this kind of belief pertain to *rational faith*? For example, if we believe travellers who tell us they have discovered a new river in Africa, is this the activity I call 'rational faith'?

Note that human knowledge is divided into two great classes, the *essences* of things and *subsistences*, which are the realisation of the essences. Now, when travellers deserving our faith tell us they have discovered a new river, they tell us nothing new about the *essence* of the river because we already know, through sense-perception, what a river is. They are not *witnesses* to the essence but simply *advisers* or stimulators of our attention which immediately thinks about a river, that is, the essence of something we already know. But relative to the *subsistence* of the river in Africa, they are true witnesses in whom we have *rational faith*. *Integration* however has no place in this rational faith which is concerned with the *subsistence*, not the *essence* of the things narrated. The activity of integration is directed to completing the *essence of being*; it does not deal with subsistence. The examples I gave of the discoveries of Leibniz and Le-Verrier concern subsistence. But the mode of reasoning is the same, and this is why I gave these examples.

Integration therefore is a kind of *rational faith*, but not the only one.

1050. *Rational creation* differs from *rational faith*. Just as faith in something perceived and conditioned is an argument for the condition, so creation assumes or imagines something whose essence has been perceived at other times, but in whose subsistence there is no real belief. This assumption or fiction is brought about by the activity of the human intelligence for various reasons which are not always rational. Hence it takes on three forms; it can be a faculty of *hypothesis*, of *personification*, or of *error*.

1051. A sound hypothesis contains a rational element and comes very close to integration, but differs from it in the following way:

1. In integration a term is present whose essence we have not perceived. But that which is assumed by hypothesis is always something whose essence has been perceived.

2. In integration argument induces necessity; in hypothesis it is conjectural.

3. In integration the non-perceived term is single and excludes all others; in hypothesis the term which is assumed to explain the facts does not exclude other terms, because the facts to be explained can usually be explained by many hypotheses.

1052. *Personification* is not rational. It has a instinctive origin, and is used by human beings almost as a symbol to stimulate feeling in themselves rather than increase their knowledge.

1053. Finally, the *faculty of error* is an arbitrary affirmation which denies the truth and is certainly not rational; on the contrary, it has a relationship of opposition to reason.

1054. Clearly, the soul's activity in rational creation pertains to the superabundant activity which the principle (subject, soul) manifests when posited in being by the term, although the activity itself does not come precisely from the term.

1055. We still need to discuss *total reflection* which, as we saw, searches for the relationships proper to universal being without attending to the relationship proper to particular entia. This reflection embraces a group of four faculties which I call 1. the *faculty of principles*, 2. the *faculty of archetypes*, 3. the *faculty of method*, and 4. the *faculty of absolute or transcendental knowledge*.

1056. Principles understood in an absolute sense, which is how I understand them, are propositions with a universal value and no other explanations higher than themselves. They are the idea of being considered in its application to reasoning, where it exercises its greatest power.[87]

1057. Just as being illuminates the mind, so it governs human activity. It equally directs *theoretical reason* and *practical reason*, providing both with their directive principles.

1058. If being were not essentially ordered and, as it were, organated, it could not of itself produce the principles of human reason which express its order. If we consider carefully the service rendered by these principles to the mind, we see 'that every principle shows the mind how an ens must be if it is to be an ens.' For example, the principle of cognition states: 'There is no thought unless it has an ens for its object.' This means that the entity called thought would not be an entity or simply would not be, unless it had an ens as its object. It describes therefore *how thought must be an entity,* that is, it describes the order of this entity.

The principle of substance states: 'There is no accident without a substance.' This describes the mode or order necessary for an 'accident' to be an entity.

The principle of cause states: 'Every event must have a cause.' It describes how an event can be, that is, the necessary order of the entity indicated by 'event'. We can proceed in the same way with other principles: each expresses how an ens must be, if it is to be, that is, it expresses its intrinsic, necessary order.

1059. Order always supposes a unified multiplicity. Unity can therefore be considered in multiplicity, and multiplicity in unity. From these two standpoints two series of principles of theoretical reason can be deduced. The first indicates how unity can be multiplied, the second how multiplicity can be unified.

[87] *NE*, vol. 2, 558–573.

1060. In addition to the three principles of cognition, substance and cause, already discussed, the following also can be reduced to first principles: the principle of substantial individual, of subject, of person and of the absolute. They state: 'There would be no ens without substantial individuals, no ens without subjects, no ens without persons and no ens without the absolute.' These principles can also be expressed by the following formulas: 'There is no multiplicity of entia, without substantial individuals'; I call this 'the principle of substantial individuals'. 'If there are substantial individuals, there are subject individuals (sentient)'; I call this principle 'the principle of subject'. 'If there are subjects, there are persons'; I call this 'the principle of persons'. 'If there is an ens, there is absolute ens'; I call this 'the principle of the absolute', from which we also extract transcendental, absolute knowledge.

1061. The relationships between multiplicity and unity result in other principles of theoretical reason, for example: 'The whole is greater than its parts', 'Two things equal to a third are equal to each other', etc.

1062. Let me say one word about the principles governing and directing practical reason. Practical reason has the two acts: *contemplation* and *action*. Contemplation is governed by the principle of beauty; action, by the principle of moral law.

1063. The *faculty of archetypes* is that in which thought carries any known essence to its ultimate, possible perfection, determining what is necessary for the essence to be fully perfect. It is the origin of the *deontological* sciences,[88] and a most noble task of reflection. By comparing the imperfect species of things given us by perception with *being*, the faculty discovers how much of the order of being can be received by their essences. This faculty supremely ennobles minds and was extraordinary in Plato, procuring for him the title 'divine'. No one can be a great human being who does not possess this faculty to a high degree. The magnanimous actions of great people are realised always through imitation of the sublime ideal they vividly contemplate in their minds.

1064. The *faculty of method* originates from reflection when it rises above all particular levels of reflection to arrange them in

[88] *Sistema filosofica*, 151–173.

suitable order. It is a kind of universal reflection which encompasses in a single glance all possible reflections, that is, an indefinite number of reflections.

1065. Finally the *faculty of absolute or transcendental knowledge* is another product of total reflection. It takes all the knowledge it wants and compares it to the essence of being. It first distinguishes what is subjective and phenomenal from things known in themselves, independently of any contribution made by our act of knowledge, and then shows that in making the distinction nothing more has been introduced relative to the subject. An example can be seen in my dialogue entitled *Moschini*.

But to summarise what has been said, it will be helpful to set out the various actions of human reason in the following synoptic schema [pp. 146–147].

SYNOPTIC SCHEMA 3

REASON AND ITS FACULTIES

Reason is the faculty of applying the *idea of being* intuited by the intellect both to what is furnished by sense and to what the intellect itself proffers (the idea of being itself or the knowledge which reason itself produces). But because universal sensitivity accompanies all that is or that is done in the human soul, reason has for its term that which is passive and active in the soul. Thus movements of instinct and will, like all cognitions, become terms of reason. Simultaneously, however, the acts of reason, and the cognitions reason produces become principles of new instincts and volitions. This explains why I think it better to deal with the derivation of the instinctive and volitive faculties after deriving the rational faculties.

Movement on the part of reason primarily pertains to instinct and then in general to the active faculties. On the other hand, reason considered as having obtained its term pertains to the *receptive* faculties. — Reason hsas three principal functions:

    1. To form and modify knowledge, and to actually contemplate knowledge after its formation.
    2. To preserve formed knowledge — *Memory (Habit)*.
    3. To recall it in act — *Reminiscence* (an *habitual activity* intervenes in its exercise).

The second and third functions are related to the first. It will therefore be sufficient to derive the different faculties from the first.

Faculty of reason which forms, modifies and actually contemplates knowledge.

These faculties can be specified and named 1. according to the different ways reason acts, or 2. according to the different kinds of formed knowledge.

I. Faculty of reason specified by the different ways in which the faculty acts:

A. Direct knowledge

1. Faculty of perception, which has three levels:
    a) apprehension, *b)* affirmation, *c)* persuasion.

2. Faculty of universalisation or of full, specific ideas.

B. Reflective knowledge, reflection, which is

1. Partial, when the aim of reflection is to discover some part of what is knowable. In this case reflection is *first level, second level, third level* and so on indefinitely because it is always possible to reflect further on every product of reflection (dialectics). Every level of reflection has its correspondingly different product in the order of systematic knowledge.

Reflection acts in the following ways:

a) by analysis, the disentanglement of knowledge.
    i) material, which is the source of numbers

II. Faculty of reason specified by the different kinds of knowledge produced by use of this faculty.

The faculties mentioned in Schema 1 produce the following kinds of knowledge, which give their name to the faculties.

A. *Faculty of persuasion* (persuasion is a state of the soul produced by means of a mental word; word is the affirmation and is pronounced by the mind 1. in *perception*, when it is complete, 2. in integration, 3. in faith, 4. in rational creation, 5. in every judgment).

B. *Faculty of variously determined ideas:*

1. *Realisable* ideas (full species).
2. *Completable* ideas (abstract species, real genera or genera of substance).
3. Elementary ideas (these are only parts of ideas to which the mind restricts its attention).
4. Negative ideas (these make something known through its relat-

i) faculty of judgment (judgments are affirmative or negative, conditional and alternative)

ii) faculty of reasoning (reasoning is categorical, hypothetical, disjunctive)

iii) faculty of argumentation (analytical, synthetical)

c) human rational faith

d) rational creation

i) faculty of hypothesis

ii) faculty of personification

iii) faculty of error (erroneous judgment, absurd abstraction)

2. Total, when the object of reflection is everything knowable or tends to integrate this knowledge.

a) faculty of principles

b) faculty of archetypes

c) faculty of method

d) faculty of absolute or transcendental knowledge

5. Relationships of ideas (an idea multiplies when some of its relationships are considered together with it).

6. Ideas of pure sign (these are solely entities supposed by the mind with the help of a sign. For example, the idea of nothing, or any concept which, although absurd in itself, is not known as such by our mind).

C. Faculty of principles or of the application of ideas. Every idea can be changed into a principle when it is used as a norm for judging. But supreme principles can be reduced to the supreme idea of being, which takes the form of many principles according to its various applications. These supreme principles are:

1. The principle of knowledge, which directs theoretical reason,

a) principle of cognition

b) principle of contradiction

c) principle of substance

d) principle of substantial individual

e) principle of subject

f) principle of person

g) principle of the absolute (origin of transcendental or absolute knowledge)

h) principle of cause

i) efficient, which pertains to real being

ii) exemplary, which pertains to ideal being (sufficient reason)

iii) final, which pertains to moral being (origin of the faculty of moral reason)

i) principle of the order of being considered relative to theoretical reason, source of knowledge of relationships, origin of the principles that

i) the whole is greater than its part

ii) two things equal to a third are equal to each other

2. Principle of the order of being considered in relationship to practical reason

a) relative to contemplation, BEAUTY (archetype)

CHAPTER 9
Instinct

Article 1
The nature of instinct; how instinct differs from will

1066. After considering the soul from the point of view of its passivity and receptivity, and deducing from this the potencies I have called 'passive' and 'receptive', I must now consider it from the point of view of its action, and from this deduce its active potencies.

We must never forget however what has been said about the internal constitution of the soul which is by nature a principle, and cannot be conceived without its terms. Principles and terms are correlative and synthesising. In so far as the principle is affected by its term, it is *receptive* or *passive*. But this *receptivity* and *passivity* involves a degree of activity proper to the principle. Thus the activity in created subjects arises partly from receptivity and passivity, and is partly their condition.

Granted therefore that the principle (whose being lies in its union with its term, as I said) has already been posited in being, its activity is not limited to receptivity and passivity. Provided the term is capable of receiving the principle's actions and being changed by it, the principle acts on its own term. If the nature of the term were pure act, all passivity or receptivity would be excluded by the essence of the term, as is the case with God and divine things. The activity of the subject therefore is carried out in the subject itself; by approaching or withdrawing from the term, the subject modifies its union with it.

1067. There are two primal terms of the human soul, the felt element and the understood element, relative to which the soul is respectively passive and receptive. Two activities of very different nature correspond to the two terms. One activity is called 'instinct'; and has its origin in sensitivity; the other, 'will', and its origin in intelligence.

The term of instinct is changeable, and is in fact changed when instinctive activity acts on it; the term of the will, in so far as it is the same as that of pure intelligence, is unchangeable because it is something divine (ideas). Consequently the activity originating from the will is limited to a varying degree of receptivity; in other words, the will acts on and changes the soul rather than the object-term of intelligence.

1068. Instinct therefore is the movement of sensitivity. Because sensitivity accompanies all the soul's potencies and actions, even rational actions, instinct extends to and is present in every part of the human being. Hence, a complete description of its subdivisions should include the special activities of this potency by tracing and classifying all the rest, and showing that each has its own special and proper instinct.

Article 2
Animal instinct and rational instinct

1069. Instinct is of its nature a blind potency. But because rational and moral potencies also have their instincts, we must distinguish between instinct that is totally blind in its movement and term, and instinct which, although blind in its *primary endeavour* or *movement*, is not blind in its *term*, or is blind purely in its movement but not in its effort and term. In fact, if we consider the instinctive movement of the will we see that it begins from a light and terminates in a known object. This movement is blind in so far as made by natural, spontaneous inclination and without deliberation or decree, as sometimes happens. For this reason alone the movement can be called instinctive. An example of instinct that is blind in its endeavour and movement but not in its term, are the acts by which we acquire our first cognitions — acts which tend to acquire the light of cognition they did not have at first. The subject, when moved to acquire his first cognitions, still does not have them, and cannot therefore move towards them except blindly, drawn by his feeling and native activity. Consequently the *start* of this movement is blind, although its term is cognition in which there is light.

1070. We need to distinguish two divisions; first, an entirely blind instinct not associated with any cognition either in its principle or term — this is *animal instinct*, which is also present in the human being because a human being is an animal — and secondly, an instinct, *human instinct*, which is blind in its movement but associated with some cognition either at the beginning or at the end of its movement.

Article 3
Subdivisions of animal instinct

1071. The different actions of animal instinct can perhaps be fittingly reduced to six classes. The soul's first act, or *principle of instinct*, is to posit itself by uniting itself to its term. But I will disregard this first act and list only the following actions which derive from it:

1. Instinct plays a role in the production of accidental animal feelings.

2. It has the power to reproduce feelings when these have lost their actuality and leave only traces, that is, habitual inclinations, in the spirit. This action is accomplished only with the help of the following instinctive faculties.

3. Through the unity of the soul, instinct has the power of associating and unifying feelings. I have called this the *synthetical force of the animal*; it can cause actions so extraordinary that they resemble those of reason. I have spoken at length about this instinct in the *Anthropology*.[89]

4. As a result of the association of several feelings in the unity of the soul, certain general modifications are brought about in the soul. These I call 'affections'. They are feelings lying midway, as it were, between *individual feelings* and *passions*. These affections are therefore the generative principles of passions, and when they are complete and leave an *habitual inclination to reproduce themselves*, are called 'passion'.

5. *Passions* are the fifth manifestation of the instinctive potency.

6. Finally, the sixth manifestation of the instinctive animal

[89] *AMS*, 416–494.

potency is the activity with which this potency modifies the sensiferous element by producing in it movements corresponding to the way in which the instinct adjusts itself.

1072. I will make some observations about *passions* and *spontaneous adjustments*, the last two manifestations of instinct.

Article 4
Rational and animal passions

1073. Passions are not purely animal. In fact, animal passions in human beings must be carefully distinguished from rational passions.

1074. Both kinds fit the division we find in Plato, that is, of passions proper to our *concupiscent* faculty and to our *irascible* faculty. By desire I mean the inclination which draws us towards good and away from evil. By frustration I mean that sudden energy which is concentrated and, as it were, built up in the soul when the soul encounters an external impediment to its tendency.[90] The soul uses this tendency to struggle and strive to remove and overcome the impediment and thus give free reign to its desiring tendency.

1075. Relative to animal passions, passions of desire tend to the possession of what is pleasant and the avoidance of what is unpleasant — for an animal there is no other good or evil. Passions of frustration are ordered to remove forcibly and overcome the difficulty that the tendencies of desire encounter against their full unfolding. Hence, properly speaking, *the irascible* faculty is simply an activity of the faculty of desire which is harmed by and defends itself against foreign impediments that oppose its progress without destroying or weakening it.

1076. We must not attribute *love*, which is a noble, rational passion, to animals. In its place, they have *unitive affection*, which can be subdivided into a *generative tendency* and that group of passions included in the *tendency to aggregation*. This

[90] Note that the only impediment arousing anger is something foreign and external to the animate body.

group includes the instinct which preserves and brings together animals of the same species, posits sympathies or antipathies in different species, unites offspring to their mother, and produces the affection which binds some animals to human beings, domesticity, etc.

1077. The same can be said about *hatred* which properly speaking expresses a rational passion and corresponds to *aversion, antipathy*, etc. in animality.

1078. *Desire* and *abhorrence* are rational, not animal passions. However, in animality, we find various tendencies specified by their respective terms, such as *voracity, hunger*, etc.

1079. *Joy* is proper to intelligence. There is a corresponding feeling in animality but without its own well-defined name because not all animal passions are individually expressed in language. Consequently the same word is often used with a different meaning to indicate sometimes a purely animal passion and sometimes the corresponding passion visible in a rational being. Examples are the two words 'sadness' and 'gladness', etc.

1080. This scarcity and poverty of language disposes a negligent mind to confuse the sensitive and rational orders.

1081. *Ownership* can also be classed among animal passions. It draws the affections of the animal to certain inanimate things, and appears identical in human beings except that they enjoy knowledge of their ownership. This adds a rational element to the feeling of ownership. Moreover, humans, with their moral faculty, raise the feeling of ownership to the level of right, of which this feeling is only the matter.[91]

1082. Although the words 'anger', 'ferocity', 'fear', 'expectation', etc. are often applied to both animals and human beings equally, they seem more appropriate to the former than the latter. On the other hand, the words 'indignation', 'fear', 'boldness', 'desperation' clearly express rational affections and passions. When authors apply these words to animals, they do so by a kind of transference and by the tendency of human beings to equate their intellective life and reason to all the entia they perceive, especially if these entia manifest phenomena normally produced by intelligence, even though they can be produced by quite a different cause.

[91] Cf. *Philosoophy of Right*, vol. 2, *Rights of the Individual*, 921–975.

1083. Human beings, because they are animal, have animal passions. But rationality gives these passions a characteristic of their own which ennobles and specifies them.

1084. Moreover, animal passions, which in beasts are moved only by stimuli and by the laws of corporeal sense, are sometimes aroused in humans by rationality itself through the influence exercised by the rational soul in animality. Thus sadness, considered as an animal passion, can be defined as 'an unpleasant feeling experienced by the animal, accompanied in certain viscera by retardation of the circulation of the blood and by diminished activity of the nervous system.' In an animal, only a physical or sensuous cause, such as retardation of the circulation or loss of nervous vigour, can produce this feeling, which in a human being, is sometimes produced by the same cause and sometimes by information that saddens the spirit; in other words, by the rational potency.

1085. Animal passions therefore are not the same as those in human beings for two reasons: 1. granted the same productive cause as in animals, intelligence is associated with them and modifies them. Thus sadness which causes an illness in an animal differs from sadness in a human being who knows his malaise. The knowledge increases the affliction. Furthermore, by using motives furnished by reason, we can ease and alleviate the sadness, even physically.

2. In human beings animal passions can, as I have said, be put into motion by a rational cause.

1086. There are also new passions in human beings of which no trace can be found in animals. Movements of the rational potency produce new effects and feelings which cannot in any way be aroused by purely animal instinct.

1087. These feelings proper to human beings sometimes seem to be purely rational or contained within the sphere of intelligence. Sometimes however it seems that animality has a place in them.

1088. In this case, animality experiences an affection that cannot be manifested in the mere animal because intelligence, the productive cause, is lacking. Here I do not intend to solve the problem about 'the presence in human beings of affections so pure that their animality has no part in them, or about the constant pressure of both intelligence and animality.' Others can solve this subtle problem; I am content to establish that in human beings some entirely new passions are revealed which cannot be produced by animal instinct, and whose sole cause is intelligence. Relative to their cause, they are intellective passions, but are perhaps never purely intellective in themselves.

1089. From this class of passions I absolutely exclude *sympathetic passions*, like compassion, etc. If something similar should show itself in animals, it can in my opinion always be reduced to individual passions and feelings. Basically, an animal moves only in virtue of its feeling-experiences, which is the opposite of human beings, who share in others' passions *purely by knowing them*. When we know others' passions, we can imagine them and so enter into them as they are. Compassion is certainly a rational passion in both its cause and in itself; if something similar becomes visible in an animal, it can be reduced to *unitive affection*; in other words, to what concerns *aggregation*, etc.

Passions common to animals have their source in what is *pleasant* and in what is *difficult*. But in human beings, because of their rationality, there are two other sources, *rapid motion of the spirit* and *that which is great*. Our spirit, which passes rapidly from one intellective state to another opposite intellective state, not only increases the vivacity of its sensitive act by means of this rapidity (which also happens in animal sense), but produces new and sudden feelings, like *laughter*, *amazement*. Again, only we with our reason can be made susceptible of feeling what is great. This feeling produces various affections like *wonder, stupor, ecstasy*, etc., all of which are human passions that are totally lacking in animals.

Article 5
Different ways in which the instinctive power proper to animal feeling adjusts itself; the resulting faculties

1090. I must now make a brief comment about the sixth manifestation of animal instinct which I placed in the power that feeling has to *adjust itself* by modifying the sensiferous element.

To understand what I mean by this power of feeling, we must bear in mind that we know feeling in two ways: 1. through the feeling itself of which we are directly conscious (subjectively) and 2. through phenomena which while produced by feeling and felt by us, are not the feeling itself (extrasubjectively). Thus sensation of pain is one thing, but the movements it causes in the body are another; these movements can be seen without our feeling pain. Pain is a subjective feeling; the movements are extrasubjective phenomena produced by the feeling and indicating pain, although of a totally different nature from pain. While extrasubjective phenomena are known by means of other feelings, these feelings have nothing to do with the feeling under discussion although they also have their subjective and extrasubjective part. All this was discussed in the *Anthropology*, to which I refer the reader who wants to follow my argument.

Granted therefore the careful distinction between subjective and extrasubjective parts of feeling, we immediately understand how subjective feeling is something totally immune from space and consequently extremely simple. In the concept of pleasure, of pain and of every other purely subjective feeling, no one can find the concept of any extension, which is only the term of certain feelings, not feeling itself. Nevertheless, extrasubjective phenomena have a simultaneity and correlation with subjective phenomena. I have said that there is no relationship of direct cause and effect between one and the other, because they are totally dissimilar. However, when subjective phenomena change, extrasubjective phenomena also change. This gives rise to the belief that the change in subjective phenomena can be at least the indirect if not the direct cause of the changes. If we restrict our consideration solely to the dissimilarity between the two series of phenomena, the argument remains uncertain. It becomes certain however when we consider that subjective feeling terminates, as I have said, in an extended element which itself is already, in a sense, extrasubjective, although individually united to the subject. Furthermore, the extended element pertains to the extrasubjective phenomena of the sensiferous element, with which it is identical in substance. Consequently, although (subjective) feeling is not the direct, proximate cause of the extrasubjective phenomena pertaining to the sensiferous element, it causes the change in its own direct term (the extended element), which is also the subject of the extra-subjective phenomena of the sensiferous element. (Subjective) feeling is therefore the remote, indirect cause of the modification of extrasubjective phenomena; in other words, it causes the cause of this modification. Having firmly established all this, I hold that 'the subject which is the principle of feeling is bound of itself to use and adjust its feeling in such a way that it obtains the best possible good and hence the least possible discomfort.' This power and activity of the sentient principle which adjusts and modifies its feeling is the cause of modifications in extrasubjective phenomena. The faculties relative to these modifications are principally four:

1. The *locomotive faculty*, by means of which the animal walks and makes different use of all its organs.

2. The plastic or *formative faculty*, by means of which human beings are made, fed, etc. In the fifth book I will describe more fully how this happens and the laws governing it.

3. The *faculty of sensitive habits*, which is the power of being able to adjust in one way rather than another. This power develops and modifies through exercise, receiving new dispositions, new conditions for its action and consequently new spontaneities.

4. The *faculty that animal instinct has to alter and harm itself*. This faculty (to which harmful phenomena pertain) is, like the three previous faculties, the same general faculty or power by which feeling can adjust in different ways to the different states given it by stimuli, habits, etc. Hence, whenever the stimuli place it in certain states, the law of its spontaneity always makes it produce the above-mentioned, harmful phenomena, about which I will speak later.

Article 6
Rational habits

1091. Human instinct, which is still the subject of our discussion, although blind as instinct, is associated with some knowledge in which it originates or finishes. It also reveals itself in rational affections, which produce both a *passive state* of the spirit, called 'rational passion', and an *active state*, which constitutes *habits*.

1092. Rational passions have been briefly, but sufficiently discussed. About *habits*, I say that a habit is 'a disposition of a potency to act in a given way'. Habits are primarily divided in the same way as the potencies or faculties which they modify and actuate.

Human, intellective faculties and potencies, classified according to their effects, can be reduced to two groups: those which produce beneficial or harmful effects in a subject, and those (extrasubjective) which, producing effects outside the subject, cause movements of bodies.

1093. There are therefore two groups of habits: those adhering to faculties which produce their effects in the subject, and those pertaining to faculties which produce their effects outside the subject.

1094. The faculties which produce their effects in the subject can be reduced to 1. *moral potency*, which gives us *moral habits*, that is, virtues and vices, and 2. to rational potency, in so far as it acts in the subject, which gives us *rational habits* such as *memory*, the *different branches of knowledge*, *prudence*, etc.

1095. But in so far as rational potency moves bodies and produces extrasubjective effects, it provides the second group of faculties which gives rise to habits of *mechanical* and *liberal arts*, of *depraved movements of our own body*, etc.

Article 7
Two ways of classifying rational instincts

1096. So far I have dealt with the principal branches of rational instinct, classifying it according to the *modes of its operation*.

Another classification is possible by examining its many subdivisions in conjunction with the different *objects* to which instinct is referred. But for the sake of brevity, it will be sufficient to present the following synoptic schema (pp. 158–159), in which the faculties and instinctive functions are classified under both headings.

[1092–1096]

SYNOPTIC SCHEMA 4
INSTINCT

Instinct is self-moving sensitivity, that is, the active part of sense. As we saw, all the soul's activities and passivities are by nature sensible affections from which an instinctive movement originates as we derived the particular activities of instinct just as we derived the particular activities of sense, intellect and reason. The soul is both essentially sensitive and essentially instinctive. Hence, the general explanation of all its instinct is in itself.

Instinct by nature is blind. But we have to distinguish between instinct which is completely blind in its initial endeavour, motion and term, and instinct which is blind only in its motion or initial endeavour but not in its term, or else is blind neither in its endeavour nor in its term. In this case, it is called instinct, not in so far as enlightened by knowledge, but in so far as it moves spontaneously. Similarly, the acts with which we acquire our first cognitions are instinctive because they are blind in their initial endeavour and principle but not in their term, since they terminate in that which gives light to cognitions. Two kinds of instinct can therefore be distinguished:

I. Blind instinct, not associated with any cognitions, whether in its principle or term; it is an animal instinct which originates from:	**II. Blind instinct, associated with some knowledge** from which it originates and in which it finishes, human instinct:

I. Blind instinct, not associated with any cognitions, whether in its principle or term; it is an animal instinct which originates from:

1. The extended felt element.
2. The intestine movement of the extended felt element.
3. The organism of the extended felt element.

Variation in these three forms of animal instinct produces a corresponding variation in the instincts which is seen in different generations of animal as well as in different individuals of the human race.

The following are the functions of animal instinct:

1. Co-operation in the production of accidental feelings.
2. Reproduction of these feelings.
3. Association of these feelings (synthetical force of the animal).
4. Production of general affections, which are the principle of
5. Passions:

A) *Concupiscent:*
  I. Libido.
  II. Aversion, antipathy.
  III. Voracity.
  IV. Ownership, by which the functions join pleasurable things to themselves.
  V. Aggregation, by which 1. like stays with and helps like; 2. a mother remains with her children, rears them, etc.; 3. domestic animals form an affection for human beings.
  VI. Cheerfulness, sadness, etc.

II. Blind instinct, associated with some knowledge from which it originates and in which it finishes, human instinct:

A) Blind instinct is either *universal* and corresponds to intellective sense (moral faculty, which develops later through will and freedom), or is

B) *Special,* corresponding to reason with which it develops. This instinct can be described in two ways, either by considering its different ways of activity, or its different objects:

1. Its different ways of action are:
   a) Rational affections, which furnish the principle for
   b) Rational passions:
      I. *Individual* passions:
         1) General affection, love
         2) Particular affections:
            i) Proper to what is good and bad. Concupiscent:
               a) Love as a particular passion — *b)* Hatred — *c)* Desire — *d)* Abhorrence — *e)* Joy — *f)* Sadness.
            ii) Proper to what is difficult. Irascible:
               a) Indignation — *b)* Fear — *c)* Audacity — *d)* Hope — *e)* Desperation.
            iii) Proper to rapid motion of the spirit, origin of the various degrees of pleasure and pain (laughter, surprise, etc.).
            iv) Proper to what is great (wonder, stupor, etc.).
      II. *Sympathetic* passions (sharing in the passions of others, compassion, etc.).

   c) Rational Habits:
      I. Proper to moral potency:
         1) Habits of vice
         2) Habits of VIRTUE

ii) Perfective habits of the will, as mover of the other potencies:
- *a*) Of reason, or PRUDENCE
- *b*) Of appetite
  1) Concupiscent, or TEMPERANCE.
  2) Irascible, or FORTITUDE.

II. Proper to rational potency:
  1) Habit of memory.
  2) Habits of intellectual disciplines, or foundations of particular disciplines and arts.
  3) Dealings with human beings, shrewdness.

III. Proper to the faculty of ordered movements, habits of the ARTS:
  1) Mechanical.
  2) Liberal.

2. Its different objects give us:

a) Human instinct for the pleasures linked with the *use* of one's potencies; corporal sensations (sensations and feelings) — intellectual — moral — mixed feelings.

b) Human instinct for the pleasant feeling linked with the *possession* of one's potencies, with the levels of their possible perfection; calm or absence of pain — feeling of perfection proper to one's person — feeling of one's greatness.

c) Human instinct for the pleasant feeling linked with actual and habitual, more enduring and more certain *communication* with good, intelligent beings different from us:

  I. Ideal entities: truth — justice — goodness — equity — gratitude — beneficence.
  II. Real beings (passive and active affections):
    i) Individual feelings and affections: sympathy (compassion, etc.) — humanity — benevolence — friendship — love (sensible-spiritual, generative, conjugal) — paternity — filial piety — seignorial love — servant's love.
    ii) Social feelings or affections: domestic society — tribe — homeland — civil society — Church.

d) Human instinct for the pleasant feeling resulting from *persuasion of one's perfection*, greatness and happiness, formed and nourished by:

  I. The favourable opinion of others: good reputation — esteem — glory (of various kinds).
  II. The signs of one's greatness: luxury, magnificence — superiority — exercise of power — uniqueness of excellence, etc.
  III. The contemplation of one's own means and goods, and of their safety (love of possession, etc.).

I. Anger, ferocity.
II. Fear.
III. Expectation, etc

6. Self-adjustment by modification of the sensiferous element, to which we can reduce:
a) the motive faculty of the body;
b) the plastic or formative faculty;
c) the faculty of instinctive habits;
d) the faculty that instinct has to change itself, giving rise to unhealthy phenomena.

Article 8
The principle of instinct

1097. To understand the nature of each instinct, we must investigate its principle, common to all its many subdivisions. This one principle, while remaining always the same, acts in different ways. Otherwise, we could not use the generic epithet 'instinctive' to mean the rational animal functions I have listed and classified.

What then is the principle of instinct and its intimate, immutable nature?

1098. Instinct indicates a mode of the subject's operation, that is, a law according to which the subject acts. To investigate this law is to investigate the principle and nature of instinct.

A subject acting according to this law is said to act instinctively. I mentioned the law when I was discussing animal instinct to which I attributed the 'power of adjusting itself in the most pleasant way.' It will be sufficient, therefore, if I make the observation more general, applying it not simply to animal subjects but to all subjects including rational and intellective subjects. In this way I will have found the one principle of instinct.

1099. I have already established that every subject is a substantial feeling and that every feeling has its own activity. I also demonstrated that this activity continually posits the feeling, whose principle it is, in the most pleasant state possible because the act which adjusts feeling is natural and proper to the activity (activity would not be such unless it had its natural act with which it posits itself and is what it is). But the activity of a feeling can sometimes be passive and dependent on something foreign to itself. This is the case with all finite activities. Such activities or sentient principles are dependent on the nature of their term, which itself is changed by some foreign cause or force. The quality and quantity of this term (foreign to the sentient principle) and its changes are sometimes favourable and sometimes unfavourable to the activation of the principle. They are favourable when they help the sentient principle to carry out some greater activity; unfavourable when they restrain its natural activity and prevent it from carrying out the whole of its natural act. In this case, the activity of the principle struggles against the obstacle.

At this point, we find the most general notion of the pleasant or unpleasant state of a feeling — a notion we have to form. An unpleasant, troublesome, painful feeling is that in which the sentient principle is prevented by the state of its term from carrying out the whole of its natural act. A pleasant feeling is present when the principle carries out without difficulty all its possible activity according to the state of its term, free from any opposition or obstacle. The activity of the sentient principle posited in act is, therefore, essentially *pleasure*. The degree of pleasure is proportionate to the actuality of the activity and to the way in which the activity is carried out. The essence of feeling, therefore, is pleasure; pain is simply that which forcefully and violently diminishes, suppresses and limits feeling.

1100. If the sentient principle's natural act is to bring about the greatest possible feeling (given the state of the term), it must do this spontaneously, that is, with the very act through which it exists and is a sentient principle. This is the principle of every instinct, and is found in the nature of every substantial feeling, of every subject; it is the activity proper to a subject. For example, why does the instinct for food manifest itself in the animal? Why does this instinct move the animal to carry out all the movements it needs to obtain food? Because these movements are efforts of the sentient principle to feel better, to enjoy a state of fuller and more pleasant feeling. We must not let our imagination restrict us to what we see externally, for example, when a wolf devours a sheep. The wolf's movements, seen extrasubjectively, are simply consequences of internal, subjective action in the wolf. We must consider the animal feelings which the wolf successively experiences in its actions. These internal feelings are the causes of its exterior movement. Everything the *wolf* does, it does internally, in its feeling. When I say the wolf does something I simply mean an acting sentient principle which adjusts its feeling in the most pleasant way. External movements which result from an internal process are only consequences relative to our visual faculty and in general to our special sensitivity. We speak about these external phenomena of our particular sensitivity as if the wolf directly and immediately produced them, whereas the wolf's action begins, continues and

[1100]

finishes in its feeling, changing the term of its own feeling (subjective body). This change presents to our vision the movements of the wolf's body (extrasubjective phenomena). These changes in the terms of the wolf's feeling and the changed terms themselves make the wolf act on external bodies (the sheep) as well. That which happens in external bodies forms new relationships with our visual or tactile sensitivity which result in new phenomena, that is, movements and changes taking place in the sheep's body and feelable by us. But I repeat, the real active cause, the first cause of all that happens, is the wolf's sentient principle, which successively adjusts its feeling in different ways until it has completed the task of feeding. Such is the action of instinct.

1101. An act of rational instinct, as we can see, takes place according to the same law. For example, the reason why we feel a natural delight in considering truth is that our rationally-sentient principle has for its pleasant, natural act the apprehension of what is true; we spontaneously apprehend it as best we can and enjoy it.

It is always the subject, the subjective feeling, which adjusts itself in the most pleasant way.

CHAPTER 10
Will

1102. I have classified instinct as a faculty, but I must point out that instinct is more a *mode* of action of different faculties than a particular faculty. As I said, instinct is a law which governs the activity of a subject and constitutes the subject. Will is the active part of an intelligent subject and can be defined as 'the power which a subject has to adhere to a known entity.'

1103. This adhesion is brought about by an internal *acknowledgement*.

But I must explain what I mean by 'willed acknowledgement'. Strictly speaking, *acknowledgement* supposes prior knowledge, which is on a par, as it were, with acknowledgement. In other words, the object of acknowledgement remains exactly as it is in knowledge. When this happens, willed acknowledgement is true, just and moral. The will, by acknowledging the known entity, does not alter the value of the entity, but restricts its pleasure to what is prescribed by direct knowledge. Sometimes however, instead of simply adhering to the known entity, the will arbitrarily increases or diminishes the degrees of being possessed by the entity. As a result, it values the entity either more or less than it is worth, acknowledging it as something which it is not, rather than as that which it is. The will supposes the entity to be different from that which direct knowledge presents, and in its place substitutes another entity which it invents and creates with its energy of free choice. This is certainly not pure and simple acknowledgement. It is first an invention and fabrication of that which afterwards we want to acknowledge. Strictly speaking, therefore, acknowledgement means an honest, true act of will. When the act is wayward and false, the will first invents and afterwards acknowledges what it has invented. Sometimes however, for the sake of brevity, we use the word 'acknowledgement' to mean the first voluntary activity whether honest or wayward. *Pure acknowledgement* and *false acknowledgement* are two ways in which volitive activity manifests itself.

1104. What is this act of will which I call 'acknowledgement', whether honest or false?

It is the pleasure, taken by the intellective subject, in a known entity. This pleasure can be enjoyed by the intelligent subject because the known entity (and therefore every entity) is its proper object, is that which makes it carry out its proper act. The act proper to a subject is that which makes it be what it is. Every subject desires to be, because the act of being proper to a living subject is pleasure itself, the essence of pleasure. Precisely because the intelligent subject tends to be and posits itself (being is its proper good), it uses the same energy by which it is to tend to be as much as it can, to increase its existence, and to enlarge and expand the act of its existence; in other words, it seeks to enjoy the objects of this act, that is, the objects through which it begins its activity, and increases and perfects itself. Every known entity is a good for the knowing subject, and its goodness is in proportion to the degrees of being which the entity has.

However, human beings are not purely intellective subjects; we are also endowed with rational and corporeal sensitivity. Consequently, we do not always act according to the inclination and law of intelligence, but according to the inclination of our animal or rational sensitivity. When the inclination of this double sensitivity prevails over the inclination of pure intelligence, we have no desire to renounce the inclination of intelligence. Instead, we seduce, deceive and persuade ourselves that the good presented by rational or animal feeling is greater than it is, greater than indicated by direct knowledge. So we invent and fabricate the object of our direct knowledge, partly by destroying it or hiding it from ourselves, partly by using our imagination to add and create in it some good which is not there. We all have this faculty for deception and sin, and although not forced or necessitated, we can and sometimes do act in this way. This properly speaking is free will.

Hence, wayward, false acknowledgement depends upon some previous feeling and affection which distracts and seduces the will in its acknowledgement.

1105. But if pure or false acknowledgement is the primal act of the will, are effects in the will restricted to acknowledgement? No, acknowledgement has a real efficacy which brings with it various consequences. These are primarily of two kinds, *decrees* of the will and *affections*.[92]

1106. If what the will acknowledges is a good we do not possess, a willed decision follows by which the will resolves to obtain the good and use the means necessary to attain its purpose. For example, a wounded man who wants to be healed acknowledges first that the healing of his wound is a good thing. He

---

[92] We cannot deny that the *Scholastics* paid almost exclusive attention to *decisions* of the will, and consequently to its free operation, which pertains to *decrees*. Modern philosophy, after falling into sensism, considers exclusively *feelings* and the affections of the will. Consequently they almost lost sight of decisions of the will and tended to destroy free will. A recent author makes the following observation about an English philosopher who was certainly influential in preparing the way for the Scottish school: 'According to Hutcheson, the question no longer concerns the Scholastics' abstract, synthetical and totally free will, but the active, affective, passionate, industrious and moral part of intelligence; in short, of the essence and rich reserve of human nature' (*Qu'est-ce que la phrénologie?*, p. 131).

then decides to apply the remedy, and as a result of his decision, uses his hands to bandage the wound. The external movement of his hands and body follows upon the decision, which has the power to move the locomotive, animal force.

1107. Sometimes, however, what is acknowledged by the will is already possessed, and the sole question is how to enjoy it more. In this case, the immediate, normal effect of acknowledgement is *sensible affection* which, moved spontaneously, is simply an increase and perfection of the pleasure already contained in the acknowledgement of the good possessed. These spontaneous effects are followed by corporeal movements which aid the effects and are revealed extrasubjectively to on-lookers. These external gestures and actions naturally reveal the joy, sorrow or other affections conceived internally.

1108. Although acknowledgement of a known good that has become more or less habitual or actual continues instinctively as an affection, the will's decision can intervene to arouse the affection. This can either make the acknowledgement actual or give it greater actuality than it would have through instinct.

1109. Hence, movements in the body can proceed from the will in two ways, by *decision* and by *affection*.

1110. We can therefore distinguish three kinds of acts of will:

1. *Instinctive acts*, that is, spontaneous affections which include both spontaneous acknowledgement as their principle, and consequent movements of the body.

2. Decisions, which determine the acquisition of an unpossessed good and the use of the means for acquiring it, or else determine the acts necessary for increasing the actual enjoyment of some already possessed good. These decrees are normally called 'elicited acts'.

3. Movements of the potencies as a result of *decisions*. These movements are normally called 'commanded acts'.

1111. *Elicited* and *commanded acts* are always *assented to* by the will; instinctive acts are assented to only when the will, which could prevent them, does not do so. Hence assent always presupposes a decision. However a decision preventing spontaneous acts can be proximate or remote. It is proximate if it expresses a will not to prevent the acts; remote, if it expresses a will not to prevent the cause of the acts, because a person who desires a cause, also desires its effect.

1112. All acts of will are called 'volitions'. Instinctive acts not put in motion by any decision are volitions devoid of choice.

Choice always pertains to the order of decisions; whenever we internally pronounce a decision, we always have the choice of willing or not willing the thing. Sometimes our choice is so free that it is determined not by its objects but by the very energy of the will. In this case we have what is called 'bilateral freedom', which is the freedom necessary for the moral merit proper to human beings in this life. The conditions for the exercise of this bilateral freedom have been discussed in the *Anthropology* and elsewhere.

I now refer the reader to the synoptic schema of the divisions of the will [p. 167].

SYNOPTIC SCHEMA 5

WILL

Will is the power which the subject has of moving itself to adhere to a known entity and to take pleasure in the entity (a negative, contrary act can be reduced to a positive act).

Will is a power or activity proper to the soul as principle; knowledge determines only the act of understanding. Anything further that the soul does as a result of its understanding comes from itself as principle. The functions of the will are:

Primary function: Acknowledgement, which is either simple or accompanied by *invention* — Faculty of Practical Reason

Secondary co-ordinate *functions*, as:
    I. Instinctive affections, when acknowledgement concerns good already possessed:
      1. Affections present in the subject.
      2. Movements of the body which result from affections through a dynamic nexus.
    II. Decisions, which can have as their object:
      1. Acknowledgement of another entity, possibly succeeded by spontaneous or decreed affections and movements — BILATERAL FREEDOM.
      2. Affections or feelings
        i) negatively: a decision is made not to impede them when they arise spontaneously from acknowledgement;
        ii) positively: a decision is made to stimulate or increase them;
      3. Acts of the rational and moral potencies.
      4. Movements of the body.

Third-level function: movements of the body resulting spontaneously from decreed or spontaneous affections.

Book 3
(synthetical)

Laws governing the activity of the soul.
How the different laws governing
the activity of the soul take their origin
from the nature of the soul

Every effort must be made to know
what REASON is.
St. Augustine, *De Immort. Anim.*, c. 6

[Introduction]

1113. Every time human ingenuity turns to the study of natural things, the analytical method gains ground. There is an explanation for this. Matter is known by us through its divisibility, through its parts and their different proximities, aspects and sensible appearances. At least, this is the knowledge aimed at by the natural sciences. They go no further than *perception*, on which they are wholly based.

This way of carrying out analysis is extremely helpful for training and gradually perfecting intellectual ability in scientific work. On the other hand, human beings are limited, and it is easy, when they devote themselves to some partial method, to forget that other good and necessary methods exist to perfect knowledge. There is a danger that such methods will no longer be appreciated.

It is also true that we tend to extremes. In this particular case, the attraction of results obtained from analytical reasoning make us imagine and persuade ourselves that this method is sufficient for every eventuality and that analysis is the only source of all wisdom. This exaggerated confidence in analysis is found in ages when natural sciences prevail. It has its advantages for the education of the spirit, which is never happy with the work of scientific synthesis unless analysis has first been perfected and, if possible, exhausted. And perhaps analysis would never have made such advances if the mind had applied itself simultaneously to analysis and synthesis.

1114. For two centuries, human ingenuity has been engaged in analysis. During this period, physical and mathematical sciences have tended to displace intellectual and moral sciences, which have felt the disastrous effects proper to analytical method when it ousts synthesis. Analysis is not capable of finding certain truths and, in attempting to work outside its possibilities, gives rise to errors.

Amongst the truths of which analysis, unaccompanied by synthesis, is incapable are many whose object are the nature and laws of spirits. Simple as they are, spirits are impossible to divide into material parts. It is quite certain that the study of spiritual natures cannot usefully be carried forward by analysis alone, and still less by material analysis. The disaster that fell upon sciences connected with spirits after the Scholastic era must, therefore, be attributed to two causes: 1. these sciences have been dealt with only analytically, without reference to synthesis; 2. the kind of analysis used in this work is proper to matter, which is multiple, not to spirit, which is simple and one.

1115. The history of the philosophy of the spirit from Condillac through to the Scottish school shows that these philosophers lost sight of the unity of the human spirit (although I do not wish to suggest that the Scots were materialists). The human spirit became a mere *aggregation of faculties*, *placed next to one another* as it were. We hear nothing, or very little, about principles of action, about first-order facts, about the principle from which faculties arise and to which they return, or about substance-principle. This is treated as an accessory, or some kind of *deus ex machina*. Yet it, and it alone, is spirit.

1116. These philosophers have in fact decapitated the psychological sciences through their exclusive use of analysis and their almost total inability to use synthesis. Phrenologists, who succeeded them, went much further. Their works are riddled with extremely serious errors that spring not only from the application of the analytical method alone to the spirit (to the exclusion of synthesis), but also from the use of the material analytical method (proper only to bodies). Phrenologists claim that the aggregation of faculties which preceding philosophers considered as the soul is nothing more than the *aggregation of* quite distinct *organs* which make up the brain.

1117. This explains why a recent author, in comparing writers of the Scottish school with phrenologists, concluded that both sides were guilty of neglecting the unity of the subject, which

[1115–1117]

they either dismembered into distinct faculties, or into organs, which are no longer the object of mental analysis but of the anatomist's knife.[93]

1118. Obviously, I am not opposed to analysis. I repeat: there can be no true scientific synthesis, no truthful synthesis, until analysis has in some way been exhausted. It is true that I began the present work with an eminently synthetical investigation about the nature of the soul, but this was authorised by the long analysis made in preceding works as a result of all possible observation of acts and faculties of the soul. The whole of this analysis was carried out in a way suitable to the spirit alone. Such analysis does not divide the spirit into separate parts, but considers individual parts without cutting them off from the single root in which they live and move and have their being, that is, in the substance of the soul itself.

1119. After dealing with the first, synthetical question about the nature of the human soul, I moved on from the soul to distinguish and enumerate the faculties and functions of which it is the root. This required analysis. Having completed this work by deriving human faculties from their principle, I now have to bring them back to the same principle in order to draw out the laws of operation proper both to the principle itself and its faculties. This is why I have called the next three books 'synthetical'; they deal with the *laws* according to which the potencies of the human spirit work. These laws are in fact derived from the intimate nature of the spirit and follow upon the first, substantial act through which and in which the spirit is what it is — or better, they follow on the act which is the spirit itself. Another necessary reason for attributing synthesis to teaching about the laws governing the activity of the spirit is this: every law that we succeed in establishing is finally nothing more than a great synthesis embracing innumerable acts carried out in the same way. The identical mode of activity is precisely the sign and substance of the law.

1120. In the preceding book, I set out to enumerate and describe the special potencies of the soul by deriving and assembling them from the essence itself of the soul. In the same way, I

---

[93] *Analyse critique des doctrines phrénologiques*, M. Flourens, honorary secretary of the Academy of Sciences, *etc.*, Paris, 1842.

[1118–1120]

now have to indicate first the single source of all the laws that the spirit and its activities follow in the acts they posit. This source is the essence itself of the soul. I shall start immediately.

CHAPTER 1

Human nature: Summary — Definition of 'human being'

1121. Let me go back to human nature as I have described it. I shall summarise all the elements composing it, and seek in the nature of these elements the laws that preside over the activity of human nature, laws through which the soul is developed and perfected. To do this, I must first consider the initial definition of 'human being'.

1122. The human being is 'an animal, intellective and volitive subject'. This definition can be summarised in another: 'a rational subject'.

The first definition has the advantage of indicating the primal potencies of the human being. In fact, intelligence is a *primal* potency; reason, a *resultant* potency, as I said. This is why I would prefer to say that the human being is an intellective subject rather than a reasoning subject. If I had put 'reasoning' or 'rational' in the first definition instead of 'intellective', it would have been impossible to place 'animality' in the definition. 'Animality' would be already contained in 'rationality' and I would have failed to offer a definition in which the primal potencies were mentioned separately.

1123. Nevertheless, as we go over the question, I find the other definition, 'The human being is a rational subject', more perfect. Given that the word 'rational' has already been explained, this definition has the following advantages, besides brevity:

1. Although intelligence is the primal potency, it does not constitute human nature. If intelligence alone is posited, we would have an intellective subject, but not a human being. As long as our thought goes no further than intelligence, the human being is in course of formation, but is not yet formed. Reason is the activity which posits the human being.

[1121–1123]

2. Reason, as the activity proper to intelligence and to its connection with animality, suitably expresses the unity of the human subject and the primal bond between its potencies. It is true that in the definition, 'The human being is an animal, intellective and volitive subject', the word 'subject' is sufficient to indicate the unity of the human being. However, the definition, 'the human being is a rational subject', besides expressing the unity of the human being, also indicates how this unity is formed, that is, in virtue of reason, which joins in itself intellect and sense.[94]

CHAPTER 2

There are reciprocal connections or relationships between entia which are essential to them and make them what they are

1124. The marvellous connection between animality and intellectuality receives light that enables us to deduce the laws which human nature follows in its activity if we recall the ontological teaching about relationships essential to entia. These relationships are called 'essential' because they form part of the constitution of entia. First, however, we must remember that the entia about which we are speaking are those which occur in our mental conceptions. If we did not conceive them mentally, we could not even speak about them.

1125. These entia which have their place in our conception possess some essential relationships in themselves without which they could not be that which they are. Consequently, they change their nature in our mind in so far as our thought considers them with some of these essential relationships or with others. The removal from a mentally conceived ens of an essential relationship is alone sufficient to make it another ens, expressed with another word. Again, the addition of some

[94] The word 'rational' in the definition 'the human being is a rational subject' does not properly express the potency of reason, but the quality of rationality proper to the essence of the human being.

relationship makes the ens something other than it was. This happens because we are dealing with essential relationships which form part of the essence of an ens, that is, the ens itself. This reminder will be clear to those who are already aware of my teaching on the synthesism of being. We now have to apply this teaching to the different entities which form part of the constitution of the human soul. If we are to deduce the laws of these entities, we have to know their nature and their intimate connection.

CHAPTER 3

The essential relationships of extension and of what is extended

Article 1
The extended element has two essential relationships: one constituting it as it is in itself; the other constituting it as term of a sensitive principle

1126. If we consider an ens furnished with extension we shall easily realise that the concept of extension results from an *essential relationship* between the parts that we can assign mentally in a given continuum, or between as many points as we care to conceive in it. The essential relationship between the parts of which we are speaking is this: one part is outside another. The essential relationship between assignable points is this: there is, between one point and another, a given continuum of varying size prevents the points from ever touching. The concept of extended ens is the result of these relationships. Extension, therefore, involves possible relationship of one extended part to another, and of points to points. This relationship is distance.

1127. But if, on the contrary, we consider the relationship of the continuum with the sentient principle, we find this relationship altogether different. It is not a relationship of part to part or of point to point. The sentient principle is neither an extended part nor a mathematical point. I called this relationship between the extended element and the sentient principle *relationship of sensility*. It is evident that this relationship is non-extended precisely because it is not a relationship of part to part or of point to point, the only relationship which alone forms extension. Consequently, I concluded that the sentient principle apprehends what is extended in a non-extended way. When I say that the sentient principle apprehends what is extended, I mean that what is extended is in the sentient principle, but not as one part is in a greater part. As a result, the extended element is not in the sentient principle with the relationship constituting extension but in some other way, that is, in a non-extended mode.

This can be proved by another argument. When we say that one ens is in another in an extended mode, we mean that it is in the other according to the law of extension. This law states that one ens is in another as a lesser extension is in a greater, as part of a body is in the whole. A part of a body is in the whole in such a way that it is outside other parts. Properly speaking, no body is contained in another body, although it may be surrounded by some other body. The precise property of extension is that every single part is outside every other. This property when considered in bodies which enjoy extension is called *impenetrability*. On the other hand, if we consider how the *extended sensible element* is in sensation or in sensitive perception, it becomes clear that it is not present in the mode we described. Here, we certainly do not find two extensions of different sizes with the lesser comprised in the greater. We find that the whole extension is present to the sentient and perceiving principle, which is not a greater extension that embraces a lesser, but something different from extension (which is its term). The extended element, therefore, is not in the sentient principle according to the mode prescribed by the law of extension; it is there in an non-extended mode. All this is given to us by simple observation. It is an undeniable fact; we simply have to pay attention to recognise it.

Yet another proof of this truth, or another indication of how we can recognise this fact, is found in what follows. The phrase 'One body contains another, one extended element other less than itself' is improper, and strictly speaking is false. Extension and that which enjoys extension is impenetrable, as I said; one part cannot be within another without destroying its own extension. Now, if what is extended were contained in the sentient principle as one extended element is contained in another, it would follow that what is extended would never be contained in the sentient principle; the sentient principle would surround it, be next to it, but nothing more. In this case, the sentient principle would never feel what is extended because the latter would always remain outside it. This is, in fact, the case between every extended element; what is extended cannot feel what is extended. But the sentient principle does feel what is extended, and the whole of what is extended. It is necessary, therefore, that what is extended should be in the sentient principle according to some other relationship, according to a law different from that of extension. In other words, what is extended is present in an non-extended mode.

Moreover, if the sentient principle had extension and perceived what is extended by receiving the latter into its own extension, one of two things would follow: either the extension of the sentient principle would be the same as that of the extended things it feels, or it would be different. If it were the same, the sentient principle would feel only itself; it would never receive any new sense-experience. If it were different, that is, if another extension were added to that of the sentient principle, the new extension, in order to be felt, would itself have to become a sentient principle. This is manifestly absurd because in sense-experience and sensitive perception, the sentient element is one thing and the felt element another.

Finally, if the sentient principle were extended, each part of this extension could feel only an extended part of its own dimension. But however small the parts assigned mentally, they could always be diminished. This could go on indefinitely in such a way that the smallest parts could never be found. There are no absolutely small parts in an extended element. Consequently, the sentient parts would never be found because no part could be felt whole and entire by its corresponding part, which itself has other parts, each of which would not feel the whole, entire part. It would, therefore, be impossible to determine one whole, entire part that felt the whole of another part. There would be no sentient principle suitable for feeling the whole of some extended element, however small it were.[95]

[95] When in the last century D'Alembert asked about the bridge of communication between the spirit and external things, his question was

The extended felt element would also be lacking, and for the same reason: there would be no sentient principle capable of feeling it as extended. Even if we supposed the sentient principle to be a mathematical point, such a point could still not feel anything other than a mathematical point; the extended element or point has no existence or action outside itself and could never feel what is extended. Indeed, the extended element would cease altogether because it cannot exist outside the sentient principle. If every part is outside every other in the extended element, every part, or better every smallest extended element, exists outside every other. If it exists outside every other part, its existence and its essence is limited to itself; it has no proper and essential relationship with any other part. But even the smallest extended element is a union of still smaller elements. This can go on indefinitely. The ultimate, extended elements cannot, therefore, be found, and thus extension itself vanishes. If extension supposes possible co-existing parts, if it supposes continuity (which has a single, simultaneous existence without any interruption), there must be a simple principle which can simultaneously embrace all possible parts. These individual parts no longer remain in their own single existence, but together are formed into a single existence, a single ens. The very nature of the continuum is that parts can be assigned in it that have individual and independent existence, although as a continuum it does not have these parts. The reason, therefore, for the continuum as a property of extension is not found in the individual existence of the single parts, but in a simple principle superior

posed absurdly. This way of asking the question presupposes as given and agreed that there is a relationship of extension between the spirit and things, just as there is a relationship of extension between one bank of a river and another, between one body and another. But once the error of this presupposition is identified, the question itself ceases to exist. It is seen to be one of those questions to which no reply can be given because the questions themselves do not truly exist. The relationship between spirit and things is not a relationship of distance but of sensility; it is not the relationship of one corporeal part to another, but of body to spirit, of felt and sentient. An important principle of logic can be drawn from this: 'All questions proposed in such a way that they include or presuppose something absurd are non-resolvable, and are annulled when the truth has been discovered.' Simultaneously with the truth we find how the state of the question has been changed, and the true question solved.

[1127]

to these parts. This principle gives all the parts a single existence and by embracing them all abolishes them, because they cease to be parts of the continuum and become simply the continuum. This is done by the sentient principle to which the continuum is present without parts, although innumerable parts can be assigned in it. This explains why I said that an extended element can exist only in what is simple (cf. 440–452).[96]

1128. What has been said enables us to reason in two ways about the nature of extension and of bodies and thus, have two concepts of them. We can consider the nature of the extension of bodies

1. *Under the relationship essential to extension*, which consists in this: one part is outside another. This consideration does not move our thought away from extension and from what is extended. It simply makes us consider extension in itself and compare one part with another.

2. *Under the other essential relationship of sensility*. This consideration compares extension or the extended element with the sentient principle, and finds extension conditioned to the principle and in-existing in it.

Normally people consider extension and the extended element under the first relationship, in which they posit the essence of extension. The philosopher has to consider it under the second relationship. He must understand that the second relationship also forms part of its essence, and consequently that extension has an *essential nexus* with the sentient principle, a principle which is not extension. These connections between two entia

---

[96] This truth was seen in some way by the Scholastics when they asked if the intellective soul were the single form of the human being. This is St. Thomas' opinion. He says: 'Through the soul this being is body and organic and a potency having life' (*S. T.*, I, q. 76, art. 4, ad 1). Cajetan, a celebrated and very subtle commentator, when explaining how the soul as a single form also produces corporeity, says: 'This question is only about quantity and what is extended *per accidens*, that is, SUBJECTIVELY.' He does not reflect, however, that the extended element, although existing in the subject is distinct from the subject; nor does he note that the principle which directly causes the existence of the extended element is the sensitive, not the intellective principle; nor is he aware that the extended element vanishes when outside the subject. Nevertheless, the commentary of this illustrious Cardinal deserves attention.

(and essential to them both) are the foundation of *ontological synthesism* and the key to more sublime philosophy.

1129. Note that the first essential relationship is not destroyed in any way by the second. Indeed, the second supposes the first. If we consider continuous extension or the continuous extended element as existing in the sentient principle, there is no danger of confusing it with the sentient principle, to which it is opposed as co-relative term. This term is an ens in itself, constituted in such a way that it can be conceived without our needing to go outside it or add anything to it. The term is, therefore, a substance because 'substance has what is needed to be conceived, and therefore exists in itself.' Note that it is not at all necessary for a thing to have a cause or a constituent principle, in order to be conceived as a substance. It is sufficient for it to be conceived by itself. We may say more briefly that 'substance is that which has its own concept.' We simply add that the word *substance* involves, in addition, a relationship with *accident* as, for instance, in corporeal substance. This allows for different accidents which exist in and through the substance. They have no separate and independent concept because we cannot conceive of a corporeal accident as existing unless we first conceive a body, an extended element, in which it is. And it is precisely to this body that we give the name 'substance'. Substance, therefore, is 'an ens (or that which has a concept of its own) considered in relationship with other entities that exist in and through it.' This is the most complete definition of substance (cf. 52).

1130. But if the continuous extended element has existence in the sentient principle as its essential relationship, it would seem that this element cannot be conceived without recourse to the sentient principle in which it exists; everything essential enters into the concept of an ens. This difficulty can be overcome by noting how we insisted that an ens changes essentially in our concept through the addition or subtraction of an essential relationship. As we said, the beings of which we are speaking are those we conceive. But the essential part added to them does not change the first part.

1131. We also need to consider that the concept of the continuous extended element, although thought of without the sentient principle, nevertheless presents in itself *continuity*, produced by the simplicity of this principle. It is precisely by reasoning about the nature of this continuity that we later induce the necessity of a sentient principle. This induction, although founded on the first concept of the extended element, pertains to a reasoning posterior to the conception of this element. Such reasoning is not necessary for the conception of an ens which as we said is posited with *the first concept.*

Article 2
Extension is one thing; the extended element another

1132. Until now, we have spoken indiscriminately of extension and the extended element because our reasoning was valid for both. But before going on to speak of the unity which the sentient principle gives to its term, it will help to clarify and eliminate all doubt in the mind of readers if we distinguish *extension* from the *extended element.*

By *extension*, I understand the same as space, considered independently of bodies. By *extended*, I understand a body which occupies a part of space, that is, of extension. Extension, that is, total or empty space, exists whether occupied or not by bodies. It is certainly not nothing, as some would have us believe. Nothing cannot be occupied by anything, nor can thought assign parts to nothing as they can be assigned in space.

This space, however, is boundless [*App.*, no. 5], immobile, indivisible, that is, continuous and unmodifiable. Only body is measurable, mobile, divisible and modifiable. But the presence or absence of the body in a given space does not modify space or extension in any way. This remains as it was previously.

1133. For me, pure space is a term of the fundamental perception of the soul (cf. 554–559).

This primal space is not a form in Kant's sense, a law of operation as it were and a production of the soul itself, but the distinct term of a natural perception. The term, however, has successively two states, the *primal* state devoid of any quantitive distinction or relationship, or of any other nature (pure, indistinct space); and *reflective space* which is brought about by the mind which compares primal space, also perceived intellectually, with various dimensions of bodies and with the possibilities of such dimensions (ideas of pure distinct space, that is, space relative to bodies). This pure, distinct, reflective space with its quantitative relationships is of another genus; it is the *idea of interminable space*, whose origin we have indicated in *A New Essay*.[97] For me, one of the terms of the fundamental feeling is an extended body and thus a distinct extension limited as the body is limited. But the animal has power to move itself, and movement means simply transporting the body into another part of space. If, therefore, some trace of the previously occupied space remains, the distinct space remains enlarged in the sentient principle in proportion to the movement and retentive faculty of the principle. When movement takes place in the human being, who is furnished with intelligence and possesses the concept of what is possible, he understands the possibility of indefinitely multiplying and extending the space of his and other bodies through motion. He thus forms the concept of reflective, distinct, pure or immense space.[98] This concept is lacking in animals, who have no concepts; it is acquired in human beings, although the indistinct space of sensitive and rational perception is innate. The instinct of motion does indeed suppose the fundamental perception of immense, indistinct space, but not the idea of distinct space. This instinct is only the bodily feeling with its limited space, of which, however, it does not feel the exterior confines. As such, the instinct tends to adapt itself in the most comfortable and pleasing way without the animal's feeling, as full and distinct, the new space to which it is to move. The animal transports itself through its activity to this space which, however, it feels as distinct, that

[97] *NE*, vol. 2, 820–830.

[98] Here we have to add that this mental operation with which we conceive interminable space would be impossible for us unless we had some movement other than absolute movement, which cannot be felt. We need relative movement. We are helped in retaining this space through which we have moved above all by surface sensations, and by sight which marks their limits so clearly. Once we know these limits, we soon think of the possibility of going beyond them again (once the limits have been passed, and we know through experience that they can be expanded indefinitely). Indeed, the concept of limit or term of space contains virtually the immensity of space in the same way as a condition is contained virtually in what is conditioned. *Reasoning* enables us to draw the former from the latter.

is, occupied or occupiable, only when it has already moved itself there, provided of course that it has some way of preserving in itself the traces of the preceding space.

Space connected with one's own body is therefore distinct space because it is occupied space, but it is not marked by limits. These cannot be distinguished because as yet nothing corporeal is felt outside the space that limits one's own body, the space of which is absolutely limited, but not measurable by the animal. Measurement supposes a relationship with some other extended quantity which is lacking until the animal exercises its locomotive power and receives new sense-experiences.

1134. This, therefore, is simply space, unmodifiable and immobile. It has no accidents, and although it can truly be called an *ens* because its concept (after the human being has obtained it) is self-sufficient and without need of body, it cannot be called a *substance*. The concept of substance is *relative* to other entities which exist in and through an ens, that is, relative to accidents. Here again, we see how unfounded is the affirmation: 'There are no entia, other than substances and accidents.' It pertains to false, material ontology.[99]

1135. Space, with or without corporeal force, is the term of feeling. This shows that space is an ens, not nothing. However, while it is only this force which changes (space remains immobile), it must be said that space is an ens having only a first act by which it is in the sentient principle it informs as term. Space has no other activity or second acts and hence no accidents. That is why those who fail to acknowledge anything until they see accidents and second acts, make the mistake of calling space nothing.

Again, in considering pure space (extension) as the immediate term of the spirit, we consider it in the very act by which it is constituted because it has no other activity beyond the activity which it demonstrates as the natural term of the sentient principle. The concept of body (of the extended element), however, as term of the sentient principle involves in addition some passivity possessed by corporeal nature relative to both the spirit whose term it is and to other powers or external forces which move and modify body independently of our spirit. In

[99] *Rinnovamento*, bk, 3, chap. 47.

other words, we can acquire the concept of distinct space, that is, of several spaces, simply by abstracting it from body.

But acquisition of the full concept of body requires the kind of experience which shows that the body is an ens acting in our spirit, which in turn reacts on the body by modifying it. Other foreign forces and powers also act on the body by producing movements and modifications in it. From all this information, the result of experience, the human spirit draws conclusions about the kind of force which, expanding in extension, is called 'body'.[100]

Article 3
The unity of extension and of the extended element comes from the simplicity of the animal-sentient principle, that is, from the soul

1136. From what has been said, we can draw the following important corollary: the unity found in extension and in the corporeal, extended element is constituted by the unity and simplicity of the sentient principle, that is, by the soul.

In fact, the only unity of which we are aware in extension and the extended element consists in *continuity*. If we remove continuity, by splitting it up successively with our mind, space and

[100] These reflections enable us to confute the error of the Cartesians who confused *space* with *body* by positing the essence of body in extension. Errors of this kind result from an inability to discover any corporeal quality outside extension. As a result, they considered extension as the *substratum* of corporeal accidents, that is, as the first thing conceived in bodies, but failed to reflect that the *extension* of bodies is not perceived distinctly except by feeling. Extension, therefore, is never conceived alone, but in the company of extended sensations in which some force is always perceived. Hence, in the order of concepts, the force which acts in us is prior to the extension of bodies. Extension, therefore, is not the first thing that we conceive in them. Rather, we conceive contemporaneously force as cause, and extension as effect. These two things do not perhaps differ relative to time, but they certainly differ relative to logical order. I grant, however, with the Cartesians that the concept of extension should be clear and sharply delineated. Cardinal GERDIL'S work *Della immaterialità dell'anima contro Locke* is helpful on this point, but does not prove that extension is the substance of bodies.

body are multiplied. This multiplication goes on *ad infinitum* because the continuum always remains; division and multiplication *ad infinitum* never provides us with a space and a body that have no continuum. Imagining this is absurd. If, then, we sweep away the continuum immediately, not successively, all extension and every phenomenal body perishes.[101]

But we have seen that the continuity of the extended element can only be conceived if we have an ens which, remaining identical, is simultaneously in all the assignable parts of the continuum. This can be affirmed of the spirit, when the continuum is considered as its undivided and indivisible term.

1137. If, therefore, the simplicity of the material world consists solely in continuity, and if continuity possesses such a concept or nature that it cannot be posited outside the sentient principle (we cannot even think it outside the sentient principle), the simplicity and the unity of the material world comes about as a result of this essential condition and relationship. In other words, the material world is the term of the animal-sentient principle, that is, of the sensitive soul.

1138. Here I trust that no one who has followed the argument will object that 'being contiguous or non-joined is a condition proper to two bodies, not to feeling'. This would show that the objector had not considered that:

1. Immobile extension is the foundation of the continuum even in bodies. Bodies are only forces diffused in extension which has its seat in the sentient principle.

2. The continuity of bodies is nothing relative to the individual bodies themselves. None of these has in itself any relationship of proximity or contiguity with another. This relationship, therefore, is extraneous to the concept. It is simply a relationship that each of them has with the term of the sentient principle, that is, with immobile and unmodifible extension. Hence, the contiguity of bodies is a relationship with the

---

[101] One of the properties of an ens is *simplicity*. This truth was known and taught by the Scholastics, who held as a principle that *esse substantiale cuiuslibet rei in indivisibili consistit* [the substantial being of anything whatsoever consists in an indivisible element], as St. Thomas says (*S. T.*, 1, q. 76, art. 4, ad 3). This means: 'Where simplicity cannot be found, there is no being'. An accident is not, properly speaking, an ens, but an entity, that is, an appurtenance of an ens.

sentient principle, which feels them in the space by which, as by its term, the principle itself is informed.

CHAPTER 4
Essential relationships of a temporary ens with the sentient principle

Article 1
Development of the concept of time

1139. Any ens whose concept excludes the *possibility* of succession is said to be eternal. Such are ideas,[102] and such is necessary being, God the Almighty.

Note that an ens can be called eternal only if it excludes the possibility of succession as well as actual succession. In other words, thinking of succession in it is equivalent to destroying it. Thus, an immobile atom of matter has no succession, but it *could have*. Changes could be thought of in it without destroying its concept. It is not, therefore, eternal.

1140. Succession implies change: consequently that which is eternal is also unchangeable.

In the same way, that which has begun to be, or even that which, without contradiction, can be thought to begin is not eternal. If something can begin, there is nothing to prevent the thought of something else beginning before or after it. One could also think of its ceasing after it had started. It is possible, therefore, to think of this thing as the term of a successive series, in other words, it allows of succession. The same must be said even of space, the concept of which easily allows a beginning without destruction of the conception.

1141. We have to consider carefully the concept of *succession*, a concept necessary to that of time.

Succession supposes a series of several events. Each single

[102] *NE*, vol. 2, 797–799 — *Rinnovamento*, bk. 3, c. 39–53.

event does not form succession or time, but all together contribute to form it. If time does not consist in each single event, however, time is outside events, each of which is essentially singular, and complete in its singularity. Its concept does not require nor has it any *essential relationship* with some other event. On the contrary, time consists essentially in the *relationship* of several events with each other.

1142. But if the relationship which constitutes time is not found in events, where is it to be found?

This *realised* relationship is found first in the *sentient principle*, which apprehends several events disposed in successive order, a fact noticeable only to interior observation. We can analyse this fact and, by considering its nature, investigate the conditions according to which the sentient principle can apprehend several successive events, for example, several of its own modifications.

1143. If the sentient principle is to apprehend several successive events as its term, it seems necessary for them to be rendered contemporaneous by remaining in it in some way. If one were apprehended but were then totally eliminated only to be succeeded by another, singular events would indeed appear in the sentient principle as they are in themselves, but the relationship of succession between them would not be apprehended; it would not exist in the sentient principle any more than in the events. Thought reflecting on these things would find no succession there.

1144. Note carefully that thought takes things as they are, as they are given to it by feeling. It does not change them.[103] It is necessary, therefore, that succession, in order to be thought, should exist in feeling before being thought. It is true that thought conceives this succession as *possible* and, as such, renders indefinite the finite succession presented to it by feeling. It does this with the idea of possibility, as we have explained elsewhere.[104] Nevertheless, it is also true that feeling must first have presented to thought some finite succession in its own reality. This will be understood better if we consider that memory itself would be impossible without the help of feelings

---

[103] *Sistema filososfico*, nn. 67–104. — *Rinnovamento*, bk 3, c. 47.

[104] *NE*, vol. 2, 776–778.

which noted things in the idea of being. It is certain that if every feeling ceased for the intellective soul, all memory of events or real things would cease in the soul. Nothing would remain present to the soul except ideal being, without any kind of determination or inequality. There would be nothing by which particular, real things were designated in ideal being. Only certain aptitudes, potentialities, habits of the soul, incapable of passing into act, would remain.

1145. To see the varying roles played by thought and feeling in the constitution of time, we have to investigate more carefully the fact of memory, a faculty which pertains to the order of intelligence, and properly speaking to the potency of reason. We shall speak about memory here. It has two principal functions, one called *retentive* and the other *reminiscence*. The task of the former is to retain information; of the latter, to recall information, when needed, to the reflective attention of the mind.

1146. We shall not delay over the second function, but must spend some time on the first, which is either unconscious or conscious.

The *unconscious retentive function* is what the ancients called 'the habit of memory', through which information remains in us without our giving it any reflective attention.

The *conscious retentive function* is the activity through which we have information present to our reflection and consciousness. We either recall the information with an act of reminiscence or we reflect upon it continuously.

1147. We say, then, that for a past event to be present to our consciousness:

1. It needs some trace of the event in our imagination or in our feeling. This trace is not the event of which we are thinking, which is already past, but a kind of *sign* of it.

2. It is necessary, therefore, that some special power of thought be added, in addition to the trace we have mentioned, which enables our mind to pass from the sign to what is signified. The mind, with the help of the trace which remains, can transport itself to the event which no longer exists and thus finish its act of thought in the past as in its term. This is not too easy to explain but, having done so elsewhere, I will summarise what has been said as a help to readers.

1148. We must bear in mind, above all, that the mere concept of an event is neither past nor future; it is present in the idea. This conception, therefore, does not give any knowledge of the event except relative to its nature and its possibility. There is no question of time, which is a relationship proper to real entia, not to pure ideas. But the conception or possibility of an event, precisely because it is immune from time, can be applied to every time. I can think of an event as *possible* in the past as in the future. We have to investigate, therefore, how we can pass from knowledge of a possible event to knowledge of a real event which is situated at a given point in time. A *real ens*, we recall, is known only through feeling. This shows once more the necessity of feeling if we are to be able to think of the time of an event.

1149. But the feeling of the perception by which we were present to an event gradually ceases. This is true, but we have to notice that perception is conceived through a judgment. Indeed, perception accompanied by reflection of one kind or another, as occurs in adults, is accompanied by several judgments which provide the spirit with information about an event. We must examine both these judgments and this information.

The judgment proper to perception is this: the event, the fact, the ens in question, subsists. Thus the spirit acquires information about the subsistence of that entity ('entity' is a word that embraces every ens, every event, fact or action). This judgment is accompanied by many others which determine the entity through the contemporaneous relationships it has with other judgments. That entity is not perceived by itself; many other entities, surrounding it and co-existing with it, are perceived with it. This provides further information for the spirit. The amount of new information is in proportion to the judgments with which it is affirmed that that entity co-exists with others.

Again, amongst the entities which exist along with the entity we have in mind, several began prior to that entity, others began after. Our entity started, therefore, while others existed. Other entities again either finished before our entity, or continued to last after it had ceased. The spirit, therefore, acquires in the act of perception (or better, in the act of many contemporaneous perceptions and the reflective judgments which accompany the perceptions) information about the chronological order in which contemporaneous entities *began*. But because the whole of life is a continuous series of perceptions and reflections, of judgments and chronological information, it follows that the spirit comes to know the chronological order of the entities or perceived events, as long as this information remains in the spirit. Everything, therefore, is reduced to explaining how this information is kept in the spirit. Granted the preservation of the information, the spirit already knows which event has come first and which later; it knows whether a given event has few or many events prior to it. In other words, it knows succession and time. Little by little, it comes to measure time more or less accurately through various periods. We need to see, therefore, how chronological information and the events acquired as a result of contemporaneous perceptions are preserved. I mention contemporaneous perceptions because it is always a contemporaneous event which indicates the beginning and end of some other event. In its turn this other event signals the beginning and end of events contemporaneous with itself, and so on successively.

What is this chronological information? It is made up of various affirmations, judgments and persuasions. But an affirmation is an act of the rational principle. If this act never ceased, it would follow that the information which it produces in the spirit would equally never cease; the information would always be present to the spirit. For example, consider this: a friend living at a distance arrived before sunset. If the affirmation we enunciated at our friend's arrival were to remain actuated, the information also would remain ever present to our spirit. Note, that in this supposition of the immobile presence of such information before our spirit, the object of the information would never vary as time went by; it would remain what it is. What we knew when we first pronounced the judgment, that is, 'Our friend reached us before evening', we would always know in the same way. These two events (the coming of our friend and sunset) would always be located one after another in our information. This is, therefore, an extremely important fact to which we must hold firm that as long as some information lasts, the object of the information does not change with the passage of time but remains identical: we are always dealing with a friend and with evening, however many centuries pass. Now, this identity of the object of some information is preserved not only in the hypothesis that the information remains before the spirit, but also if we are able to recall it after it has ceased. It is true that our spirit, by turning its thought once more to the information, would carry out a new act different from the first. Nevertheless, the object of that new act would be identical with that of the old act which had ceased, and it is the identity of the object which constitutes the identity of the information. This is true not only relative to chronological information, but relative to information of any kind. I may think a thousand times that $2 + 2 = 4$. If I do, I carry out a thousand different acts, although the object of all these acts is always the same and the information identical. I may think a thousand times that 'Alexander, the son of Philip existed'. Once more, I carry out a thousand acts, but always with the same object. In each of these acts, I think always of the same Alexander, the same Philip, and I think of them as father and son; the multiplicity of my acts does not multiply the objects. This is true whether we are dealing with a necessary object of information, such as the arithmetical truth that $2 + 2 = 4$, or whether the object is contingent, as for example the truth of the existence of Alexander, son of Philip. This means that the object of information is immune from time because time (which passes) and events (which succeed one another) do not change the object. Note, however, that this object although immune from time as an object of information, is not immune from time in itself because what is contingent is subject to time. In fact, there was succession and consequently time between Philip and Alexander. We have to conclude, therefore, that thought apprehends time, but not temporally. It apprehends what is temporary, but outside time. This is very similar to what we have said about the extended element's being apprehended by the spirit in an non-extended way. If the object of information, therefore, is temporary, and yet in so far as it has become an object of some information in the spirit is no longer subject to time, and is thus apprehended by the spirit outside time, where does the spirit apprehend it? We have to conclude that thought apprehends time and what is temporary in what is eternal. If we exclude the possibility of time, as we said, eternity remains.

[1149]

1150. We can explain this if we reflect that, granted feeling, we see in *ideal being*, which is necessary and eternal, even what is contingent and successive. We also see reality itself as able to subsist (idea of reality). We affirm subsistence by joining this reality with the essence of the thing. Consequently, every time affirmation makes some judgment about subsistence, it indicates the reality of the same essence and, therefore, the identical thing. This shows that thought, judgment and affirmation, when repeated, do not change their object; they take hold of it and place it before the mind in an eternal, unchangeable mode.

1151. We have now introduced two hypotheses. First, that the judgment producing the chronological information about entia for the spirit when perceptions take place lets this information remain in the spirit, as though it were deposited there. The second hypothesis is that the judgment reproduces the information after it has vanished. Relative to both hypotheses, we concluded that once a succession of several entities has been known, we can then know many others in the same way. The passage of time is no obstacle to this. But to avoid leaving anything that could disturb the mind of those who are following these investigations, I have to ask: 'Which of the two hypotheses conforms to fact?' The second is generally preferred because experience shows that a great deal of information is first forgotten, and then recalled through reminiscence. Consequently, it does not appear to be preserved in the spirit continuously. Here, however, there is a real difficulty. If this information is not retained, at least weakly, we would have no explanation for its recall. Where or how would our spirit have found what was lost? We cannot say this would come about through the association of this information with other present information. If the previous information were altogether lost, there could be no association. Nor could the recall be made as a result of instinct. Instinct supposes sense, whose movement it is, and consequently also supposes information retained in some way in feeling. In addition, the recall is often made not instinctively but through an arbitrary decree of will. On the other hand, there is no doubt that we lose *consciousness* of this information, and then revive it again.

All these difficulties vanish for persons who know the theory of consciousness. They will easily understand that acquired information can remain present, actual and alive in our spirit without, however, entering consciousness. I have already shown, that 'no act of the spirit is known to itself'. Such an act is always directed to knowledge of its own object, not to knowledge of itself. To know that we know a reflective act by which the act of the spirit becomes object must be followed by another reflective act. We must, therefore, choose the second hypothesis. We have to say that it is not sufficient to have information, but that in addition we have to have it preserved in ourselves if we are to become conscious of it. Hence it is not absurd to say that information once received in the spirit remains there. What ceases is the act of *attention*[105] that the spirit gives to the information, and the act of *reflection*. Without these acts, we have no consciousness of anything in our spirit.

1152. We return now to the argument. Thought knows succession, although not successively, provided that succession has already been offered to thought in perception and in the reflective judgments which accompany perception. But, as I said, perception and its concomitant judgments offer succession to thought. While we perceive one entity, others are perceived which begin or end. These successive perceptions leave in the spirit chronological information about events. This, however, presupposes *the duration* of perception. In fact, we could not conceive any *succession* of events unless there were some duration between one and the other. But duration supposes that which endures, for example, the perception itself. Duration is proper to that which exists. Nothing can exist in an instant which has no duration; an instant is only the principle and term of duration. The succession of events, that is, of their beginning and end, presupposes the duration of an ens. This duration is like a thermometer marked with all the events that have begun or ended, or changed and succeeded in that duration. Time, therefore, can be defined in itself as 'the relationship between *duration* and *succession*'. The concepts of duration and succession are correlatives; one can neither be known nor exist without the other. Just as there is no succession between one event

---

[105] *Attention* is the activity of an intelligent subject. Without attention, the subject receives, but does nothing; it has not yet undertaken a second act. The primal intuition is a *receptive act*, it is not *an activated act*.

and another (which always means a beginning or an end) without some duration, so duration is not understood except through the *possibility* that there is a certain succession of events to which it may be referred.[106]

1153. We need, therefore, to consider the nature of *duration*. First, the duration of thought, then of intellective perception, then of feeling, and finally that of material ens. When our understanding has been satisfied as a result of our consideration, the nature of time will have been sufficiently explained for us.

The duration of thought consists in the identity of the object. We have seen that every object of intellective information is, as such, immutable. If thought turns to some other object, it is immediately another thought; it is not what it was. But because the object is unchangeable, thought remains unchangeable until the spirit turns to some other object. In fact, the object, which determines a given thought to be what it is, is never lacking because the object of any information is eternal and thought is possible whenever the object is present. It follows that the duration of thought is a participation in the eternity of its object. It is the *limitation* of the thinking subject which causes the thought to cease and finish while the ens which is its object remains. This cessation is precisely the instant which terminates the thought's duration.

1154. The information that one event has preceded another is received by the spirit through perception. But how do we explain the duration of perception? — Perception can only endure if the feeling to which it is referred endures.[107] Nor can the feeling last if

---

[106] The concept of *duration* arises, therefore, from the concept of *eternity*, considered in relationship to some possible succession. Consequently, when we say that God the Almighty endures, or that an idea endures, we are referring to a relationship of opposition between the being of God (or of the idea) and contingent things subject to succession. In himself God the Almighty does not *endure*, but is.

[107] Relative to the duration of perception, note that 1. some elements can endure in perception while others change. This is sufficient to bring about some duration to which the changes can be referred. For example, although the accidents of light are changed during perception of the sun, the perceived sun is always the same at every hour of the day, or is considered as such; 2. renewal of the perception takes the place of its continuation because the identity of the object is preserved. For example, we do not keep our eyes on the sun all day; sometimes they are even closed for a while. Nevertheless,

the sentient ens and the felt ens do not last. We must, therefore, explain the duration of the felt ens which is the object of perception. How can the duration of entia be explained?

1155. The subsistence of a contingent ens is simply the realisation of its idea. This realisation is brought about by creation, the first cause of things. But the supreme cause is necessary and eternal, and the *idea* is also necessary and eternal. The supreme cause creates or realises contingent entia by way of understanding; this is an act of God's practical reason, of his acting thought. God, the Almighty, makes things subsist with an act analogous to that with which human beings think of things as subsisting. We saw that human thought, from the point of view of the known (although contingent) object, that is, of the *information*, is immutable and eternal. It ceases, however, because of deficiency in the thinking subject. On the other hand, while the immediate object of God's thought is indeed eternal, the thinking subject, that is, God, is also eternal and never-failing. Hence, created things can last as long as God wills. This will does not in fact regret what it has done. Entia, therefore, once created, never cease because they are the work of God. Their actions and passions, on the contrary, do cease, because their subject and proximate cause are the contingent, deficient entia themselves. Actions and passions begin and terminate; they begin again and again with unceasing variety and succession.

We have to say, therefore, that *duration* is a participation in God's eternity, and that *succession* is the effect of the limitation and deficiency of creatures. Time, therefore, is precisely succession brought back to and gradually marked on duration.

1156. Thus, it is clear both how entia *last* and *succeed* one another and how their duration is measured by the number or series of their successive actions.[108]

every time we come back to perceive the sun we consider the perception as the same in so far as it has the same object and its information remains identical; 3. in every lasting perception it is always an *ens* which remains identical. The actions and passions of the ens change. It is these actions and passions which provide the *succession* which is referred to the *duration* given by the same ens.

[108] The *unity* of these actions must be found by making them all equal, that is, of the same extension, as I have shown at some length in *NE*, vol. 2, 764–799.

Article 2
Time is not found in material things

1157. Having expounded the nature of time, we can return to our question. We want to know if time is in material things, in feeling and finally if thought alone forms time.

It is clear from what has been said that time cannot be in material things; their unity, and hence their duration, is due to the sentient principle in which they exist. They have no unity or duration of their own. The relationship between succession and duration is not, therefore, something that can exist in any assignable part of matter, as matter, because no parts are posited without continuous extension. This, however, is not proper to matter as matter.

1158. Moreover, if we set aside the phenomenal changes which appear in matter as a result of its relationship with the sentient principle, and take matter in its own pure concept, we find it impossible to conceive any change in it except that of motion, which is a relationship with space. But space, the continuum, does not pertain to pure matter. It is impossible, therefore, to conceive in it, purely in it, any change or even succession.

1159. Again, matter has no multiplicity because each portion of it is one and remains one. Each portion finishes in itself without being able to form a single unit with any other portion, from which it has an entirely separate existence. These portions have no reality in common.

1160. It is true that if a sentient principle were present in a material ens, the ens could carry deep within itself a succession of events which would have a physical nexus with the immutable, lasting principle of the ens. In such a case, time would, as it were, be realised. If, however, we remove feeling from corporeal matter (feeling does not pertain to the concept of corporeal matter), simplicity and unity of every kind is no longer present in corporeal matter. Any *corporeal principle* we admit cannot be either body or matter, precisely because it is their principle. Even if we suppose that this corporeal principle had time in itself, the purely material ens would not have it.

Article 3
Time is found in simple entia which are subject to modifications. The sentient principle is such an ens

1161. We return, therefore, to the sensitive ens where we find a simple principle as the source of different sense-experiences and modifications, of activity and passivity. The concept of this sensitive ens contains *duration* pertaining to the principle, which itself remains identical; the concept also contains *succession* in its particular sense-experiences; finally, the concept contains a physical nexus between the duration of the principle and the succession of its passions and actions. These passions and actions are contained virtually in this principle; given certain conditions, they arise from this principle, and pertain to it as to a subject. These three elements, *duration, succession* and their *nexus*, complete the concept of time which exists in the nature of feeling. But when we begin to discuss this, our mind encounters points of great difficulty that will undoubtedly cause hesitation and unease.

1162. It will be useful if we discuss these difficulties. If we passed over them, our argument would not fully persuade us of the truth.

When transient and successive acts of a sentient principle cease, they either leave some trace in the principle or not. If they do not, there is no possibility of any succession of acts remaining contemporaneously in the principle. This, however, is necessary for the existence of time. As we have seen, time implies succession which is not present unless it can exist altogether and, therefore, contemporaneously. In other words, something is needed to unite the links of succession. But if successive acts do in passing leave traces of themselves in the sentient principle, these traces are not the acts themselves. The sentient principle does not, therefore, retain in itself any succession of acts, but the succession of their traces through which time would have to be created. Now, the succession of these traces is not their duration because there is no succession in simple duration. The succession of these traces is simply the way in which one begins before another or, if they finish, the way in which they finish. Our supposition, however, is that they remain permanently. The beginning of each trace, however passes in an instant, without leaving any trace; it is the trace which lasts, not the instant in which it begins. The 'before and after' of the beginning of the traces, which forms succession, is simply a series of instants, the first of which is no longer present when its successor arrives. We have to say, therefore, that succession does not endure; it is not obtained from some ens which holds it present to itself. The sentient principle does not retain the various beginnings of its traces. These beginnings pass because of their essentially instantaneous nature. Consequently, we have the same difficulty in understanding how the sentient principle can assemble in itself the entire succession of traces left by its acts as we have in understanding how it can assemble and retain in itself the succession of its passing acts. We must find another way to overcome this difficulty.

1163. We shall find the right path by considering the nature of *duration*.

The concept of duration that we have given is: 'A participation in eternity.' Ideal being, as we know, is totally immune from time. Its realisation shares in this immunity, although in a limited way because it is incapable of anything else. This participation is duration, which therefore supposes *identity*. The essence of an ens is identical in whatever instant it is considered. In the same way, a real, simple ens is equally identical in every instant in which it acts and suffers. Granted this, it follows that the identical sentient principle which carries out an act is also that which carries out all successive acts. Because of its identity, it is present to all the acts it does. It is, therefore, present to the whole of succession without itself being subject to succession, or being a link in succession. When we consider the sentient principle in this way, we easily understand how it assembles in itself both the entire succession of its acts and equally the succession of the traces which its acts leave in it, even though the terms of the succession of the acts and of their traces pass in such a way that one is not present to the other. Yet this is necessary if they are to form succession. We have to grant, therefore, that the principle, if it is to accept succession in itself and thus place time in existence, is outside time. I must insist that 'time cannot exist except in that which has no time as its term.' Here again, the entire difficulty consists in persuading ourselves that the sentient principle (like every other simple ens) is not subject to time. Properly speaking, it is in eternity, or as we normally say, it pertains to the metaphysical world.

1164. As far as I can see, this entire argument is inviolable unless we want to impugn the *duration* of the sentient principle, that is, its *identity* relative to all its successive acts.

Let us suppose, therefore, that this duration is under attack. We now have to sustain it. If I do so with invincible arguments, I shall have confirmed my conclusion. This is the essential point of my argument.

The first proof that I shall give of the identical duration of the sentient principle will be a general demonstration of the necessity of the duration of entia. Let us suppose that an ens had no duration. It is clear that it would no longer exist. Instantaneous existence is absurd. An instant is nothing other than the beginning or end of some duration. But if an ens endures, even though the duration may be very limited, it must be identical as long as it endures. Otherwise, there would be no duration in it but a succession of equal entia, each of which remained for an instant. This, I have to repeat, is obviously absurd. We could not even think that any of those entia would exist because in the same instant in which they were, they would cease, they would not be. But to be and not be is a contradiction. Moreover, these entia could not form any succession because there would be no duration between them. Duration, as we said, is impossible without the possibility at least of one enduring ens.

1165. A second, particular proof of the duration of the sentient principle is drawn from the following fact. Often the successive acts of an animal are carried out in order; this shows that there is some entity in animal instinct, some cause that produces them. If there were no single cause of all the successive acts, if each act had a different cause, a different sentient principle producing it, there would be no reason for their order, no explanation of the singleness of the aim to which they often tend so admirably. In this case, each principle would be able to produce only a single act without any connection with the other acts. We would either have to have recourse to some pre-established harmony or to the immediate action of God as an explanation of the actions and passions of the animal. This, however, cannot be granted because of the innumerable absurdities produced by such systems.

[1164–1165]

1166. The third proof. If the duration of identical entia had been removed, the existence of new actions of entia would be impossible. Action is a second act which presupposes the first act of existence. Consequently, it presupposes at least two instants with an interval of some duration; otherwise there would not be two instants.

1167. The fourth proof, and here we arrive at the human being, is found in consciousness of the identity of the sentient principle relative to its acts. Reflective thought does not in any way alter things in their being, as I showed; it simply makes them known as they are. Reflection is a faithful witness that the sentient principle endures numerically the same.

It is not absurd, therefore, for the sentient principle to possess some *duration*. This means that it remains identical relative to all its successive acts. Indeed, this cannot in any way be denied. But it is in the sentient principle that the relationship, later called *time*, is generated.

Article 4
The unity of succession is due to the sentient principle

1168. We conclude, therefore, that the unity of *succession* of acts, modifications, passions, beginnings and ends is due to a simple principle that possesses duration. In other words, this principle is identically present to all the terms of succession. Without this, there would be individual links, but never succession and hence never time. Nor could the links be explained as links.

Article 5
Time in the rational principle

1169. As a simple being, the rational principle carries out successive acts of which it is the cause and the identical, lasting subject. Consequently, in this principle also we find all the conditions required for the existence of time.

1170. We have to conclude:

1. Space and the extended element receive their unity from the *animal-sentient principle*; their succession, on the other hand, as well as time and temporality, receive their unity from a *sentient principle* of any kind, that is, either *animal* or *rational*.

2. Space is a concept consequent on the concept of *animal ens*. Time, however, is consequent on *real ens* as such, as soon as it becomes a subject of change. *Identity*, or *duration*, pertains to an ens as it undergoes change.

3. The concept of time is not found in the concept of pure space or of matter. Here we can think of duration, but not succession, and consequently cannot think of the relationship between duration and succession.

Article 6
Real time: real time as known: ideal time

1171. We have to distinguish, therefore,

1. *Real time*, that is, time in so far it really exists in the nexus between an identical principle and the succession of its modifications.

2. *Real time as known*, which is time present to the thought that apprehends it. And

3. *Ideal time*, which is the concept, or mere possibility, of a nexus between duration and succession.

CHAPTER 5

The essential relationship between feeling and idea

1172. We now have to demonstrate how the rational principle joins and unifies idea and feeling. Feeling is of three species: animal, intellective and rational. We shall have to show separately how each of them can be joined to the idea. Moreover, there are two elements in feeling, the sentient element and the felt element, each of which can be known in the idea.

We shall, therefore, divide our questions as follows:

1. How are the extended element and succession perceived

by the intellective principle which thus takes the name of rational principle?

2. How is the animal sentient principle perceived intellectively?

3. How is the intellectual principle, whose term is the idea itself, perceived, and how is the rational principle perceived?

4. How are the different affections of the rational principle perceived?

Article 1
How the felt extended element and the succession of events
are perceived by the intellective principle
which thus takes the name 'rational principle'

1173. We have already seen that the extended element and extension does not communicate with the sentient principle by way of extension that is, as something extended could be contained in some other extended entity. Indeed, if the extended element and extension possessed only this property of extension, it could have no nexus with a sentient principle, which is non-extended. But the extended element and extension is also sensible, and through the *relationship of sensility* is received and contained in the sentient principle. This relationship is, however, produced by the very nature and activity of the sentient principle whose nature is such that it joins with the things appropriate to it by way of feeling. Thus, it makes *felt* that which is *extended*.

1174. This *relationship of sensility* lies at a higher level than the *relationship of extension*. As a higher-level entity, possessing more degrees of being, it embraces the lesser-level entity which has fewer degrees of being. In doing this, it communicates its own nobility to the lower entity. Thus, the concept of the extended element is embraced by and contained in the concept of *felt* element, and not vice-versa. The extended element itself, by becoming felt, or considered as such, is raised to a higher level in the scale of being.

1175. *Being* itself, which is the object of the understanding, stands above every entity. Its concept, therefore, embraces all inferior entities, whatever degrees of being they enjoy.

[1173–1175]

Everything, therefore, is joined to the understanding through an *essential relationship of entity*.

1176. But because we perceive intellectually only that which falls within our feeling,[109] things cannot be perceived by the understanding unless they first possess the condition and relationship of felt element.[110]

The extended element, therefore, is in the felt element, and the felt element in the ens intuited by the understanding. We need to consider that ideal being comprehends *possible-reality*, that is, the essence of real things. Hence, when the principle which sees an ens is set in counter-position to an extended-felt element, it can only see this element in the ens as in that which shares in being. This explains the perception of the extended-felt element, as I explained more at length previously.

1177. When the principle that sees an ens sees in addition the entity shared by the felt element, that principle which was previously called 'intellective' only, now begins to be known as 'rational'. The *rational principle*, therefore, perceives the felt element in its quality of ens, that is, it joins in one what it sees in the idea (being) and what it feels. Thus, the felt element becomes an *ens* to the intelligence; it becomes an object to the intelligence.

1178. If no intelligence perceived the felt element, the latter would not have the concept of ens, but only of felt. It receives the concept of ens from its relationship with the essence of ens. This essence dwells in the supreme mind, and in all inferior minds to which the supreme mind communicates it and, in communicating it, creates those minds.

I call this relationship *essential* precisely because it forms part of the extended-felt element as ens, and provides it with a greater degree of entity. Indeed, it gives the extended-felt element that final act by which it is that which it is. The felt ens,

---

[109] *Teodicea*, n. 153.

[110] Knowledge of what is in our feeling and of what is acquired by way of intellective perception is called *positive knowledge*. Knowledge of entia which are not perceived, but argued to from perceived things, is called *negative knowledge*. Feeling enters both kinds of knowledge, either as *matter* or as *means* of knowledge, in so far as it serves as a point from which to launch reasoning.

exists, therefore, as an ens in the mind, although human beings, when they talk about it, rightly attribute the condition of ens to what is felt. Although we speak of things only as they are in our mind, what is in our minds is an ens, and an ens substantially different from the mind which, in positing it, perceives it.

1179. The same simplicity of idea and information, through which the mind is immune from space and time, explains how the mind can conceive successive events, past and future, as we saw.[111]

Article 2
How the animal-sentient principle is perceived intellectually

1180. It is necessary to indicate this heading here because my intention is to show how the rational principle is that which gives unity to all human operations. However, I have already resolved the question and will summarise the answer here. It is sufficient to say that *reflection* in turning back on a felt-ens, finds that a sentient principle must in-exist in it. As I said, the

---

[111] I would like to refer once more to D'Alambert's question which caused such confusion amongst the philosophers of the last century. He asked: 'What is the point of communication between the spirit and external bodies?' We have answered this question by showing its absurdity relative to the spirit as a sentient principle. I showed that the sentient principle communicates with an extended element through a simple relationship of *sensility*, not through a relationship of extension. Here, I have resolved the question in a similar way relative to the spirit as intelligent principle. I have shown that intelligence does not communicate with bodies through a relationship of extension, but through *a relationship of entity*, which is a simple relationship. Thus, the question is entirely resolved from both points of view. In fact, bodies are perceived in two ways, sensitively and intellectively, not in one alone. The proposed question was defective, therefore, in this way also: it supposed that 'the spirit communicates with bodies in one way only.' This defect arose from sensism, in which sense and intellect are confused in a single potency. Moreover, the question posed by our learned mathematician made no mention of time, although the same difficulty is present in explaining how the spirit perceives the extended element, as in explaining how the spirit perceives past and future. Anyone who understands clearly that idea and information are immune from space and time will also have understood how the mind can know what is extended and reach out to all time.

extended felt alone would not possess the unity it has if no sentient principle were present. And consciousness tells us that we are sentient principles.

Article 3
How we perceive intellectively 1. the intellectual principle whose term is the idea, and 2. the rational principle

1181. Consciousness tells us without any doubt of the existence in us of a sentient principle, an intellective principle, and a rational principle in which sentient and intellective principles are united. But consciousness itself is a *reflection* on our own feeling.

Our own feeling, however, is known directly through perception, without need for reflection (cf. 71–80).

This is true, but it is one thing to perceive our own feeling, and another to distinguish in our feeling — distinguish accurately I mean — *principle* from *term*. We perceive this principle within our feeling, but if we are to have a separate, distinct concept of it, we must turn to reflection.

Reflection finds the principle precisely by considering the nature of feeling. Everything, therefore, is reduced to explaining the nature of reflection, and the way in which it proceeds.

1182. Reflection is defined as 'the faculty of applying the idea of being to our cognitions and their objects.'[112] To explain this operation of the spirit, we have to consider carefully the nature of the idea of being, the means of both *perception* and *reflection*. The difficulty which presents itself is this:

'In perceiving an ens, I use the idea of being which I bind in with what is felt. How, after that, can I go on to apply the same idea of being to perception and its object, and draw further information from this new application (that is, from reflection)?'

We have to base our answer on accurate, factual observation. Close attention to facts shows that what we have described actually occurs. We have to conclude, therefore, without hesitation that what happens is possible. The idea of being can always

---

[112] *Sistema filosofico*, 69, 77, 82–87, 104.

be applied by the mind to the idea itself, or to any cognition whatsoever in which the idea is already contained. This admirable fact cannot be denied or impugned, but it can be analysed. We can draw from it useful consequences which enable us to know better the nature of the idea itself (cf. 570). Here are some of these consequences.

1. However we bind the idea of being in perception, we are still free to use it again, to apply it once more to the perception which contains it. We must say, therefore, that it is totally immune from all *passivity*; that our seeing something in it does not properly speaking bind or coerce it to what we see in such a way that the idea is no longer as readily available to our needs and uses as before.

1183. 2. We are always able to use the idea of being as if it were unattached, and as if we were using it for the first time. This fact shows that the idea of being, identically the same, is always present to all the acts of our spirit — acts of perception, of reflection, and so on. Its identical presence to many acts proves that it is *simple* and, as simple, stands over against the multiplicity which it accepts in itself. Its presence to many successive acts of the spirit shows that it is not subject to time but is, as we said, *eternal*. In fact, the property of what is eternal is 'to be present identically to many successive entities'. When I intuit being, it is present to my intuiting spirit; when I reflect on being, which I intuit, being itself is present to my act of reflection. Identical being, ever the same, is present, therefore, as object to both the first act of the spirit and the second, to intuition and to reflection; being is one, but related to two acts. In its relationship to the intuitive act, it reveals itself to the spirit indistinctly; in its relationship to the reflective act, it reveals itself to the spirit with those distinctions and conditions which analysis and synthesis (the two ways in which reflection operates) find in it. The fact that it reveals itself in the second way, does not prevent its being revealed in the first way. Hence, the *simplicity* and *eternity* of an ens explains reflection; without these two attributes reflection would be impossible.

1184. 3. What we know through *reflection* is different from what we know through *intuition or perception*. We know, that is, in a different way, and at different levels, etc. In reflection, an ens simply communicates greater information about itself to the spirit, that is, it communicates information of a different kind. The *information* that the spirit has must be distinguished, therefore, from the *idea of an ens* considered in itself which produces the information. Information is in some way limited and subjective; the idea is unlimited and totally objective, or better, object. This object is always present in all *information*, whether information comes through intuition, or perception, or reasoning, that is, through reflection. But the object is present in different ways in various kinds of information [*App.*, no. 6].

1185. 4. From the same fact we can deduce and confirm this truth: being is loaned, as it were, to finite things because of the necessity we are under of knowing them, and our impossibility of knowing them unless they have first become entia, that is, unless they have been joined by the mind to some ens. The essence of an ens is neither confused, therefore, nor made one with sensible realities; it is simply joined to them and thus renders them intelligible. This truth radically destroys pantheism. It shows that the essence seen in the idea always remains unconfoundable with reality, as long as we are dealing with finite things. This is a most important corollary.

1186. We should not be surprised therefore if, having perceived intellectively the animal-felt entity, we can apply the idea of being to it, and thus through reflection draw out of it the concept of sentient principle. We can carry out this operation as follows. The felt element is an extended-continuum. This entity, however, would be impossible without a simple principle in which it can exist. I show this truth by comparing the extended felt element with *being*, which I attribute to it. Knowing by nature what being is, I know that it can never be in contradiction with itself, that is, *being* cannot be *not being* (because of the *principle of cognition*). But the extended felt entity would not be extended and felt if it had no simple principle. Therefore, etc.

We should not be surprised either if, after intuiting the idea, we can in a similar way draw out the concept of an intuiting principle by applying being to intuition. We can say: the intuited idea has the entity of intuited idea; but it could not have this entity unless an intuiting principle were present; granted therefore that this entity cannot be and not be, I must admit the presence of an intuiting principle.

Finally, we should not be surprised if, reflecting on the extended felt element perceived intellectually, we discover the necessity of the existence of a rational principle. If, in fact, we do not admit this principle, it would not be true that we had perceived the extended felt element intellectively. But it cannot be true at one and the same time that we have perceived it and not perceived it through the nature of being (known by nature). Contradiction excludes this. Hence the rational principle exists.

It is also possible to arrive at an affirmation of the sentient principle, the intellectual principle and the rational principle through simple abstraction or analysis, as well. These operations are carried out, as I showed elsewhere, through a hidden, scarcely noticeable application of the idea of being.[113]

CHAPTER 6

The unity and hence the nature of the human being lies in the rational principle

1187. From what has been said, we can conclude:

1. The animal-sentient principle has reference only to the extended element.

2. The intellective principle has reference only to the idea.

3. The rational principle has reference equally to the felt-extended element through perception and reflection, to the idea and to the sentient and intellective principle, and finally to itself. It is, therefore, the rational principle which binds and embraces everything within the human being and extends to everything.

4. The unity of the human being is present, therefore, in the rational principle.

5. Finally, human beings are such only because they are single beings. They are human through the rational principle in which, therefore, as in its proper seat, humanity is completed and wholly ennatured.

[113] *NE*, vol. 3, 1454–1455.

[1187]

CHAPTER 7
Every human activity begins from the rational principle

1188. Having summarised the teaching on human nature, and seen how it is completed in the rational principle, the seat of unity in human beings, we now have to turn our attention to the activity which springs from this human principle. Our aim is to investigate this activity and consider its laws.

First, however, we must separate out those activities which are mixed with human activity, but are not human activity itself. Confusing these two kinds of activity would be a real obstacle to our discussion. Confusing concepts necessarily leads to error.

Article 1
Five activities can be seen in the human world.

1189. What we have said shows that five activities are seen in the human being. Only one of these is proper to the human being as such.

1. We recognised the existence of extension, the term of the animal-sentient principle, which although residing in this principle is not the principle. Such activity, although immanent, does not produce second acts. Consequently, it cannot be thought of as substance, but only as entity. We did not investigate the cause of this activity, but were content to note that it has an *essential relationship* with the sentient principle. It is, therefore, absurd to think of this activity outside the principle.

1190. 2. We recognised the existence of a corporeal activity which shows itself in extension, in which it becomes the term of the animal-sentient principle. As extended, this corporeal activity also has an *essential relationship* with the sentient principle. In other words, it must have its seat in this principle. It cannot be thought outside it. This activity, however, which is seen in extension, is not extension, just as it is not the sentient principle. Such corporeal activity has not only its first act of existence, but second acts also. It does not present itself to the sentient principle as an immobile and immutable term, but with movement and varied appearances. The proximate cause of this activity, which is foreign to the sentient principle, was named *corporeal principle*. When this principle makes its action felt in the soul, it is called *sensiferous power*. We did not investigate the nature of this principle but did ask ourselves what it might be or not be in itself. We considered the cause which prompts bodies to move according to the law of attraction and, as terms of our sentient principle, to change position and aspect. This cause was located, with highly probable arguments, in the animation of the elements. Hence, 1. sometimes the activity itself of the sentient principle changes and moves its term; 2. sometimes the corporeal term of a sentient principle is changed by a principle which the sentient principle does not perceive and is probably another sentient principle. We leave aside the cause of mechanical movement, which has its origin elsewhere.

1191. 3. We also recognised the activity of the animal-sentient principle. It is this activity which constitutes the animal. From what we have said, it is clear that this activity has the power of changing the extended-felt element. It is also clear that the rational principle perceives feeling as entity, and hence can act in it; this however does not destroy the activity of the sentient principle. Consequently, although the activity of the rational principle can act in feeling and change it according to certain laws, the activity of the sentient principle, which is an essential element of feeling, remains. We also saw that simple perception changes nothing in feeling; perception does not alter or counterfeit perceived objects. Nevertheless, the rational principle, although it perceives the felt element, cannot act on it directly because it perceives this element essentially in the sentient principle and, therefore, as constituted by this principle. The rational principle must change and move the sentient principle so that the latter in turn may change what it constitutes, that is, the extended-felt element. Two activities, therefore, are found to operate in the same felt element: one (the sentient principle) acts directly; the other (the rational principle) acts indirectly, that is, by moving the sentient principle. Sometimes, these two activities clash and give rise to the battle of concupiscence. Moreover, the activity of the sentient principle is limited, nor is it the only activity that forms and moves the felt, extended element. Other activities, such as the *sensiferous force*, and various sentient principles also play their part. In the same way, the sentient principle is sometimes in harmony with foreign activities which have the power of constituting or of changing bodies; sometimes it is out of harmony with these activities and either prevails, or is overcome. Everything depends on the degree of force exercised by the opposing principles, which gives rise to the battle called 'disease'. In the same way, the rational principle is sometimes out of harmony with all these activities. It could join forces with the struggling sentient principle, or even with the activity of the foreign principles when these bind and dispossess the sentient principle and thus prevent it from subjecting itself to the activity of the rational principle and serving it.

1192. The opposition to the rational principle may arise, however, from the sentient principle itself rather than from the foreign agent. In this case, the primal perception which serves as bond between the rational soul and animal body is defective. This explains why the rational principle is sometimes without its full, natural forces, and cannot ensure obedience from its inferior.[114]

1193. 4. We also recognised intellective activity, which consists in the intuition of being. This intuition has not and cannot have any reaction to being.

5. Finally, we recognised and described at length the activity of the rational principle.

Article 2
The first three activities are not, properly speaking, human activities, but conditions or instruments of human activity

1194. We proved that the first three activities are not properly speaking human activities by noting that sometimes they are in

---

[114] This explains the mysterious nature of the defect which theology calls *original sin*. I have already written about this in an appropriate work.

opposition to the human being. If they were human activities, they could never oppose rational activity, which is human.

Nevertheless, they are of assistance to the constitution of the human being. The first activity, extension, serves as the *condition* by which man can perceive bodies; the second and third activities, that is, the sensiferous power and the sentient principle, help as *instruments* of the rational principle. The sensiferous power acts as direct and the sentient principle as indirect instrument.[115]

1195. We also saw why the rational principle is not always able to make use of its instruments by controlling and dominating their power. What we said can be reduced to the following two reasons.

1. The weakness and imperfection of the rational principle which cannot rule the force of the animal-sentient principle, granted the imperfection of the fundamental perception.

2. The weakness of the sentient principle which is not sufficiently well connected to and harmonised with the sensiferous principle, on which it depends.

Article 3
The other two activities, that of the intellective principle and the rational principle, form a single activity in human beings

1196. The first three activities, therefore, are not proper to human beings. The same cannot be said of the other two if we consider them in their nexus, through which they form a single activity, that is, the rational activity.

In fact, intellective activity, the simple intuition of being, although the first act constituting an intellective principle, is not yet the complete principle of the *second acts* in which the activity of the soul is manifested. We are speaking, however, of the activities of the soul in order to explain the laws governing their operation; in other words, we are searching for the cause of

---

[115] Aristotle makes a similar distinction. He speaks of *two classes* of 'things which occur relative to the soul'. Some seem to be passions proper to the soul, others seem to in-exist in animals for the SAKE OF THE SOUL. *De An.*, 1: 1.

second acts without confining ourselves to the first act which finishes totally in itself.

Considering the rational principle, we see that it always contains the act proper to the intellective principle. The rational principle could not perceive any real ens without first intuiting ideal being. The subject, therefore, which intuits ideal being (and to this extent is called intellective principle), is the same as that which perceives real ens, and to this extent is called rational principle. The intuition of ideal being does not exhaust the activity of the subject. Consequently, the intuition of ideal being is an act of the subject, but not of the whole subject, not of the whole man. A subject, as we know, is posited by that first act which potentially embraces in itself all second acts.

The intuition of ideal being can also be considered as a necessary *condition* for acts of the rational principle. Here, we notice an admirable analogy between the animal and intellectual orders. In the former, the apprehension of space is present as a condition for the apprehension of body. In the latter, the intuition of ideal being is present as the preliminary condition for the perception of real being. Pure space, therefore, is a highly satisfactory symbol of indeterminate, ideal being. In space, bodies are perceived sensitively; in being, real entia are perceived intellectively. Ontology asks the following question: 'Are the symbols, scattered in sensible nature, of what happens in intelligent nature the necessary consequences of the intrinsic order of being, or an effect of the supremely wise will of the Creator?' But we must return to our own question.

1197. How must we define the rational principle in order to include fully in its definition the first act of the human subject with its different forms? — We define it as follows: 'The rational principle is the power by which we apprehend being as being, under its three forms. This power is wholly in act relative to the ideal form, partly in act and partly in potency relative to the real form (it is in act relative to fundamental animal-feeling which it perceives, and in potency relative to different terms of this feeling which successively change the feeling) and in potency relative to moral being.

1198. Hence, in the *rational principle* which is rendered one by the unity of being, there is first the intellective principle as the first form of its act. Also present radically are the three supreme orders of the human potencies and faculties, that is, the orders of potencies and faculties which are referred to the idea, to things (real), and to eudaimonological-moral good.

1199. The rational principle, therefore, has one, single object, *being*. But as being is in three forms, so too the *first act* of the rational principle is also in three forms respectively. The third form, however, is initially in potency, not in act. This can be conceived because the presence of the act of the first two forms necessarily gives rise to the relationship between them, that is, to the third form.[116]

CHAPTER 8

We have to find the explanation of the laws of human activity in the rational principle and its relationship with lesser agents

1200. From all that has been said, we can conclude that the *potencies* of the spirit are diversified according to the relationships that the rational principle has with other activities and lesser entities. In the same way, we have to find in the nature of such relationships the laws which the various potencies observe in their activity.

What we call *law of nature* is the constant mode shown by entia in their operations. If, therefore, we are to prepare the way for an explanation of these laws, it is not sufficient to have found the font of all human operations and all laws in the rational principle. We also need to have dealt previously with the theory of operations of entia in general. In other words, we have to present an accurate concept of *operation*. The mind, when furnished with such an accurate, well-analysed concept, will be able to understand the necessity of those constant modes which are noticed in the operations or modes to which the name of laws is given. This argument pertains in fact to *ontology* and *cosmology*, but so far insufficient work has been done on them

---

[116] There would be no potency without a first act. This is clear from what we said about the concept of potency in *NE*, vol. 2, 1005–1019.

for our purposes. We have to deal with them, as we have done on other occasions, by taking from them the teaching we need. We begin, therefore, by explaining the concept of operation, and demonstrating its possibility, which common sense admits without any difficulty or wonder, although the concept has proved such a great obstacle to philosophy.

CHAPTER 9
The concept and possibility of operation

Article 1
Immanent acts and transient acts

1201. When we conceive a determined *ens*, we simultaneously conceive an *act*, that is, the act of its existence. This act is simple and lasts as long as the ens. It is, therefore, one of the acts we call 'immanent'.

1202. But is conceiving an ens and conceiving the act of its existence one and the same?

The act of the existence of an ens does not differ from the ens itself except through certain relationships which our mind adds to it.

1. When we say *act*, we add to it a relationship with potency, to which the concept of act is correlative through opposition.

2. When we say *ens*, we conceive a completed, finalised act. When, however, we say *act of being*, we conceive mentally or imagine we conceive the entire *path* by which an ens has been unnatured. In the act itself, we distinguish a certain kind of principle (the initial act), a means, and an end in which the being rests as complete and absolute. This explains certain sayings of philosophers, such as 'in an act, there is not yet act', and so on.

3. Moreover, the act itself of being is conceived by us as preceded or followed necessarily by certain other immanent acts, as we shall explain soon.

1203. When an *ens* is constituted with all its necessary, immanent acts, we then think, as a result of our experience, that the ens now has its complete act of existence and that it moves towards other acts which are also called its actions and operations. The act of existence and even the immanent acts which normally accompany it are usually called *first acts*; subsequent acts are usually called *transient, second acts*.

1204. The nature of the *transient act* consists in the passage made by an ens from one state to another. This may happen in an instant, or last for a while in some continuous motion. The characteristic of the transient act, therefore, is *passage*; it is unceasing motion.

Article 2
Different kinds of immanent acts

1205. An immanent act is one that endures along with an ens until there is some kind of substantial change. Amongst immanent acts, the act of existence is certainly the first, as we said.

Nevertheless, we do find, other than the act through which a given being exists, other immanent acts which can be divided into two classes.

1. Immanent acts which *precede* (not in chronological order, but in the intrinsic order of ennaturation) the act of being. For example, we saw that the act of being proper to human nature, that is, the act of the rational principle, results from two preceding acts (as it were, from its form and its matter). One of these acts is the intellective act, the other the act of the fundamental animal-feeling. These acts also are immanent.

2. Immanent acts which *follow* the act of being, but which are indivisibly joined with it. For example, the stable accidents of a substance, such as, habits.

1206. There are, therefore, three classes of immanent acts: 1. those which precede the act of being in an ens; 2. the act of being; and 3. those which are subsequent to the act of being and remain stable.

1207. Moreover, analysis and abstraction often split up an act further as a result of the different relationships under which they consider it. Consequently, immanent acts are multiplied in language and in human conception.

Article 3
Difficulties in explaining transient acts

1208. Great minds first began to raise highly difficult questions in Italy, the homeland of dialectic. Here, it was first understood that it was not as easy to explain as to accept what the whole world admitted, that is, operations of entia as transient acts. It was not easy to reconcile these acts with other truths administered by human thought. But truth, as we know, cannot be split in two or contradict itself.

1209. The difficulty, clearly perceived by the ancient Italian philosophers, was relative to the popular concept of transient acts, according to which 'the transient act, continually changing, endures for some time.' This concept of continual change involved insuperable difficulties which, when subjected to extremely subtle dialectic by the illustrious school of Elea, disturbed the whole field of philosophy. The battle, which flared up on several occasions, always ended through exhaustion on the part of the adversaries, never as a result of some decisive victory. It seems to me that these arguments contain something solid. Five of them can profitably be used against the continuity of an act.

Arguments against continual change presupposed in the transient act

1210. I. *Argument.* — If, during its transient act, an ens changes continually, none of the states which it undergoes successively during these changes has *duration* of any kind whatsoever. But that which does not endure, is not. Consequently, none of its successive states is. Hence, the concept of continual change is absurd.

1211. II. *Argument.* — If the transient act, taken as a whole, has some duration, during which an ens changes its state continually, the number of the successive states it takes does not exist, because a number of instances does not exist. For example, take any number of instances you wish that, put together, may form some duration.[117] If there is no number of states for the ens to pass through, it is absurd to think that it can pass through them. To pass through different states, there must be a determined number of states because there is nothing given in nature which is not determined. Hence, continual change involves absurdity. It is, therefore, impossible.

1212. III. *Argument*. — But perhaps a given duration is actually divisible *ad infinitum*. If this were so, it would be possible to have an infinite number (this is certainly absurd despite its being affirmed by great men such as Leibniz!). In this case, I would have to ask if each of this infinite number of parts (into which, it is claimed, duration can be divided) endures a short time or no time at all. It must be one or the other. If each part endures, we would need an infinite time to move through an infinite number of durations, no matter how small they may be. In this case, the transient act would never be completed. This is one of Zeno's arguments against continuous motion [*App.*, no. 7]. If, however, each part of the duration does not in any way endure but is an instant, the transient act would have no duration, which is against the hypothesis. Infinite instants, each of which has a duration equal to zero, give only a duration equal to zero when added together.

1213. IV. *Argument* — Bodies which move with continuous motion can never move with different speeds. If we suppose that a body is not stationary anywhere, it must pass from one place to another at the greatest speed; we cannot conceive any speed greater than that which passes without cessation from one place to another because it does not lose even the slightest time in passing.

1214. V. *Argument* — I take this argument from the time which motion requires to communicate itself to all parts of a body. Almost all physicists hold as indubitable that this communication requires time; it is not done in an instant. This, for example, is the reason why a bullet fired from a gun makes a

---

[117] Aristotle knew that the continuum in space, in time, and in motion cannot result from an aggregate of indivisible things. The great philosopher's argument for this can be found in the sixth book of *Physics*, and is worth reading.

hole in a plank. The extreme velocity of the bullet breaks the cohesion of the parts of the wood which it strikes. The time the bullet takes to do this is less than the time required for the motion to be communicated to the whole plank which, therefore, remains stationary. This indubitable fact provides two arguments which prove equally that motion is not continuous.

The first of these arguments affirms that if motion were communicated without pause to the places through which it passes, the total time employed would have to be nothing because the sum of so many zeros equals zero. In fact, an instant does not endure; it has zero duration only. But because this argument is similar to the preceding, I consider it simply as confirmation of what has gone before.

The second argument, however, is new and runs as follows. My supposition is that we have a perfectly hard body which receives an impetus to motion from another perfectly hard, moving body. The first body does not move until the impetus has been communicated successively to all its parts. For this communication to take place, some time is required, as we have seen. The length of time depends on the size of the two bodies and the speed of the body which imparts the impetus. During this time, the hard body receiving the impetus resists the moving body which provides the impetus. For a brief moment, the moving body is halted; then, both bodies, the one which strikes and the one which is struck, continue to move according to the laws of motion. Here we have an undoubted case of rest during the seemingly continuous movement of the first body. We have, therefore, motion, then rest for a moment, then motion again. But according to the law of inertia a body when at rest remains at rest unless there is a new cause of motion. The fact that we have indicated is opposed to this law. We have to say, therefore, that there is some kind of pause and rest which harmonises very well with the motion we think continuous, and to which we apply the law of inertia.[118] Moreover, if the body which is struck is unable to move until the impetus has been propagated to all

---

[118] If we suppose the body which is struck to be of immense size, the two bodies will be halted for a noticeable period. Indeed, this respite can last as long as we wish because we can imagine the body which is struck to be as big as we like.

its parts, and if the propagation of the impetus is not halted at any point (as supposed by those who believe motion to be continuous), motion would be impossible. If communicated to a point in an instant, it would either produce movement immediately or, if there were some obstacle to motion, it would be smothered and wiped out. In fact, it is necessary for the impetus to be retained in the individual parts and points of the body for the whole time needed for all the parts to acquire the same impetus, and thus be moved together. Each part of the body, therefore, which receives the impetus waits for some time before beginning its effective motion. After this time, motion begins. Consequently, the communication of motion itself, but not of the impetus [*App.*, no. 8], is made to each part of the struck body in a given time, not in an instant. But all bodies, however small, have some continuous extended element. The same thing must happen in all of them, therefore. Motion is not communicated to any body in an instant, but with some interval of rest.

What can we say about these arguments? — As far as I can see, they are insoluble. Each contains a demonstration that the transient act is not carried out by means of continual change, but in instants between each of which there is some duration. I have already demonstrated this when I denied the continuity of real movement,[119] despite its phenomenal continuity.

1215. Minds unaccustomed to philosophical speculation have immense difficulty in conceiving how the movement of some real being, that is, change in the transient act, is not continual. People tend to believe in the phenomena of their senses to such an extent that they cannot think anything as possible which does not appear to their senses. It is not to be wondered, therefore, that we hear so often: 'Observation shows us that movement is continuous and, as you yourself constantly say, we cannot go against facts which we observe.' It is very difficult to convince people that observation cannot decide the question under discussion. We are dealing with something beyond all sensible observation — something which cannot be proved by observation. As we know, every size smaller than a given measure escapes our sense.

[119] *NE*, vol. 2, 813–819.

1216. Let us imagine that I succeed in persuading these people that observation can tell us nothing about those measurements of space, of time, and of motion which are so small, as they must be in our case, that human sensitivity is unable to perceive them,[120] or at least that no mental advertence is capable of considering them in feeling, even if feeling provided them. People would then ask: 'How therefore is it possible to conceive a transient act or some real movement done at intervals?' This question, however, is not drawn from observation, but from reasoning which considers the possibility of non-sensible things. It would be sufficient to reply that there is nothing to demonstrate the impossibility of what we have suggested, even if we do not know how to explain the way it occurs. Moreover, if there are two opposite opinions and we have shown the absurdity of one, but not of the other, we have to hold the second and reject the first. It would be sufficient, I say. Nevertheless, it would not persuade the majority who have little faith in what reason demonstrates. To assist such weakness of spirit, which withholds simple, firm assent to speculative proofs contrasting with sensible appearances, I shall first show that sight, to which we normally give credence when it gives or seems to give witness to the continuity of the motion of a body (the same reasoning can then be applied to the other senses) does not and cannot properly speaking witness to the *continuity* of motion.

1217. It is indeed a fact acknowledged by all physicists and provided by experience that sight sensations have some duration in the optic sensory. They do not pass in an instant. If this were not a truth of indubitable experience, the necessity of duration could be demonstrated by considering that sensations which had no duration could not exist. But we do not need such a proof from reason.

However, although all optic sensations last some time, people normally think them instantaneous because their duration is very limited. But, granted the truth that every optic sensation has some tiny duration, it follows inevitably that the eye cannot

---

[120] Sense, in perceiving the continuum in space (where it is certainly found) also perceives as a result every small space assignable in a space of significant dimension. This, however, does not mean that it perceives every minimum space separated and isolated from a greater space.

witness in any way to continuous movement because it cannot testify to what it does not see. Continuous movement is in fact a continual change of place in such a way that a body never comes to halt in any place. If continuous movement were to be seen, the eye would have to have a succession of different sensations, each of which possesses no duration at all. But this is not what happens. When a person thinks he sees a body in continuous movement, the eye experiences only a series of sensations. Each of these sensations follows on from another (or with an insensible interval); each of them lasts a small time. Hence even phenomenal motion, which is sensible to the eye, is reduced to a series of states of what is movable. Each of these states lasts a little time. The mistake is in our mental advertence when, by neglecting to observe those minute durations, we suppose that one follows another without any interruption [*App.*, no. 9].

Starting from these principles, natural scientists eventually invented some ingenious gadgets with which they made it seem to the eye that a body was moving. They did this simply by successively placing before sight a certain number of bodies, each of which appeared with the same form in places very near each other. The body which appeared first seemed no distance at all from the succeeding body. But all these equal bodies presented successively to sight in extreme proximity are taken for a single body moving with continuous motion. This device enables us to compose any apparent motion whatsoever, linear or circular, etc., although the body which apparently moves is not in fact identical, but a complex of several equal bodies seen in different places and representing the motion that we take for continuous.

1218. This experiment alone is a sufficient reply to the somewhat indiscreet question: 'How is it possible for a body to pass from one place to another without moving continuously through all the intermediate spaces?' The question is sufficiently answered when we demonstrate the possibility of motion's appearing continuous to sight without actually being such. This possibility has been demonstrated provided we have proved the fact in a single case.

Nevertheless, I want to offer another experiment, one amongst many provided by physics, principally astronomy.

When a person passes in front of a mirror, the movement of the image corresponds to the motion of the person. Both motions seem continuous. But how does the apparent motion of the image come about? It certainly does not pass from one place to another. This appearance is produced by means of continually new rays of light which depict ever-new images, that is, physically different images, on the mirror when previous images have vanished; nevertheless, the same image seems to walk and pass in front of the mirror. Hence, the phenomenon of the continuity of motion can be explained without any absolute necessity that all the points of a given, moving body should touch the intermediate points of the space through which the body passes, or seems to pass.

1219. A time will come perhaps when we will be able to appeal in favour of this teaching to intermittent light, suspected by some physicists although not fully demonstrated. For the moment, I want to offer a final objection.

1220. The examples I have used show clearly that the phenomenon of continuous motion can arise without any actual motion. This comes about as equal, multiple bodies are substituted successively for one another. This applies also to equal, multiple operations. Now, is it possible that moving bodies do not retain their identity, as Leibniz said? He supposed that the full and empty areas of space were made up of immovable matter, which constituted infinite space. This matter hardened itself, as it were, successively, and thus appeared as an identical, moving body.

This supposition, although extraordinary to normal thought which restricts itself to the phenomenon without investigating reasons and causes, has never been shown absurd, still less factually false. It is a metaphysical question which leaves physical things as they are, whatever solution is given. Consequently, it can scarcely be proved true or false with physical arguments.

1221. Leaving aside an examination of Leibniz's supposition, I want to ask if the elements making up the identity of a body have been clearly defined. This is a more difficult question than appears at first sight. I shall deal with it briefly here, but in a way sufficient for our purpose. Two things are distinguished in body: extension and force. When a body moves, it is certain that extension is changed; the body changes place, and one place, which is always outside another, is never identical with the other. This truth may not be understood if we are prejudiced by the thought that a body carries around its own extension, as though extension could be moved from one place to another, or as though the extension of a body and that of the place occupied by the body were two extensions rather than a single, extremely simple extension. It is the measure of quantity of extension, which is always preserved identical by a body, which leads our thought in this direction. Extension itself, however, changes. It constantly takes on another extension, although one of equal measure with that previously present. Because the different extensions in which the body successively expands are totally equal in size and uniform in quality, the illusion is easily aroused of some extension adhering to and carried around by the body.

1222. The identity of body, therefore, cannot consist in any element except bodily force. This, however, is only the term of an act of the hidden agent I have called *corporeal principle*, which can only be simple. But the identity of the term of an act consists in this: the term is equal in everything. We are looking for a specific identity in relationship with the act, because the term is constituted by this essential relationship. Thus, if I smell a rose one hundred times, these acts although numerically different have a specifically identical term. They always terminate in the same sensation of the scent of the rose, granted that this sensation is invariable. In all these acts, we have no other sensation than that of the scent of the rose. This scent is referred to multiple acts. Now, the corporeal principle is simple and as such can embrace the whole of space in a single moment (as we have seen in the case of the sentient principle). In our case, if the corporeal principle were to actuate a body intermittently, it could make the body appear successively in tightly packed places in such a way that these places appeared continuous and uninterrupted. Thus, the body would appear to move with continuous movement, although this would not in fact be the case. Nevertheless, it would be the same body because it is a totally equal term of the intermittent acts of the simple, corporeal principle. The individual diversity that the body could possess would be wholly indiscernible. If, however, we were dissatisfied with maintaining a specific identity for each body, and required numerical identity, there would be no difficulty.

The sensiferous force could be considered as an identical power of the corporeal principle, a power which operated intermittently and in a way unobservable by sense.

1223. My conclusion is that transient acts are formed in an instant, or are a complex of lesser acts formed in very close instants between which there is a tiny duration totally unobservable by human beings.

CHAPTER 10

The connection between transient and immanent acts

1224. There are many other difficulties which present themselves to the mind of the speculative thinker when he attempts to explain the concept of transient act, or even to form its concept accurately. We will encounter these difficulties later, however, and do our best to overcome them. Bringing them forward now, one by one, would retard our argument as it presses on to its goal.

Here we have to consider the connection between transient act, according to the concept we have recently outlined, and immanent act.

For me, this concept is found in *passage*, that is, in change made in an instant.

1225. Keeping this concept in mind together with the teaching on *instant* and *duration*, we have a definition of transient act which points clearly to its *essential relationship* with immanent act. Our definition of transient act is this: 'A transient act is always the beginning or end of an immanent act;' in other words, 'A transient act is simply the beginning or end of an enduring act.'

CHAPTER 11

'Corollary I' — Granted the existence of transient acts, we can demonstrate the existence of God

1226. An extremely important corollary can be drawn from the definition we have given. Here, I want to comment on this corollary which we shall need as we go on if we are to proceed with total clarity and distinction of thought.

This corollary concerns the existence of God, demonstrated only from the existence of transient acts. To my mind, the demonstration is utterly clear, and can be set out as follows.

If transient acts exist, immanent acts also exist; the former are only the beginning or termination of the latter. But no immanent act can be the cause of its own termination because no act can be the cause of its own non-act, that is, of its own cessation. Nor can the immanent act be the cause of its own beginning because no act can give itself existence. If it did, it would act before it was.

Now, the transient act also needs a cause because it is change, passage. It needs a cause according to the principle of cause.[121] Nor can this cause be the transient act itself. As I said, that which is not, cannot give itself existence.

But if the transient act is not caused by an immanent act whose beginning and end it is, there must be another immanent act which causes it.

This immanent act which causes the transient act will either itself begin, in which case it would be caused by a transient act, or it will have no beginning of any kind and hence no end.

If it is caused by a transient act, we shall have to go back to another immanent act. But to avoid seeking causes *ad infinitum* (in which case no act would be produced because an infinite time, which is never traversed, would be needed to produce it), we have to stop at an immanent act which has neither beginning nor end. If, then, this act is not caused by a transient act, we have again an immanent act without beginning and without end. An

[121] *NE*, vol. 2, 567.

immanent act exists, therefore, without beginning and without end; and this is God.

If, therefore, transient acts exist, Almighty God necessarily exists.[122]

1227. This demonstration of the existence of God has the advantage of leading directly to God as *immanent act*, and totally pure act.

CHAPTER 12

'Corollary II' — Demonstration of creation

1228. This truth is extraordinarily productive. It is the principle which gives rise to all teaching about the divine nature, as natural theology must show.

Amongst the other truths which it contains embryonically, is a direct, rigorous demonstration of the necessity of creation. As far as I know, this demonstration has not yet been noted. The following propositions provide briefly some notion of it.

All immanent acts which have a beginning and end are mingled and connected with transient acts which are precisely the beginning or end of immanent acts.

Such immanent acts, which begin from a transient act, cannot cause this transient act. The transient act, therefore, which provides a beginning for an immanent act, must be caused by an immanent act which has no beginning and no end, and is not mingled with any transient act.

This immanent act, as we saw, is called God who, in producing the transient act which gives rise to an immanent act, must operate in such a way that he produces the transient act outside himself. He must do this without any passage, any mutation or any transient act arising in himself.

This way of acting is called *creation*, relative to the transient act produced as the principle of the immanent act.

---

[122] The demonstration of the existence of God from motion, which St. Thomas took from Aristotle, *Physics*, 7 and 8, and is, he says, 'The first and most obvious way of demonstrating the divine existence' (*S.T.*, I, q. 2, art. 3), receives its force from the principles we have given about the nature of immanent and transient acts.

Creation, therefore, must be. In other words, creation is necessary to explain the existence of the world, which is a complex of immanent and transient acts bound together.

I have no doubt that the careful reader will understand that this proof is on a par with any of Euclid's proofs [*App.*, no. 10].

CHAPTER 13

No ens moves itself, that is, makes transient acts solely by itself; it needs the concourse of something different from itself.

1229. We move now to another difficulty presented by the concept of transient act.

Transient acts cannot be other than acts coming from immanent acts. That which is, is immanent. As we saw, an *ens* without duration is absurd. An instant is the limit of duration, and thus supposes duration; it does not stand by itself. It is like a mathematical point which is the limit of a line and does not stand on its own. Now, an immanent act which produces a transient act either produces it with an eternal act, which is also immanent, or produces a transient act of which it is the subject. In the first case, the immanent act is not the subject of the transient act which it produces. This, as we saw, happens only in creation. In the second case, the immanent act produces a transient act of which it is the subject. For example, the act with which the sentient principle acquires a new sensation, or the act with which the rational principle elicits some thought. These are transient acts whose subject is the sentient principle or the rational principle. These transient acts modify the subject which carries them out; they produce something new in the subject and, as we saw, their explanation presents difficulties, one of which can be expressed in the following way.

If an ens, an immanent act, becomes the subject of transient acts, that is, modifies itself, there has to be a sufficient reason, a cause of this modification, according to the principle of cause.

The ens, that is, the immanent act itself, does not contain this sufficient reason or full cause of the new happening. If it did, the act produced would be immanent, not transient; in other words, it would always have been in the immanent act. Granted the *full cause*, the effect exists. But the immanent act existed before the transient act appeared. The immanent act, therefore, is not the full cause of the transient acts which, as its accidents, are manifested in it. This is a new proof that the immanent act, as the subject of a transient act, cannot be the full cause of the transient act. This proof must be added to that which we have already given.

1230. Consequently, no ens is truly and rigorously *self-moving*. Some foreign agent must concur in its movement, that is, in its change.

1231. This consequence appeared to pose difficulties to many ancient philosophers who, to avoid it, posited the essence of the soul in movement [*App*., no. 11]. Movement, however, is not substance. It needs a substance as its subject, and it also needs a cause. Moreover, such movement would always have to be equal. If it varied, recourse would be necessary to the intervention of yet another cause to explain the variation. Aristotle concludes, therefore, that rest, rather than motion, is proper to the soul.[123]

1232. Aristotle observes that these philosophers came to their conclusion because of their inability to conceive how a mover can itself not be in motion.[124] He arrives at a contrary conclusion

---

[123]   The arguments used by Aristotle to show that the soul does not move of its nature are reduced more or less to the following:

1. If the soul moved of its nature, it would have to make use of some force, in other words, it would have to do violence to itself. The same would be true if it wished to pass from motion to rest. In the nature of the soul, however, we find spontaneous, not violent motion (bk. 1, *Sum*. III, c. 1). — This would be contrary to the well-being of the soul; the soul would be unhappy by nature because violence is contrary to happiness.

2. If the soul is in motion because the body moves, the motion of the soul ought to be like that of the body. It should be a kind of passage. In this case, the soul should be able to leave the body and then re-enter it.

3. If the soul moves itself, it is mover and moved at one and the same time. Now, if what is moved goes a certain distance, the soul in so far as it is moved could go some distance from itself, from its own substance, as mover.

4. If the essence of the soul consisted in motion, its rest could not be explained. Now, it is certain that the intellect, when it has intuited principles, comes to rest in them. When it has come to the conclusion of a syllogism, it rests there.

5. Finally, the nature of the intellect is unalterable and hence immobile. It does not suffer corruption when the body corrupts.

[124]   *De An*., bk. 1.

after proving that the soul does not move of itself:[125] *non necesse est id quod movet, ipsum quoque moveri.*[126]

This opinion raises many difficulties, however. Either the word 'movement' is understood in its proper sense of local movement of bodies, or in a wider meaning. In the former case, it is easy to prove that the soul, as simple and spiritual, is immune from movement; it can move bodies without moving itself. The soul is principle and bodies, where space, place and motion have their seat, are its term. In the second case, movement is a transient act of change, an act in which something new occurs. This is the meaning often given to movement by Aristotle. Unable to deny that the *potencies* of the soul break forth into transient acts, and noting that Democrites spoke of the soul as moving, he confuses the soul's potency, to which motion belongs, with the soul,[127] to which it does not belong.

If however potencies are only activities of the soul, residing in

---

[125] Nevertheless, he attributes movement to the soul *per accidens*, like people on board a ship who do not move of their own accord, but move because the boat moves. Thus the soul, although immovable in the body, moves when the body moves. This way of conceiving movement in the soul shows, however, that even Aristotle did not attain a pure, distinct concept of spirit. His defect lay in not distinguishing with sufficient care and constancy the *principle* from the *term* of the human individual. If he had seen or sensed the supreme importance of this distinction, he would have realised two things: 1. the soul is *principle* and, although essentially connected with its term, is not its term, but something distinct from and even opposite to the term according to substance; 2. every movement arises in the *term*, not in the principle. Consequently, the soul is immune from all local movement both *per se* and *per accidens.* If it were to move like the voyager in the boat, it would have local movement, and there would be no contradiction in the possibility of self-movement.

[126] *Ibid.* — Aristotle said that the soul moves without being itself in motion. Aureolus and others then commented that the argument about the existence of God, which proves the necessity of something immovable to move what is movable, does not strictly lead to God, but only to a world-soul. But, as Cardinal Gerdil says: 'The first ways (of proving the existence of God) from motion are sufficient for their purpose. Their conclusion, 'Therefore a first unmovable mover exists', does not ask whether this is the soul of the heavens or of the earth. We have to go to the following question for that.' This is what St. Thomas intended when he explained the demonstration of the existence of God from motion (*In S.T.*, I, q. 2, art. 3).

[127] *De An.*, 1.

its essence, we have to say that the soul itself is modified by the acts of its potencies not only when they are in act, but afterwards. Habit remains in the soul as a kind of residue of the act. Although the soul possesses the nature of *principle*, this principle receives or loses some of its activity. Consequently, change arises in it. Some motion is present metaphorically in it, therefore, in the sense that the soul is the subject of all the acts of the potencies, and the subject is modified through its transient acts.

Aristotle does indeed say that the soul is act (the act of the living body), but he cannot deny that this first act is in potency to other transient acts. As such, the soul is not pure, immutable act, but passes from potency to act.[128]

1233. If, therefore, the word 'movement' is taken for every passage from potency to act (the nature of the transient act lies precisely here), we have to say that the true opinion lies between that of those philosophers who posited the essence of the soul in motion, and the opinion of Aristotle, who denied all motion to the soul. In other words, 'the soul, like every ens other than the first, is an immanent act and the subject of transient acts, but not their complete cause.'[129] If it were the full cause, the acts, which could never cease as long as the cause endures, would be immanent. This is the case with God's creative act which, as eternal, neither has nor posits in God change or passage of any sort. Otherwise, the soul would be a *self-mover* — a contradictory concept, as we have seen.

1234. If it is impossible for any ens to be a true self-mover,

---

[128] St. Thomas agrees that true self-movers are impossible. His principle is: 'All that moves is moved by something ELSE' (*S. T.*, I, q. 2, art. 3). But the soul is *moved*, that is, it passes to *transient acts*. Hence the demonstration of the existence of God from motion does not conclude only in demonstrating *the soul of the world*, as Cajetan grants to Averroes and Aureolus when he takes as true Aristotle's opinion that the soul does not move or suffer change from transient acts. The soul does not in fact move itself locally, but from potency to act, which is sufficient for us to appeal to some mover without transient acts, some mover who does not move from potency to act.

[129] Cajetan writes very subtly: 'Efficacy belongs to the explanation of cause. Unless cause brings something about, it cannot be called cause in act. The explanation of cause has to be preserved if its causality is to be complete' (*In S. T.*, I, q. 2, art. 3).

that is, a full cause of its own transient acts, we have to investigate how these acts rise. In other words, what is their complete cause?

To do this, we have to recall what has already been said. The soul is by nature a principle, and the concept of principle involves that of act. But no principle exists without its term, from which it receives its actuality and activity.

The sensitive soul has space and body as its term.

The rational soul has an ens as its term.

Now, if the term is changed, the actuality and activity of the principle is also changed. Our investigation, therefore, concerns the cause of transient acts which take place in the soul as its terms change, as we said. Thus our principle is essentially act and indifferent to its terms, nor does its activity cease, whatever term it is given. Rather, it is activated in various degrees according to the term.

1235. This teaching, which is provided by internal observation, explains the apparent contradiction of the presence in the soul of some possible potency, although the soul as principle is essentially act. Granted that this act receives varying degrees of entity according to the nature of the terms which are given it, we realise on the one hand that it always remains pure act, although in varying degree, nor properly speaking does it ever have united to itself any potency as part of its essence. On the other hand, because it is capable of increase and decrease, we say that it is in potency to this increase or decrease.

1236. Thus we have explained the true *concept of potency* as a *negation of act*, not as something positive constituting a substantial part of the principle-ens.

1237. It is true that there is a middle state between giving and totally denying a term to a principle. This state consists in the term's being given imperfectly so that the principle cannot be fully actuated. In such a case, the *deficient state* of the principle itself is revealed as well as the *struggle* between it and its term. I shall speak of this elsewhere.

1238. We can now conclude that the explanation of transient acts must never be sought in principle-entia but in term-entia. We have to examine carefully the forces or powers or causes that change the term-entia to see how such forces operate. Only then shall we have explained the possibility of transient acts because we shall have shown how they are formed. However, because their formation is different in different entia, we must consider the individual kinds of entia and their transient acts. We shall do this in the following chapter.

CHAPTER 14

Different natural agents, and their different way of operating. First, the action attributed to bodies

1239. All that has been said was, I believe, necessary as a preface to the explanation of movement in the rational principle. The condition proper to this movement is not clear conceptually unless 1. we understand the nature of movement in general of all entia, especially of entia which are subjects of transient acts; and 2. we compare the movement of the rational principle with that according to which other agents in nature move. We have already dealt with the first point in the preceding chapter; we shall now deal with the second.

1240. The only full space (that is, a distinct space given by means of the body which expands in it) presented to human beings through nature, is that of the fundamental feeling.

The limits of this space, which are not felt initially, are found by means of surface sensations.

These limits could not be perceived unless we felt some space beyond them.[130]

Here we must pause for a moment. What has been said already needs some explanation if we are to make headway. — How can we feel something beyond our body?

1241. Although we truly perceive unlimited space, this space is indistinct. In other words, it has no relationship for the moment with the bodies which either fill it or can fill it. This space is not sufficient, therefore, to explain how we acquire knowledge of distinct space which exceeds the limits of our body, that is, of the relationship between our body and immense space.

[130] *AMS*, 154–155.

The solution to this difficulty must be found in the distinction between the two ways of feeling, *subjective* and *extrasubjective*.

The subject spreads itself as proprietor in the corporeal fundamental feeling where it is at home as though it were a part of itself, a continuation of itself. The subject acts in it and needs it as an essential condition of itself. No linear or surface limits are manifest here. We are dealing with a solid feeling, outside of which nothing corporeal is felt, nothing can be felt; there are no sensible relationships with any foreign body.

Extrasubjective sensation, however, is of a totally different nature. It betrays the presence of a force foreign to that of the felt element. This force acts energetically (although sometimes pleasantly) on the fundamental feeling. The foreign force acts in the extension itself of feeling, in the fundamental felt element, which is then outlined and shaped. It is necessary to understand carefully the nature of these surface limits which our fundamental felt element thus acquires.

First, when our touch is affected by a foreign body, we realise that this body *is* foreign because we feel its action is not that of the sentient principle. Rather, the foreign body is in the action of the sentient principle in the sense that we feel not the foreign agent in itself, but only the effect and term of its action, because we feel a surface, not a solid. We feel the term of the action, therefore, but not the foreign body. This is quite different from what occurs in the fundamental felt element, which is not felt as a surface term of action but is the agent in the whole of the solid space in which it expands as agent. The term of the foreign action is, therefore, in our fundamental felt element which receives this action. Consequently, the sensible surface which is the term of the foreign action is perceived as limit to the fundamental feeling. This surface is thus distinguished from the remaining part of the fundamental feeling, and becomes the term of two agents, the foreign agent and its own agent which is the fundamental felt element (in so far as it is sensiferous). This all happens through touch which is the proper measure of bodies (we prescind for the moment from sight and the other senses).[131] Consequently, if our body were immobile we would be unable to know simultaneously with our touch the surface of

[131] *NE*, vol. 2, 922–924.

a foreign body larger than the surface of our own body, which serves to measure the surface of the foreign body.

If therefore we want to explain how we can perceive a body larger than our own we have to take cognisance of the movement of exterior bodies and our own body. Let us take the movement of exterior bodies first. If different bodies act successively on the same part of our body, these bodies are either perfectly equal in extension, form, etc., or are different. If they are perfectly equal and applied successively to the same part of our body, we will be unable to distinguish whether the agent is one and the same body, the same power operating with repeated acts, or several bodies (if we rely on touch only without the help of other senses). But if the bodies vary in extension and shape we will take them for different bodies. This happens not in virtue of the sentient principle alone and of the retentive faculty proper to it (I prescind from this for the moment because there is no need to consider such a subtle question), but through our rational retentive faculty. By comparing one sensible, sensiferous surface with another, we find that they differ. Thus we have in our spirit information about several surfaces. For example, we may have ten surfaces each of six square centimetres, but varying in shape. This alone is sufficient for us to begin to conceive an extension greater than the corresponding extension in our body. In fact, the surface, in so far as it pertains to our fundamental feeling, cannot ever be multiplied. We always feel it as the same. A single surface of six square centimetres of our body is the field, as it were, where we can feel six square centimetres of extension in the exterior force. This measurement can be multiplied as often as we wish, according to the number of sensations of different shape which are repeated and multiplied successively.

1242. We come now to the movement of our body. It is certain that by moving our body and constantly receiving new and different sensations from bodies around us which differ in figure and activity, we can by means of our rational retentive faculty acquire information of indefinitely extended space. This space has no assignable limit. But the difficulty lies in explaining the movement of our body. We said that the feeling and rational principles are immovable relative to local motion. How, then, can we move our subjective body? What is this movement?

We need to consider that we perceive our body in two ways, *extrasubjectively* and *subjectively*. We feel our body extrasubjectively as we feel every other body, that is, in so far as it too has sensiferous power which makes it visible, touchable, etc. Subjectively, our body is the *felt element* of the fundamental feeling. But our extrasubjective body does not form part of the fundamental feeling. Indeed, its sensiferous power is foreign to and in opposition to the fundamental feeling. Let us imagine, therefore, that we have perceived our body only subjectively, not extrasubjectively. In this case, our body no longer has motion. In fact, I have already shown in my treatise on ideas that our motion is not sensible.[132] But if our fundamental feeling feels no motion, motion does not enter it. Our fundamental feeling is essentially feeling, and only what is sensible enters feeling.

It may be objected that when we ourselves move our body, for example, by walking or jumping, we feel the effort that we make in moving. This is true, but the effort that we make to move is not motion, but its cause. Motion, by which we pass from place to place, does not therefore enter the fundamental feeling, although the force and cause of motion are found there.

The motion of passage is only a change made outside the subject, a change in our extrasubjective body, a mutation in the sensiferous force. But it is not present in any way in the fundamental feeling, which remains immobile.

1243. Nevertheless, the extrasubjective body moves in such a way that we notice, through extrasubjective experience, that it has changed place. We realise this by means of its different relationship with surrounding bodies. At these moments, our fundamental feeling, and hence our subjective body, is still present to the extrasubjective phenomena given by our moved body. Our subjective body has not changed its relationship with our extrasubjective body. If our extrasubjective body now occupies a different space, we normally say that our subjective body also occupies this other space. The subjective body, it would seem, has been transported, has been moved.

Aristotle was led by this observation to posit in the soul the kind of movement which he describes as *per accidens*. He likens

[132] *NE*, vol. 2, 806.

it to the motion of colour which moves not as colour, but as adhering to a body which moves. But this, as we said, is an error. Going back to the fundamental felt element, we see clearly that motion must either be felt and thus enter into feeling itself, or not be motion proper to feeling, which is closed in itself by its very essence so that change of things outside it is not movement springing from itself. We have to say, therefore, that local movement is an entirely extrasubjective phenomenon, that is, a phenomenon revealed only through extrasubjective experience. It is not some subjective phenomenon experienced either as an accident of the subject itself or of its fundamental felt element. Now, extrasubjective phenomena are produced by the *sensiferous force*. We can say, therefore, that the relationship between our fundamental feeling and the sensiferous force scattered throughout nature — for example, in external bodies — changes with the movement of our own body. But feeling itself does not change or move.

1244. We come now to a series of objections.

The surfaces of the fundamental feeling itself are felt in the fundamental feeling through the action of the sensiferous element. These surfaces move. — I answer: 1. Surfaces are felt when the sensiferous force is actually applied to our body, but there is no local movement of the surfaces during this action; 2. when the sensiferous force no longer acts on our touch, and our body has been moved from one place to another, the change consists only in a change of relationship between the sensiferous force and our fundamental feeling, as I said.

1245. But our body is seen when it is moved. — I answer: sight experience is totally extrasubjective. What we see is our body in so far as it lies within extrasubjective experience. I have already noted that motion is present in the body considered extrasubjectively. Such a body, however, is totally different from the fundamental felt element.

1246. But surely we feel motion on the surface of our body whenever a particular sensation moves from one point to another of that surface? — I answer: This moving sensation is produced by sensiferous power and hence pertains to the body perceived as extrasubjective. Motion is present in this order of perceptions.

1247. But you have distinguished a simple sentient principle and an extended term in the fundamental-animal feeling. In addition, you have acknowledged the condition of the *felt element* and of the *sensiferous element* in the extended term. Even granted that motion is not proper to the sentient principle, which is simple and incorporeal, it must be granted to the extended term for two reasons: 1. because the extended term *is* extended, and something extended can be moved from one place to another; 2. because the sensiferous element, in which, as you agree, motion is present, is in that same extended element.

I answer: The term of the fundamental feeling purely as sensiferous power in itself is not the term of the fundamental feeling. Rather, it is the power capable of changing the term of the fundamental feeling, that is, of constituting it in a way other than what it actually is. Let me explain. The fundamental felt element, simply as felt, is in the sentient principle. As we have seen, it is present in the way that the extended element is present in the sentient principle, that is, as contained in container. Moreover, there is such a perfect union between sentient principle and extended element that they form a single feeling. It is different for the *sensiferous force* which is not in the sentient principle in this way. This force simply acts in the extended term of feeling and changes it. Consequently, the sentient principle is neither united stably with the sensiferous force, nor receives the force's action directly. It receives this action indirectly because the felt element of the sentient principle is changed by a force which is not its own. Moreover, when the sensiferous force actually acts in the extended element, in the term of feeling, it does not present in itself any movement from place to place, but simply action in the felt element itself, the term of the sentient element.

The second of these two objections is this: The felt element, because it is in the extended fundamental feeling, is capable of moving. I answer: not every extended element is capable of motion. As we saw, infinite space itself, which is essentially immobile, is not suitable for motion. If there is to be some possibility of movement, some other space must be present besides the space occupied by the extended element, into which this element can be transported. But we have seen that the proper extended element of the fundamental felt element has no boundaries; only when surface boundaries are perceived is it necessary, in order to perceive them, to perceive some other space beyond them. The fundamental felt element is, on the contrary, of such a nature that beyond it, beyond its felt element, no other extension is perceived. All extension finishes in the fundamental extended element with the result that it is impossible for it to be subject to some movement of its own; there is no other space in which it can place itself except that which it occupies. In order to conceive some change of place, it is necessary to go outside this felt element and enter the extra-subjective world. But when we come to know the phenomena of this extrasubjective world, it seems to us that the fundamental extended element moves. This motion, however, consists, as we have said, only in a change of relationship between the felt extended element of the fundamental feeling and the extrasubjective world. This relationship is not a relationship of place to place, of extended element to extended element, but of extended element to feeling. The change takes place, therefore, in an unextended relationship of sensility and, properly speaking, in a relationship between the cause, the agent in feeling (the sensiferous element) and feeling itself. Movement, on the contrary, is a change in relationship between extended element and extended element.

1248. Another objection. If the whole fundamental felt element has no motion, if it is not transported from place to place, you have at least to admit that the extended element of the fundamental feeling can be increased and diminished. But this implies a kind of movement either through extension or restriction. — My answer is this. Although the fundamental felt element can be increased and diminished, this happens through *naturation*. not through motion. The felt element begins to be in a greater extension, or ceases to be in a part of it. This, however, is not local motion, but a kind of creation or cessation of a new felt-extended part.

1249. Another objection. The fundamental feeling is not uniform. If some part of it is felt more than another, or in a different way, it will be able to move from place to place within a fundamental felt extended element. — My answer is this. What you have described can perhaps be called movement, but it is the only movement that can be admitted in the fundamental feeling. We have to explain it, however, and in explaining it we realise that it is not true movement because it prescinds from every action of the sensiferous element which can be mingled in it. In fact, we have already seen that if the corporeal particles in which the fundamental feeling terminates are moved without losing their continuity, the feeling is stimulated, that is, gains greater, different vivacity. But when we speak about movement of corporeal particles, we are speaking first of all about an extrasubjective phenomenon. The subjective phenomenon corresponding to this is the greater vivacity and variety in feeling which we have mentioned. The question, therefore, consists in knowing if this change in the subjective phenomenon can be called motion. But 1. The movement of each particle is not sensible, as we have seen, because the movement of the felt element does not take place in the felt element, and is therefore totally extrasubjective; 2. the movement of two or more particles which move without losing continuity does not produce any other change in the felt element, as far as extension is concerned, except for increase on one hand and diminution on the other. But this is not movement, as we have seen again; finally, 3. if the particles constitute an organ and the intestine movements of the particles succeed one another so that the particles in the first line move before those in the second, and so on, we have a succession of motions which must have a succession of stimuli distributed in the various parts of the organ. The stimulated movement then produces the phenomenon of internal movement because the same sensation appears to pass from one extreme to the other of the organ, which is felt in its totality through the feeling of continuity. This is the only movement which can be conceived in the fundamental felt element. But granted the animal retentive faculty, which preserves the trace of the preceding sensation, and even more the rational retentive faculty which preserves the memory of already experienced sensations and compares them, this movement is subjective. Nevertheless we should remember that no sensation is numerically the same. When one sensation ceases another takes its place so that it appears as a series of sensations representing a movement, just as the image in the mirror moves although no identical body is transferred from place to place in the mirror.[133]

[133] A body is said to be *identical* even if successively in different places

Here we are dealing with phenomenal movement, that is, movement residing in feeling. Consequently, there is nothing contradictory in its having a kind of continuity in so far as the felt element is continuous and the new sensation can begin where the former sensation finishes, or can mix the extremes of these sensations.

1250. Relative to the sentient principle, therefore, that is, to the sensitive soul, we have shown that it is immune from any movement whatsoever.

But while we deny *local motion* to the fundamental felt element, as we have said, and to the sentient principle, this is not to be taken in the sense that we predicate *rest* about these things. Rest can be assigned only to that in which motion can be present. Rest is relative to motion. We should say, therefore, that the fundamental felt element and the sentient principle have neither motion nor rest. This is similar to situations where there is no extension. No extension means no point, which is the term of extension.

1251. From all these things we can conclude:

1. Space, because it is without second, transient acts, needs no explanation relative to its way of action.

2. Body presents two activities, *what is felt* and the *sensiferous*.

3. Properly speaking, the felt element has no local motion; its action depends upon its being given to the sentient element and, as it were, posited in it. This kind of action can come originally only from the Creator, the Maker of feeling. As I said elsewhere, the animated being is not formed, but posited in nature.[134]

4. Only the action of the sensiferous element, the cause of movement, now needs to be explained. This action depends for its cause on the *corporeal principle* which, however, does not fall within our experience. We cannot, therefore, indicate how it acts with second acts, whether they are immanent or transient.

---

because place does not form part of the essence or substance of body. But the sense-experience which is aroused in different parts of the fundamental felt element cannot be called identical as a result of the relationship the experience has essentially with the felt element of which it forms a part. One part of the felt element is not identical with another.

[134] *AMS*, 323–325.

1252. Knowing only that movement and consequently the endeavour to move,[135] that is, the corporeal force, depends on the sensitive principle and an unknown agent is sufficient to conclude that the body does not pass to its transient acts alone. It receives motion and force from the *sensitive principle* as it receives existence from the *corporeal principle*, which itself can be a principle of motion, although the way in which it produces this motion may be altogether hidden.

1253. Force is considered as an immanent act in bodies; motion as a transient act. It will help, therefore, if we indicate the relationship between this corporeal force and motion.

We said that the extended-felt element does not contain the cause of extrasubjective movement. If it did, this cause, now become the extended-felt element, has lost the nature of force, dominated as it is by the sentient principle. We now have to consider this force as distinct from the felt element; we have to determine it from its effects, which are:

1254. 1. Communication of motion. — When one body strikes another, the body which is struck and free moves in the same direction as the body which strikes it. This effect is reduced to *impenetrability* and to *inertia*. Because one body cannot penetrate another and motion has to be preserved through inertia, one gives way to another with a velocity in direct proportion to the quantity of motion in the body which strikes and in indirect proportion to the mass of the body which

---

[135] The endeavour to move, or the living force, would seem a fact from which the *continuity* of movement could be inferred. Careful consideration, however, does not necessarily lead to any conclusion about the existence of continuous motion. First, we have to admit *impenetrability*, an undeniable quality of bodies. *Impenetrability* limits the force which produces motion in bodies in so far as it impedes this force from producing the effect called motion. But the force (the sentient principle, let us say) can nevertheless continue to operate according to its laws. The result is an endeavour to move, although not to continuous motion. Let us imagine that one body is weighing down another. If the first body wishes to penetrate a millimetre into the place occupied by the second, contiguous body, it will press down upon it and, if it has the strength, will even force it to move over. In other words, the body cedes its place to the stronger body so as not to be penetrated. We would, therefore, have to know the laws according to which this force operates in order to gain an adequate explanation of the laws which govern the movement of bodies.

is struck. This fact is relative to the communication of already existing motion, not to the beginning of motion.

2. The conservation of motion. — A body in motion continues through inertia to move in the same direction. This effect supposes that the cause of the motion persists. This cause cannot be the body itself because it is indifferent to rest and to motion. It must be, therefore, an incorporeal force which, different from the body, acts in the body.

3. Attraction. — This incorporeal force is simply an endeavour to move, a permanent endeavour, on the part of one body towards another. The permanence of this endeavour indicates a cause of motion different in its activity from the *cause of the conservation of motion*. The fact behind the cause which conserves motion is this. Two bodies of equal mass move with equal speed towards one another in the same line. When they strike, motion is destroyed. They become stationary so that the same quantity of motion remains in the same direction. The two bodies now at rest are in contact with one another. The endeavour to move in the directions which they previously held is no longer present. They no longer bear down upon one another. On the contrary, the *cause of attraction* produces pressure in them by which they tend to penetrate one another.

Experience shows, therefore, that three causes of motion concur in the nature of motion:

1. A *cause that simply produces motion*, that is, which makes a body pass from rest to motion, and vice-versa.

2. A cause that governs *conservation* and the communication of motion between one body and another.

3. The *cause that produces a constant endeavour* of one body to move towards another (that is, phenomena of attraction).

1255. As far as I can see, the first and third causes are sufficiently explained by the movement-activity of the sentient principle joined with elements of matter and by the laws according to which that activity operates.

1256. The second supposes another principle foreign to bodies. This principle constitutes bodies and in constituting them imposes laws of inertia.

According to these laws, motion in one direction is annihilated by the same kind of motion in the opposite direction. The endeavour that bodies possess to penetrate one another ceases in this case with the cessation of movement because it arises from movement and not from the force which causes it. This force has ceased. All the laws of conservation and communication of motion are consequences of this first law.

The force which produces motion remains even after the production of motion. If this cause is connected with bodies, as in attraction, the endeavour that bodies make to penetrate one another does not cease with the cessation of movement because it is not produced by movement, itself an effect of the force, which does not change its own nature of force.

1257. *Motion* is renewed at every single moment in the conservation of *simple motion*, but no new endeavour is added to that which arises from motion itself. Consequently, *motion* is *uniform*.

1258. The renewal of the *endeavour* towards motion at every moment is an effect of *attraction*. The endeavour produces new motion, while the body is already moving as a consequence of conservation of preceding motion. The result is *accelerated motion* dependent upon *the square of the brief intervals*. Accelerated motion, therefore, is made up of two principles: 1. the principle of the production of motion and 2. the principle of its conservation.

1259. *Impenetrability*, although destroying motion and the endeavour proceeding from motion, does not destroy the *constant endeavour* which precedes motion and causes its production. If two equal bodies move in opposite directions with equal motion but without attraction, all their motion, together with the free endeavour which comes from motion (always an instantaneous endeavour) ceases when they come into contact. In other words, it ceases during the brief interval which is necessary to extinguish motion. On the other hand, if two bodies draw close as a result of attraction, all their motion ceases when they make contact (granted that their mass is equal) although it has increased according to the square of the brief intervals during which the bodies have moved towards one another. Nevertheless, there is no cessation of the *constant endeavour* with which they tend to penetrate one another or at least (and this seems to me closer to the truth) to touch one another at all their points, to centre themselves.

[1257–1259]

1260. It is clear that two powers are at work in bodies: 1. a constant cause of already produced motion; 2. a constant cause of endeavour to produce motion.

1261. We said that the *cause* of motion is certainly distinct from bodies because motion is excluded from the essence of bodies. Can the same be said about the cause of the endeavour to move?

We have to say that the cause of this endeavour, which is also called *attraction* or *living force*, must act incessantly in bodies because all bodies attract one another (I leave aside so-called weightless bodies concerning which the question is still open). But it is easy to show that this endeavour does not form part of the essence of bodies. We simply need to consider that each body has its own essence in itself; it finishes in itself; nothing outside of it pertains to it. Attraction, however, is directed by the *relationship* of one body with another. Necessarily, therefore, the cause of attraction is not a body, but an agent capable of embracing the relationship between several bodies. This seems to confirm once more the opinion that such power may be a sentient principle united with all corporeal atoms. This opinion would, in fact, remove the difficulty. Moreover, because experience proves that the sentient principle can be a cause of motion, the hypothesis, if it is such, possesses the two conditions required by Newton: it is something existing in nature and has sufficient power to produce its effect.

However, we have certainly demonstrated that matter is *per se* inert and needs to receive motion. In itself it has no faculty for producing motion.

CHAPTER 15

'Continuation' — The action of the sentient principle and the origin of its transient acts

1262. The case is different with the sentient principle, which has its own activity and is the cause of its acts. However, no cause of transient acts is a full cause. If it were, it would produce acts as immanent as itself. We must, therefore, investigate how the sentient principle can posit its transient acts.

We have already said that the activity of the sentient principle is aroused by its terms. Once aroused, however, the activity is proper to itself and directed in its operation by its own laws. The activity of the sentient principle, therefore, has two parts, and transient acts can arise in it from two causes:

1st cause. Change of its term, that is, of its *corporeal felt element*. This change does not come from the sentient principle but from foreign causes. Here we must remember the opinion previously mentioned that every particle of matter has some feeling joined to it. This helps us to understand how the term of a sentient principle can grow as one feeling unites with another, granted the law that the sentient principle is single where the felt element is continuous (rather like two mathematical points which merge to form a single point, neither more nor less). Diminution of the felt term is explained in the same way: the extended elements break off from one another and lose their continuity. This enables us to understand how the sentient principle, although properly speaking remaining the same, seems to go out to a new transient act. It is only the term of the sentient principle that increases or decreases. Note, however, that we can observe only two changes as one extended felt element joins with another: 1. the subjective change when two felt elements are united through apposition (this is explained as a result of what has been said); and 2. the extrasubjective change of movement in the two extended elements which have separated or come close in apposition. We explained the cause of this movement previously. Every change, therefore, that is recognisable in the fact under observation must be explained by us in this way.

2nd cause. By the change produced in its term by the activity of the sentient principle. Explaining this change, we have to consider that the sentient principle placed in being has an act determined by its nature. Sometimes, however, this act is partly impeded by foreign causes. When these blocking causes are removed, the sentient principle carries out its act completely. This explanation of its natural act is taken as its transient act and is thought to be a change in it. But, properly speaking, it is the first act itself. It is its own nature which was previously discomforted through constraint by adverse agents but now is placed in its own convenient, natural attitude. Thus, the whole transient act in the sentient principle is not reduced properly speaking to some new activity, but to the primal activity. What is new is the removal of impediments. This enables it to be what it is, what it must be by nature. Let us clarify this concept of the transient act in the sentient principle.

1263. First, we have supposed that the sentient principle is placed in its first immanent act which constitutes it the ens which it is. We explained how this came about: it depends upon its term and the conditions of the term. The second transient acts have no part at all in this term. They follow later because they are acts of the already ennatured principle. But the principle itself is placed in being in different ways: 1. according to the degree of extension in its felt term; 2. according to the intestine, stimulating movements of feeling.

If the principle is placed in being solely through continuous extension without stimulating movements, its activity is restricted to feeling the extended element given it as a term.

But if it is placed in being through stimulating movements also, it has another act. The stimulated feeling is an act which, like every act, endures. In other words, it has a force of self-conservation and of development according to its own nature. This depends upon the principle already stated that 'every activity, every first act, has a natural state in which it is in the most perfect and complete mode that it can be.' The stimulated feeling, however, can be held back from its full, perfect naturation and development. I pointed this out previously (Ch. 1, Article 6) when I said that 'between a principle's being given a term and being denied it, there is a middle state which consists in the imperfect donation of the term and the consequent incomplete self-actuation of the principle itself. In this case, the *bad state* of the principle itself is manifested together with its struggle'.

1264. 1. If an intestine, stimulating movement compatible with perfect stimulation begins in the term of feeling, the sentient principle acts to conserve and continue the movement.[136] This activity which perpetuates the movement (when it finds no obstacles) is not something new, but the same activity present prior to the stimulated feeling and possessing the power to conserve itself and endure as it is.

---

[136] *AMS*, 419–429.

1265. 2. But not every intestine movement in the extended felt element is sufficient for explaining the natural act of the stimulated sensible principle. This act requires

a) a harmonious, single movement;

b) a kind of movement which circles back on itself (otherwise it could not perpetuate itself);

c) a movement which is as frequent as possible, granted the first two conditions;

d) the preservation of the contact and gravitation of one molecule towards another, but in a way which does not impede the three conditions explained previously.

1266. The first act of the stimulated feeling is a power whose energy is limited. It has to be adjusted in the most pleasing, perfect and natural way. Despite its limitation, it exercises its influence to ensure that the stimulating movement of the felt element has the four conditions set out above.

1267. But sometimes as a result of contrasting force and opposing powers it cannot attain this aim.

For example 1. imagine that contact is made between one extended felt element and another. The second, let us say, is extremely small and as such capable of coming sufficiently close to the first to form some continuation with it. This second extended element has its own organisation and is dominated by another stimulated sentient principle. It is stimulated, therefore, by intestine movements which are in harmony with its own sentient element. These movements, however, are out of harmony with the intestine movements of the first extended element to which the second has been joined. The inevitable consequence is war to the death between the two sentient principles, both of which endeavour to draw within the maelstrom of their own activity the corporeal atoms which they share. This is perhaps what happens in the case of poisons and the chemical changes they produce in the living body;

1268. 2. Let us imagine that an extended element, as small as necessary but without movements or vincible movements, draws near to a felt element in which the stimulating movements of the sentient principle are perpetuated. The stimulated sentient principle must, in order to assimilate the small extended element to its own felt element, cause in it suitable stimulating movements. It does this by drawing it within its own ceaseless vortex of activity, by dividing it into its smallest parts and arranging it as necessary to suit the organisation of its own felt principle. This organisation, the source of the movements, is itself formed by the movements themselves. During the whole of this period, the sentient principle only carries forward its first act. It adjusts the first act to the state it should occupy by nature, and does this with an immanent, continuous act which constitutes it in being, but which until now has been impeded and withdrawn solely because of a lack of opportunity to extend itself, or through some impediment dependent on the condition of the term to which it is bound and by which it is conditioned.

This theory explains all instinctive movements which, in the last analysis, are only movements of the fundamental feeling as it endeavours to constitute itself in its most natural, comfortable and pleasant disposition.[137]

CHAPTER 16

'Continuation' — The action of the rational principle and of its transient acts

1269. I want now to explain the transient acts of the rational principle. This, as we have seen, has several activities:

I. Intellective activity, which has the intuition of being as its first immanent act. The term of this activity is ideal being.

II. Perceptive activity, which consists in perceiving real ens. This activity has the perception of its own fundamental feeling as its immanent act. It also has many transient acts which are explained as soon as we know that they arise on the occasion of the modification of the fundamental felt element. Because this element is perceived naturally, its modifications must also be perceived.

External bodies, in their turn, are also perceived necessarily as a sensiferous force because of the violence they exercise in the fundamental feeling.

---

[137] *AMS*, 367–369.

III. It also has reflective activity. We have already given at least a partial explanation of the transient acts of reflection. Reflection begins from the same principle, that is, 'the transient act is the very activity of the first act when this is given an opportunity of moving and adjusting itself in its most natural way.' In fact, reflection is moved to its transient acts:

1270. *a*) by animal instinct, whose acts are transient acts of the animal fundamental feeling. Because this feeling is naturally perceived by us, all the instinctive movements are also perceived. When human animality rouses itself and moves towards the satisfaction of some need, rational perception accompanies all these movements and actions. But because man is a single, rational principle, he endeavours with all his powers — even his rational powers — to obtain the desired satisfaction of his animal needs.[138] This obliges him to fix his attention on means and ends, that is, to reflect on his own perceptions. This whole work of the understanding is always moved to action by the principle we have noted: 'The subjective feeling adjusts itself in the most commodious and pleasant way.' Reflection is attention whose act encompasses all the terms proportioned to it. Disquiet, however, and need are new terms for reflection. It constantly finds new outlets, as it were, open to it. It is like water in a container: as soon as a hole appears in it, the water flows out, not as a result of some new power, but through the same gravitation and pressure which it exercises in the container as long as the continuous sides of the container held it compressed;

1271. *b*) by the rational instinct in a similar way. An example of this is curiosity. When something unexpected happens, we spontaneously desire to know why the cause, which first produced one effect, now produces something quite unexpected. We reflect upon this and are not at ease until we find the solution to the difficulty. As we know, 'when the mind is faced with an apparent contradiction, its rational act is not complete and at rest until the contradiction has been resolved. The term of thought is being, and being is devoid of contradiction. Consequently, thought is not at rest until it has removed the contradiction and thus restored its term.' The same can be

[138] *AMS*, 530–534.

said about any question, about any scientific difficulty. When this new object appears before the intelligence, the way is open to an act of reflection which wishes to grasp the object in its totality;

1272. *c*) by a decree of the will which, having proposed some end, necessarily moves reflection to seek the means. Otherwise, the act of will would remain unfulfilled and disenabled relative to the need of its primal activity.

1273. IV. Will and practical activity can also be explained in other ways. — But the rational principle moves to the kind of transient acts which are called 'willed' through the new objects given to it by other potencies. These objects, which are new terms, call for and provoke the development of new activities according to the principle already laid down: 'The first, immanent act of the soul whenever it receives new terms is no longer in a satisfactory state, but naturally carries out its activity which previously had been held in check and existed only as an active endeavour because of the obstacle, that is, the way in which it is restrained.'

1274. V. Finally, we have bilateral freedom. As we saw, transient acts of this freedom are the most difficult to explain. — The difficulty is this. If the first, immanent act of the soul is carried out naturally when it receives new terms, and the furthering of the primal activity is the same activity which by a law of nature adapts itself to its most commodious and convenient state, transient acts are necessary. They are determined by the nature of the first immanent act and by the quality of the terms applied to them. In this case, bilateral freedom, or indifference, is no longer present. — In considering the potency of bilateral freedom, it seems necessary to say that it is moved by the subject itself in complete independence of the terms given to it. If this is so, we find ourselves in the same difficulty which we have endeavoured at great length to overcome. If this difficulty is not removed, the transient act remains unexplained. It either has a full cause in its subject (immanent act) and then must co-exist with the subject and no longer be a transient, but an immanent act, or it does not have the full cause in its subject and depends on the terms of the subject itself (every stimulus given to the subject by a foreign agent is itself a term) and is necessitated. Or again, it arises from the subject without any possibility of finding the full cause. In this case, it comes into collision with the principle of cause. This difficulty, which is apparently very grave, led many leading philosophers to deny freedom.

They were wrong. Their investigation into the nature of this faculty was insufficient. But careful consideration of the faculty as I have described it in *Anthropology*[139] will provide a suitable way for dispersing this terrible difficulty, as we shall see immediately.

First we have to determine the precise term or proper object of freedom. We already know that this term is 'the choice between two contrary volitions.'[140]

But the essence of freedom does not consist in choosing or not choosing; it consists in the *way* we choose one of two volitions.

When two volitions are presented as a choice to the spirit, either we make a choice or not. If not, there is no act of will; if we do, there is an act of will.

Granted, therefore, that we are determined in making or not making a choice, and granted even that we are moved to carry out this act by some spontaneous necessity, we are not deprived of our freedom provided that in doing the act we remain free to choose one volition rather than the other.

Again, we may find that the two volitions from which we have to choose are present to our spirit and that we are necessarily moved to the transient act by the new term given to our immanent activity (this term is formed by the two contrary

[139] *AMS*, 636–643. The wise reader should not attribute to immodesty or discourtesy my frequent recommendation to pay serious attention to certain difficulties. Very often, questions arise whose subtlety and delicacy make them hard and difficult to understand by even the cleverest people. Let me say very simply with St. Augustine: 'This comes about because what I write will be read not only by you and those who think like you, but by others who lack your intelligence and experience. Nothing can dissuade them, so determined are they, for better or worse, to know my works. You see how much care must be taken in writing, especially about things so great that GREAT MEN HAVE TO WORK HARD AT THEM' (*Ep.* CLXII).

[140] This is not intended to exclude choice between different but not contrary volitions. Several acts are posited when a choice is made between different volitions. The choice consists in deciding whether to do one of them or not. This means choosing between contraries, the elementary choice to which any choice between volitions is always reduced.

[1274]

volitions from which we can choose, and the need to make the choice).[141] Nevertheless, we are not necessarily moved to carry out the act in one way rather than another, that is, to choose one rather than the other of the two volitions; we can choose whichever of the two we wish. We are free, therefore, perfectly free. This freedom does not appertain to the part of activity coming from the term, but to the part pertaining to the already constituted and actuated principle.

1275. But what sufficient reason explains the choice of one volition rather than the other? This kind of question shows a deficient grasp of the force of my definition of bilateral freedom. If 'freedom is the faculty to choose between two volitions', the act of this faculty is the choice. The act of the faculty consists precisely in determining oneself to one rather than the other of the two volitions; it is not the faculty positing the volitions themselves, but the choice of one of them. The reason for the choice, therefore, is the faculty itself, the very activity of the choosing principle. But this faculty, when moved by the presence of its term, comes into act, that is, it chooses between the volitions. Although it is drawn to act necessarily just as other powers are, the cause which draws it is completed by means of the new term, that is, the two volitions, to which the faculty is drawn. It is drawn necessarily to a free act which is its very own; that act is precisely the choice of which we have spoken.

CHAPTER 17

The subject of the following two books

1276. So far, we have 1. reduced all the potencies of the soul to unity, that is, to the essence of the soul itself; 2. we have overcome the ontological difficulties impeding the explanation of

---

[141] It will be said that we are free even in making or not making the choice. This is true, of course, but in this case a distinction has to be made between the choice which becomes the *object* of our choice and the *act* with which we choose between making or not making the choice. I place necessity in the *act-choice*, not in the *object-choice*. I agree that we are free relative to the objects of choice.

the soul's transient acts, that is, of its operations; 3. at the same time, we have investigated the nature of these acts, their explanation and the way in which they appear and disappear. We are now on sure ground and able to deal with the argument we have undertaken, that is, the exposition of the laws which govern different operations of the soul.

The soul, however, is one and simple, and all its actions are ultimately reduced to the *rational principle* in which the final and complete essence of the soul itself properly consists. Consequently, if we succeed in suitably expounding the laws according to which the *rational principle* acts and suffers, we shall have kept our promise and carried out our purpose.

1277. There are, however, two principles of action in the human being, one is the human being, the other is in the human being. The former is the rational principle, the latter the animal principle. When we say that the human being is composed of body and soul, we have to understand that we are speaking of an *animated body*, and of a *rational soul*. The human being is not divided by placing brute matter on one side and the sensitive, rational soul on the other. The intellective soul is the form of a sensitive body, not of naked matter.[142] This does not destroy, but rather confirms, the unity of the soul, which is the supreme principle of feeling in so far as it perceives feeling as entity. This also explains, as we have said, why sensitive activity in the human being is sometimes opposed to the rational, human principle. The fundamental perception, although destined to dominate sensitive activity, does not destroy it. Otherwise, there could be no contradiction and struggle between animality and reason without the existence of two souls.

I shall, therefore, dedicate the following book [Book 4] to explaining the laws according to which the human being acts. By human being I mean the *rational principle* which has in itself feeling under the *essential relationship of entity*. In the next book, the fifth [*Laws of Animality*], I shall explain the laws according to which the animal principle considered *per se* acts.

---

[142] In the Bible, the human being is *flesh* and *spirit*. The Bible always speaks of the flesh as living and fighting with the spirit; it does not speak of dead flesh. This is the true, philosophical division of the principles which make up the human being.

In other words, I shall deal with the animal principle under the *essential relationship of sensility*. This animal principle is not the human being, but is in the human being. In dealing with the sensitive principle, I shall also speak when necessary of the activity, the sensiferous power which, although different from the sensitive principle, is nevertheless manifested in it and sometimes struggles with it.

Book 4
(synthetical)

Laws governing the activity of the soul —
laws according to which the rational
principle operates

[Introduction]

1278. Logic and Christian feeling are the two characteristics of the people of Italy. Writers true to logic and religion were, therefore, acceptable to the nation. This was not the case with others who, abandoning right reasoning and faith, were either censured or forgotten by the public despite their intelligence and erudition. These characteristics explain the progress made in the natural sciences by Italy as she sat at the feet of Galileo; they also explain her tardiness in heeding the call of philosophy in the 16th century.

Logic was an inevitable part of the mathematical sciences. The immortal Galileo ensured its presence in the physical sciences where the study of nature, entrusted to rigorous reasoning, could never clash with religion.

Unfortunately, the nature of metaphysical investigations is not on a par with the nature of mathematics. Illogical metaphysicians are not immediately condemned as mistaken. Nor did heaven grant to philosophy a scholar like Galileo. 16th century philosophers, tainted with the human passions and vices from which philosophy as a whole is not immune, were unable to shake off the unwholesome influence of northern heresy. But such sophists were rejected by the Italian spirit which sometimes went to the excess of burning the impious. For her part, Italy, a desert philosophically speaking, was incapable of attaining nationhood.

Peoples of different blood and talent, brought up in more restricted traditions and less venturesome, were able to unite and cultivate a national spirit almost instinctively, without the developed culture proper to systematic knowledge. This was not the case in Italy, which could achieve nationhood only under the guide of truthful philosophy. The Italian people must first be brought together by intellectual principles which, because they are logical, are also religious. This is the first bond uniting the peoples of the peninsula, and it is hopeless to presume that other ties can achieve the same end without this primary uniting factor.

If religion and logic are the only feelings which remain common to the Italian family, it is inevitable that philosophy must demonstrate its capacity for uniting the peoples of Italy in the school of truth. From the depths of the nation it must draw religion and logic, two extremely powerful seeds of good civic order, and make us realise that our minds aim at the same rectitude, our spirits at the same belief and our ambition at the glory of the Christian pontificate. Harmony amongst Italians will thus spring from their own intimate character and nature; truth, and the Almighty himself, will act as their mediators. This harmony will be firm and lasting, capable of development and of fulfilling every civic need; it has its source where man resides as lord, that is, in reason; here alone he is a noble servant worshipping his Creator. Geometry and physics, studied with such passion by Italians, is only a delightful apprenticeship for this.

1279. Divine Providence has, I think, kept Italians exclusively occupied in mathematical and physical sciences to train them for the higher, more important philosophical and civil sciences (sciences for which we were also prepared by our literature and arts, the envy of other nations). Plato was wise when he excluded from his divine lessons students who had not already been trained in geometry; Socrates' courtesy and grace, seen at their best when employed in the service of philosophy, were very suitable for adorning the philosophical schools.

The logic of natural sciences is not proper to them; it does not differ from the logic required by metaphysical disciplines. Logic is one, just as the art of thought is one, and truth is one. Taking the logic of natural sciences as peculiar to them has led many of our best scientists to despise metaphysics which, they think, rejects the exact reasoning that always goes hand in hand with sciences of mere quantity. And such scientists would be right if my attackers — those who blame me for wanting Italian philosophy to faithfully obey the common laws of human thought, to begin from observation and the verification of facts, to reason exactly on the basis of facts — were themselves correct. But attacks of this kind will not lead me to repudiate the quasi-experimental method which I have recommended to those of our nation who have already begun to philosophise, and whom, as far as I know, I have supported in their philosophical investigations. There is no other method. Certainly, I have no regret in leaving to the devotees of the ancient oracles the divine intuition which, it would seem, led them to contemplate and receive from the voice of their god everything created and uncreated. Let them, and those drunk with poetic inspiration, be banned from entering the temple of philosophy. Without such a prohibition, Italians will never be philosophers, but rest content with their natural state as poets.

1280. This is why I have headed the new book: *Laws according to which the rational principle operates*. Here, too, I want to imitate natural scientists who collect similar facts about which they take accurate, careful notes to see what is identical in them and to discover the *constant modes* of operation of their frequently hidden causes. Such constant modes are called 'laws'. What our scientists call *laws of nature* are simply the identity and constancy of effects as they appear in the reciprocal action and passions of the corporeal substances making up the world. Scientists then reasonably induce the way in which things act from the sameness discovered in effects. From there, they go on to argue that the cause is so formed or natured or disposed that it can only be used in that way. They rightly call such necessary action, always carried out in the same way, 'law'. Law 'indicates necessity that determines action' although the necessity may sometimes be physical, sometimes moral; it first points to moral necessity before being transported to the field of physical necessity.

I have to follow the same path in studying operations and effects dependent on invisible and spiritual causes. Thought as dialectic requires the same process: first, extremely accurate observation to bring together the operations of the rational principle; then, careful examination of what is identical in these operations; next, induction about the constant way in which the cause operates; and finally a conclusion showing that this constancy and uniformity of operation must have a correlative necessity obliging the cause to conform its operations in this way. This necessity, which we call 'law', must have its root in the very nature of the operating substance or cause. Nature and substance are immutable, immanent acts relative to their passing actions and effects.

1281. Because the laws we bring together will be very numerous, I shall try to put some order into the work by first considering the principal sources, the principal elements, which give rise to the operations of the rational principle, operations which we have to observe. These elements, when accurately distinguished, will immediately give us a first, general classification of the laws we intend to investigate.

CHAPTER 1

Classification of the laws of the rational principle in its operation — ontological, cosmological and psychological laws

1282. 'Anaxagoras alone said that the intellect cannot be divided into parts and has nothing in common with other things. But despite that, he did not say, nor is it clear from what he said, *how* the intellect knows, or what causes it to know.'[143]

The great step forward was taken by the Ionian school when Anaxagoras or Hermotimus, both of Clozomenae, recognised the extreme simplicity of the intellect. But, as Aristotle observes, the way in which the intellect knows and its *means of knowledge* were still unknown. An explanation was also needed of

---

[143] Aristotle, *Metaph.*, 1. Shortly before this, Aristotle had written: 'But it seems that Anaxagoras maintained that the soul and the intellect were different. — Nevertheless, he uses both as though they constituted a single nature, except that he made the intellect the PRINCIPLE of all things. He says that the intellect alone, amongst all entia, is simple, unmixed, pure. But he attributes to the same principle both knowing and moving, saying that the intellect had put all things in motion.' — It was said, however, during Aristotle's time that Hermotimus, a fellow-citizen of Anaxagoras, had previously posited the intellect as the cause of the universe. *Metaph.*, 1. Hermotimus and Anaxagoras provide a date for the interchange of teaching between the Ionic and Italic schools. From the time of these philosophers onwards, both schools dealt with the same questions and differed in name rather than opinion. Cf. *Rinnovamento*, bk. 3, ch. 51.

the causes which enabled the totally simple intellect to be moved, especially to knowledge of corporeal things.

1283. These questions were of supreme importance, and neither Aristotle nor any of the other ancient philosophers was able to provide an adequate answer. Aristotle, in confining himself to the question about the means of knowledge, applied to the spirit limited ontological principles drawn exclusively from material ens, not from all entia. Aristotle saw that matter and form are present in material nature. Matter is passive, form active; matter becomes everything, that is, all special corporeal entia; form does everything, that is, by configuring matter puts these entia in being. He believed that the same teaching could be used to explain the constitution of the intellect.

> THROUGHOUT NATURE, there is something which is matter for each genus, and it is matter because it is all these things in potency. There is something else which is cause and efficacy because it does all things. It is, as it were, art relative to matter. In the same way, IT IS NECESSARY for these differences to be found even in the soul. Indeed, there is one such intellect which becomes all things, and another which does all things. The latter is a kind of habit, like light which somehow makes colours exist in act which previously were in potency. This intellect is separable, unmixed, unable to be divided into parts; and its substance is action. The agent is always more noble than that which is passive, and principle more noble than matter. Knowledge, then, in act is the same as the thing.[144]

Aristotle thus agrees with Anaxagoras in saying that there is an unmixed, immaterial intellect. This, however, according to Aristotle, is *knowledge* itself in act. Prior to this, there exists in the soul a certain kind of matter of all cognitions. He thought that in this way he had overcome the difficulty about Anaxagoras' teaching which, by admitting only an immaterial intellect, had been unable to explain how this intellect could know, and be moved to know, material things.

1284. Several observations have to be made about Aristotle's reasoning.

　1. First, this reasoning contains defects against the rules of

---

[144] *De An.* 3.

good method. From the very beginning, Aristotle supposes that everything *throughout nature* is composed of form and matter. But he does not demonstrate such a universal principle except by recourse to experience and to the experience of material things alone. He then concludes that this *must be* the case for the soul also, although he should have been satisfied with observing if this were in fact the case without imposing *a priori* limits and laws, which are always arbitrary and fallacious, on the nature of the soul.

1285. 2. By going on to say that the *possible intellect* becomes all things, that is, all cognitions, he makes cognitions subjective. All of them, without exception, would be nothing more than the soul itself modified in various ways. Hence, these cognitions would be contingent, etc., as the soul is. They would be mere feelings of the soul without the power to testify to any object distinct from the soul.

1286. 3. If the last words have to be translated: *idem autem est scientia quae actu est, quod res ipsa* [knowledge in act is the same as the thing itself], as Michele Soffiano and other translators put it, we have to conclude that because all our information is simply the soul modified and actuated, so the soul would be all things. This is the *panpsychism* of many German philosophers.

1287. 4. If the *acting intellect* is cause, efficacy, a principle which operates in the form of an art or habit, it is not entirely in act. Although Aristotle did indeed indicate, with his possible intellect, the material cause of cognitions, about which Anaxagoras had been silent, he did not sufficiently explain with his acting intellect either the full-efficient cause of cognitions or their instrumental cause. Habit needs a stimulus if it is to come into act, especially if it must be determined to produce from matter one thing rather than another, if for example a statue of Apollo has to be made from a piece of stone rather than a statue of Hercules. In the same way, art needs instruments to produce the statue.

1288. 5. On his philosophical journey Aristotle encountered the beautiful likeness of light, which could have shown him the right way. But he used it very badly. Colours in potency, which he introduces, are not colours, and colours in act are the light itself modified and broken up. Moreover, the eye which sees is

[1285–1288]

one thing, the light which makes us see is another. In Aristotle, however, the intellect, which is the eye, is confused with the light which makes us see. The *object* is confused with the *subject*.

This great distinction between object and subject, which alone was capable of completing that which Anaxagoras had left to be discovered, was lacking in Aristotelian philosophy.

1289. I have shown what the light of the mind is; the *idea of being*, which is the *means of knowledge*.

The human intellect, although unmixed, as Anaxagoras affirmed, possesses a duality which removes Aristotle's difficulty about the teaching of the great philosopher of Clozomenae. The intellect has been given a *means* of knowledge. At the same time, the way in which Aristotle thought the difficulty could be overcome has been shown to be erroneous.

1290. The differences between my way of overcoming the difficulty and Aristotle's are these:

1. Aristotle, in affirming that the intellective soul was composed of matter and form in the likeness of material nature, made it result from two elements, each of which was a substantial part of the intellective soul, although form was even more substantial than matter. For my part, I did not make *ideal being* a substantial part of the soul, but simply the object given to be seen by the soul. Ideal being thus places the soul in act and in being without confusing itself with the soul. It simply posits cognition in the soul. For me, therefore, the intellective soul remains altogether unmixed, despite its being joined with something different from itself which illumines it.

1291. 2. Aristotle makes the soul result from a *form* similar to the forms of real being. This form is itself a *reality*, it is the act of reality. For me, *ideal being* does indeed inform the soul, but in a completely different way. It conserves its own being, which is totally different from that of the soul. It simply gives itself to the soul to be known.[145] Forms, or informing causes of this kind, I call *objective*. Present in the spirit as essential light, they provide it with an act of intuition which could in some way be called a *subjective form*. From this point of view, objective forms are *causes of subjective forms*.

---

[145] *Sistema filosofico*, n. 35.

1292. 3. Aristotle grants to the intellective soul something which corresponds with the matter of bodies. Consequently he says that the soul becomes all things. This I repudiate entirely. The soul always remains a principle of extreme simplicity. It is not made up, properly speaking, of form and matter, but of act and potency. It is indeed act before it is potency. And it is potency not *per se* but as a result of change in its terms, as I have explained. Aristotelians can now press the following objection: 'In this case, how do you account for the rise of special cognitions?'

My answer is: the rational soul apprehends ens, which is *ideal* and *real*. *Ideal ens*, which is essentially unlimited, is given to the soul by nature. The soul also receives by nature a limited, *real ens* in the *animal fundamental feeling* which is perceived rationally by the soul because it is already comprehended in its own way in *ideal ens*, which comprehends everything. The relationship between a *limited-real ens* and *unlimited-ideal ens* constitutes *concepts*, that is, special and generic ideas. But neither ideal ens nor any real ens perceived naturally by the soul is the soul itself; it is something joined to the soul through its proper relationship of *rationality*, as I have called it to distinguish it from everything else. In this way, the Aristotelian difficulties vanish without breaking up on the rock where Aristotle foundered.

1293. Having established the composition of the soul, and explained how it is able to work and develop, I have opened the way to a suitable classification of the laws followed by the soul in its operation. The soul's activities spring and as it were burst forth from two sources, its term and its principle (it has this in common with every other finite ens). The term of the soul is twofold: Ens and the World (what is real but finite). Hence there are three sources for the laws governing the soul's operation: Ens, the World, and the activity proper to the rational principle. The laws of operation proper to the rational principle can therefore be classified of themselves into three extremely noble kinds: *ontological*, *cosmological* and *psychological*. I shall begin by discussing the laws imposed by the nature of the object on the rational principle in its action, that is, the ontological laws, which can never be lacking whatever ens is present as the object of the soul's operation.

The ontological laws followed by the rational principle in its operation and imposed on speculative reason — the supreme law

Article 1
Statement of the supreme law of thought

1294. The rational principle acts in two ways, speculatively and practically. While its speculative action produces no effect outside the mind; its practical action does. I now intend to consider the ontological laws imposed by the object on both speculative and practical reason.

1295. First, we have to consider the *principle of cognition*, the supreme and most general law.

All other laws are indeed contained and summed up in the principle of cognition which is formulated as follows: 'The term of thought is an ens,'[146] that is: 'Thought is such that its primal, natural law is to have an ens as its term. In other words, thought either has an ens as its term or ceases to be.' Considered from this point of view an ens is, therefore, the condition under which thought, the speculative operation of reason, exists.

1296. It follows that the qualities and characteristics essential to an ens correspond to conditions of thought. They are laws of thought. Every thought, in order to exist, must have a term furnished with all the qualities and characteristics possessed by an ens.

Note that when we speak in general of laws of thought, I do not mean that such laws must be observed in every act of thought separated by abstraction from all other acts of thought. I am considering the complex, total thought which results from the sum of the single, partial acts which a person carries out in his mind at every moment. For example, a man thinks of a real line. This is a particular act. But he cannot think of a real line

---

[146] *NE*, vol. 2, 559–566.

without thinking of the surface of which it is the term. If I said that the need to think of surfaces or solids is a law of thought applied to corporeal extension, it could not be objected that we also think of lines and points which we find through abstraction in the surfaces and solids we perceive. The special act with which we think of the abstract point or line, is not an act that stands alone. It is simultaneous with and conditioned by the thought of the surface or the solid in which we see the line or the point. It follows that the surface or solid is not lacking in the complex thought of corporeal extension. Thus the law of thought is fulfilled. When we say, therefore, that accepting an ens with the qualities which constitute it as ens is a law of thought, I do not mean in any way that we cannot, through abstraction, think of some quality of an ens separate from some other quality, even though the quality cannot stand alone. Rather, I mean that this abstract element cannot be thought unless we first think of an ens. We know that the element pertains to an ens and is in an ens. It is true therefore that 'we think of an ens together with its essential conditions' in complex, human thought. This is so true that if, through sense, we receive an accident of an ens (for example, a colour and nothing more), the soul can think of this accident only by adding to it the substance which it does not receive. This comes about because the accident would not be an ens without the substance, as I have shown elsewhere.[147]

Article 2
The supreme law expressed in two propositions

1297. What has been said is sufficient to overcome the objection against the principle of cognition which could arise from seeing that abstract thought is concerned with accidents which, taken on their own, lack the properties of an ens. Abstract thought is a part of a thought; it is not thought in its entirety. Abstract thought never exists alone in the mind without some kind of presence of thought in its entirety. I must add here

[147] *NE*, vol. 2, 567–569.

another extremely important observation. Thought has many species of acts, not all of which apprehend an ens in the same way and with the same completeness. To show how this comes about, I must explain more distinctly the efficacy with which the principle of cognition gives form to intellections. This efficacy can be set out in the following two propositions:

1298. I. 'Human understanding cannot think anything which has properties contrary to those essential to an ens.'

1299. In virtue of this law, the human spirit cannot think anything which is and is not at the same time because no ens contradicts itself. The principle of contradiction expressed by the Greeks, τήν ἀντίφασιν οὐ συνκληθείειν,[148] has its origin here.

1300. It may be objected that we think nothing, we think negation. But nothing is the opposite of an ens, which expresses something. It is not necessary, therefore, that an ens should always be the object of thought.

I answer. 'Nothing' indeed is contrary to an ens, but if we think carefully we see that nothing is not and cannot be thought as nothing. When we think of nothing, we really think of a relationship proper to a contingent ens, a relationship that an ens has with thought and with itself. By means of this relationship, we think that an ens either is, in which case it is thinkable, or is not, in which case it is unthinkable. 'It is not' simply signifies that two acts are combined in the same thought, one of which thinks of an ens, the other of which removes the ens and, by taking it away, abolishes the object of thought. If we consider all the argumentation that mathematicians bring to bear on 'nothing', and the different species of nothing which they set up, we can see that *nothing* as thought is not properly speaking nothing, but a relationship of an ens. Giuseppe Torelli spoke very subtly about this in his beautiful book, *De nihilo geometrico*. The same can be seen if we examine the ways in which ascetics express themselves. When they say, for example, that man is nothing, that everything is nothing outside God, they are speaking the exact truth. A spiritual person often used this prayer: 'My God, I am a sinner, a sinful nothing. Make me innocent, an innocent nothing.' There is a marvellous truth and exactness in this prayer where we see that the nothing of which

---

[148] Aristotle, *Metaph.*, 3, c. 6, 7.

it speaks is not pure nothing, which is incapable of fault or innocence, but a relationship pertaining to human beings who are nothing of themselves without the Creator. Without the Creator, they would cease to be.

1301. II. 'Human understanding, although it always has an ens as its object, is not forced to think in the same way of all the properties of this ens. It has to think of some properties actually, and others virtually. It is obliged not to deny those properties of which it thinks virtually, but be prepared to examine them. Human understanding must think actually, however, of the *ideal essence*. It is not obliged by any law of thought to consider actually the properties and relationships which, although pertaining to an ens as real, are virtually comprised in the ideal. This is so, even if such properties and relationships are necessary for the constitution of the ens of which we think. It is simply obliged not to deny them and to leave them as matter for successive investigation.'

1302. This extremely important law makes possible the different kinds of intellections proper to the human being, and assigns its special laws to each of them. Let us examine the ontological laws obeyed by each kind of intellection. The principal kinds are: 1. intuition; 2. perception; 3. reflection exercised through abstraction and integration, and consequently divided into *a*) reflection as abstraction and *b*) reflection as integration.

Article 3
The law of intuition

1303. *Intuition* has ideal ens as its object. This act of thought, while extending to ens in its ideal form, totally prescinds from reality and morality, the other two forms.

1304. Here we have to consider an important ontological principle, that is, 'an ens, although it may be in three modes, is complete in each of them because each in its own way embraces the whole ens.' Intuition, therefore, embraces all that an ens is, and can only be predicated of an act which, referring to all that an ens is, lacks nothing required by thought which, in turn, only requires an ens as its object.

1305. Moreover, because an ens is simple and indivisible in its ideal form, it can only be given to the understanding as *whole* or *nothing*. Under its real form, however, an ens can be given in part to the understanding because it is divisible and multipliable although in this case it cannot be thought of on its own since it lacks one of its parts (it is not a complete ens).[149] But the human understanding, granted that it already has the whole of an ens in the ideal form, can no longer lack the full, entire object which it requires. Granted this object, the parts of what is real can also be thought because their presence simply adds some other term to thought without removing the ideal ens. Thought is possible as soon as it receives the ens in its entirety under the ideal form. As I said, it is ideal being which forms thought and constitutes the potency of thought.

Article 4
The law of perception

1306. Prior intuition of ideal being, the light, the means of knowing everything real, is needed if we are to explain *perception*, the operation of the rational principle by which a *real ens* is apprehended.

This truth is seen only by those who meditate profoundly on the nature of perception. Many are persuaded that the object of our perception when we perceive something real (for example, a body), is a *particular* and nothing more. They never succeed in resolving the perceived object into its two elements, *possibility* and *reality*, that is, into the *idea* in which the knowable essence of a body is seen and the contemporaneous *apprehension* with which reality is affirmed.

Our mind does not in fact perceive a body without calling upon both elements in its act. This truth will be seen by answering the following question: do I *know* what I have

---

[149] But if the whole of what is real were given to an intelligence, would intelligence be able to understand it? — Note, what is ideal resides in the depths of what is absolutely real. Hence the whole of what is real cannot be given to the intelligence without its being given at the same time what is ideal. The same has to be said, and even more forcefully, of what is moral, which requires union between the ideal and the real.

perceived? Yes, I do. It was a round body, the size of a pomegranate, yellow, clear, hard, a ball of ivory. This is the concept of the body that I have perceived. — But does this concept include the subsistence of the body? This is an important question, and the answer is 'No'. As long as I think only of the concept of the body, which is expressed in the definition I have given, I still do not know whether the body subsists. — I conclude that knowing the subsistence of a body is different from having its concept.

As a result of perception therefore, we acquire two cognitions of a body, that of its concept and that of its real subsistence. Hence every perception is twofold, and results from two contemporaneous acts of the spirit, the intuition of a concept, and the persuasion that something subsists. Obviously, we cannot be persuaded that something exists unless we first have its concept. In the logical order, the concept precedes the persuasion that what is in the concept and known through the concept actually exists.

Another way of convincing ourselves of the same truth is to consider that we know immediately the *possibility* of every contingent thing that we perceive. If I am asked: 'Is something possible?', I reply without hesitation: 'It must be; if it exists it is possible.' But how do I know that what exists is possible? Where do I get the concept of possibility? I get it, this is quite certain, from the concept I have of some thing. The concept, as we know, gives me information about the knowable essence of a thing, but does not tell me that it subsists. I conclude, therefore, that the thing contemplated in its concept may or may not subsist. To know if it subsists, I need some further indication which, in the perception, is the feeling I have of the thing. The possibility is contained in the pure concept of the thing in so far as this concept does not necessarily show the thing as subsisting. Now, this concept is the ideal being of the thing. If, in perception, I did not think the ideal being of the thing, I would not know its possibility. The origin of the thought of possibility supposes, therefore, that in every perception I intuit the ideal concept, in addition to perceiving the reality of the perceived thing.[150]

[150] Another proof that in perception the idea of a thing is intuited simultaneously with feeling or affirming what is real can be drawn from the

1307. But what is the ideal concept of an ens? It is simply the universal concept of being, limited and determined by the action of a thing in us, that is, by the feeling produced in us by the thing. When I say: 'The concept of an ivory ball', I simply say: 'The concept of a being determined by the sensible qualities of this ball.' Every perception of an ens includes the intuition of its ideal being, and every ideal being supposes the intuition of *indetermined* and *universal ideal being*. Perception cannot be explained, therefore, unless we suppose that the soul first intuits *ideal being per se*.

1308. Thus the object of perception, although a limited, real thing is nevertheless an ens. It lacks nothing essential; it accords with the principle of cognition. If the limited, real ens were separated from ideal being, it would no longer have all the conditions and qualities of an ens. It cannot exist of itself alone, nor does it have in itself the explanation of its own existence. Separated from what is ideal, it is divided from its own essence. But united with what is ideal, what is real has received its essence; it is a complete ens. It can, therefore, be perceived.

1309. But we still have to explain how perception is limited in this way. Why do we not perceive the whole of reality? Why does understanding apprehend in perception one part of reality of an ens and exclude every other? — This portion of what is real and perceived is not chosen abitrarily by the understanding, but furnished for it by feeling. Individual feelings are separated in such a way that what is in one is not in another. Moreover, they are mutually incommunicable. In perception, the rational principle, therefore, remains limited by feeling. This we posit as an undeniable fact. Its explanation will be given in *Theosophy*.

1310. But if real ens is *per se* unlimited, will it not always lack some essential or necessary quality when it is perceived as limited? If limited, real ens has no explanation for its subsistence, can we conceive it as subsisting? — Everything lacking to a real ens is already supposed and admitted virtually and indistinctly in ideal being which joins itself to the real ens, and in which the real ens finds its essence. Reality, without which

undeniable fact that the pure idea of a thing remains in our mind even when we have forgotten that it has been really perceived. No other operation is needed for us to have the idea as I showed in *NE*, vol. 2, 519–520.

the real ens cannot be complete in the thought we have of it, is not excluded but, as it were, left behind. One example of this is the way mathematicians express an indefinite series. After having written some of the terms, they add: 'and so on'. In doing this, they indicate and suppose what is lacking, but without expressing it. Thus, in the perception of a limited, real ens, the conditions indispensable for its subsistence are not denied but left vague. These conditions are its essential or at least necessary relationships with other limited entia or with the unlimited ens. All this later becomes the subject of ontological and theosophical reflection.

1311. An argument of this kind confutes the error of the *panidealist* philosophers who claim that man must, in his first intellection, perceive everything which he will afterwards find through reflection. They do not distinguish sufficiently between ideal and real being. Confusing them, they claim that THE WHOLE OF REALITY also enters the first natural intellection and, therefore, every perception. The truth is that only THE WHOLE OF IDEALITY enters the first natural intellection. When what is real but limited and partial is compared with the whole of ideality, reflection finds what is lacking to what is real.[151] We now move on to explain the law of reflection.

Article 5
The law of reflection

1312. Reflection is the faculty which, turning back on a perception or its object, abstracts or integrates.

§1. *Reflection as abstraction*

1313. Relative to reflection as abstraction, we have to distinguish three accidents:

1. Simulated abstraction. This is properly speaking nothing more than imperfect perception. Its foundation lies in the imperfection of sense. This accident deceived the Aristotelians

---

[151] *Sistema filosofico*, 75–81.

who were led to attribute the universal to sense as though it were an accident of sense.

2. Abstraction which simply divides the ideal part from the real part of the object of perception. This is called 'universalisation', and is sometimes carried out naturally without any positive act. The act of affirmation ceases and is forgotten.[152]

3. Finally, abstraction exercised on the idea of a thing and only consequently on the real thing, in so far as it corresponds with the idea (realised form). In this abstraction, attention is limited to one part of a conceived and perceived ens without abolishing in the mind other parts to which we simply pay no attention.

1314. Let us consider the first accident. — Aristotelians noticed that the notions of children and uneducated people are very general. They also noticed that an object presented at a distance from the sensory organ conceals some of its differences. For example, a stationary person seen at a distance is not distinguished from a column because our sense does not apprehend the smaller parts which differentiate the human being. They concluded that sense presents first the most common *qualities*, and then *proper* qualities. They also concluded that the intellect, following sense, first conceives what is universal and then what is particular. This is an illusion of sensists. But it was at least a much more subtle illusion than many of those proper to modern philosophers. It was also characteristic of the Aristotelian spirit. Here I think it worthwhile explaining the matter in the words of Zimara, a 16th century Italian philosopher and professor at the University of Padua. He discussed the question; 'What do we first know?' and answered:

> If we want to see what is first known in confused cognition, we must have recourse to sense. This, I think, is the principal foundation on which Averroes based himself.[153] — Things known to us which give rise to systematic knowledge are rather confused; universals are better known than the species of which they are composed; the names of the species are better known than the parts which define them for the intellect. This comes about because the

[152] *NE*, vol. 2, 519–520.
[153] Prolog. *I Phys.*, nn. 4–5.

singular, which is a kind of whole, is known by the sense before its parts. Contemplating this basic source, we notice how it gives rise to the following truth: the more universal accidents of time and place are better known to sense than less universal accidents. Relative to place, as Themistius says,[154] the whole body of a distant animal is clearer than its head, hand or other part. Similarly, distance shows us first an animal, then a man. In these things, universals and common characteristics are clearer to us than things which are close and particular. Relative to time, as our philosopher says in the text, children call all men 'Father' and all women 'Mother'.[155]

This sensistic illusion arises because sensists always speak of things as felt-known, never merely of things as felt. Consequently, they find what is common and proper in what falls under the senses, and have no hesitation in saying that sensible entia possess universal and more or less common accidents. To avoid mistakes, we need to take the felt element and despoil it of everything added to it by the act of knowledge and of perception. Nothing universal and common now remains. 'Universal' and 'common' express only the relationship between the felt element and ideas. All that remains is particulars. In sense, the whole, the part, the animal, man, are all equally particular. Moreover, the eye has only a particular sensation whether it sees a confused object at a distance without distinct parts, or sees it nearby with distinct parts. A distance sensation is different from a nearby sensation, but they remain sensations; the comparison between the two felt elements is made by reason after it has grasped them and they have become known, contained and measured in the idea. There is no doubt that we find common and proper parts in these known-felt things. But, at the same time, we see that what is common corresponds to the first sensation, and what is common and proper corresponds to the second sensation. Various arguments can be used to prove this besides the principal argument drawn from observation and contemplation of the thing in itself. I add

[154] In *I Phys.*, text. comm. 4.

[155] M. A. Zimara, *Quaestio de primo cognito in Gymnasio Patavino publice examinata.*

here several arguments in addition to those I have given elsewhere.[156]

I. *Argument.* — Sense does not first perceive the whole and then the parts in a nearby object; at one and the same time it perceives the whole with its parts. All parts of a human being are contained in the sight and image that we have of him. Nevertheless, the rational principle first attends to the whole rather than the parts, and needs to pay special attention to perceive clearly the parts from which the whole results. It is characteristic of rational attention to embrace first the whole and then the parts. Babies, for example, initially call every man 'Father' and every woman 'Mother', although through sense they perceive distinct images of people whom they have seen. Their sense-perception is in fact perfect, and better than that of adults. Nevertheless, their rational attention first grasps what people have in common. They leave aside whatever else they may have perceived through sense. It seems as though they have not felt anything else; in fact, they have simply not considered it mentally.

II. *Argument.* — Babies first fix their attention on more common sensible qualities (without however ignoring other qualities) with the help of words, which are the instrument of reason, not of sense. Without such instruments of thought, through which they can concentrate on the common element and forget the rest, they would never arrive at such abstraction. This is so true that Aristotelians themselves noticed with great acumen that the child does not turn his attention to common, universal characteristics not indicated by a word, even if these are present in sensible things. Unnamed universals are not more known than particulars nor prior to particulars. But these philosophers did not profit from the light of this beautiful observation as they should have done, although it focuses exactly on the point at issue.

> According to Aristotle,[157] there are several unnamed intermediate genera. For instance, there is an unnamed genus close to horse and ass. Now, there is no doubt that

[156] *Rinnovamento*, bk. 2, ch. 31, 33.

[157] *Metaph.*, 7, text. comm. 28.

accidents consequent on the specific natures of these beasts, that is, of horse and ass, are better known than the accidents consequent to such an unnamed genus.[158]

The Aristotelians say that this depends on the weaker impression made in the sense by such genera. They give no proof of this, however, and often it is not the case. On the other hand, it is clear that these genera remain unnamed because they are less necessary to human life and, if not signalled by words, apprehended only with difficulty by the intellect.

III. *Argument.* — It is not true that the baby possesses the abstraction which all Aristotelians and sensists suppose him to have; abstraction, which is posterior to the child's first operations, comes with reflection. Abstraction means dividing what is common, what we call *abstract*, from what is proper. The baby does not divide and abstract with his first operation, but unites and synthesises, that is, unites what is most universal (the idea of being) to the concrete fact that falls under the senses. The words 'paternity', 'maternity', 'humanity', which express abstracts, remain unintelligible to the baby for a long time. Nor do the words 'father' and 'mother' first indicate what is common, what is abstract, to the baby, but the real individuals (perceived by him) who have been indicated by these words. It is incorrect to imagine that they have the same meaning for the baby as they do for us.

To perceive such individuals, however, the baby first has to unite to them the universal which he has in himself. As a result, the object signified by such words, although particular, is associated with the universal, in which it is seen by the mind.

When other people make an impression on his senses, the baby does not halt to note mentally the differences which do indeed exist in the sensation; he either takes them as though there was no change and uses the same word, the one which comes easiest to his lips, or he uses the same words because he has united to them the *thought* of certain more obvious qualities which have attracted his attention in the first men and women he has known. For example, his attention may have been attracted by beards worn by the first men he had known and by

---

[158] *Quaestio de primo cognito, etc.*

the head-covering of the first women. When he sees a man, he calls him 'father' but means 'the being with a beard;' when he sees a woman he calls her 'mother', but means 'the woman with the head-covering.' The same thing happens if the baby's attention is fixed on some general, total configuration of male or female body, rather than on some special characteristic. In this case, he calls 'father' the ens with a total, masculine configuration, but takes no notice of minute differences; he calls 'mother' the ens with a total, feminine configuration, and again takes no notice of minute differences. He is still ignorant of the true meaning of 'father' or 'mother'. Although this seems to be abstraction, it is in fact synthesis because 1. an ideal ens is united with the sensible configuration, or with a more apparent, sensible mark; 2. an individual, an ens, is determined by means of the configuration or mark which serves to distinguish it from other individuals. — But, you may say, this configuration, or sensible mark, is common. — No. Initially, the child does not see it as common. It is a felt particular, taken as a sign and connotation of an ens; it draws attention to the universal, which it determines but does not form. A similar mark indicates several individuals successively through particular acts of the spirit. Only later, through reflection, when the mind is stimulated by some need, does the baby note more specific differences. He then discovers that the *mark* which initially served to restrict and particularise the universal, and to name individuals, is itself *common* and universal, considered in relationship with those differences which, after perceiving them, he re-uses to restrict and particularise all the entia possessing that *mark*, which is thus seen as common to many individuals.

The sensists are wrong, therefore, when they attribute this false, apparently primal abstraction to sense, as though sense first perceived what is common and reason then took it ready-made from sense.

1315. We come now to abstraction's second accident, universalisation. This kind of abstraction, rightly called *universalisation*, simply analyses intellectual perception by placing *ideal being* on one side, and the felt element, what is *real*, on the other.

1316. There is a difficulty here: 'If what is real is considered in its fullness as infinitely real, it cannot, of itself, be divided from what is ideal; both are simply a single being. If, however, we are speaking of what is finitely and contingently real, *what is real* divided from what is ideal is not a complete ens, and is consequently unthinkable. How then can abstraction divide them?'

Note first, that what is infinitely real is not given to the human being. When by means of a judgment we abstract what is ideal and separate it from what is infinitely real, as we imagine we do, we actually divide nothing. The object of our reflection as abstraction is not what is truly infinite and real, but a negative, analogical concept which takes the place in the human mind of what is infinitely real. A person who has the vision of heavenly glory and apprehends what is infinitely real would never try to separate the ideal from the real by means of an abstractive judgement, just as we would not try to do something mentally absurd if we knew it were absurd.

This serves to refute the teaching of pseudo-mystics who claim that the object of natural, human intuition is God himself, who contains infinite reality. According to them, we then draw ideal being, through abstraction, from what is infinitely real. Such a system, besides contradicting common sense, involves many other absurdities and consequences harmful to Christianity.

However, I want to continue with this direct confutation of the sect of pseudo-mystics. First, we have to consider that either through abstraction or in some other way, the human being does in fact intuit what is ideal without what is real (even our adversaries do not deny this). Now if we were to see God the Almighty, the absolute and infinite reality by nature, we would have to see two things together: 1. that what is ideal is in the depths of what is real; 2. that it is absurd to consider it as separated from what is real by way of judgment. But it is clear that, because we do not see this absurdity in the present life, we think what is ideal without thinking what is real. We find no difficulty in this. This shows that we do not apprehend what is absolutely real by nature, as the pseudo-mystics maintain. It is true that what is ideal is conceivable *per se* because it includes the whole of being, although under a single form. But the reason why we intuit what is ideal is different from the reason why we think and judge, without absurdity, that ideal being is alone and separated from what is real. The reason we conceive ideal being is that it has everything needed to be conceivable; the reason why it can be thought and judged alone, without our realising how absurd it is to admit such a state, is our lack of apprehension of what is infinitely real and hence of its necessary nexus and identity with what is ideal. Consequently the absurdity remains hidden.

1317. We come now to what is real but finite, to *universalisation* exercised on the finite object of perception. Here we must note that dividing this object into its two elements (what is ideal, and what is real but finite), means that only the ideal element remains conceivable as an ens. The second element remains solely as felt, and outside mental conception. In other words, this kind of division dissolves the real object. What is real remains, but without its condition as object. It is an illusion to imagine that what is real may be conceived on its own. If we do make an effort to conceive it on its own, our very conception shows that we have mingled and bound it up with the idea that completes it as an ens. It is false, therefore, that we conceive it as separate.

1318. How, then, do we come to speak about it? How do we speak about it as united and separate? — We speak about it as united to the idea, while seeing that it is separable. In other words, real, finite ens is annulled as the object of cognition because we understand that it is not the idea. This negative cognition is sufficient for us to be able to speak about it without our having to conceive it as an actually separate object of knowledge.

We can also understand that as separate, what is real is not a complete-ens. This, too, is a negative cognition independent of perception or positive conception. We come to such negative cognitions by contemplating what is real in the idea, and by comparing it with the idea. The separability of what we consider united is itself thinkable, just as the annihilation of a thought object is thinkable.

1319. Abstraction's third accident: abstraction properly speaking.

Finally, we come to the third accident of reflection as abstraction. This is abstraction in the strict sense, and is present when, by reflecting upon some concept, we separate different elements or relationships, for example, when we abstract (from the concept of a finite ens) substance from accident, or accident from substance, and so on. The products of this abstraction (for instance, substance or accident taken separately) are not entia and cannot, therefore, be objects of thought. They are parts of entia, or imperfect entia (entities). They are thought not with all-embracing, but partial thought, which is the kind of abstraction that we exercise on ideas. These parts or elements of thought are not completely separate from the concept, but are contemplated in the concept itself. Attention of the spirit is specifically restricted to each of them. However, the whole concept on which we reflect, and whose unity and simplicity makes it possible for us to consider each part, remains in the spirit. If the whole concept were removed from the spirit, its parts would also be removed, and the spirit would be unable to focus its attention on any of them.

The act proper to this kind of abstraction cannot be found on its own in the spirit. It is not a whole, complete thought, as we have already seen, but part of a thought, and has to be seen in the whole thought. An ens is the object of an all-embracing thought; it is not a part of thought, nor of one specific act necessarily joined to another because such a specific act does not stand on its own. It is not, of itself, a thought.

1320. It is true that, in fixing our attention on certain elementary parts of the ens which we see in the idea and to which we have given a name, we often change it into a true ens. This is another illusion, an error that we make because we add unconsciously something to an element which is not an ens. Hume did this when, in claiming that the universe could be composed of accidents, he was forced unwilling and unwittingly to change accidents into substances.[159] This is a very frequent illusion. Through it people change abstractions into entia, they personify them, and so on.

We have another class of errors when, by applying such abstracts to real entia, we imagine that what has been divided and separated in abstraction is divided in these entia as well.

1321. I have shown that this kind of abstraction has its own laws springing from the idea of being. Consequently, this idea necessarily precedes all abstractions because it directs them.[160] It

[159] *NE*, vol. 2, 598–614.
[160] *NE*, vol. 3, 1454–1455.

cannot, therefore, be formed through abstraction. This is a new argument to destroy the error of *sensists*, as well as that of their comrades-in-arms, the pseudo-mystics. Sensists believe that the idea of being can be drawn by abstraction from real-felt things; pseudo-mystics claim even more absurdly that it can be drawn from real-absolute being, intuited naturally by the human spirit. The second group do not realise that the abstraction under discussion is exercised only on the idea and that the idea, therefore, must be first in the logical order. Nor do they realise that the idea of being directs abstraction in its operations. Without this direction, abstraction would operate haphazardly, which is not the case. The pseudo-mystics might perhaps have recourse to the second kind of abstraction, but I have excluded this previously.

§2. *Reflection as integration*

1322. We have to maintain therefore:

1. that the understanding perceives finite realities, which of themselves alone are not complete entia, in ideal being, which does complete them;

2. that the understanding does not nevertheless apprehend *actually* their essential or necessary relationships with complete real being. Without denying them, it leaves them aside as an appendix to be developed later.

This development is precisely the work open to reflection which, turning back on the perceived, real thing, confronts it with ideal being, the type of every reality. Reflection then discovers what is lacking to the real being, known through perception. For example, it realises that this being is contingent and has a relationship with what is necessary; it finds that this real being is limited, and could not be, unless there were some unlimited being, and so on.[161]

1323. *Reflection as abstraction*, therefore, compares the ideas of entia with one another in order to establish what is most common by applying the results of this comparison to the entia themselves. In the same way, *reflection as integration* compares the idea of entia with the idea of being in general and discovers

---

[161] *Systema filosofico*, 82–104.

the ontological relationships, that is, the relationships that finite entia have with the essence of being itself.

1324. This integrating work of reflection is abolished in the pseudo-mystic system. They claim that reflection never discovers anything new because human beings are given the fullness of real being by their natural intuition. Consequently, the only reflection open to pseudo-mystics is reflection as abstraction. This, however, is contrary to common sense and to what we know of ourselves. We all know very well that *new* truths are discovered through reflection. This is the way sciences develop. There is no need, as these philosophers falsely claim, that such truths should already be present in the object of intuition. It is sufficient that the object of intuition be ideal being which, by containing, according to its own mode, the whole of being, is the universal rule used for judging what is real, knowing its order and relationships, and finding what is lacking to its completion. Acquired cognitions and all the sciences arise from these judgments about what is real.

1325. This arbitrary, exaggerated system, which I hope will always be rejected by Italian good sense, arises from two equally false suppositions: 1. The object of the mind cannot be an ens under its ideal form alone. This is obviously *contra factum*. The mind which thinks of a *possible* ens does not need in any way to think simultaneously of its reality; 2. Unless the mind could apprehend what is absolutely real, reflection would be unable to discover scientific truths about determined, real beings. This, too, is false because, as I have shown, ideal being already contains the supreme rule for understanding felt, real things, all of which are contained *virtually* (and therefore in the ideal mode) in what is ideal. The pseudo-mystics are also unaware that what is real is present in feeling, and that we do not perceive it unless we relate it to the idea. They add certain theological arguments in their favour, but these only show that they are as ignorant of theology as they are of philosophy.[162]

---

[162] The theological arguments used by a recent Italian author against me can be seen reduced to syllogisms in the *Impartiale* of Faenza (15 July 1845), with their answers. They would make profitable reading.

CHAPTER 3

Continuation — Derivation of the special ontological laws which govern human thought

1326. Having explained the supreme, universal law of human thought, 'Ens is the essential term of thought,' and having applied it to different kinds of intellections, I must now determine the special laws arising from it. This can be done easily by considering the special endowments of ens, each of which impresses its own characteristic on human knowledge in such a way that it contributes greatly to our understanding of the intimate nature of the ens necessary for the purposes of our investigation.

1327. The principal qualities of any ens (and I limit myself to these) are that it is 1. object; 2. possible; 3. first act; 4. one; 5. lasting, and 6. finite or infinite. Each of these qualities gives rise to a special law which determines the nature of the cognitive act. I will begin with the first: 'The term of thought is an object.'

CHAPTER 4

Continuation — Special laws — First law: the objectivity of thought

1328. It is commonly believed that all potencies have an *object*. The truth is, however, that they all have a *term*; only understanding has an object. But because we understand everything and speak only about what we understand, we change the terms of potencies into objects by the very act of perceiving the terms or thinking about them. The terms therefore of non-intellective potencies are subsequently called 'objects' in so far as they relate to our thought. But what does 'object' mean?

1329. The term of a potency is object when it is neither passively nor actively modified by the potency; the term is simply contained in the act of the potency. Only through this act does the potency enrich and benefit itself, without modifying the term in any way, as I have said.[163]

Moreover, if a potency is to have an object, it must possess that term for what it IS in itself, not for what it DOES in the potency.

1330. Hence three conditions are necessary for the object: 1. it must be immodifiable yet united to the potency in its own way; 2. it must unite and communicate itself in such a way that the effect of the union and communication is not the potency's apprehension of the object's *action*, but the apprehension and use of the object itself by the potency; 3. the potency which apprehends the object, must apprehend the object alone, not itself and the object. Hence the object is always separate from the potency by virtue of the very act of union and apprehension. This act places the object before the potency, hence the name '*objectum*'.

1331. These three sublime conditions are not found in any of the terms of other potencies, only in the term (ens) of understanding. The terms of all potencies are: 1. passive relative to the potencies and receive modifications; 2. active and produce modifications in the potency in such a way that what the potency receives is only the *action* of an ens, not the ens itself; 3. sometimes modifications of the potency itself (for example, sensations, the terms of feeling, are simply modifications of the fundamental feeling); 4. united with the potency in such a way that they fuse with it, becoming a kind of continuation or actuality of it, etc.; in the act of union they are neither separate

---

[163] The ancients, who did not sufficiently distinguish between *receptivity* as such and *passivity*, were incapable of knowing how an ens is united to the soul. Even Plato, it seems, did not fully know the nature of the totally objective relationship between the soul and an ens. In *The Sophist*, he introduces a guest from Elea who represents Eleatic philosophy:

'*Guest*: If knowing is *acting*, it would follow that being known means *suffering*. An essence (οὐσία), therefore, when known and in so far as known, must suffer as a result of knowledge, and in so far as it suffers, must be moved. The same cannot be said about something stable.

Theaetetus: True.'

Plato uses this principle to refute the Eleatic school which admitted only immobile ens. — I have demonstrated that the mind neither acts on nor modifies its objects. Cf. *Rinnovamento*, bk. 3, c. 47.

from nor opposed to the potency. On the contrary, a potency, when apprehending its term, simultaneously apprehends itself as modified, and therefore does not leave and apply itself totally to something different from itself.

1332. Careful consideration shows in fact that objectivity is such an essential condition of an ens that an ens which is not object, is not an ens. At the most it will be only a vestige of an ens conceived through an abstraction but unable to exist entirely by itself. Indeed if we carefully note the contents of the *concept of an ens*, we see no relationship in it between one ens and another. On the contrary, the concept excludes all relationship as something extra; it indicates the thing *in itself*, not as *acting in another*. But the thing is only *in itself* when in a mind. In fact, if we speak about a body not conceived by a mind, this body lacks the condition of being something *in itself*; it has no selfness. The same is true of a purely sensitive being; it also lacks SELF. Being, in ITSELF, is simply being conceived *absolutely* by an intellect, without relationship to anything else. To consider things not conceived by us as having an absolute existence is to fall into a kind of transcendental illusion. In the very act of conceiving and reasoning about them, we consider them as not conceived. Consequently, without realising it, we speak about things conceived in themselves. They certainly exist *in se* without our needing any other act to conceive them. It is sufficient that they present themselves to our thought to fulfil the condition required for their being in a mind. But we can never say that entia which we have neither really conceived nor imagined as conceived by another mind, in other words, entia unknown by every mind, are complete entia, are something in themselves. Objectivity is therefore an ESSENTIAL property or relationship of an ens.

1333. To say that *objectivity* is an essential relationship of an ens means that the ens is essentially knowable, that is, *intelligibility* is a necessary property of it. Entia therefore which are not known *per se* and require some *means* of knowledge to be known are incomplete. They need to be completed and finalised by a kind of marriage in the mind, that is, by the union of essential ens, ens *per se* intelligible. In fact *objectivity* is found in entia only in so far as they are in the mind. Hence *objectivity* and *intelligibility* present the same concept and mean the same thing under two aspects: 'object' means an *ens understood* in itself; 'intelligibility' is the property an ens has to be understood when this property is separated through abstraction.

1334. Aristotle states in several places that *ens* considered *per se* is the first thing understood; without it, other things cannot be understood. I will comment only on the fourth book of *Metaphysics*, where he teaches that 'the relationship of a thing to being is the same as its relationship to truth.' 'The most certain and known principle, about which it is impossible to lie,' he says, 'is the principle of contradiction', that is, 'Being cannot not be.' This supposes that the mind first knows what *being* is, as Alexander of Hales noted.[164] According to him, the principle of contradiction is necessary and not something hypothetical: 'Anyone wishing to study a discipline must know this principle beforehand and not search for it while studying.' It is 'this first truth without which we cannot know any ens whatsoever.'

1335. This gave rise to a subtle difference of opinion among the Aristotelians. They all agreed that ens was the first intelligible, but disagreed intensely whether this intelligibility pertained to an ens as ens or to an ens in act, which they saw as a special genus of ens. The fine Italian philosopher whom I have quoted above, Marc'Antonio Zimara (shamefully unknown in Italy), expresses the following opinion:

> Relative to the discussion, the intellect is divided into acting and possible intellect. It is characteristic of the acting intellect to make itself all things, and characteristic of the possible intellect to make all things.[165] But because the nature of the possible intellect is solely to be in potency (called *intellect of the soul*)[166] it follows (granted that an ens in potency is drawn into act only by an ens in act)[167] that what is understood by our intellect is understood in so far as in act. This is clearly the opinion of Aristotle expressed in book nine of the *Metaphysics*.[168] According to him and also to Averroes, *intelligibility* must be a passion which

[164] *PE*, 8–12.

[165] Arist., *De An.*, 3, text. com. 17.

[166] *Ibid.*, text. com. 5.

[167] *Metaph.*, c. 9, text. comment.

[168] Text. com. 20.

originally and *per se* pertains to an ens in act in so far as it is in act, not to an ens purely as ens. I have myself on occasion demonstrated the same: passion which originally pertains to a thing, does so by reason of the thing itself. In other words, once the thing is posited, passion is also immediately posited; if the thing is removed, passion is removed as well.[169] But exactly the same happens in the case of actuality relative to intelligibility: once actuality is posited, intelligibility is immediately posited; there cannot be an ens in act which is not intelligible. Similarly, once actuality has been removed from anything whatsoever, even if some preceding quality remains, the thing is no longer intelligible. This is the case with first matter considered separately and in itself. Taken in this way, matter is an ens, but according to Aristotle, unintelligible; in book 7 of the *Metaphysics*[170] he says that matter, although *per se* unknown, is an ens.[171]

1336. This statement (that matter considered separately and in itself is an *ens*) is erroneous. As far as I know, neither Aristotle nor any of the ancients knew the doctrine *of imperfect entia.*[172] The doctrine is founded principally in the ontological law of *synthesism.* According to this law, finite entia sustain and support one another in such a way that, if they are divided and separated by abstraction, they are annihilated, and properly speaking no longer entia. Whatever remains of ens becomes an object of abstraction and can be called, at most, *imperfect ens.* This ens is something on the way, as it were, to being an ens; it is completed and becomes really possible when another ens on which it depends is added to it. Hence matter is an ens considered as term of the sentient principle; separated from this, it is a vestige of an ens, which in reality is nothing because it cannot exist in this way. Even in the mind it is an *imperfect ens* because, although the mind gives it some completion, without which it

---

[169] Arist., *Poster.*, bk. 1, *cap. de universali.*

[170] Text. comment. 35.

[171] M. A. Zimara, *Quaestio de primo Cognito.*

[172] Nevertheless the doctrine had been glimpsed, as we see from the Aristotelian principle that not *forms* but only *composites* can be placed in a genus or species (St. Thomas, *S.T.*, 1, q. 76, art. 3, ad 2). The reason is because they understood that the forms of composite things are not complete entia.

could not be thought, abstraction follows and removes anything not belonging to it. The mind can then consider it as naked matter, although matter is not naked in complex thought as a whole. 'Ens' therefore means 'act'; there is no ens as pure potency. Potency, as we saw earlier, is something negative and therefore more a non-ens than an ens.

CHAPTER 5

Continuation — Law of synthesism of thought

1337. The law of objectivity gives rise to the law of synthesism (cf. 34–44). Although the object is united to the subject, there is no fusion whatsoever between them; by the very act of union, the object keeps itself separate from the subject and posits itself for what it is in itself. At the same time it initiates an act in the subject which terminates in the object, not in the subject. Subject and object are therefore united in such a correlative way that their union is essential to both;[173] it constitutes them both in such a different way that one is not only separate from the other but also opposed to it.

1338. Because the ancients did not know this law,[174] they fell into inextricable speculations and very serious errors. Ignorance of the law shored up Parmenides' ἓν τὸ ὂν καὶ πᾶν, as we can deduce from a place in the dialogue which Plato named after that truly great Italian. In the dialogue, Socrates urges objections against Parmenides' system that 'all things are one single ens'. He maintains that although *species* is one for many individuals,

[173] It must be understood that the object is necessarily in a mind, not essentially in a human mind but an eternal, divine mind.

[174] Aristotle, noting that some accidental forms are ordered *ad invicem*, distinguished two kinds of *predicating per se* one thing of another. In the first kind, what is predicated is understood in the essence of the thing of which it is predicated, for example, 'The intellective soul is incorruptible'. In the other kind, what is predicated is not understood but necessarily found with it, for example, 'The surface is coloured', where the surface is not a coloured being but is found inseparably with colour, or according to the Scholastics, 'Surface is the preamble to colour'. In observing all this, Aristotle noted a special case of the law of synthesism. Cf. St. Thomas, *S.T.*, 1, q. 76, art. 3.

[1337–1338]

species are distinct from individuals and from each other; they are entia in themselves. In reply, Parmenides points out the absurdities that would result from such a supposition. For him, the supposition is not justified, and even if it were, there would be great difficulty in showing how species can be known and, through them, individuals. To prove his point, he makes Socrates grant that every *essence which exists in itself* cannot be in us. Granted this, Parmenides concludes that species are unknown to us because we do not share in them.

However, if Socrates had known the law of synthesism, he would never have accepted Parmenides' claim that *species* were something in themselves and could not be in us. On the contrary, he should have determined that the intellective species (not to be confused with the image) is *being* itself in its ideal form. Being is so totally in itself that it cannot not be in itself nor can it receive anything from us. However, it can be intuited by us exactly as it is in itself, and not otherwise. We share in it, and in this sense it is in us. This proves that the species must be united to us if we are to intuit it and use it to know other things. But it does not prove the impossibility of its being intuited by us and remaining a being of a nature different from ours. This would certainly be the case if it were proved that what is in us has to be a part or modification of ourselves. But this is false and gratuitous. We see therefore that Parmenides' error was a result of the same arbitrary principle from which modern thinkers have derived their *subjectivism*. But his logical mind went much further and concluded that all things had to be one single ens. This argument, which Plato puts in the mouth of Parmenides, is clearly Parmenides' own. In the extant verses of his work, Parmenides endeavours to explain cognition by saying that knowing and being are the same thing,[175] and again (according to Karsten's translation):

> Thinking is the same as that of which the cause is thought.
> You cannot discover thought apart from ens in which it rests.
> Nor is it or ever will be anything other than ens.[176]

[175] Karsten, v. 41 [*Philosophorum graecorum veterum reliquiae*].
[176] *Ibid.*, vv. 93–96.

These places can throw considerable light on the passage in Plato's *Parmenides* to which I have referred.

1339. Furthermore Parmenides uses another argument to prove to Socrates that things cannot be known if species are given an existence in themselves and distinguished from each other. He grants that what exists in itself cannot represent things, because existence which is in itself is not relative to anything else; it is closed within itself. Hence, he reasons, not even God would know human things or have power to govern them. The very art of disputation would be annihilated if things had to be known through these kinds of species, each of which would have a proper essence distinct from the thing itself. Parmenides goes on to say that some thinkers, having seen these consequences, held back and doubted whether ideas existed, because ideas cannot explain knowledge. This is precisely the case of the modern Scottish school, which denied ideas. I myself have explained, perhaps with even greater efficacy, the uselessness of ideas when we claim that their only function is to be representative and that everything is known through representation.[177] But this is manifestly false because the essence of the idea is not seen in the idea. Instead we see the essence of ens, and ens is identical under both its ideal and real forms. Hence, in my opinion, the idea is simply *being intuited by the mind*[178] in its own essence, which is eternal. This essence however can include the realisation of being (in which case it is infinite being, that is, God, who is not seen), but can also not include the realisation of being (in which case it is *ideal being*, to which we refer the realisation apprehended by us through feeling). Hence the known, real thing is simply *realised ideal being*. Consequently

---

[177] *NE*, vol. 1, 104–108.

[178] It has been objected that I use 'idea' in different meanings. But those who think this have not considered that I define idea as 'being, intuited by the mind'. According to this definition, I distinguish in the idea the act of the mind, which I call 'intuition', from the object of this act, which is *being, ens, essence*, as it is more appropriately called according to the different relationships under which it is considered (*NE*, vol. 2, 646–659). Thus, when I consider essence in itself, I call it 'essence'; when I consider it as object of the intellect (*intuited essence*), I call it 'idea'. But because the *idea* has many relationships, it is given various names which however do not affect the definition 'intuited being', or even 'being known per se'.

the object of knowledge is the result of the two elements described above, 1. the ideal element, and 2. the real element, which is the complement of the ideal element. What is ideal is not representative in the same way as a real thing, for example, as the form of a statue represents another form, that is, the person whose statue it is, but as the essence of a thing represents the realised thing. The realised thing is not separated from its essence; if it were, it would no longer be a complete ens. Essence therefore is the act by which an ens exists in the ideal world. Realisation is another act of the same ens as act by which the ens is in feeling, that is, it feels or causes feeling. This feeling is added to the ens in the perceiving spirit as the completion of the ens. We must also bear in mind that existence in the spirit does not remove existence in itself; on the contrary, it constitutes it.

CHAPTER 6

Second special law: the term of thought is that which is possible

1340. The word 'possible' in its logical sense means free from contradiction, but an *ens* admits no contradiction whatsoever. This characteristic, which makes an ens essentially concordant and harmonious with itself, is the source of the principle of contradiction that 'being and at the same time not-being is not being.'

If 'being and at the same time not-being is not being', thought is impossible, because the object of thought is being. In this sense logical possibility constitutes the thinkability of things.

1341. But where do we look for contradiction (if there is contradiction) deep within an ideal or real ens? We must look into the essence of the ens as seen in its idea. If the possibility of an ens is that which makes it thinkable, and if this possibility or freedom from contradiction is in its idea, the truth I established in the previous chapter is once again confirmed by a new, sound argument: nothing is thought without an idea. This does not mean that every human thought comes about *exclusively* through an idea, as some inattentive thinkers have attributed to me. In rational perception, where we think something real, the object of our thought is both ideality and reality; every perception has both an ideal and a real element. But sensism, by stopping at what is real and recognising it alone as the object of thought, is an erroneous system and so deficient in philosophical insight that it renders thought impossible by excluding thought in the very act of establishing it.

Moreover, granted that possibility is thinkability, and thinkability is in the idea, any reality separated from its idea is no longer thinkable. The idea cannot in any way originate from it, because the real thing is in the understanding solely by virtue of the idea.

1342. Again, what is real and divided from the idea is not of itself an OBJECT of the mind, because what is real receives thinkability only from the idea to which it is united in the human spirit. Thinkers who consider what is ideal as nothingness, claiming that the human mind would not have a true object unless it had something real as its term, show how little they have progressed in philosophical investigation. In fact the opposite is true: only ideal being, the essence of an ens, is OBJECT. Outside of or apart from this, there is no object. If what is real is to be thought, it must first be OBJECTIVISED, that is, contemplated in the idea, in the essence.

1343. Saying that something is object or thinkable or intelligible *per se* means more or less the same thing. Only *ideal being* is INTELLIGIBLE *PER SE*; real being is INTELLIGIBLE BY PARTICIPATION. There is only one exception to this principle (although properly speaking it is not an exception): God is intelligible *per se* in his reality also; his subsistence is understood in his ideal essence. Consequently in God, subsistence (that is, reality) can never be unaccompanied by ideality. It is a serious, pernicious error to say that God is an idea or even that he is THE IDEA. In human language 'idea' does not mean reality, yet God is EXTREMELY REAL. Why do we use the word 'idea' in this way? Why has 'ideal' been coined in opposition to 'real'? Precisely because we do not naturally have a vision of totally real being and do not have any experience of the necessary nexus between ideal being and complete, real being; we can only reason to this nexus. The very existence of the word 'idea'

[1342–1343]

and its constant use refute the error of those who attribute to human beings the intuition of God in the present life.

1344. But what about the word 'possible'? In its logical sense, as I said, it means that which does not involve contradiction. But God himself involves no contradiction. Is he therefore possible?

The repugnance we find in affirming that God is possible shows that another concept, besides the absence of contradiction, is present in this use of the word 'possible'. Neither the creature nor God involves contradiction. The divine essence however is not only free of contradiction, but necessarily real, whereas the essence of the creature does not necessarily subsist. Hence the essence of the creature can be conceived without the inclusion of reality in the concept. This explains why the reality of contingent being is said to be possible: 'Contingent being can be realised because its essence does not involve contradiction.' This truth completes the concept of *what is possible. Logical possibility* is therefore the explanation of *metaphysical possibility.*

1345. Everything therefore can be objectivised, that is, idealised, because everything that is not necessary and does not involve contradiction is conceived as possible. In this sense all things have an idea as their counterpart. What is individual can be considered as possible; the same is true of subsistence, when considered in relationship with its idea, that is, with its essence, of which it is the realisation.

1346. When a thing is considered possible, it is universalised. But not all things can be universalised in the same way. The word 'possible', as we saw, has two meanings: one, purely *logical*, when it signifies the essence of something that involves no contradiction; the other, *metaphysical*, when it indicates the realisability of an essence. The same can be said about universalisation.

Sometimes universality is not present in a pure *essence*, as in the case of things which are essentially single; for example, the essence of what is individual, of what is one, of *myself*, of what is subsistent, etc., includes particularity and singleness. Consequently, what is individual, what is one, *myself* and what is subsistent can only be single. On the other hand, if we consider the possibility of the subsistence of many *myselfs*, many ones, many individual things, many subsistent things, etc., we see all these things universalised by metaphysical, not logical *possibility*.

It may be objected that a multiplicity of each of these things corresponds to a single essence, that is, to the essence of *myself*, of what is individual, etc. But if the multiplicity corresponds to a single essence, essence must be the means of universalisation.

I deny that each of these things corresponds to a single essence. In fact the essence of *myself*, of an individual thing, etc., is not the essence of some other *myself*, of some other individual thing, etc.; the essence of one *myself* has nothing to do with the essence of another *myself*. It is characteristic of a subsistence not to have anything in common with another subsistence. The contrary seems to be true because the *nature* in which one subsistence participates is confused with *subsistence* itself; nature is *common*, but subsistence is *single*.

1347. Someone may further object that if many *myselfs* share the same *myself*, that is, have the same *selfness*, they have something in common.

I agree that *selfness* is indeed a common essence but it is not the essence of *myself*, etc. *Myself*, considered as such, is something real, something subsistent and therefore has no ideal essence. When many *myselfs* are conceived, the universalisation involved depends upon abstraction which, in the absence of a *specific essence*, sets up a *generic essence*. This *universalisation*, founded on *metaphysical possibility* (that is, on the existence of a will as efficient cause, and not upon an idea as exemplary cause), is referred to a generic essence, which represents only a part of the essence in question. The other part is produced directly by the efficacy of the will. In this way the *generic idea* of *myself* is the idea of human nature in so far as the efficient cause makes it subsist in several individuals. The generic idea does not represent the individual itself, which it makes subsist in reality.

1348. 'How then can we know whether a given essence may be realised in several individuals or in one only?' This question can be answered only by considering the particular *essence* itself under discussion. It is the *essence* of a thing which either excludes or permits varying multiplicity of individuals.

Thus the essence of God and of matter excludes multiplicity of individuals: the essence of God, because it is being itself, which is one and totally simple; the essence of matter, because it is the extended term of feeling and as such has only a generic ideal essence which expresses the whole of matter, not a part of it. Thus the individual has no place in matter. When for example we say 'water', we express the total nature of water. Its nature is simple, like the real essence itself to which the concept of water is restricted.

1349. Similarly, there could be essences which determined a certain number of individuals. All the entia known to us through *specific essence* are indeed unlimited in the metaphysically possible number of their individuals, but it is impossible to show the absurdity of some essence unknown to us which could contain limits of this kind. One example would be the essence of any order resulting from several finite things.

CHAPTER 7

Third special law: the term of thought is a first act

1350. Because our discussion concerns human thought in its entirety and complexity, the meaning of this third law is 'Thought cannot have second acts alone as its term; these must be accompanied by thought of the first acts from which they arise.' Although we can think of second acts by abstracting them from first acts, abstraction is not complex thought. Indeed abstraction is impossible unless the mind first contains that on which abstraction is exercised. Furthermore, abstraction does not discard the thought from which it originated. If I abstract second acts from first acts, the first acts remain in my mind and enter into the complex thought, even if I do not give them the active attention which I give to the abstract element. Although I restrict my attention to a part of the thought, the thought itself does not cease.

1351. The reason why we cannot think anything without thinking a first act is that the term of thought is an ens, and an ens is always constituted by a first act.

1352. If we observe entia directly to discover their total constitution, we find that some have an essence prior to and distinct from their subsistence, while others have subsistence as their first, original act. The former are multiple and contingent, the latter is only one and necessary. However, when subsistence is the first act, an ens obviously cannot be perceived without the perception and thought of its subsistence. Thus, God cannot be thought solely in an ideal way, nor as possible, in the way that we can think of contingent things. Either we think of him as subsistence or we are not thinking of God. Hence anyone who said that *ideal being*, which informs our reason, is God, would commit the most serious error and end up in rationalism, pseudo-mysticism and many other monstrous absurdities.

1353. Contingent entia on the other hand have their own essence, which is manifested in the *idea*. This fact, and the fact that nothing can be thought without its essence, demonstrates once again the often stated and still little understood truth, that our understanding cannot perceive a real, contingent ens except through and in the idea. The idea itself cannot be given by sensation because sensation is precisely the real entity to be perceived and known.

Furthermore, we do not perceive what is real through the idea alone. The idea contains the pure essence of an ens, separate from its reality or subsistence. Consequently, as long as we intuit only the essence in the idea, nothing is understood of the reality. As I said, only feeling, rational apprehension and affirmation apprehend subsistence.

1354. But how do we apply the principle that nothing can be known unless the *first act* of the thing known is itself known? Strictly speaking the *first act* is not in the reality because, as we saw, first act pertains to essence. Hence, in *perception* and *universalisation* the spirit takes as first act that which it indicates by a word and to which it directs its attention. Second acts are seen as those which happen to the thing indicated by the word and taken as the subject of the definition and the focus of attention. They lie either outside the elements included in the word, definition, or object abstracted by our attention. This is how the spirit forms its knowledge of real things and of their knowable essences: it determines and limits them, as I said, by that which it first perceives through feeling.[179]

[179] *NE*, vol. 3, 1203–1208.

1355. Furthermore, the intelligent spirit finds an order in feeling itself because 1. certain sensible qualities cannot be perceived independently of others; for example, colour or shape cannot be perceived independently of extension; 2. some qualities are anterior and, because they are conditions, remain unchanged, while others which are conditioned change; for example, extension, which is anterior, remains unchanged, while colour, which is posterior, can change. Thus, when we see things with this kind of connection and interdependence, we take the first condition or quality logically prior to the others and consider it as first act; when we take it in relationship to other qualities already united to the essence, we call it 'substance'. In bodies this first act, without which the other corporeal qualities cannot be felt, is the *sensible and sensiferous force*. Hence, even in the sphere of reality there is a kind of *first*, but hypothetical *act* because, as I said when discussing perception, it is relative to sensitivity itself. The understanding therefore conceives the essence of an ens capable of being perceived, that is, an ens with all the conditions for being a term of perception (which I have already dealt with). It goes on to break up the ens by abstraction in order to find the first act called substance, without which it cannot perceive the rest. But this order itself, present in reality, is reflected in the ideal essence actuated and determined before the eyes of our spirit by this relationship with what is real. It is in this ideal essence that knowledge is found.

1356. To perceive a contingent, real thing, therefore, the following is necessary:

1. The essence intuited in the idea, because essence is a *first act* relative to realisation.

2. The *first act* of reality itself, because without this act reality cannot affect feeling or be named. Note however that the first act of reality to which feeling is conditioned is hypothetical, that is, we consider it such, and it is in fact such, but only in relationship to the felt element, not to the whole of being.

CHAPTER 8

Fourth special law: the term of thought is one

1357. Another property of an ens is that it is one. If it were not one, it would not be an ens. It is necessary therefore that *one* be always present in the object of thought; otherwise there would be no ens. An ens is always an individual and, without attributing an individuality to it, cannot be thought with entire, complex thought.

1358. What is the origin of the idea of one or unity? It is given with the idea of an ens and is obtained from the ens by means of abstraction.[180] Without an ens no idea is possible; with an ens the idea of one is immediately in the mind.

1359. This explains why the Scholastics said that one and ens are interchangeable.[181] The ancient philosophers, particularly the Pythagoreans, took 'one' to mean 'ens in the abstract', without determining anything else in it. But anything abstract is an incomplete ens, and many of the things they said about this kind of ens apply only to a complete ens. This mistake is the real source of the errors of the Pythagoreans.

1360. The Scholastics also said, 'Everything is one by its essence',[182] and asked, 'Can the mind understand several things

---

[180] *NE,* vol. 2, 575–578.

[181] St. Thomas, *Quodl.,* 6: 1; Aristotle, *Metaph.,* bk. 4: 2.

[182] St. Thomas, *S.T.,* I, q. 5, art. 3, ad 1. Is this principle true relative to the divine persons? I answer negatively, together with St. Thomas, who defines oneness as 'that which is undivided in itself and divided from other things'. In the divine persons there is no difference of essence that can divide one person from the other; each person has the same essence and nature. Hence the principle that distinguishes them is not essence but *relative property.* 'Personal unity is the RELATIVE PROPERTY which distinguishes one person from another, not the essence of the person himself' (*In 1 Sent., Dist.,* 19, q. 4, art. 1, ad 1). — Nevertheless *unity* or *one* can be considered under two aspects: 1. what it is in itself (*ens divisum* [undivided ens]); 2. what it is relative to something else, that is, as a principle of division (*divisum ab aliis* [divided from other things]). If we consider unity as that which it is in itself, each person in the holy Trinity is one because the essence is one and most simple. But this unity and simplicity of person is not a principle of distinction

simultaneously?' They replied in the affirmative but on condition that the mind thinks these things *per modum unius* [as one]; for the Scholastics, one must always be present in the object of thought.

1361. The first philosophers (who also influenced Plato) could not find unity in body because they looked for it in matter, that is, in body separate from the sentient principle and therefore divisible *ad infinitum*. Unable to arrive at a first, extended element possessing unity that could not be lost through further division, they denied that body was an ens and could be the object of knowledge. Thus they changed body into a phenomenon which they said people in general take for an ens but which philosophy sees as a mere phantom. In short these philosophers fell into idealism or, more correctly, posited the ontological principles from which platonic idealism originated. But I have placed the unity of body in its *essential relationship* with the sentient principle. I fully agree that the felt and sensiferous elements, when separated from this principle, can no longer be conceived. However I said that this necessary relationship of body with the sentient principle does not in any way deny its reality; it simply demonstrates that by nature body must be united to a sentient principle from which it receives perfect continuity and therefore the necessary unity for being an ens.[183]

1362. Because ens is one:

from the other persons. The principle of distinction between them is purely the *relative property*, as I said. It is not absolutely true therefore that that which constitutes one, that is, a substantial ens, is that which distinguishes what is one in the substantial ens from some other one which is also in the substantial ens. The same substance subsists in the three, that is, in the three divine persons.

[183] Apparently Parmenides was aware of the part played by *continuity* of body. We can gather this from the attribute he requires for an ens to be such, that is, continuity (τὸ συνεχές). Aristotle disagrees with Parmenides; he says the continuum is that which holds together by means of a continued series of parts and therefore can be divided *ad infinitum* (τὸ θίαιρετον εἰς ἀεὶ θίαιρετά). For Parmenides on the other hand, ens cannot have parts (*Phys.*, 1, 2; *De caelo*, 1, 1; *Categor.*, 6). But Aristotle is mistaken because the continuum is not in reality divisible but only limitable by *human imagination*. Strictly speaking, the continuum is immobile space, whether occupied or empty, as I have said.

1. It is interiorly harmonious and concordant, and excludes all contradiction or repugnance. As I said, this makes it logically possible. Hence the principle of contradiction expresses simply the unity and concordance of ens with itself. This immunity of ens from all contradiction and intrinsic repugnance was seen by the ancient thinkers. Parmenides expressed it in the fragment preserved by Clement of Alexandria:[184] 'You will never sunder being from its hold on being.'[185]

2. It is *simple* in such a way that if it lacks anything constituting it as ens, it is no longer one. Parmenides saw this and expressed it in a fragment given by Theodoret: 'If something is lacking, all ens must be lacking.'[186] Precisely for this reason I induced the conditions and laws of thought from the principal properties of ens. But Parmenides did not see that something can be called 'ens in the course of formation' when separated from its *essential relationships*, as I explained when speaking about matter, etc.

3. It is immune from space and time by reason of its simplicity, and constitutes what I call the 'metaphysical world'. This also was seen by Parmenides and mentioned in the fragment recorded by Clement in his *Stromata*:[187] 'With your mind contemplate attentively what is absent as though it were present.'[188]

CHAPTER 9

Fifth special law: the term of thought endures

1363. We have seen that an *instant* is simply the beginning or term of what endures (whether it is an ens or an act of an ens). There can be no instant therefore without duration. An instant can be conceived only as the limit of duration and in duration, in the way that a mathematical point is the term of a line and conceived only in the line and by means of the line.

---

[184] *Strom.*, 5, p. 652.
[185] Οὐ γὰρ ἀποτμήξει τὸ ἐον τοῦ ἐόντος ἔχεσθαι.
[186] Theodoretus, *Therapeut.*, Serm. 1, p. 13.
[187] Clem. Alex., *Strom.*, 5, p. 552.
[188] Λεῦσσε δ'ὅμως ἀπέοντα νόῳ παρεόντα βεβαίως.

Believing that there is an ens which can exist for a single instant is a base illusion of those who have not formed an accurate concept of an instant. Such an ens would have no duration whatsoever because the instant would not have any duration, and what does not endure is not an ens.

1364. The Italian schools of *Magna Graecia* noted this important truth and from it deduced the principle of cognition. Let us see the controversies it caused.

Parmenides distinctly expressed 'the principle of cognition' in the following verse preserved by Simplicius[189] and by Proclus:[190] 'You do not know non-being, because it cannot be,'[191] and in another fragment, also preserved by Simplicius:[192] 'It cannot be spoken, nor can the mind reflect on it. It is nothing,'[193] which is a principle so obvious and so patently in agreement with common sense that only an extremely corrupt sophistry could refute it. The first and most famous Italian philosophers therefore made the 'principle of cognition' the firm foundation of their philosophy.

1365. But as soon as they applied it, they encountered great difficulties. They understood that if some *ens* is the only object of thought, its qualities and conditions must be investigated. This investigation is necessary if we are to know whether something expressed in a proposition is thinkable or not, that is, whether it is or is not, whether the proposition says something or nothing, and whether what we believe we are thinking is an appearance or a truth.

Unity and *duration* were among the first properties which they saw. They concluded that anything which is not *one* and *does not endure* is nothing, and cannot be the object of thought. I will deal here only with *duration*, as I have already spoken briefly about *one*.

These thinkers quickly found themselves with a result

---

[189] *Phys.*, 1, f. 25.

[190] *In Timaeo*, bk. 1.

[191] Οὔτε γὰρ ἂν γνοίης τό γε μὲ ἐόν, – οὐ γὰρ ανυστόν.

[192] *Phys.*, 1, f. 34.

[193] Οὐ γὰρ φατὸν οὐδὲ νοητόν ἐστιν ὅπως οὐκ ἔστι , which Bessarion translsates as *Nec dici ore potest, nostra nec mente revolvi. Quod nihil est* (*Adv. Plat. Calumn*, 2).

repugnant to common sense. The philosophical concept of motion, as I have given it, was not yet established. The concept held by people in general and then uncritically taken up by the schools, supposes that motion takes place without interruption and through continuous change — the briefest interruptions which make it intermittent have escaped all sensible observation, at least up to the present. Common opinion, which follows what the senses present, could not even suspect these interruptions. Philosophers themselves did not suspect them because their reflection had not offered them any reason to do so. Later, motion was denied simply to avoid the embarrassment it caused philosophical systems, a fact which is not without its importance. But the problem was not solved; the appearance of continuous motion, which was undeniable, remained unexplained. It appeared more of an aberration than of a truth that harmonised with nature. Aristotle refuted the subtle arguments of Zeno without seeing that although they overthrew the continuity of movement, they did not harm movement itself according to its true concept.

The insuperable difficulty therefore that threw the whole field of philosophy into confusion was the following: 'If something continually changes state and each state has no duration of any kind, the thing can neither be conceived nor be an ens.' Peace returned only with the death of philosophy, when barbarism silenced the philosophical schools.

The ancient Ionians, who were limited to the study of nature and had not yet risen to the heights of metaphysics, were unaware of this great difficulty. Instead of finding the concept of continuous movement difficult, they supposed that life and intelligence must consist in continuous movement. Aristotle attributes this crude opinion to Thales, and after him, to Diogenes, Heraclitus and Alcmeon, in this passage:

> Thales, according to what is recorded about him, also considered the soul as something in motion. In his opinion, rock has a soul because it attracts iron. Diogenes and a few others thought the soul was air; according to them, there was nothing more subtle than air. Hence the soul knows and moves. Air, as principle of other things, knows; as very subtle, it moves. Heraclitus also holds that the soul is a principle; he says it is vapour which makes up

all things; totally incorporeal and continuously in movement. According to him, that which moves can BE KNOWN precisely BECAUSE IT MOVES. HE MAINTAINED, AND PEOPLE IN GENERAL HOLD, THAT THINGS WHICH ARE, ARE IN MOTION. Alcmeon, it seems, also judged the soul in the same way: the soul is immortal because similar to immortal beings. The reason is that the soul is always in movement like all divinities (the moon, sun, stars and heavens), which are continuously in motion.[194]

Between the first Ionians and their successors however there is a great divergence. Among the latter, Heraclitus, a compatriot of Thales, had already heard about the Italian metaphysicians' opposition to continuous motion. On the one hand he saw the difficulty of admitting that what moves is an ens, and on the other he was unable to relinquish the Ionian opinion that everything moves — his language became so obscure that he was nicknamed σκοτεινός. He granted that all things lay between ens and non-ens, and were continuously composed and decomposed, as we see in these two opinions preserved by Heraclides Ponticus in his work, *The Allegories of Homer*. The first is: 'Both gods and humans are mortal; as mortal they live out (they are or make) their death; as dying (they are or make) their life'; the second, 'We step and do not step into the same rivers; WE ARE AND ARE NOT.' This seems to mean that when human beings return to their origins, they are changed into gods and thus live the life of gods who are the origins. Becoming human, on the other hand, they acquire human life, and with this bring about the death of the gods because they cease to be origins. The second alludes to the perpetual transition of things, which this philosopher supposes (ῥοή).[195] It is clear therefore that Hegel's system, which has BECOMING as its principle, was obviously derived from Heraclitus' 'We are and are not'. But 'We are and are not' is a contradiction and therefore repugnant to ens; it

[194] Arist., *De Anima*, bk. 1. — θεός comes from the verb θέω, 'I run', which in its poetic form is θείω. This origin highlights the *astrolatry* of the first settlers in Greece.

[195] Plato, *Cratyl.*, ed. Bipont. p. 267. — According to Plato in the *Sophist*, Heraclitus stated that 'an ens is always dissipation and reconciliation' or as Ficinus translates, 'What is breaking up always comes together' (*dissidens semper congreditur*).

necessarily destroys ens, whose origin is now nothing! This crazy, absurd system, if it can be called system, has been dubbed, not inappropriately, NIHILISM.[196]

1366. How then did the minds of these pseudo-philosophers arrive at such absurdities by which thought destroys the universe? By starting from two common concepts, from two prejudices unworthy of philosophy: 1. movement is continuous; 2. sensism.

Experience certainly tells us that all bodies move. Granted therefore 1. that all bodies move and nothing stays still, 2. that the movement is continuous, and 3. that nothing is known except through feeling and that, as a consequence of the principle of sensism, the only entia that fall under our perception and knowledge are bodies, then all known entia are continuously changing and their states have no endurance whatsoever: they ARE NOT but continuously BECOME. Now that which *becomes* is not; therefore no entia exist in the *universe*. This is Hegelian *nihilism*, which is highly logical in deducing consequences, but basely defective in its uncritical acceptance of the false principles on which it is based.

1367. Today, modern physicists accept that the whole corporeal world is in movement; we need only read Boyle's book to be convinced of that. But what I find strange is that Leibniz's great, energetic mind accepted the *continuity* of movement without even suspecting the insuperable difficulties involved, or glimpsing its most unfortunate consequences. I think this was the effect of his vivid imagination, which readily furnished him with hypotheses. He embraced these so willingly and impetuously that he often missed links in the chain of his reasoning.[197]

---

[196] Sextus Empiricus reports that Democritus refers to a certain Xeniades of Corinth, whose dates are unknown. This Xeniades was precisely of the opinion that everything came from non-ens and continuously returned to non-ens (he was thus one of the first authors of nihilism): ἐκ τοῦ μὴ ὄντος πᾶν τὸ γιγνόμετον γίγνεσθαι, καὶ εἰς τὸ μὴ πᾶν τὸ φθειρόμενον φθείρεσται (Sext. Emp., *Adv. Math.*, 7: 53, 388–389; Pyrrho, *Hypot.*, 2: 18.

[197] For example, to defend Locke against the Cartesian opinion that 'the soul always thinks', Leibniz said, 'I maintain that a substance cannot naturally be inactive, and even that there are no bodies without movement' (*Nouveaux essais sur l'Intendement humain* etc. bk. 1). It is true that no substance can be inactive, in so far as it necessarily has at least a primal, immanent act.

1368. But let us return to the debates of the ancient philosophers. They sailed between two hazards. On the one hand, the opinion that all things were in continuous change was driven forward by the invincible logic of Heraclitus and came to grief on the obvious absurdity that anything moving in this way does not exist. This great dialectician was hounded by opponents whose principle was: 'There is no ens without duration'. On the other hand, to deny motion (whose concept seemed at that time to involve the idea of continuity) and consequently continual generation and destruction of beings which fall under our senses, meant at least the renuntiation of common sense, a most authoritative judge. More probably, though, such denial would incur mockery and derision. The early philosophers of Mileto thus accepted continuous change and unsuspectingly followed the appearance of the senses, like the commonalty. But then came Parmenides who established the principle proffered by the idea of ens, 'That which has no duration does not exist'. With this principle to hand, he took to task those who thought that sensible phenomena were truths. Parmenides asserted that *reason* alone, the only potency whose object is truth, must be followed:

> Do not follow this way,
> Nor turn aside down the unsafe path
> Of mistaken practice of the common people.
> They put their trust in the blind eyes of the body,
> In deaf ears, or in the sound of the voice.
> You must judge and thoughtfully weigh
> This prudent reasoning I have given.[198]

To add that 'there are no bodies without movement' is a fatal step. If there were such bodies, it would be a truth of experience but never a consequence of the principle, because 1. movement of bodies is not a first, immanent act, relative to which alone the principle is true; and 2. movement cannot be said to be an action of bodies that are moved, but are not movers. The principle of movement has to be sought elsewhere, as we saw earlier, even though movement once imparted is communicated from one body to another according to certain laws. Hence Leibniz jumps from the metaphysical principle of the activity of substances to the entirely empirical necessity that bodies move.

[198] Cf. Karsten, vv. 52, 56. Simplicius (*In Phys.*, 1, f. 7) thinks that Parmenides, when speaking about those who accepted the simultaneity of being and non-being, was attacking Leucippus who posited two conjoint elements as the principles of things: *atoms*, which he called *being*, and the *void*, which he called *non-being*.

[1368]

Although Parmenides' argument was insoluble, it was not accepted for long, partly because he drew some extraordinary consequences from it, and partly because it was repugnant to the senses and the opinion of the multitude. People preferred to deny every truth and espouse scepticism and nihilism. Thus philosophy fell into the hands of the coarsest of sophists, of whom Protagoras was the most famous.

After Parmenides it became impossible for anyone with understanding to accept that what is perpetually subject to changes is an ens. Because the senses see only things subject to continuous change, people preferred to deny the existence of all things than to admit that the senses were mistaken in presenting continuous change. This, according to Plato, is the description given by Socrates of Protagoras' system and that of many others:

> Nothing one in itself is certain, nor can it be correctly called some determinate thing or nature. If you say something is big, it can in fact appear small, and if you say it is heavy, it can appear light. The same can be said about everything: there is nothing one, nothing that is something, nothing that is some kind of thing.[199] All things are composed of extension, motion and reciprocal actions and reactions. We call them existent but this is a mistake. NOTHING EVER IS, BUT ALWAYS BECOMES. All later sages, except Parmenides, agreed: Protagoras, Heraclitus, Empedocles,[200] together with all the greatest comic and tragic poets, Epicharmus, for example, in comedy and Homer in tragedy. When Homer said that Ocean was the father of the gods, and Tethys their mother, he proclaimed that all things are generated by flux and movement.[201]

This quotation from Plato is important because it tells us that:

---

[199] It is clear that Protagoras generalises what applies to corporeal, feelable things, and applies it to any ens whatsoever. He thus constructs an ontology which says nothing about the appurtenances of every ens or the essence of ens, but only about the appurtenances of a special ens which is phenomenal, relative, corporeal and sensible. This kind of *sensist ontology* is still deeply engrained in minds, and is the source of all modern errors, of all false systems and of all impediments to the progress of legitimate, true philosophy.

[200] Cf. Sturz, v. 34.

[201] *Theaetetus*, 69–70, ed. Bipont.

1. Parmenides, having formed the opinion that what exists must as an ens have the essential property of immobility and duration, denied generation and movement [*App.*, no. 12].

2. Except for a few of his first followers, he alone held this opinion.[202]

3. The philosophers who followed him could not on the one hand deny that duration is an essential property of an ens, and on the other did not want to deny continuous change, that is, generation and movement. Lacking the drive to rise above the senses and oppose common sense which accepted continuous change, they were forced to deny ens, that is, to deny that anything truly exists, and fell into nihilism.

4. Denying the existence of anything was a blow to that very common sense for the sake of which they had believed in continuous change. Hence, Protagoras and his fellow sophists, after deducing the extreme consequences of their system, were forced to hide from the commonalty. A few lines earlier in *Theaetetus*, Plato says that Protagoras spoke in two ways: to his closest followers he openly declared himself a sceptic and nihilist; to others he talked ambiguously to conceal such a repugnant absurdity.[203]

5. Finally we learn that Plato was the first to attempt to show expressly how Parmenides' teaching (if a thing is to exist it must endure) could be held without denying common sense about continuous movement. Things that ARE (ideas) could be accepted together with other things that BECOME (things in flux which have *in themselves* continuous change). However, not even he could solve the problem of this very curious mystery that some things *become* and *are* not. He did not see that *continuity* of change, which causes such great difficulty, was a false supposition, unsupported by any reason and

---

[202] It is extraordinary that Plato makes no mention of Anaxagoras. He says, with characteristic Attic irony, that all *wise men* (πάντες οἱ σοφοί), so-called to distinguish them from philosophers (φιλόσοφοι), upheld the nihilism of Protagoras. Yet Anaxagoras was the first to admit the unity and simplicity of the mind (ὁ νοῦς μόνος αὐτὸς εφ'ἑωῦτοῦ ἐστιν, *Fragm.*, ed. Schaubac., p. 110). Plato's silence on Anaxagoras was perhaps due to the fact that Anaxagoras did not sufficiently develop his concept, or did not deal strictly speaking with the general, ontological question raised by Parmenides.

[203] *NE*, vol. 2, 1127–1131.

accepted gratuitously as a result of phenomenal illusion [*App.*, no. 13]. And I see no evidence that he saw that the *continuum* is in fact rooted in the simplicity and unity of the sentient principle.

1369. Moreover, simply by reading the fragments we have of Parmenides, we can easily see that they contain nothing about the doctrine of ideas as it has come to us from Plato whose Parmenides seems to lead to the same conclusion. Socrates is the first to introduce the argument about species or ideas into the dialogue when he discusses the matter with Zeno, a disciple of Parmenides.[204] Zeno and his master seem to show some contempt for the formidable reasoning of the young Socrates. The fragments of Parmenides' poem definitely indicate three systems: 1. that which accepts only ens (the Eleatic system); 2. that which accepts only non-ens, that is, sensible things subject to continuous change (an opinion widespread in Ionian philosophy and ultimately the system of Protagoras and the sophists); and 3. that which accepts both ens and non-ens (Plato, Aristotle and their followers, who attempted a reconciliation between what is eternal and what is generable). At the beginning of his poem, Parmenides speaks of the first two systems as the principal and most precise, and the only well-defined systems at his time:

> Listen and take note of what I say.
> I will tell you the only ways open to thought.
> One way is the mother of persuasion,
> And truth discerns it.
> Its motto is 'That which is, and cannot not be'.
> The other way proclaims 'That which is not, nor can be',
> A way which, I affirm, is totally wrong.[205]

He then subdivides the second way, whose characteristic is to admit non-ens, into two, that is, the system of those who admit only non-ens and deny ens, and of those who claim that non-ens can be admitted simultaneously with ens:

> First, withhold your mind from this way of investigation,
> (a way that admits non-ens, which is nothing).

[204] Page 76 ss., ed. Bipont.
[205] Cf. Karsten, vv. 33–38.

Then from the way down which mortals wander uncertainly,
Their minds, deaf, blind, weighed down by stupor,
Creating inconstant doubt in their hearts;
An insane race of people, for whom
Being and non-being are the same and different.[206]

Parmenides is describing popular, common sense which, because it admits simultaneously that which endures and does not endure, trusts the senses. It makes no distinction at all between that which truly is and that which, through continuous flux, only appears to be so.

1370. The Eleatic teaching however does not come from a single principle but from the two following principles: 1. that which continuously changes and does not endure is not ens, and 2. ens cannot come from nothing.

So far I have spoken about all the teaching Parmenides deduced from the first principle, a teaching which shows that the sensible world, because *continuously changeable* (as everybody supposed), was appearance, non-ens.

1371. From the second principle he deduced other properties of ens: it is *eternal*, *necessary*, the *all* (because nothing could be outside it) and the *universe* which was called 'BEING, one and unmoved.'[207] In a word, he deduced all the pantheism of enophanes. We can see therefore what he had taken from his master and what he had added himself: directly from Xenophanes came the teaching deduced from the principle *a nihilo nihil fit* [nothing is made from nothing]; the teaching about the *necessary duration* of ens was apparently his own, as we can surmise from the fragments we have of these two philosophers, and particularly from Aristotle's book, *Xenophanes, Zeno and Gorgias*.

Indeed, the sole principle that ens must *endure*, that is, be in continuous change, does not in any way allow us to draw the consequence that there is a *single ens, eternal*, the *all*, etc. On the other hand, if we are to demonstrate that several entia exist in fact, we must prove that sensible things have duration. To do this, we must overcome deeply ingrained prejudice about the

---

[206] Vv. 45–51. Although Simplicius presents the passage in the sequence shown, a few lines seem to be missing between verses 44 and 45.

[207] Οἷον ἀκίνητον τελέθειν τῷ παντὶ ὄνομ' εἶναι.

continuity of motion, or more generally about continuous change, which is what I have tried to do.[208]

CHAPTER 10

Sixth special law: the term of total, complex thought can never be indefinite

1372. *Finite* is that than which something greater can be thought.

1373. *Infinite*, absolutely speaking, is that than which nothing greater can be thought.

1374. The *infinite* must not be confused with the *indefinite*.[209]

---

[208] Aristotle attributes the Eleatics' error to their having seen only that which is *ens per se*, which is one, and not having distinguished between *simple ens* (*simpliciter ens*, τὸ ἁπλῶς ὄν) and *potential ens* (τὸ κατα δύναμιν), between *ens in potency* (τὸ δυναμει ὄν) and *ens in act* (τὸ ἐνεργέιᾳ). His argument however is a vicious circle. The Eleatics did not admit these distinctions, precisely because they were establishing (or thought they were establishing) the absolute unicity of ens. Not even Aristotle therefore could destroy their arguments because he himself 1. held the *continuity* of change in nature, without suspecting that it had to be rejected, and 2. did not know that the first cause could not produce transient acts in itself, but of necessity produced them outside itself. This was creation, a concept which really destroys Xenophanes' principle.

[209] Ancient languages did not make this distinction, which is so necessary in philosophy. The Latin word *infinitum* means both that than which we cannot think anything greater, and that than which we can always think something greater without determining the amount. The Greek πεπερασμένον means both what is limited and what is not indefinite or indeterminate, although nothing greater than it can be thought. Hence Parmenides applies this epithet to *ens*, although he calls it ἄναρχον, ἄπαυστον and acknowledges nothing outside it. By calling it πεπερασμένον, he clearly intended to exclude indetermination. Melissus, on the other hand, a philosopher of the same school, calls it ἄπειρον, which also has a double meaning: it expresses both that which has limits, but indeterminate limits (the indefinite), and that which naturally has no limits because nothing limits or circumscribes it in such a way that some addition is possible. This explains why these two philosophers are in apparent contradiction. Aristotle himself, possibly following his usual practice of understanding preceding philosophers literally, takes Melissus' *infinite* in the sense of *indefinite*, and therefore commends

That which is indefinite can always receive a further increase; it has no fixed measure because it is considered susceptible of a continuously increasing series. Hence *that which is indefinite* does not express an ens but an abstract idea, for example, the generic idea of *number*. This idea corresponds to all numbers which, no matter how large, can always be increased by a unit. Clearly, an *ens* can never be *indefinite*, because what is abstract (formed by abstraction strictly understood) is not an ens but, as we saw, an object of abstractive reflection, something seen by the spirit. This reflection limits our attention to a quality of an ens and always presupposes in the mind information about the ens from which the abstraction is made and in which what has been abstracted is seen.

1375. I have been accused of accepting a universal, indeterminate and abstract being (ideal being) as the first object of intuition, but I have explained my opinion in many places. For example, in *A New Essay* I said the following about universality and indetermination:

> There is nothing that can be *universal in itself*. Everything, in so far as it is, is particular and determined. A *universal*, therefore, is something through which many things, or rather an indefinite number of things, can be known. Universality is purely a *relationship* present solely in ideas which, as we have seen, are things with which we know an indefinite number of things. This number is called 'species'.[210]

Again it is said that I attribute abstraction to the idea of being. But in *A New Essay* I explained as follows:

> When in the course of this work I call ideal being in general *most abstract*, I do not mean that it has been produced by the operation called abstraction, but simply that of its own nature it is set apart and separate from ALL SUBSISTENT BEINGS.[211]

But I think it a waste of time to go on recalling what is already in print. I would simply refer those who honour me with their

Parmenides for having called the all, that is, ens, *finite* in his condemnation of Melissus (*Physic.*, 3, 1).

[210] *NE*, vol. 2, fn. 139.

[211] *NE*, vol. 3, 1455.

objections to many other places in my works. I am convinced that the public and I would best be served if critics were more attentive in their severe judgment. Let me add a few new considerations, or considerations presented in a new way.

1376. Is it possible for us to think of the abstract idea of colour without knowing some particular colour, or to think abstractly of sound without ever having known a particular sound, and so on for all other sensible things? I do not think so. Note, I do not induce this from experience alone, but from the intimate nature of colour, sound, taste, etc. In fact, abstract colour, abstract sound or abstract taste simply mean that which is common to particular sensations of colour, sound, taste, etc. Now, that which is common, purely common, to several things and not proper to each, cannot be thought without reference in some way to the particular things in which it resides.

Is this also true of being in general? — At first sight, it seems so, because being in general is extremely common to everything that is particular and real. But closer examination shows that this is not the case. Being in general is not *purely common* in such a way that it excludes what is *proper*. Rather, it includes what is proper in a common way. Ideal *being* is that which is realised not only in the substance of things but in accidents as well; not only in what is generic and abstract-specific to things, but what is full-specific, that is, proper to them. Consequently ideal being extends to the whole of an ens and to all that is in it (although not in the same way); it is not purely a common element of the ens to the exclusion of what is proper to it. *Ideal being* has an entirely different nature from abstractions. These express only what is generic or abstract-specific to an ens, and exclude differences. Abstractions cannot exist entirely on their own, contemplated by thought, without their seeking some support in perceptions or in the full species which perceptions leave in the spirit; abstractions alone are not ideas of entia. On the contrary, the idea of an ens has eminently and essentially the characteristic by which it reveals an ens together with all that it must have in itself to be an ens, although a part of this 'all' which the ens must have is only virtually contained in it.

This first difference gives rise to a second difference which shows the supreme diversity between *abstractions* strictly speaking and *ideal being in general*. Abstractions express something about an ens, something which does not have and cannot have its own act of existence. In fact no abstraction, considered in itself, could supply an artist with the model for a statue or with the sketch for a painting. The act of being is outside what is abstract, or certainly made impossible by it. No one can ever conceive any act of being proper to an abstract colour or sound, or even to an abstract substance (excluding the accidents). On the contrary, the idea of being is precisely that which manifests every act of being; its object lacks nothing for its intuition by thought. As I have noted, thought neither determines anything special in the idea of being, nor excludes anything; on the contrary, it presupposes and demands something special, and expects to find it whenever opportune.

The characteristics of *ideal being* and of *abstractions* are not therefore the same, but rather total opposites. Ideal being, precisely as the idea of an ens and conceivable by itself, has everything to constitute an ens. Abstractions on the other hand lack and even exclude many things necessary for the ens to which they relate; as such, they cannot be an object of complex but only of partial thought, of abstracting reflection.

1377. This enables us see what is true and what is false in the teaching of Stewart and other nominalists. They maintain that abstractions are only *names* which the mind uses to pass freely from one particular idea to another. As an example they point to the use which algebraists make of the letters of the alphabet for their calculations. But these philosophers are mistaken:

1. They do not see that an idea, although revealing an ens with all its conditions and accidental qualities, is *universal*, and can be called *particular* only when considered in the perception joined to it. This condition is extrinsic to the idea and relative to the spirit that joins it to the perception. Although an idea is naturally *universal*, it is not naturally *abstract*, because it can manifest everything that can occur in an ens. We can think of ideal being, that is, a non-abstract *ideal being*, without having to think of a *subsistent being*. We do not need signs to think of a non-abstract being, that is, a *full idea* which must be either given to our spirit by nature or extracted by the spirit from perception. Names are by no means necessary for this.[212]

[212] *NE*, vol. 2, 514–427.

1378. 2. Abstract ideas cannot be thought by the mind if *full-ideas*, to which abstract ideas are related, are totally lacking to the mind. However, it is sufficient for *full-ideas* to be present in the mind without the spirit's giving them any attention. In fact, as we saw, abstraction is simply concentration and limitation of the mind's attention on some quality present in the full-idea, to the exclusion of everything else in it. The psychological fact that ideas, or part of them, can exist in the mind without the mind's attention is certain and of supreme importance. Such ideas are continuously intuited but without our advertence, or without advertence to one rather than another. We can therefore pass freely and with varying ease from an abstract idea to awareness of the full ideas to which it relates[213] — this is the truth seen or glimpsed by our nominalists. However, when they said that an abstraction was nothing in the mind, but purely a sign outside the mind, they made a mistaken induction from the fact that an abstraction can be thought in the mind without the full-idea (which they confused with a particular idea). This mistake was also the result of the following.

1379. 3. To ask 'What is necessary for an idea to be *thought* or thinkable?' is one question; to ask 'What is necessary for a person to *form* an idea or be able to form and think it?' is another. An abstraction is thinkable when the mind has the full-idea to which the abstraction relates and from which it is taken. For the spirit to move to this act, it must be propelled by an object, term or motive, because its activity is always aroused by the term. But an abstraction, purely as such, does not exist and therefore cannot draw the spirit to itself. On the other hand, if the abstraction is joined to a sensible sign, it can stimulate and activate the mind's attention towards itself. I have already used this fact to prove the usefulness of language, or better, of signs for forming abstractions. This usefulness

---

[213] Note that when we perceive with our different sensory organs a corporeal ens and acquire the full idea of it, we do not need to clothe the corporeal ens with all its sensible qualities but simply with those found in each perception of this ens. A perception is always limited to a single sensation. The fact that we understand how an ens given us by several perceptions of the same sensory organ or by several organs, is identical, results from the association of sensations and perceptions through the identity of space, and through reasoning. Cf. *NE*, vol. 2, 941–960.

consists solely in presenting to the spirit a stimulus and term which moves it to concentrate and fix its attention in the way I have explained at greater length in *A New Essay*, and which I will again discuss further on.[214] Nominalists erred because this fact too escaped their observation. They moved from the usefulness of language to the *formation* of abstractions, and concluded that abstractions were nothing in themselves and therefore could not be formed or thought without the signs of language.

1380. 4. Finally the example they used to confirm their teaching (the use made by the algebraists of the letters of the alphabet), far from proving their teaching, proves its contrary. Indeed the meaning given to the letters of the alphabet by the algebraist is one thing; the truth he wishes to establish with their use is another. Algebraic symbols certainly indicate abstract quantities (a discrete quantity, even when determinate, remains an abstraction). However, the algebraist does not use them simply to indicate these quantities, but to discover their relationships.

What in fact is his intention when he writes $a + b$, and $d - c$? In the first case he wants to express the relationship of addition between any two quantities (abstract and indeterminate) indicated by the two letters a and b. In the second case he wants to express the relationship of subtraction between any two quantities indicated by the two letters d and c. When he makes an equation between the two functions of $a + b$ and $d - c$ $\{(a + b) = (d - c)\}$, he finds that $a = d - (c + b)$, that is, that the value of a equals the value of d less the sum of c and b. When performing this task, his mind directed its attention to the relationship of equality between the two functions, and the result of his attention was to join them with the sign of equality. He then directed his attention to the result, which was a discovery of the value of a relative to the other three letters. If the algebraist made his calculation by directing his attention to the relationship, and after noting the relationship joined the letters with various signs, it is clear that before he put the signs on paper, his mind thought of the *relationship* and the results, and that he wrote down the signs expressing the relationships only after he had

[214] *Loc. cit.*

thought of the latter. In other words, he had thought of the relationships without their signs; these followed as a result of the relationships already thought by his mind. But *relationships* are themselves abstractions, far superior to the simple quantities involved.

The use of algebraic signs therefore clearly demonstrates that abstractions are *thinkable per se* without the need of signs. This use would in fact be impossible if a mind did not think of abstractions without signs. Their use implies that the mind already possesses abstractions at a very high level, but does not in any way explain how the mind formed them, and much less does it answer the question 'What is necessary for abstractions to be thinkable?' Signs simply help the mind to keep its attention on a series of relationships, which because of its length and multiplicity would easily be lost.

CHAPTER 11

Seventh special law: the term of complex thought is something finite or something infinite. Neither can be changed into the other

1381. An ens cannot be indefinite. That which is indefinite does not have everything necessary for it to be an ens, and therefore on its own cannot be an object of thought. However, although an ens can never be indefinite,[215] it can be finite or infinite.

1382. A careful examination of this law shows us that *finiteness*

---

[215] How then do I say that ideal being, which essentially constitutes the object of the mind, is *indeterminate*? — It is not indeterminate in itself, but relative to contingent realities. It is a means of knowing these realities but makes one known only when it receives some addition of feeling. The *indetermination* of being is not a quality proper to being but an enduring indeterminate relationship with contingent things; it is an indetermination foreign to being. For example, a portrait which showed a great likeness to several people is said to be indeterminate, although not indeterminate in itself. Similarly, if the person portrayed is unknown, we say the portrait is indeterminate, although the portrait itself is always determinate whether the original is known or not.

or *infinitude* is an ontological quality so proper to an ens that if the quality is removed, the ens loses its identity. A finite ens, no matter how much it increases or multiplies, will never change its nature; it will always remain finite. On the other hand, an infinite ens can never be divided in such a way that it becomes finite. If our mind could distinguish several things in what is infinite, each would have to be infinite and contain all the others virtually or in act, with or without advertence.

1383. There is another consequence. If we think of the infinite, we must think of it as a whole or not at all. Although we can think of it in a *limited way*, this limitation must be attributed solely to the *way* in which we think of it, not to the object of thought. A subject thinking of an infinite ens knows he cannot think of the ens totally; in other words, he knows that the nature of the ens extends without confine or measure far beyond what he apprehends. Moreover, he knows that, although the thing occupying his thought contains everything, its totality appears only implicitly or virtually. The reason lies in the *way* in which the subject knows: just as a person with weak sight will not see a human being as perfectly as someone with excellent sight, although both see the whole human being.

1384. The matter will be clearer if we consider that the object of thought is: 1. ideal ens which, as we saw, cannot be measured, and 2. real ens, which can be measured.

We therefore have two questions:

1. 1. How is it possible for us to think of infinite ideal ens? — I reply: the fact itself shows how we think of it. Anyone who reasonably examines ideal being sees immediately that its extremely simple infinity admits no division or splitting. The question therefore is not even possible. Instead we should ask: 'When we think of ideal ens, why must we think of it as infinite?'; the reply however would be the same: ideal ens is perfectly simple and one.

1385. 2. How can we think of a real infinite ens? I reply: that which is infinite and real is the same ens seen in the idea under the form of reality. But if it is not absurd to see what is ideal and infinite, it is not absurd to be able to see what is real and infinite, because it is the same one perfectly simple ens as that intuited in an ideal ens.

1386. These replies, although sufficient for those who

thoroughly understand them, are susceptible of further helpful development.

The perceptions which most attract our attention are those of bodies and other contingent things. Our reasoning about the perception of what is real is founded on the example of bodies, etc., as if there were no other way of perception. But taking bodies as an example will never explain the perception of the infinite. This is why it is so difficult for us to understand perception in the supernatural order.

We perceive bodies through the real *action* they exercise on us. Hence, what we think in their concept is a mixture of *subjective* and *extrasubjective* elements. This corporeal ens, composed partly of our feeling and partly of something acting in our feeling, is not the object *per se* of our thought, but is thought of *in* the object. The object is foreign but the mind unites it to the corporeal ens as a necessary means of knowledge.

Once more, if we consider perception of ourselves in so far as we are a substantial feeling, we see that the thought contained in this perception is purely of a *subject*, which we objectivise in order to perceive it. The subject however is finite, so that everything known about it or its modifications or the agent modifying it, can only be finite. What is finite can feel in itself only a finite *modifying* action; the modification itself must also be finite.

Furthermore, the perceiving *subject*, that is, ourselves, is multiple. Nothing therefore that we perceive as a passion or modification of what is multiple, and as an immediate agent or cause of this modification, can be perceived as something totally one and simple; it must be perceived with some multiplicity. In fact multiplicity is found wherever there is limit. Consequently that which is infinite, to which supreme unity and simplicity pertain, cannot be perceived as a modification of ourselves or as the force that directly produces the modification.[216] If this kind of perception existed, perception of the infinite would be inexplicable. But there is another kind.

Infinite ens is essentially *object*. Nothing subjective can occur in the perception of what is infinite. To be object means that we know the object by distinguishing and separating it from ourselves and putting it in counterposition to ourselves. What is

---

[216] *NE*, vol. 2, 672–691.

infinite is perceived simply as *ens*; it neither produces a *passion* in the subject nor is perceived as *agent*. The transient acts it may cause cannot be confused with it; they are outside it and do not in any way constitute the concept. The object therefore is not confused with the subject but intuited and perceived in itself; nor can the subject impose any limit or multiplicity on the object.[217] In perceiving the object, the subject does not receive the latter as an agent; it simply sees the object distinct from itself. The subject, in perceiving the object, does not need to impart its own measurements, as in the case of contact where a part which touches is measured by the part touched; in our case, the subject attributes nothing of its own limitation to the object. This explanation overcomes the difficulty and repugnance present in understanding that a finite ens perceives an infinite ens (in the supernatural order, of course), and topples Protagoras' principle: 'Man is the measure of all things'.[218]

1387. This manner of perceiving objectively is certainly mysterious. There is no other example of it in all the perceptions of finite things from which we arbitrarily draw the law of perception. But the fact is nevertheless undeniable, and we have an example of it in nature: the intuition of ideal being. The fact, which must be admitted despite its apparent mystery relative to our normal way of reasoning, contains nothing repugnant to the human mind; as I said, it is merely contrary to our habit of reasoning. The contemplative mind, rising above habits of this kind, which limit the sphere of reasoning, will see the fact as evident and so necessary that without it none of our mental operations can be explained — all thought, of any kind, would be impossible.

1388. It is true that afterwards the subject derives a feeling of delight and happiness from his perception of the infinite. This feeling, which is so special that it cannot be confused with other

---

[217] *Rinnovamento*, bk. 3, c. 47.

[218] Note, the *intellective principle* as such is entirely actuated in the object and therefore receives from the object this unique condition: as an intellective principle it cannot act nor even suffer from another agent, but can only intuit, know. If it acts, it does so because it is sensitive as well as intellective (this explains why it is called rational). Its action, regulated by what it knows, can also consist in the enjoyment of what it knows.

feelings, makes the subject understand that its source is infinite. Although an effect of the objective perception and closely bound with it, the feeling is not the perception itself and can never be confused with it. The feeling is finite but appears to be infinite because indivisible from the objective perception. In the unity of the human being the objective perception is joined with this feeling in such a way that the perception forms, as it were, its completion and apex.

Granted therefore the objective perception united with the feeling produced in the subject by the perception; granted again the whole formed by this communication of the infinite with the finite, it follows that knowledge of the infinite is both infinite and finite. It is infinite relative to the intuited, perceived *object*, and finite relative to the *feeling* it produces in the subject.

1389. For the same reason we are fully justified in saying that those who perceive God's glory in heaven perceive God *whole* but not *wholly*. The *object* is all God, but the feeling which the object produces in them is not the whole *action* which God could cause to be felt. The whole of God is perceived as *ens* but not totally as *agent*. But I must explain how God can be *agent* in the intelligent creatures who perceive him.

1390. The concept of God as *agent* in the subjects that perceive him can be falsified in two ways. In the first, God is seen as doing nothing; only the subject acts, deriving from the infinite object of his perception the joyous feeling which makes him happy. In the second, God is seen as acting subjectively in the subject, similar to the way in which finite *entia* act in human beings and simply modify them.

Granted therefore that God as perceived acts supremely in the person who perceives him and that God in acting does not immediately *modify* the subject, what kind of action is this in the finite subject which is proper to God alone but does not consist in producing a simple modification or passion?

When I say *modification* or *simple passion*, I mean that the substance of the subject is neither changed nor increased, still less produced; it remains quantitively what it was, but in a new mode. In other words (and this expresses the concept better), the agent simply modifies but does not produce the substance, which is seen as already produced and capable of receiving in itself the agent's action. Divine action however is always performed by means of a kind of creation,[219] that is, with an action which posits an ens with its nature and quantity, but does not suppose a pre-existing subsistent ens in which the divine action can take place.

I say this because God as the cause of every ens makes everything with one perfectly simply act. The accidents (no matter how short lived) are posited at the same time as the substance; they are not produced by a different act. If God did otherwise, his action would contradict not only the unity and simplicity of the act with which he does all that he does, but also the perfect simplicity of his substance.[220] His substance and his action are the same; in creatures, substance and acts are different. We have in fact seen that transient acts can occur in created substances and that God can be the cause of transient acts. These, however, which can never occur in him, must remain clearly distinct from him. In created natures, on the other hand, *activities* are distinct from *substance* so that when one acts in another, it does so with its activity alone, not with its substance; the activity of one can modify only the activity of the other, but never produce substance itself. If therefore God were the direct agent in already existing substances, he would not create them but modify their activities. His activity but not his divine substance would enter into contingent substances, because what is passive and modified never receives substance but only activity from what acts and modifies. In this case, there would be a real division in God between his action and his being, which is absurd. God can act only by means of creation, that is, by creating at every moment the whole of a contingent ens together with all its modifications. It would also be absurd to say that God entered with his substance into an ens which is not. Substance can never be received in an ens which acts as patient.

Granted all this therefore, it will no longer be difficult to understand how God as perceived can act, and act supremely, in anyone who perceives him.

---

[219] *Teodicea*, 547–548.

[220] When I apply the words 'substance', 'action', etc., to God, I do not mean that these concepts are in God as they are in creatures. I use the words in the sense given by theologians, which was illustrated particularly in the book *De' divini nomi* and in the works of St. Thomas.

Two things occur in this fact:

1. The intelligent subject, to whom the perception of God is given and who possesses God as *object* of his intellect, can with his own activity cling to and enjoy God with all his strength in loving contemplation.

2. At the same time the measure of the strength with which he enjoys God is allocated to him by God as his Creator, that is, as the cause which produces him totally with all his acts of enjoyment.

1391. The enjoyment is limited because it is an act of the subject (the act and the subject are created by God), but the *object* of the enjoyment is infinite. It is in this sense that God, because he is indivisible, is perceived as *a whole* and cannot be perceived otherwise. Nevertheless he cannot be perceived *wholly* in the good which the subject derives from him, because the nature of the subject, the strength of his nature and the acts of his strength are limited.

1392. Although what is enjoyed of God is always God because the whole of God is enjoyed, the limitation of the act with which the intelligent subject adheres to God is such that God seems to be divided. Indeed different subjects endowed with different strength enjoy God differently. All of them however enjoy the *infinite*. In this sense I said that 'infinite being or finite being pertains to ens, that is, to the object of thought', and that neither can be changed into the other. But because what is infinite is enjoyed in varying degree, it seems to be divided, diminished or increased in our concept when this takes as its measure the relationship between infinite ens and its enjoyment. This apparent diminution, however, never deprives what is infinite of its infinity. If it did, such an ens as object of the mind would immediately be something else.

1393. This also explains how God can be conceived (always in a negative or virtual way) under various concepts, as of subsistent wisdom, subsistent goodness, holiness, etc., because in each of these the infinite is always equally present. The multiplicity of concepts (except the concepts of the Persons) has its origin entirely in the subject and in the varied and many experiences he has of them through his own limitation and multiplicity.

1394. But because the perception of God pertains to the

supernatural order, a very difficult question arises: must the multiplicity of concepts under which the human being can think of God cease entirely in the beatific vision? I reply tentatively.

We should first note that, if we mentally divide something essential to God from the object of thought, the object is no longer God. It is essential to God that *subsistence* and *essence* are the same thing, the same perfectly simple being. The *essence* of being, separated from *subsistence*, is not God. By nature, human beings intuit only the essence of being, ideal being, and not its real subsistence. Consequently this essence cannot be called the essence of God. Hence human beings do not by nature intuit God. This is a truth which is proved equally by experience, reason and Christian faith. Indeed, we have simply to reflect upon ourselves to ascertain that there is naturally no divine subsistence in the human intellect, but only a pure idea of being. A large part of the human race will not only find that the natural object of their understanding is not the *subsistence* of being, but also that they cannot observe even its essence in themselves. If they had divine subsistence as the object of the their thought, it would be of such value that no one would be ignorant of it. On the other hand, reason shows that this need not be supposed in order to explain the actions of the human spirit. Furthermore, if we intuited God, beatitude would depend solely on our own will because we would possess its source, which is not the case. Finally, to say that human beings by nature see God is a MANIFEST ERROR CONTRARY TO CHRISTIAN FAITH, which reserves the vision of God to heavenly beings.

If on earth mankind is not granted to see the identity of the essence and subsistence of being and therefore not to see God, we must acquire knowledge of the supreme Being BY REASONING and not by direct intuition. This reasoning leads us to know that God is, but not the *mode* in which he is, concealed in his subsistence.[221]

In the beatific vision, however, where the subsistence of being is perceived, the connection of identity between the subsistence and the essence of being will be seen; this connection will reveal God. God will be seen *sicuti est* [as he is], when the imperfection

---

[221] *Teodicea*, 55–74.

of reasoning will come to an end *et scientia destruetur* [and knowledge shall be destroyed].

If we want to use reason to investigate whether the divine subsistence will appear to us devoid of all relationships with creatures, we must say, in my opinion, that it will be seen only in its creative relationship with creatures, not otherwise. God's infinite perfections will be contemplated in this relationship, as I have stated elsewhere.[222] But because his relationship with creatures is multiple (not on his part but on that of creatures who are multiple), his divine perfections will appear multiple, and different from the way they appear to us on earth. In our present state we cannot attain to the perfectly simple source of the divine perfections, where they identify with each other, and all identify with being. We shall do this in heaven. There, we will see that the divine perfections which appear in creatures now and hereafter as multiple, will in God be his perfectly simple essence alone. On earth we can see that this must be so, but *how* it is so remains a mystery because we find no example in nature. Thus, although we will be able, even in heaven, to use different concepts to express the divine being, we will see the same being in each concept. Their multiplicity will not prevent us in any way from seeing God as he is. We will see simultaneously how the divine perfection is diffused in many relationships and how there is one single, identical, primordial and essential perfection in all of them.

1395. Furthermore, when we think of a perfection in our present condition, for example, wisdom, we see it as limited. Only by 'eminent' *reasoning*, as the theologians call it, do we understand that this perfection must be unlimited in God. This is why I said that when we think of God as subsistent goodness, etc., the concept we form of him is virtual, not actual. In heaven we will not use reasoning to induce this necessity but see directly that the case is so, is a fact, because we will see wisdom as infinite and necessarily infinite; above all, we will understand directly how it can be so.

If then in heaven divine perfection appears to us as one (just as the one, identical centre of a circle is also the beginning and term of all the radii), each of the divine perfections will obviously be

[222] *Ibid.*, 660–698.

sufficient to make us know God as a whole. As the term or beginning of a single radius is sufficient to indicate the centre of the circle, so in each of the perfections we will always see the same infinite ens.

Thus, infinite ens, although seemingly divided through the various aspects under which it is considered, never ceases to be infinite ens. Infinity is a condition which pertains to infinite ens, just as finitude is a condition pertaining to finite ens. The law of thought which I have proposed is therefore valid.

CHAPTER 12

The ontological laws which govern practical reason in general

1396. After discussing the principal ontological laws which govern the rational principle in its actions, I must now discuss those governing the actions of practical reason.

According to me, practical reason is something more than the kind of reason (speculative) which determines what may or may not be done, what may or may not be fitting. Practical reason is a *rational, decision-making principle*[223] governed by the ontological laws under discussion.

1397. These laws must be the same as those governing theoretical reason (that is, reason in its first acts) whose subsequent acts pertain to practical reason. If these laws are lacking, reason is lacking. *Practical reason*, however, is *reason* because there is only one rational principle which as knowing is 'theoretical', as acting 'practical'.[224] Obviously, therefore, the laws applicable to speculation are also applicable to decision-making because they have their source in the nature of a common principle. In a word, theoretical reason becomes practical when it acts. But because it acts as knower, the laws governing it as knower must be those which govern its activity.

---

[223] Cf. *PE*, 1–14 and *Conscience*, 18–22.

[224] Cf. *Teodicea*, 161, concerning Kant's error: he made theoretical and practical reason two radically different faculties.

1398. These laws are *natural* to reason, just as the laws of the communication of motion are natural to bodies. But here a difficulty presents itself. Sensitive nature and even purely sensible nature always obey their laws. Why then does reason infringe them by falling into *error*, which is a violation of the laws of theoretical reason, and by falling into *sin*, which is a violation of the laws of practical reason? The simple reply that reason, being free, can infringe the laws, does not solve the difficulty. It merely states the fact which seems to contradict the concept of the law. On the one hand, the difficulty requires the contradiction to be eliminated; we have to demonstrate the existence of truly natural laws which can nevertheless be violated. On the other hand, the character of *natural law* seems to require the impossibility of its violation.

The solution to the difficulty will be found if we note that foreign agents subject to laws different from those of reason are involved in the actions of the rational principle. Violation of the laws of reason arises therefore from the collision between various laws of different character. This also explains the wonderful fact of human freedom, which I have already discussed,[225] and to which I will return after explaining the supreme law of practical reason.

CHAPTER 13
Continuation — The supreme law of practical reason: 'Acknowledge ens'

Article 1
Statement of the supreme law

1399. We must show that the principle of cognition which constitutes the supreme law governing theoretical reason also furnishes practical reason with the supreme law according to which *it must act*. Thus, if the law of theoretical reason is 'An

[225] *Teodicea*, 384–415.

ens is the object of knowledge', the law of practical reason is 'An ens must be the object of practical knowledge'.

We say that theoretical reason acts according to the principle of cognition because it either does not act at all or, if it does act, is bound to this principle. Even errors therefore must be attributed to practical reason, as we have seen.

On the other hand, we say that practical reason MUST act in conformity with the same principle because its action can be carried out in two ways, either in conformity with its law or not. If it acts in conformity with the law, it is upright; if not, it is wayward. This is precisely what is to be explained, as I said, but before giving an explanation, let me set out a few notions.

Article 2
Explanation and demonstration of the supreme law

1400. An insensitive ens is not a subject of good or bad. It acts according to its own necessary laws and always in an ordered way. Only human beings require it to act differently and, due to a kind of mysterious illusion, attribute bad and good to it. We do this by binding it to our own ideas, to which of course it is not bound. For example we say, 'This must be a pear, but it has been eaten by worms. It is bad.' The statement would indeed be true if the pear should have been perfect and possessed what is contained in the idea of pear, but it lacks this requirement. If we measure the pear against the *full-specific idea*, we would find it to be what it should be. On the other hand, measuring it against the *abstract idea* means we are considering in the object a relationship which enters into the constitution not of the pear's intrinsic order but of a hypothetical, extrinsic order linked to an idea imposed on it.[226] In short, matter, whatever its shape, is not a *subject* because a subject is always a *principle-ens*, while the concept of matter is solely that of *term-ens*.

1401. Sensitive entia and rational entia are however subject to good and bad.

The good proper to both consists in some activity to which

[226] *Teodicea*, 434–464.

[1400–1401]

their badness is also reduced. Each can have an activity which does or does not conform with its essence. If it conforms, it is in a good state; if not, it is in an bad state. The essence of the sentient principle requires the performance of its activity without its finding obstacles on the part of its term. If the principle encounters obstacles, pain results.

The same happens in the rational principle which, depending on the aim and endeavour of its essence, acts in a given way. If for any cause it does not act in this way, there is disorder. It suffers because, being feeling throughout, it must feel its own disorder.

1402. But if up to this point one formula suffices to express the good or poor state of the sensitive and rational principles, the infinite difference between what is good and bad for these two principles becomes apparent immediately. I must explain. The difference between good or bad in one principle and good or bad in the other is rooted in the difference of their terms, from which their activities originate and their nature is determined. As I said, good and bad proper to an ens which is susceptible of good and bad depends on the disposition of its activity.

The term of the sensitive activity is the *material, extended element* together with its passions; the term of the rational principle is an *ens*. Consequently sensitive activity is the seat of what is good for the sensitive ens, and takes place when it can diffuse its passions into the extended element in proportion to its instinct. Rational activity is the seat of what is good for the rational principle when, without any opposition or struggle, it adheres to its term which is ens. We now have the first law of reason: 'Adhere to an ens'.

1403. In fact the rational principle can never cease to be rational and therefore can never cease to have an ens as its term. If it has an activity of its own, as it certainly does, it is not purely receptive; this also must have an ens as its term. The law of this activity must come to it from the ens, according to the principle that every subject susceptible of good and bad possesses some good when it adheres perfectly to its term, and some bad when it fails to adhere to its term in the way required by its essence.

The rational principle therefore, whether purely receptive (called 'theoretical reason') or active (called 'practical reason'), must as one and the same principle have the same term from which it necessarily receives the laws of its operation.

Article 3
The moral freedom of practical reason

1404. But in so far as it is receptive, the rational principle receives purely in its own way, which is through intuition. Union with its term does not depend upon the principle precisely because it is receiver, not agent; union depends on the term itself, on the ens given to the intuition of the principle whose constitution is fixed and determined by a necessity foreign to it, that is, by that necessity which constitutes it as it is.

But as active, the rational principle itself posits its act. If an act is performed, the rational principle performs it; if not performed, the rational principle does not perform it; in other words, the rational principle is the cause. The necessity of this act can never be the same as the necessity of the principle's receptivity of an ens. Even if the activity of the rational principle were not carried out properly and uprightly, the principle would still be. However, it would not be, if it did not receive ens. Hence, the first difference between the rational principle as theoretical and the rational principle as practical is that while a first theoretical act is *necessary for the constitution of the principle, a practical act is not.*

As I said earlier, this fact alone would be sufficient to explain fully how the principle can deviate from its own *natural law.* The most complete explanation however is found by examining the nature of moral freedom, the way this potency is constituted, and the way it results from the collision of categorically opposed agents. But all these things have already been discussed and I must presume they are known to the reader.

Article 4
Specific difference between theoretical and practical acts of reason

1405. Because the word 'activity' is common to every ens, we must now examine the rational principle's own particular nature and kind of activity. We must first distinguish its activity from all other activities, and then from the primordial, receptive activity of theoretical reason.

A rational principle must be rational activity, that is, some way of knowing, but first knowledge is proper to theoretical reason. The activity of practical reason must therefore be another way of knowing, a way of knowing that takes pleasure in the known object, of appropriating the object and of discovering one's own good in it. Hence an *ens* relative to practical reason gains the notion of *good*.

1406. To indicate this active, lively knowledge I use the phrase 'practical acknowledgement'.

This act of practical reason is the first act of *will*.

The supreme law of theoretical reason is therefore the supreme law of practical reason. The difference is purely in the relationship of each reason to the *same* term: the relationship of theoretical reason is 'receptivity'; of practical reason, 'adherence'. I have explained both.

Article 5
Total thought and abstract thought considered in relationship to practical reason — The supreme rule of prudence

1407. What I have said about the supreme law of theoretical reason must be applied to practical reason.

First of all, I have distinguished between *total thought* and *abstract thought*. I noted that the latter can indeed draw our attention to itself and become the exclusive term of our attention. But it cannot exist alone in the human mind where *total thought* must always be present, even if neglected and unnoticed. Granted that 'an ens is the object of knowledge', there is clearly no knowledge unless all that is essential to an ens is in the mind, although one part of it can be in the mind in one way, for example, accompanied by attention, and the other part in another way, unaccompanied by any actual attention.

This teaching is extremely important in practice because practical reason contains a very noble rule, 'the supreme rule of prudence'.

[1406–1407]

1408. Attention, although energy pertaining to practical reason, is an activity influencing theoretical reason and strengthening its acts. As we shall see more clearly later, practical reason possesses an action which effects theoretical reason in various ways. But practical reason is already active at the start of attention, and the cognitions to which the spirit attends become more easily and efficaciously norms and principles of human action.

1409. Human beings can therefore direct their actions in two ways, either in conformity with what they know through *total, complex thought*, or exclusively in conformity with what they know through *partial, abstract thought*. If human actions correspond to complex, total thought, they are themselves complex and total; if their norm is abstract thought, they are defective and imperfect. It is here precisely that we find the supreme rule of prudence, which can be stated positively as: 'Act in keeping with total thought' or negatively: 'Be careful not to act according to partial, abstract thought.'

1410. However we must bear in mind that acting according to the norm of complex, total thought can be of two kinds of varying perfection. If thought is total but without analysis and abstraction, action, although substantially prudent, will lack some accessory element. The action will be imperfect in its accidents. The result is two degrees of prudence: the prudence of those who act according to complex, total thought but without analysis and abstractions; the other, more perfect, of those who act according to both total and abstract thought. They do not take abstract thought alone but unite it with total thought, that is, they consider the abstractions as joined to the objects on which the abstractions were made.

1411. I will not develop this teaching any further, although it is of supreme importance. The reader can find a most enlightening example of its efficacy in the way I have applied it to political prudence in *Society and its Purpose*,[227] where I called the faculty of total, complex thought simply *faculty of thought*, and the other faculty, faculty of abstraction.

1412. This general rule gives rise to the more special rule, 'When acting, keep to the substance and never sacrifice it to the

[227] 839–843.

accidents,' which I discussed in another work.[228] Substance, which is the first act of every *ens*, must be present in the object of total thought; it can be lacking only in abstract thought.[229]

Article 6
Application of the supreme rule to the different generic acts of theoretical reason in relationship to practical reason; first, to intuition — The law inclining human beings to contemplation

1413. Theoretical reason has various acts which I reduced to three: *intuition*, *perception* and *reflection*. Similarly the laws which govern these different acts must be reproduced or have their corresponding laws in *practical reason*, which I must now discuss.

1414. The object of intuition is an *ens*, a total *ens*, but under the ideal form. The only way in which we can enjoy and unite ourselves to an ideal *ens* is by contemplation. The law proper to practical reason is therefore the *inclination to contemplation* of the idea which, according to different relationships, becomes truth, type, beauty, etc. Every *inclination* proper to an *ens* is a law of its action because its action, and its activity in general, is in a good state when in conformity with its essential, natural inclination.

1415. Certain conditions are required if the inclination to the contemplation of ideas is to be activated. Without these conditions natural intuition lacks the effort for activity and remains theoretical, not practical.

1416. The single, principal condition is 'the comparison between a real *ens* and an ideal *ens*'; properly speaking a real *ens* is the term of *rational* activity. But because every real being is given to the rational principle by means of the idea and in the idea, the rational activity, which is moved by the real term, can also affect the idea and, when moved, fix itself on it. *Active*

---

[228] *The Summary Cause for the Downfall or Stability of Human Societies.*

[229] Prudence is a moral virtue when complete, not when incomplete. The law of prudence which I have given applies equally to the virtue of prudence and to prudence, understood simply as 'the ability to achieve any purpose'.

contemplation is developed in this way, and can also be called simply 'contemplation' as opposed to simple 'intuition'. Furthermore, just as pleasure is present in every act of the rational principle, so is love, which can be defined in general as 'fruition of the object'.

Article 7
Continuation — The law inclining human beings to every real ens

1417. In the second place, because the essence of every real ens is understood in what is ideal, intuition also produces in the rational principle an *inclination* or predisposition to every real ens. However, the essence is only virtually understood; the *mode* of the ens is not seen until it is perceived. This is the usual teaching of philosophers, who say that 'the object of the intellective appetite, that is, of the will, is good in its common notion'.[230]

1418. Ideal being therefore, the object of intuition, *per se* produces in human beings inclinations and propensities but not acts, which come later when suitable stimuli have been received. The inclinations can be reduced to two: 1. the inclination to contemplation, and 2. the inclination to every knowable, real good.[231]

Article 8
Perception considered relative to practical reason — The law of moral order

1419. Let us now consider perception and see what the laws governing perception contribute to practical reason.

The law of perception is: 'A limited ens perceived in feeling is referred to and seen in ideal being' in such a way that the

---

[230] St. Thomas, *S.T.*, I, q. 59, art. 4.
[231] *Teodicea*, 389–394.

perception contains 1. a feeling or reality, 2. an ideal ens, and 3. the (imperfect) relationship of identity between these two.

An ideal ens is infinite and *per se* complete. If a real ens is rationally perceived and referred to it, the limits of the real ens are also perceived because, by referring a real ens to the totality of being, we see the degree to which every real ens participates in and realises being in itself.

1420. Because the term of practical reason is an ens given by theoretical reason and all its functions, a perceived ens must also be the term of practical reason. Furthermore, if the act of practical reason consists in adhering to its term, it must adhere to the perceived ens in the way this is perceived. But ideal being perceives these entia as measured so that one is perceived as greater and another as smaller. Thus, it is a law of practical reason that it adheres to entia according to their measure. Even when the subject perceives only one real ens, it sees whether it is limited or unlimited by comparing it with what is ideal, and must adhere to it exactly as it is, that is, with an affection measured and proportionate to the ens.

This is the moral principle, 'the law of moral order'. It prescribes that the affective acknowledgement given to known, real entia be proportionate to their limits considered relative to the ideal, complete ens and, in the case of several, in comparison with each other.[232]

Article 9
Continuation — The object of every moral act is the infinite

1421. There is another very noble consequence: moral good has an infinite nature in so far as its object is always an infinite ens.

Perception never presents us with an isolated, limited ens, relative only to itself. What is limited is always united with and measured by what is ideal, complete and infinite. The object of practical reason is never confined to a finite-real ens, but always

---

[232] Cf. *NE*, vol. 1, 180–187, where I explained how what is ideal is always the measure of what is real.

joined to what is ideal and infinite, with which it constitutes the good proper to practical reason. Consequently, the act of adhesion found in practical reason is subject to ideal being in general as its supreme norm and rule, which it reveres more than any finite real ens.

1422. This is precisely the *essential characteristic* of what is moral: it always embraces the TOTALITY OF BEING in which it ends and according to which it regulates itself. Moral good, therefore, is of its NATURE INFINITE; it cannot be compared with any other finite good such as eudaimonological good which, unaccompanied by what is moral, terminates in what is finite. Moral goodness, which *orders* human beings to the whole of being, to infinite being, furnishes this order with infinite worth. And this is the constant, uniform judgment of mankind.

It cannot be objected that the real ens adhered to is finite. Adherence depends on prior adherence to what is ideal and infinite and, as such, measures and determines the quantity of adherence due to any real ens.

1423. If the real ens were itself infinite, the moral good would be infinite in both respects, that is, relative to the infinite dignity of the norm revered above all finite things, and relative to the real object. Here morality, because it acquires an infinite value, would be infinitely greater than in the case above, where however there is an infinite value. As we saw, 'infinite' is an ontological property which cannot be partly lost; either it is all lost or it all remains, that is, infinity remains because it is such by nature, not by addition or according to quantity.

Article 10
Reflection as an act of practical reason

1424. The act proper to practical reason is the practical acknowledgement of what is first known theoretically. This is morality, and its first act is carried out by means of reflection. Reflection however is twofold, *abstractive* and *integrative*. But a third function can be added, that of simply acknowledging what is known without any abstraction or reflection being exercised on it.

[1422–1424]

Consequently *practical reason* must also have three functions: 1. the willed acknowledgement of what is known, 2. acknowledgement accompanied by abstraction, division and separation, that is, acknowledgement of only a part of what is known, and 3. acknowledgement with integration.

1425. If practical reason acknowledges a known ens purely for what it is in theoretical cognition, its action is natural. It unites itself to the term determined for it by its own essence, by its essential inclination — its act is good.

But if instead of simply acknowledging its term as a whole, it wills to abstract from one part while willing to adhere to another, it does not reach the totality of its term — it is wayward and its act is evil. Every immoral act therefore contains an arbitrary abstraction contrary to nature. I have explained elsewhere how human beings can be drawn to act in opposition to the essence of their rational principle, which is themselves.[233]

1426. Furthermore, when practical reason limits and restricts its attention and activity to a part of the known object, it deprives itself of some light, it blinds itself. The ignorance and blindness present in every vice and wayward act also produces erroneous consciences, from which it is very difficult to free ourselves. Even awareness of them is difficult.[234]

1427. *Integrative reflection*, as a function of practical reason, contributes most nobly to human perfection. It raises us to God, where moral order attains its ultimate perfection, and practical reason reaches its ultimate, divine term which, as *essential being* and the beginning and end of things, completes the order of known ens. Its term is now not only all that is under the ideal form but also under the real form, although the second cognition is negative. Religion is therefore the crown of morality, and just as morality opposed to religion is not morality but rather extreme wickedness, so without religion it is like a roofless house whose roof is nothing more than a outline on an architect's plan!

---

[233] *Teodicea*, 396–410.
[234] *CS*, 406–458.

CHAPTER 14

The special ontological laws of practical reason. The first special law: objectivity

1428. I now come to the special ontological laws of practical reason. The first is that of objectivity.

We have seen that through the law of objectivity reason 1. does not modify its term, 2. apprehends its term but not the action of the term, and 3. apprehends the term without simultaneously apprehending its own self; its act finishes in the term outside itself. These three qualities of rational action must be present in both theoretical and practical reason because both are reason. These laws, relative to theoretical reason, are constitutive and necessary. They are therefore essential (Art. 2, §1 [Ch. 2, Art. 1). Relative to practical reason, which is subject to agents foreign to its object, they do not constitute its essence but its perfection, its proper good, and in this sense are fitting but not necessary. They are *morally* but not *physically* necessary.

1429. That which is *essential law* for theoretical reason is *moral law* for practical reason. It follows therefore:

1. As it is an essential law for theoretical reason not to modify its term, so practical reason must abstain even from trying to modify, alter or make the term different from what it is. If practical reason were not to do this, it would deviate from the law of the rational principle and no longer act rationally. This explains precisely why I posited a faculty of *error* and *malice* different from the faculty of knowledge. By maliciously altering the limits and value of entia, the activity of practical reason opposes rather than produces an act of knowledge .

2. As it is an essential law for reason to apprehend an ens without receiving from it any action which may enter and modify the subject, so the rational, practical principle must, according to its law, consider the value of the ens in itself, independently of the accidental real action which the ens exercises on the principle. The ens must be measured against ideal being, not against subjective advantage, and then esteemed according to the measure it receives from this comparison. In other words,

its *real* action on us must not move our practical reason to value it differently from what it is worth in itself when considered relative to and in the ideal ens. It is one thing for us to act as a result of the *real action* exercised on us by an ens, or rather by an agent; it is another to act as a result of the true measure of the ens (manifested by comparison with the essence of the ens intuited by the mind in ideal-universal being) in which is included the activity of the ens and its aptitude to act on us and others. To act in conformity with this measure is to act *rationally* and therefore *morally*; to act through the impulse of a real action on us is to abandon the law of reason in order to follow that of real or blind being, that is, of purely sensible being.[235] Practical reason must be directed according to the OBJECT, not the SUBJECT.

1430. 3. As it is an essential law of reason to apprehend an ens to the exclusion of itself as apprehending, so practical reason, to act rationally, must follow its term-ens in such a way as to forget itself (subject) totally, unless it is contained in the ens, that is, is understood in the object (objectivised). This is equivalent to the preceding law of acting in conformity with the *object*, but also indicates why a virtuous person forgets himself. It is the origin of *generosity, magnanimity, sacrifice* and *simplicity*, that noble, beautiful endowment of a just person, which consists in doing good without regard for subjective stimuli.

CHAPTER 15
The synthesism of practical reason. Moral good is twofold: ontological and psychological

1431. We now come to the law of synthesism proper to reason and its consequences for practical reason.

The rational principle has a twofold quality. It comes out from itself, fixes itself upon and takes up residence, so to speak, in the object, that is, in something different from and opposed to itself as subject. In the same way, whenever practical reason acts in conformity with its own law of reason, it is ordered and

---

[235] *Teodicea*, 384–415.

satisfied in itself (psychological-moral-good) and gives what is due to its ens-object. Thus the *exigency of ens* is satisfied (ontological-moral-good).

Vice versa, practical reason, if it deviates from the law proper to reason, produces two evils: 1. it disorders itself by not uniting with and unfolding its activity towards its term as required by its nature (psychological-moral-evil), but even worse, 2. it posits a disorder between itself and the ens, because the natural relationship between the two terms has not been observed (ontological-moral-evil).

1432. Moral evil therefore cannot be fully repaired by the simple correction of the disorder left in practical activity, which simply restores the *psychological order.* Satisfaction must also be given to the ens whose *exigency* has not been respected, so that the ontological order is restored. This explains the origin of punitive and vindictive justice, as well as that of penal satisfaction. If anyone has within himself the whole of the ontological order and therefore necessarily presides over its conservation (this is God), it is clear that his justice would demand penal satisfaction for an *ens* harmed by a moral evil.

The same must be said about upright action. In addition to the psychological good effect which comes in the lower order proper to the subject who has done moral good, there must also be an ontological reward.

1433. But this effect varies according to the *particular ens* whose exigency has been respected.

If upright persons do good relative to themselves (objectively considered), they will have the ontological good of an increased love and esteem of themselves (testimony of conscience, which differs from the feeling of moral-psychological harmony).

If they do good relative to their fellows, the ontological reward to which they have a right is the love and gratitude of their fellows. If the love and gratitude are denied, the supreme Ens who presides over the ontological order must compensate. Equally he must punish the unjust refusal of love and gratitude.

Finally, if they do good relative to God, he reserves for them rewards worthy of both himself and the moral virtue they have exercised towards him.

The same argument is also valid for harm.

It will be helpful if we see more clearly the twofold quality, psychological and ontological, of moral harm and good by comparing the good proper to the activity of the rational principle with the good proper to the activity of the sensitive principle.

The term of the sensitive principle, undivided from the principle, has a union or relationship of *reciprocal activity* with the principle; the term of the rational principle is essentially in opposition to its principle; here the union is an intuitive relationship, not a reciprocal activity. Hence all harm experienced by the sensitive principle is reduced to what it produces in itself; what it produces in another does it no harm. The material, extended element as term of the sensitive principle is, as I have said, not susceptible of harm and good, because anything not joined to it is not its term. If a dog bites a man, we do not say that the dog suffers any harm from the action, and if we say it is a bad dog, the description refers solely to the harm done to us. This is metaphorical, not literal language. In the case of the rational principle, however, the term is an object distinct from ourselves, so that whenever we harm another (for example, our fellow), we act contrary to the law imposed on us by an ens as term of our activity. This results from the above-mentioned laws of objectivity and synthesism, through which the term is present to the rational principle. The sensitive principle is therefore subject to harm for the sole reason that the activity of its natural instinct can be disturbed. On the other hand, the rational principle can cause harm in two ways: 1. by upsetting the ontological order when the principle alters the natural relationship of entia and thus tends on its part to destroy ens in general, which possesses this intrinsic order — this action is imputed to it as cause; and 2. by not adhering to its natural term according to the law of its constitution and thus causing disturbance in itself. Consequently moral necessity is simultaneously objective and subjective.[236]

---

[236] *The Essence of Right*, 189–193, 211–222.

Chapter 16

The second special ontological law of practical reason: its object is that which is possible

1434. We now apply the second law of reason which states: 'The term of thought is that which is possible.' Two extremely sublime consequences are immediately apparent. The first states that practical reason has as its term the essence of entia in relationship to the essence's realisation.

Article 1
Practical reason has as its term the essence of entia in relationship to the essence's realisation

1435. In speaking of the law of perception, we saw that practical reason must adhere to a real ens according to the measure of the ens, and that its measure is determined by ideal-general being.

This measure is the *specific idea* of any ens with which we are dealing, and the specific idea is always ideal being, considered as manifestative of this real ens.

We have, therefore:

1. ideal being in general, the first absolute measure, the measure of all measures of real entia;
2. the specific idea, the proximate measure of a real ens;
3. and a real, measured ens.

The first law is that of the first measure which measures all others. In other words, the practical reason must act according to the indication given by this measuring element and embrace the measure which ideal being assigns. The second law is that of the proximate measure. In other words, the practical reason, having received this measure from the absolute measure, must hold it as the norm of its esteem for and adhesion to any real ens. These norms of practical reason are, therefore, superior to real ens. It follows that the moral order comes to practical reason from those laws which prescribe for it the attitude it must have towards each real being. The ultimate reason for moral respect is an idea, and an ens is esteemed only in so far as this *idea* prescribes.

But an idea contains the essence of an ens. The respect of rational reason terminates, therefore, in the essence of the ens. The real ens is appreciated not in itself and for itself, but in its essence and for its essence. But the essence of an ens, when we are dealing with contingent entia, is ideal, and is called *possible* when considered relative to the realisation of the essence. The final, necessary term, therefore, for practical reason is the possible essence of a thing in relationship to the realisation of the essence.

1436. The moral act, as we see, consists not only in respect for a real being according to the measure of its ideal essence, but also in a tendency to realise this essence. If practical reason has as its object the realisation of an essence, it follows that practical reason tends to produce it if such a realisation has not yet come about, or has come about imperfectly. It also tends to produce it in the most complete and perfect way. If the realisation has already come about, practical reason will tend to adhere to such a perfectly realised ens.

There are, therefore, two moral acts: 1. adhesion to a real ens (special-justice); 2. realisation of an ideal ens (beneficence, charity). The second act is divided into the two *acts of production* and *perfecting*.[237]

We can conclude, therefore, that there is a law of *complete realisation of species* or of *excluded equality*, which the Creator follows in the formation and government of the world.[238]

1437. We have been dealing with contingent entia. A similar argument can however be applied to supreme, necessary, absolute Ens. Although the supreme Ens has subsistence and reality in its essence, this essence is nevertheless not less manifestative of its subsistence and reality. Or, better, the subsistence of the supreme being, in so far as it makes itself known with its own light, is the *law* imposed on practical reason; and, in so far as it lives complete in itself, is the real *object* of practical reason itself.

---

[237] For the distinction between the moral acts of production and perfecting, cf. *PE*, 197–211.

[238] *Teodicea*, 617–641.

We also have the second consequence deducible from our knowing that the term of reason is that which is possible: practical reason has, as its law, harmony in the object.

Article 2
Practical reason has as its law adhesion to an harmonious term

1438. Any essence which does not have in itself the subsistence of an ens is called 'possible' considered in relationship to the realisation of the essence.

Logically speaking, 'possible' is everything which does not involve contradiction. Hence the object of reason, ens, is as I said immune from every contradiction; it is self-accordant, fully harmonious.

Practical reason, therefore, which itself is reason, must have a harmonious term immune from contradiction if it is to act according to its own nature.

1439. Careful consideration shows that the malicious human being, on the contrary, always has some contradiction as the term of his activity; he endeavours to do the impossible. In fact, it is impossible to destroy the intrinsic order of universal being. Because essences are immutable, it is impossible to make an ens, considered according to its essence, different from what it is. When a person, instead of acknowledging some conceived ens according to its measure, wishes to acknowledge it according to another, arbitrary measure, he re-presents to himself the essence of an ens changed relative to its measure, and consequently possessing greater or lesser value than the true ens. He re-presents something false as the object of his activity. He does not present it as false, however, but as true. No one can want to deceive himself fully and absolutely; every malicious person tends necessarily to persuade himself that the good he wants is true good. If he could convince himself fully *hic et nunc* that it were not good, not true good, he would never follow it. He would not abandon true good for that which he would know not to be good. Although there is no doubt that he can with his speculative reason know that he deceives himself, he does not want to acknowledge this with his practical reason. He tells himself that the good which seduces him is not good in general, and that it brings in its wake greater harm. At the same time, he wants it as good for him here and now, abstracting from future consequences or from a multitude of other considerations. As we said, it is through abstraction that practical reason mistakes the path prescribed for it by its natural laws. If, therefore, a person wants practically, and at the very moment of his action, that evil be good, he will try with his activity to denature and destroy truth, and to make what is in one mode be something very different for him. In other words, he attempts to change the order of an ens.

Now in this case, an ens would contradict itself. It would be one thing and have one measure relative to theoretical reason, but be something else and have a different measure relative to practical reason which, by tending through malicious activity to put an ens in contradiction with itself, attempts the impossible.

1440. Here we see the origin of the incessant struggle and implacable battle which every malicious person fights within himself, and of the peace and concord found in the just.[239]

CHAPTER 17

The third special law of practical reason: practical reason has an intelligent substance as its term

1441. The following four laws of reason simply define that which cannot constitute the term of reason. They are equally effective, in a negative sense, for practical reason. They show that there can be no term proper to practical reason when this term lacks either a first act, or unity, or duration, or determination. This all means that the term of practical reason must be some substance. An accident cannot constitute the proper term for practical reason which must refer what is accidental to what is substantial. We have already seen this when speaking about the law of prudence.

1442. Moreover, that which is corporeal, because it has no

---

[239] Cf. *ER*, 94–107.

unity of its own (it borrows this from the sentient principle in which alone it has continuity), cannot be the true term of practical reason.

The same applies to the merely sentient-animal principle which, because it is not a complete ens but only a rudiment of an ens, cannot constitute the final term of practical reason. As such, it is on its way to being an ens. Moreover, practical reason, having always to thrust towards the infinite in order to be moral, cannot have the animal principle (totally devoid of anything infinite) as its term. Intelligent being, on the contrary, has its seat in the infinite, in ideal being, in the essence of ens as universal and, in so far as it focuses on and rests in this essence, shares in the infinite dignity of ideal being to which it is ordered. Consequently, it is known as *end*, and as term of practical reason.

1443. Moreover, there is an order among intelligent-real beings. What is finite and real is produced by the infinite, which creates it. Thus practical reason has to adhere to a finite, intelligent ens in such a way as to refer it to its principle, to God the Creator, in whom alone this ens rests totally as in its final, complete, absolute term.

We have dealt sufficiently with the ontological laws to which the rational principle is subject. We now pass to the second kind of laws, that is, to psychological laws.

CHAPTER 18

The psychological laws of the rational principle corresponding to the ontological laws in general

1444. Although it is the term which arouses the activity of the principle to which it is joined, the principle has its own activity. In our natural life the term of the rational principle is twofold: ideal ens and the finitely real (the world). This double term therefore must arouse in the rational principle a double activity which must receive a large part of its mode of action from the nature of the principle itself, that is, from the soul. The psychological laws therefore must divide into two classes: those corresponding to the ontological laws, and those corresponding to the cosmological laws. I have spoken about the ontological laws but not the cosmological. It will be helpful therefore if I discuss only the psychological laws corresponding to the ontological, and postpone discussion of the others.

This cannot be done however without some reference to the cosmological laws. What is said about them here will serve as an indication of what must be said later when they are discussed expressly.

1445. The general ontological law which summarises all the others is: 'The term of the rational principle is an ens'. If some essential condition is absent from this ens, the term of the rational principle no longer exists. On the other hand, if no condition is lacking, the principle exercises its activity on its term.

In order to apply this law properly to the human being, I needed to note the essential conditions of any ens, which are:

1. It has three forms, and is complete under each. Thus under the ideal form, it can be given to a subject without its being given under the other two forms.

2. Under the real and moral forms however, it cannot be given without the ideal form, because ideal ens manifests the *essence of ens* and without its essence no ens can be the object of thought under any form.[240]

3. Because an ens under the ideal form is *per se* object, the rational principle informed by it can have a term only under the form of object.

1446. These truths teach us:

1. The rational principle as naturally intellective has only the activity given it by ideal ens.

2. If the principle were in fact divided from animal-fundamental feeling, it would find satisfaction in ideal ens, its natural term.

3. It cannot be moved to another act except by a new object.

These propositions contain the seeds of the psychological laws which I propose to explain. I will begin with the last proposition.

---

[240] Thus it would be an absurdity to maintain that we saw God but not his essence.

CHAPTER 19

The first psychological law: rational inertia

1447. The last proposition means that if the rational principle remains at rest, the only object moving it to action is what is ideal. Its only act is the intuitive act, which unites it to its term.

1448. In fact investigation of the subjective laws governing the action of the rational principle involves two questions:

First question: According to which laws is the principle moved to its second acts?

Second question: Granted that the principle is moved, which laws govern its movement?

1449. The answer to the first question is that the rational principle is moved to a second act only when given a new object, in addition to an ideal ens; it must be given something real.

A real ens however, as term of thought, can be finite or infinite, complete or incomplete. If it is infinite and complete, its essence is seen realised in what is ideal. In this case, real ens is *per se* object, and the infinite real ens, if communicated to the rational principle, would arouse in it truly *ontological* activity. This would allow us to investigate the nature of the ontological-subjective laws of the rational principle. Maximum, but extremely simply activity would be aroused in the rational principle and totally reduced to an act which would be at rest and find satisfaction in its term alone. With the completion of this act, the only other movement possible would be the passage from what is ideal to what is real, a pleasurable act caused by seeing that what is real completes all that is ideal, and what is ideal expresses and, as it were, illuminates all that is real. The rational principle could be moved to this incessant passage of attention and contemplation by what it would find to be identical and distinct in the ideal and the real.[241]

---

[241] *Teodicea*, 694–698. The objection that God, although not coming out of himself, performs distinct things, is not valid. The truth is that the Creator touches the creature with his creating act in so far as the creature is the term of creation. I am speaking about the hypothesis that the soul intuits God to the exclusion of all union and contact with creatures.

1450. But leaving aside the communication of infinite real ens, every communication of what is finitely real can arouse only a cosmological activity and be the source of solely cosmological, not ontological laws. Once this activity has been aroused, the *way* that the rational principle acts certainly originates from ideal ens and is thus ontological. Subjective-ontological laws are now possible, although the only act relative to purely ideal or infinite-real ens is that which terminates and rests in it.

1451. This need for new objects if the rational principle is to perform new acts I call the *psychological law of inertia*. According to this law the principle cannot move itself from rest to another act unless the object itself draws it and permits it to move. Once in motion, it can do different things in conformity with the other law of spontaneity.[242]

CHAPTER 20

Psychological inertia can be reconciled with the various actions of the soul through the law of spontaneity

Article 1
How the spontaneity of the rational principle is aroused

1452. If the human soul or rational principle is moved only when a term is given it, how can we explain its immense activity in the various actions contributing to its extraordinary development? It would seem that the soul has either been given or not been given an object. There is no middle choice. But if it has received an object, it does nothing else but rest in it; if it has not, it does not act. It is true, of course, that the principle would have no activity of its own if it lacked an object. Nevertheless, granted the object, this activity is present with its own laws, that is, the *psychological* laws which we are now investigating.

---

[242] In the *Anthropology* I discussed the two laws of *inertia* and *spontaneity* which govern an animal. The same laws can be seen in a rational being, to whom freedom is added.

First of all, union with the object takes place in two ways, *speculative* and *practical*, as I have already indicated. The merely speculative union is the first act of union, an *ontological union* determined by the presence of the object. The *psychological union* takes place through the activity proper to the subject.[243]

1453. We saw that the ontological laws of speculative reason are physically necessary because they arise both from the object and the creative power posited by the soul intuiting the object. They are not drawn from the soul's rational activity which, on the contrary, is created through them.

Investigation showed, however, that the ontological laws[244] governing practical reason were only morally, not physically necessary. In other words, they determine the moral, not physical action of practical reason; they determine what it *must* do if it is to be perfect, not what it actually does.

Practical reason therefore has two kinds of laws: those which govern its natural action (*psychological* laws), and those according to which it must act if it is to be perfect (*ontological*, moral laws). I have already explained the latter; I need only discuss the former.

1454. Practical reason, however, which is a kind of continuation of theoretical reason (just as second acts are a kind of continuation of some first act) never acts independently of theoretical reason, from which it originates. The laws of theoretical reason are therefore already fulfilled in the action of practical reason, although such fulfilment does not identify these two very different kinds of law which must be very carefully distinguished.

1455. Consequently, *psychological activity and spontaneity*, that is, the soul's varying degree and manner of union with the

---

[243] Note however that this *psychological union* is itself partly determined by the information given by the object as stimulus, with the result that a diversity of objects moves the soul to varying degrees of activity. In general the following principle, which I will discuss elsewhere, is valid: 'Certain complex objects whose elements are ordered to one another arouse a complex, multiple activity in the soul, resulting from several mutually ordered acts. But while the intrinsic order in the complex object is simultaneous, the order in the soul's activity unfolds in successive acts.'

[244] Anything physically necessary proceeds from the nature of any ens whatsoever, that is, from φύσις (nature).

object (granted its presence) harmonise very well with *psychological inertia*, that is, the soul's inability to act without an object.

Article 2
Psychological development described

1456. A clearer understanding of this harmony will be obtained if I briefly summarise the totality of *psychological development* by drawing on the various places where I have discussed it. It unfolds through the following stages and modes of action, for each of which I add its sufficient reason:

1. The rational principle does not move unless it is given an object to which it can unite itself.

2. If this object is purely infinite, ideal ens, the principle rests in it; its action is utterly simple (intuition), just as the object is utterly simple. The principle goes no further with its movement, which has attained its complete term.

3. If the object is something real, given in feeling, the feeling seconds the perception, which is multiple in nature and consists of *a*) what is infinite and ideal, *b*) what is ideal in so far as it shows the essence of what is real, that is, the concept and measure of what is real, and *c*) the affirmation of what is real, that is, the realisation of the concept. But all this is, so to speak, organically united.

4. If the *affirmation* or memory of what is real ceases for any reason, the concept of the thing remains in the mind, preserved by some real vestige of feeling, which takes its place.

5. But anything real perceived by our *theoretical reason* can become the object of our will (psychological activity) not only as *conceived* but as *real*. These are two different ways of the soul's *union* with the object.

In fact the *will* sometimes simply takes delight in actually knowing a thing (delight of contemplation). In this case it is sufficient for the object to be present in the *concept* possessed by the theoretical reason; the will is content to contemplate the object. This is an act of practical reason.[245]

---

[245] This *contemplation* was considered by the Scholastics as an act of theoretical reason. But as an enjoyed, willed and loving act, it should be

6. But sometimes it is not sufficient for the will to contemplate the known object. It desires to feel the enjoyment of the object, that is, it desires the object as real, as a term of feeling, not as a term simply of cognition.

Relative to this real union, two kinds of volition can take place: *affective* and *appreciative* volitions.[246] In *merely affective volitions*, the rational principle simply seconds instinct and behaves negatively relative to the term of instinct which it conceives in the ens without distinctly appreciating it as good. In *appreciative volitions*, the act of appreciation intervenes and becomes operative.

1457. *Appreciative volition* (to which I will limit my observations) desires what is real as a term of feeling. Consequently it varies according to the diversity of the sensories and the ways in which the sensories unite with their term. Therefore:

a) In the case of the sensory of sight, the appreciative volition takes place when what is real is present to our eyes. The *visual perception* of what is real will be the object of our appetite. For example, all we need do to desire a luscious fruit is contemplate it as it hangs on a tree.

b) In the case of touch, the real thing needs not only to be at a certain distance where it can be seen, but also close at hand. For example, a child will want to pluck and hold the luscious fruit it sees.

c) In the case of taste and the alimentary sense, there will be a wish to be able to eat the object. The child will want to be able to place the fruit in its mouth and eat it.

The same can be said about every other feeling. Generally we want the desired term to be united, in the particular way required by the nature of the sensory, to the sense to which it pertains.

7. Hence, whenever theoretical reason conceives what is real, which is then desired by the will as the real term of feelings,

placed, I think, among the acts of practical reason. However, it is nearest to theoretical reason, which it reinforces. I think that bliss should be placed in this act of the practical reason which reinforces and completes the act of theoretical reason, not in a mere act of theoretical reason without the intervention of human will.

[246] *AMS*, 612–635.

the real thing receives the nature of *end* relative to the will. The activity of the will is immediately aroused to find the *means* to obtain the end. Either *purely affective volitions* can be used to obtain them, or the *practical reason* can move to obtain them by appreciative, calculated volitions.

8. In this last case, *practical reason* moves *theoretical reason* to discover the *means*.

1458. We cannot conclude however that the abstract concepts of *end* and *means* are formed in this way. Theoretical reason still contains nothing truly abstract. It acts according to the relationships it sees in entia, but does not abstract the relationships or see them separate from the entia. Its acts have a complex, multiple term, whose parts, like the organs of a single, understood whole, are in the whole and through the whole.

Action of this kind, without abstract knowledge of ends and means, pertains to *multiple*, not *abstract* thought. *Multiplicity* can be present in the object of thought irrespective of abstraction. Thus, we have seen that perception is a single action despite the three elements distinguished in the object of perception which itself is one, although organated.

1459. 9. This relationship of means and end is already a bond between ideas and perceptions. Later, other bonds are revealed which associate ideas and perceptions in countless forms and make a single thought of them. The instrument which gives new activity to thought is the association and spontaneity of phantasms. We have seen that it is a law of the rational principle to unite the idea to every feeling. Consequently phantasms stimulate thought. But it is proper to phantasms to have a kind of spontaneous motion so that a single phantasm gives rise to many others.[247] Hence, such a stimulus causes a whole series of thoughts.

1460. Furthermore phantasy is subject to the law of habit, which is partly imposed on it by thoughts. Just as phantasms move corresponding thoughts, thoughts move phantasms, and just as thoughts are joined by their logical connections, so corresponding phantasms are usually represented in what could be called a reasoned series. The series of reasonings already made by the mind joins together and produces the corresponding series of phantasms. Afterwards these reasoned series

[247] *AMS*, 416–494.

of phantasms, joined together in keeping with the different reasonings, are aroused in us habitually as soon as the impulse is given to our internal sensory. We then make appropriate reasonings about them. In this way the habit to which the phantasy is subject passes into the faculty of thought, which is tied to the phantasy. This is what I call 'reasoning phantasy' or 'reasoning habit'; we use it to explain the phenomena of dreams, of distractions, and so on. Note, the *reasoning habit*, already initiated at this level of intellectual development, increases greatly and expands with other levels of thought which I will now describe.

10. The association of perceptions and ideas makes one real thing a sign of another and the perception of another perception. This explains the natural formation of language. Moreover nature (instinct) teaches us to use the association of perceptions in the company of our fellow human beings. Sometimes we may want to attain an end, and need to let them know about it. The knowledge we impart to our fellows is a *means* with which we obtain our desired end. Again, the wisdom of the Creator has endowed us with many ways of communicating our needs and will to others. One very suitable instrument is the faculty of articulate sounds which, through another gift of God, we *produce instinctively* as a simple physical consequence of our feelings and thoughts. When we are quickened by a rather strong feeling we instinctively emit sounds, even when alone. The movement of our tongue, the emission of air and the apposite alteration of our throat are effects of our internal feeling, independent of the aptitude which such sounds have for imparting meaning. This aptitude is soon discovered however, and is a great step in our intellective development. But abstraction strictly speaking is not yet present.

11. Are these signs or sounds which we use to reveal our needs, feelings and volitions, proper or common names?

By nature they are common names because they express a concept (otherwise they would be instinctive sounds, not intended signs), but in the beginning they are *used* as proper names because they express the concept still bound to the feeling, the perception.[248]

[248] *NE*, vol. 1, 134–210.

Although they begin as proper names at the moment they are applied to an object of perception, which is by nature singular, they are very soon used as common. The perception contains what is common, that is, the concept which is essentially common. Very quickly, the idea, although first tied to the object of the perception and thus particularised, is separated from this external bond.

To see how far the human being, or rather human beings living in association, can progress in the formation of speech, we must consider carefully the nature of perception, the first fount of names.

The three elements of perception are: 1. the idea (unlimited, ideal being), 2. the concept (ideal being limited by the relationship of sensitive perception with it), and 3. the act of the spirit which affirms the subsistence, that is, the realisation of the concept. Although this triple object of perception is indicated by the name when it is first imposed, the spirit soon abandons *subsistence*, which is no longer needed, and is left with the concept intuited in the idea. From this moment, the name, which does not change, is used as common.

1461. 12. But what is the nature of the *concept* acquired in the perception?

First of all, intellective perception takes place on the occasion of sensations and sensitive perceptions. The different sensories which perceive the real thing split it up naturally into many real things and, by means of separate perceptions, furnish us with its different sensible qualities. Hence we can apply one sound to indicate a coloured object and a different sound to indicate the same object as tasted [*App.*, no. 14]. But this is still not pure abstraction. Each of the sounds indicates a real substance proffered by the relevant sensory; they are *qualified substantive* names. Even when we are aware of the identity of the individual thing, there is still no abstraction, only synthesism. Nevertheless, this step taken by the human spirit is important.

1462. 13. It can happen that two or more different real things perceived in different ways give us similar pleasure or similar pain. In the first case our joy, and in the second our pain is expressed by fitting movements. People will see pain or pleasure on our face and in our gestures. Our feelings can also be expressed by spontaneous, instinctive sounds which strictly speaking express something real, that is, our pleasant or painful feeling. They can however be very quickly associated with the real objects which are their cause and form, according to the Scholastic saying, *sensibile in actu est sensus in actu* [what is sensible in act is sense in act]. Let us suppose that a mother wishes to keep her child away from various harmful objects. To make the child understand that such objects are harmful, she will make gestures and sounds expressing pain, fear and other similar affections. She will use these signs to make the child understand that he must keep away not only from fire, but from razors, ponds or precipices, etc. Because the feeling produced by the objects is the same, it is always natural for her to use the same signs, especially in light of the law that 'animals and human beings always follow the easiest way to produce their action', and that it is easier to repeat the same sound than to find new ones. Thus a sound will gradually become fixed as a common name for all harmful objects. On the other hand, if a mother were to invite her child to enjoy pleasant objects, such as eating fruit and sweets, playing, etc., she would use signs which express joy, and by repeating the same signs in very many different circumstances and for very different real objects, will finally determine a *common name* for all pleasant or useful objects.[249]

The names given by the mother would mean 'that which causes pain, sadness' and 'that which gives pleasure, joy'; they would express entia, characterised and distinguished by the effect they produce in the child's feeling. They would therefore be *common names* of very extensive meaning because they would include innumerable kinds of effects. Granted this faculty, nothing prevents us from inventing common names of more limited meaning in accord with our need, determined not by pleasure or pain in general but by a genus or species of pleasure or pain, of enjoyable or unpleasant feelings. Words like *good* and *bad*, *useful* and *useless*, *healthy* and *unhealthy* are classified by grammarians as *substantivated adjectives*. This classification is incorrect, however, because such words precede adjectives in the development of human language. Their philosophical name would be *qualified substantives* since they

[249] *Rinnovamento* , bk. 2, cc. 31–33.

express the concept of a substance determined by one or more species of its accidents.

According to the same law, it seems that the common name which initially means the full species, must be transferred to signify not only very extensive genera but the least extensive and even most limited genera. For example, the sight of grass covering a stretch of land moves us to name it 'meadow', thus indicating the object of our perception by a proper name. Later, we give the name 'meadow' to every similar stretch of green, that is, we use the name as common; we abandon the thought of the subsistence of the first real meadow and make the concept and name common to every stretch of grass. The word 'meadow' now indicates the object of our *concept*. In the first perception of the meadow it is true that we perceived qualities other than the colour green: we perceived the size, the shape, the intensity of colour, etc. But these qualities did not strike our gaze as vividly as the *colour green*. We ignored the other qualities without naming them, being content to name the object of sight according to its most vivid quality, 'a green ens'. Consequently, if we were to see a *green* tapestry and had no other words to name it, we would not look for a new word — this would take too much effort and not serve our purpose — instead, we would immediately use the same name, *meadow*. The name would now have an extended meaning and be generally understood as 'that which is green'.

The conclusion is that naturally we think genera and species and produce *common names*. All the first substantive names must therefore have been *qualified substantives*, but never simply substantives. The most ancient languages bear clear traces of this, a fact which Leibniz noted. It will therefore be helpful to add his examples to mine.[250] He was at work in Germany before the caustic spirit of sophism had penetrated that nation, a spirit introduced by Kant, a son of his times and a corrupter of true philosophy. Leibniz says:

> But I would add, as I have already noted, that proper names were originally adjectives, that is to say, had a general meaning in the beginning, like Brutus, Caesar,

[250] *NE*, vol. 1, 138–155.

Augustus, Capito, Lentulus, Piso, Cicero, Elbe, Rhine, Ruhr, Leine, Ocker, Bucephalus, Alp, Brenner, Pyrenees. We know for example that the first Brutus was so called because of his apparent stupidity, that Caesar was the name of a baby born by cutting the maternal womb, that Augustus was a name of honour, Capito means a large head, as does Bucephalus. Lentulus, Piso and Cicero were names given at the beginning to people who were professional cultivators of certain kinds of vegetable. I have already given the meaning of the rivers, Rhine, Ruhr, Leine and Ocker.[251] We also know that all the rivers in Scandinavia are called *Elbe*. Finally the Alps are mountains covered with snow which corresponds to *album*, just as *brinck*, among the Lower Saxons, means *height*, and there is a *Brenner* between Germany and Italy, just as there is a *Pyrenees* between France and Spain. I would say that nearly all words are originally general in meaning because it would very rarely happen that the name of a plant, for example, were invented without any reason to indicate the individual thing. We can say therefore that the names of individuals were names of species given to an individual for its excellence or otherwise, just as the name *large head* is the person in the city who had a large head or stood out most among those with a large head. Similarly names were given sometimes to a species, sometimes to a genus, by applying a more general or imprecise term to designate a more particular species whenever there were differences. For example, the generic term *absynthium* is sufficient although there are so many species of absinth that one of the Bauhins filled a whole book with them.[252]

1463. In this passage however Leibniz does not deal with the cause which inclines human beings to form *common names*, and form them so easily that they do it effortlessly; furthermore, the

[251] He derives Rhine, Rhône, etc., from ῥέο, to flow; Leine from λύο, to melt, applied to snow; Ocker from *aha*, *auue*, *eau*, *acqua*, etc. — Hence *lanum* in *Mediolanum* probably means water, as if to say 'in the middle of the water', and the torrent Leno which flows through Rovereto also originates from λύο. A great many words therefore can be reduced to the same origin.

[252] *Nouveaux essais sur l'entendement humain*, bk. 3, c. 3, §1. Although some of the etymologies given here by Leibniz can rightly be criticised, his reasoning is valid and could be enriched by numerous, indisputable examples.

less developed the human race is, the more readily it forms common names. The cause is always:

1. The nature of *perception*. Perception apprehends things in their special action on particular sensories, and does so only partially, in unilateral activities, not in their whole being and activity. The perceived ens is therefore determined by these sensible qualities.

2. The nature of *feelings*. Here disparate objects produce the same or similar feelings. The different causes of these feelings are attached to the feelings as to real things, and receive a *common* name. This name is more common than that which expresses an aptitude for producing particular perceptions, because it indicates several disparate real things through their aptitude for causing the same feelings.

3. Finally, the nature of *appetence*, which is also something real and to which the mind joins distant desired objects as well as those suitable as *means* for obtaining these distant objects. The result is other names that are still more common. All these names indicate multiple real things which have a more or less indirect, common aptitude for making the appetence obtain the object to which it tends as to its end. For example, we could use the word *vehiculum* for all things capable of carrying something, and *instrumentum* for all things suitable as a means for doing something, etc.

1464. Some comment about the potency that Aristotle called common sense, admitted by all the Scholastics, will be helpful. According to Aristotle, *common sense* is an internal potency with its own organ in the brain which receives the sensations of the five external senses. That this potency has its own organ in the brain is a gratuitous proposition. In fact, reason proves the opposite, because every corporeal feeling must have a particular corresponding movement. If sensations of different senses happened simultaneously and they were all received by the organ destined for common sense, this organ would have to produce simultaneously different movements, which is clearly absurd. Furthermore, if the organ were composed of several parts, each of which received one of the movements, there would be several organs and several senses, not a single, common organ; we would still be unable to explain how a single sensory organ could govern all the different sensations. Again, if a

[1464]

common sensory were present in an organ different from and in addition to the special sensories, all the special sensations would have to be double. They would first have to be separate in the special sensories, and then united in the common sensory. This is contrary to fact. Finally, if we add all that was said in the *Rinnovamento* against the unification of sensations in a common sensory, we will clearly see that solid philosophy cannot admit the common sense of Aristotle and the Scholastics.[253] Consequently, the faculty Aristotle allotted to common sense for discerning and *judging* the difference between the sensations of the various special sensories disappears. The same reasoning also invalidates the faculty which he and his followers attributed to the special senses for discerning or judging between their own different sensations.[254] Finally the Aristotelian definition of phantasy as the faculty which preserves the species of both the special sensories and common sense is corrected.[255]

1465. Nevertheless, although we can exclude these errors, there must be something in reality that corresponds to the 'common sense' of the Aristotelians. Without such a sense the animal could not direct itself according to its various sensations and feelings. But no new sense can be admitted. We have seen that animal feeling has an *extended term* and a *simple principle*. The multiplicity and variety of sensations and feelings pertain to the extended term; the animal's governance of its sensations, feelings and sensories pertains to the simple principle. All sensations and feelings exist in this immaterial, simple and identical principle. The animal not only feels each but is moved by them all, and performs its actions according to its total feeling, as I have explained at length in *Anthropology*.[256]

The animal has a single, fundamental feeling which can be modified in different ways. The modifications are particular sensations[257] which do not exist in separation from all the rest of the feeling, but are its most vivid parts; they are variations

---

253 *Rinnovamento*, bk. 2, c. 38.

254 Cf. St. Thomas, *S.T.*, I, q. 88, art. 4, ad 2.

255 St. Thomas, *S.T.*, I, q. 88, art. 4.

256 Book 2.

257 *NE*, vol. 2, 692–748.

which take place in its extended term. Hence the animal always acts as a result of the state of this single feeling, not as a result of a mere sensation (although the special vividness of the sensation can give the opposite impression). The total sensation therefore is something real, to which, as an object of intellective perception, a name can be given. The sensations themselves are as it were different facets and attitudes of this feeling and can also be named. Similarly, because the term is distinguished from the principle and confused with the stimulus when this is applied to a sensory, the stimulating object as stimulant is itself named. This name then becomes the *common name* for all the objects capable of stimulating us in a given way, or for all objects if our attention, in the intellective perception, extends to the whole feeling without being restricted to what is most vivid in the feeling. In this case the invented, common name will be *that which is sensible*.

1466. As I said, however, we normally restrict our attention to what strikes us most or to what we need. In our natural state it would therefore be difficult and time-consuming to invent for felt things a name as common as *that which is sensible*. We first invent less extensive common names for things that fall under our senses, and then unconsciously use these names with more extensive meaning, according to our need. Moreover, because our attention is activated more by the vividness and convenience of sight-sensations than by any other sensation, we invent, from the very beginning, a name which equates with *what is visible*. Later we extend this meaning to everything that falls under our sense. This is what happened in fact, as we can see by examining languages, particularly ancient languages. All languages used the words applied to sight-sensations to mean not only the objects or terms of these sensations but *everything* that falls under the senses. Thus, we generally speak about *visible things* to indicate all that acts on our senses. This history of words, of which the clearest traces are preserved amongst peoples and in the most ancient languages, is well worth our consideration.

The following are examples of how words are applied to hearing while retaining the use they had when first applied to sight. In Exodus, Moses says: 'All the people *saw* the voices';[258] in

---

[258] Ex 20: 18 [Douai].

Deuteronomy, 'Forget not the words your eyes *have seen*',[259] and later, 'You *saw* no form but only voices'.[260] Calmet correctly notes that 'the Hebrews use the verb *to see* to indicate all the senses.'[261] The Greeks did the same, especially the ancient Greeks, like Aeschylus who used the phrases 'to see noises'[262] and 'to see the voices of a human being.'[263] Examples are numerous, many of them in Latin and modern languages. But the closer we come to modern times, the more the meaning of words moves away from perception and nearer to the common concept.

1467. The name given to a perception, and then transferred to mean the full species (which can be defined as a *perception of the phantasm*), is the origin of all allegorical, metaphorical, figured, transferred and other kinds of language.

In fact, in the most ancient languages, people used the functions of life instead of the verb 'to live', which applies to the fundamental feeling as a whole. These characterised the perception because they attracted the attention more. In Genesis (16: 13), the Hebrew text says, 'Do I still *see*, after him that "sees me"?', where 'I see' replaces 'I live'.[264] Elsewhere 'to eat and drink' means 'to live', as in Exodus,[265] where we read that the Hebrews 'did eat and drink' after seeing the Lord. To express a peaceful, prosperous life, Scripture speaks about everyone 'dwelling under his vine and his fig tree'.[266] This expression does not in itself indicate *everything* present in the concept of a happy life, but is transferred to give this sense. It is sufficient to name that which caught the attention most in life; the rest is understood as present. 'To make someone a slave' is expressed as 'bend his back'.[267] This part of the concept engraved itself more deeply on the

[259] Deut 4: 9 [Douai].

[260] Deut 4: 12.

[261] Deut 4: 9.

[262] Cf. *Septem contra Thebas*.

[263] Cf. *Prometheus*.

[264] Calmet says, '"see" is used here for "live", that is, a function of life considered as life itself' [*Commentarius,* vol. 1, pt. 1, Venice, 1774].

[265] Ex. 24: 11 [Douai].

[266] 3 Kings 4: 25 [Douai].

[267] *Et dorsum eorum semper incurva* (Ps 68: 24 [Douai]).

[1467]

phantasy; the remaining parts were implicit. 'The city will be deserted and filled with sadness' becomes 'No more will the voice of bridegroom and the voice of the bride be heard.'[268]

For the first human beings, therefore, the application of general precepts was ineffective. Particular precepts had to be given, as a kind of example and representation of general precepts. The Decalogue is composed entirely of particular precepts; for example, 'You shall not commit adultery', means we must not sin by lust; 'You shall not kill', means we must not harm our neighbour, and so on for the other commandments. It was of no value to legislate for the human race in general terms; particular precepts were given, like the following:

> If the ass of your enemy lies under its burden, you shall help him.[269]
> If you come upon a lost sheep, you shall go and return it to the flock.[270]
> You shall not speak evil to the deaf, nor put a stumbling block before the blind.[271]

In Scripture, 'to seize or kill a mother and her children' indicates tremendous cruelty. The sacred writings are full of such phrases, the Old Testament more than the New. The oldest books of antiquity have practically no other kind of expression. After Scripture, Homer abounds in them. The lesser frequency of such expressions in the sacred books of India and China is for me new proof that these books are not necessarily as old as was thought, or that they were altered and translated, although their style was perhaps less metaphorical because thought, which then came to a halt, had made such rapid progress. The characteristic of the words and ancient forms of speech we are discussing is that they 'express the concept given by perception'. This expression, because so particular, was later transferred to mean an ever more common and general concept or opinion.

1468. As I said, the explanation of all metaphorical speech and grammatical turns of phrase lies here. It also explains why the

---

[268] *Auferetur vox sponsi et vox sponsae* (Jer 7: 34).

[269] Ex 23: 5; Lev 19; Deut 21–22: 2.

[270] Ex 23: 4.

[271] Lev 19: [14].

style of the ancients is more poetical than that of modern authors; they described things for the senses. No other fact is required to explain the natural development of thought and the application of words to thoughts. The ancients, forced to form a language they did not have, had first to name concepts bound to perceptions, and then name concepts severed from perceptions. In perceptions however they did not name everything, but only what struck and attracted their attention most. This was taken as an indication and sign of the whole perception. The name expressed the perception and referred to it as an indication or natural sign. The word itself always meant 'that which produces this feeling'; for example, 'that which is beautiful' produces the feeling of beauty; that which is healthy is 'that which produces health'. But because the same indication was found in other objects, the word was suitable for indicating them as well. This was true also for disparate objects, because they produced the same feeling and, I must insist, the meaning of a word refers to feeling. 'The unity of feeling is the primal instrument for the formation of genera and species signified by words.' The feeling is an effect produced equally by several causes and hence a common *natural sign* of them.

1469. Furthermore the *unity of feeling* also explains the *association of partial feelings* which, as I have said, is the source of metaphors and particularly of metonymy. The element that we name relative to a perceived feeling is that which attracts our attention most because it strikes our *sense more vividly* or responds to our *need*, the two guides of our attention. Sometimes the feeling contains the cause and effect, the container and the contained, the sign and the thing signed, etc. The word, precisely because it is suitable for arousing other feelings through association, expresses one of these elements and is then transferred to mean them all or another element.

We say 'I did not see his face' to mean 'I did not see the man'. The part that attracts our attention more is his face, so the word is suitable for arousing the thought of the whole person. We say 'I will draw steel' to mean 'I will draw my sword', that is, the material is used for the whole instrument (material and form). 'The whole earth exulted' means the inhabitants of the earth, the container for the contained. The same can be said about every case of metonymy.

[1469]

1470. We must also note that change in meaning never ceases, precisely because association of thoughts and feelings never ends or stops. This explains changes in languages. Association unfolds in a continuous series which sometimes regroups and returns on itself. Both the human mind and its accompanying use of the signs makes continual progress in this way. Signs which sometimes change from common names to individual names, revert once more to common and even very common names. The same is true about transferred and proper names which are continually interchanging. For example, in the logical order, 'Adam' must have first meant a perceived tract of red earth and been applied to the individual object of the perception. Later it meant 'all red earth', which is the specific idea understood in the perception; it was now a common name. Next, it expressed the first created man because he is formed from red earth. The common name has once again become individual. It was then given to women as well as men, and thus took on the general meaning of 'that which is formed from red earth', but its use[272] remained tied to the more limited genus, human beings.

1471. 14. So far we have seen how human beings in society were able to think what is common and invent words to indicate it.

But what is common is still not pure abstraction. This comes later, and we have great difficulty in understanding its origin. Elsewhere, I concluded that we were unable to think and name pure abstraction because nature provided no stimulus for us to do so. From here, I went on to deduce the divine origin of the abstract part of language.[273] Now, however, more mature reflection shows me that the demonstration is not irrefutable. We have to distinguish the question of *fact* from that of *simple possibility*. Relative to fact, there is no doubt that the first human was taught to speak by God himself; God spoke first and, in doing so, communicated a part of language, as I shall show elsewhere. Relative to simple possibility, the case is different. I now think it possible that the human family, not an isolated individual, could

---

[272] The distinction between the *use* of a word and its *nature*, that is, the way in which it indicates things, must always be kept in mind.

[273] *Teodicea*, 100–115; *NE*, vol. 2, 514–527.

with time come to think these abstractions and at the same time, by some complex action, indicate them vocally or through some other sign. I think I have found the stimulus which moves the human mind, the stimulus I had previously sought in vain.

This must certainly have taken place after the processes mentioned above; *abstract names* must have come after *common names*, as ancient languages clearly demonstrate. They had very few abstracts (perhaps of divine origin); in their place they frequently used *common names*, that is, *qualified substantives*. This characteristic is still found in the language used by Plato who however took abstraction much further when he entitled his dialogues 'On what is just', 'On what is beautiful', 'On what is holy', 'On what is good', rather than 'On Justice', 'On Beauty', 'On Holiness', 'On Goodness', etc.

1472. But how could the human family, simply with its own resources, arrive at pure abstracts, or at least at some abstracts? There must be something in real nature, some natural sign of the abstract, to which the abstract can be joined. Without this, the attention of the human mind cannot rest in abstracts nor draw them together. Let me explain what this is and how it was given to humanity.

We invent names to arouse in others' minds the concept of the thing we are indicating: a part is used for the whole, the container for the contained, etc. When the name given to the part or to the container is sufficient to arouse the concept of the whole or of the contained, no other name is needed. Granted the natural association of feelings, this is precisely what happens.

Granted moreover that corporeal entia have several parts, each of which can be perceived on its own, it is clear that each part can, without any difficulty, also be named on its own. Thus relative to the human person, in addition to the name 'man', other names were easily invented, like 'head', 'face', 'arm', 'hand', etc..

Each of these parts however has its own particular qualities and properties, perceived together with the part to which they belong. For example, one of the properties could be strength. This can be named in two ways: either with a neutral, common name, meaning 'that which is strong', or with the name of the part where it is most frequently seen and engages our interest, for example, the hand or arm, or horns. A name is of course applied in the easiest way, and surely it is easier to use 'hand', 'arm', 'horn', etc., to indicate strength than invent a new name, a neutral common name? The strong parts of the body had already been named, and it was clearly easier to use them with a metonymical meaning. The extension or transference of the meaning of a word already in use is, as a general rule, easier than the search for an entirely new one. But the names of these parts, which indicate objects of perception, were among the first to be invented and can therefore be understood as meaning 'strength'.

This is precisely what we find in ancient languages: 'the hand of the Lord'[274] or 'the arm of the Lord'[275] are continually used in Scripture to mean the strength of God; 'a horn to David' indicates the strength of David.[276] A sign is found to which the mind can attach an abstract concept, and then the name, as it gradually loses its first meaning, becomes ever more abstract until it results finally as an abstract name. 'Face' or 'visage', parts of the body which reflect human affections, are applied to God, and taken to mean his benevolence or even his anger.[277] *Path* is taken for his Providence, etc. In this way we can even arrive, in the formation of pure abstracts, at extreme abstraction.

Let me take more general abstractions as an example. First of all, in metonymy the sign is taken for the thing signified. This is very common and very natural. Suppose we are asked what something is and reply: 'A body, a light, an elephant'. Here the sign is taken for the thing signified. We simply use the word itself instead of a long rigmarole such as: 'It is the ens signified by "body" or "light" or "elephant", etc.' We should not be surprised therefore that *word, verbum*, λόγος, *debir* are used in Scripture and in Greek and Latin authors to mean any fact or event whatsoever, and even most generally 'thing', as we see in the lexicons. Moses says, 'Lest you forget the WORDS which your eyes have seen'.[278] In the first book of Samuel[279] we read, 'I

---

[274] 1 Samuel 5: 6 [Douai].

[275] Is 51: 9 [Douai].

[276] Ps 131: 17 [Douai].

[277] Ps 26: 8–9 [Douai]; Lev 20: 3, 5–6.

[278] Deut 4: 9.

[279] 1 Sam 3: 11.

am about to do a WORD in Israel', a very frequently used form of speech in the holy books. 'Expression' or 'word' itself is taken to mean the most general abstract by which we can conceive an *efficient and real ens*. It was also applied to mean the second of the divine Persons.

Even *ideal being* can be indicated as representing something real by transferring 'image' to it or 'something seen', as ancient languages did.

1473. So the human mind, with the help of these kinds of sensible signs provided by nature and hence denominated, determines certain abstracts and names them according to these signs. Thus there is no longer any obstacle to impede the mind's progress, and its whole development is explained naturally.

CHAPTER 21

Second psychological law: limitation and concentration of attention

1474. The soul, granted that it has been given the necessary *terms* and *stimuli* to express its acts, maintains a *mode* of its own in these acts.

This mode is such that the soul, when it wishes to unite itself more closely to its term, concentrates its limited activity on a single point of the term while withdrawing its activity from the other parts. This is the origin of both material and formal analysis, which in turn depends upon the extension or non-extension of the object on which the activity is exercised.

Formal analysis is *abstraction* in the strict sense. In an ideal or spiritual object it considers one element independently of the rest. This is the psychological law corresponding to the onto-logical laws described above.

1475. But how can an ideal or spiritual object, extremely simple in itself, be analysed and as it were divided into parts by the application of human attention? Are these parts real, or simply apparent and false?

Before replying, I must make the following observations.

1. A simple thing is often multiplied by the spirit which

considers it in relationship to many others things. For example, when we say: '*Ideal being* is the possibility of things', we are simply considering this being relative to its realisation, without predicating possibility of ideal being itself. Thus the ideas I have called 'elementary ideas of ideal being'[280] can be reduced to relationships of ideal being. The *many relationships* that a simple being may have do not deprive it of its simplicity, just as the centre of a circle does not lose its simplicity when seen in relationship with all the assignable, innumerable points in the circumference.

These relationships clearly show that that simple ens is not alone: other entia exist to which thought can refer and compare it, and vice versa. Indeed, if there were only *ideal being* and no real ens (which is impossible), nothing could be distinguished in ideal being, which would remain internally uniform. If Parmenides had understood his one ens as an ideal ens or the idea of an ens, the objections made against him by Plato[281] and Aristotle[282] would have been effective. They claimed that he contradicted himself by attributing to that ens immortality, immobility, uniformity, integrity, perfection, etc. In their view, if the ens were simply one, nothing else could be added to it. But because the ancients did not realise that an ens is under several forms, they inadvertently reasoned about it now under one form, now under another. These great minds were thus lost in inextricable labyrinths. Generally speaking, however, deeper reasoning ended in the *idea of an ens*, while the properties of the idea were attributed to the *ens* itself. Hence, because this idea does not have internal variety except in the presence of what is real, the ancients denied internal variety and order to ens. This explains the objections which appear so difficult to solve.

1476 2. An ens can be simple but still have variety deep within it. Any argument supposing the contrary shows that our only concept of simplicity is that taken from a mathematical point. This is a negative concept which totally denies extension. But simple entia do not consist in mere negation; they are

---

[280] *NE*, vol. 2, 575–578.
[281] In *Sophist*.
[282] *Phys.*, 1.

positive, more positive even than extended entia. A thing is simple when nothing can be taken from it without destroying it.

1477. According to this definition, an ens containing many different things is not contrary to simplicity, although everything in it must be so unified that the removal of one element alone is sufficient to destroy the ens.

1478. Hence, various classes of simple entia.

A mathematical point is not an *ens* but a *negation*, as I said. It is not an *object* of our spirit, but an *act* carried out by our spirit on an object (extension).

An *ideal ens* is totally uniform. As long as it remains one ens, nothing can be discerned in it. Only by comparing it with a real ens can something be distinguished within it.

A *spiritual ens* is simple and not internally uniform; on the contrary, it is organated in such a way so that none of its organs, of its essential elements, can be removed without destroying it. This must be understood in several ways:

a) If we are speaking about the reality of a spiritual ens, its accidental parts can *be changed into others* without being divided by the change. It can also *be multiplied*, if its term is multiplied, as in the case of the animal principle. But this is still not division into several parts.

b) If we are dealing with the idea of a spiritual ens, we can: 1. conceive multiplication of the ens and changes in its accidents, and 2. divide the elements by *abstract thought*, although not by *all-embracing thought*, which always remains in the mind. The fact that abstract, partial thought can find these distinctions does not contradict either the simplicity of the ens or the truth, because the elements, although truly distinct in the ens, are not separate; abstract, analytical thought merely distinguishes them without separating them although, at the moment of their distinction, they are kept individually united by total, all-embracing thought. We may perhaps mistakenly believe we separate them, but in this case our belief originates from judgment, the source of errors, not from thought.

CHAPTER 22

Third psychological law: the absence of consciousness

1479. We know nothing except the object of thought (idea) or what our spirit says about the object of thought (word).

When the object of thought is ourselves, or what is or what happens in us, we know ourselves, or what is or what happens in us. This kind of knowledge is called 'consciousness'.

Consciousness differs from *feeling*. The former is knowledge and has the duality proper to knowledge (the knower and the thing known, as separable entia). The latter is simple; it has only the duality, proper to itself, by which two correlative terms are distinguished, such that one cannot be thought of as an ens if separated from the other.

1480. As long as the object of the human spirit is ideal-infinite being alone, the spirit has no consciousness of itself because both it and what happens in it have not yet become an object of its attention.[283]

Consciousness therefore is produced by *attention* directed to oneself. The human principle, which is afterwards called *myself*, must attract its own attention to itself.

1481. But the human principle is moved to attend only through *need*, which we define as: 'The instinct to complete an action already begun, that is, the instinct for completing an activity already in motion.'

1482. All human activity begins to move by means of its real term, as I have said. Hence, only when a real term has been added to the intellective principle, can the principle be moved to focus on itself and form consciousness. Granted the conditions for forming consciousness, we can separate ourselves positively from the ideal object and know ourselves as a subject in contradistinction to the object.

1483. There is therefore this difference between our human

---

[283] Contrary to the truth of the fact, Spinoza and the German philosophers claim that human beings are always conscious to themselves of all that happens in them.

initial state, anterior to all development, and the state in which we are conscious of ourselves — the difference, I mean, when we distinguish ideal being from self. In our initial state, we know only ideal being, not ourselves. We *do not confuse* ideal being with ourselves because we do not know OURSELVES; OURSELF is not yet formed. We cannot distinguish it, because one thing cannot be distinguished from another without knowledge of both.

In the state of consciousness, we know ideal being and know ourselves as a subject opposed to this object; we thus *distinguish* ourselves by a positive act.

1484. We can therefore assert that to know without consciousness is a psychological law of the spirit, and that consciousness originates in the spirit solely as a result of real stimuli which draw the spirit into action.

CHAPTER 23

Fourth psychological law: knowledge obtained through affirmation or denial (word)

1485. But what the spirit adds is the *word*, that is, the interior word with which it affirms or denies.

With this act the spirit acquires a new cognition but not, we must carefully note, a new *object*. What the spirit pronounces presupposes the object given it through intuition, perception or reasoning. The object is as it were the matter of the spirit's pronouncement.

1486. Because the word, the judgment, the affirmation (or whatever we call it) is moved by the influence of practical reason upon theoretical reason, it has its cause more in practical than in theoretical reason. Nevertheless by a kind of psychological instinct the act of affirmation sometimes follows immediately upon theoretical vision.

1487. The spirit cannot perform this act of the interior word unless it finds in the object a duality which can become predicate and subject. Simple intuition allows no pronouncement or judgment because *infinite, ideal ens* divided from all reality is so uniform that it does not admit multiplicity.[284] If the spirit is to be able to affirm or deny, it must be put in communication with some real being, the source of plurality.

1488. But if the word adds no new object to the spirit, what is the nature of the spirit's cognition acquired through the word?

The cognition produced by the mental word differs totally from that produced by the *idea* (ens). The former is *subjective*, the latter essentially *objective*, as we have seen. By *subjective cognition* I do not mean false cognition; I mean that this cognition, unlike the cognition coming from the idea, does not have its truth within itself but must receive its truth from the idea, from the object, by harmonising and adapting itself to the object.

1489. The object, the ens, the idea, which is truth itself and as it were synonymous with the truth, is superior to true and false.[285] 'True' and 'false' pertain to the pronouncements of the spirit, not to the object.

1490. We now have a solution to the famous sophism of the ancients, which runs as follows:

'We think only an ens and therefore can pronounce only an ens, because a non-ens is neither thinkable nor pronounceable.

But an ens and what is true are the same thing.

Therefore everything we think and pronounce is true.'[286]

I deny the major when understood in its totality. In other words, when distinguishing its parts, I say:

'We think only an ens.' Here I make the following distinction. If the sentence is used to express objective thought, I grant its accuracy; if it is used to express all thought, including subjective thought (which pronounces something about the ens), I deny it.

'And therefore can pronounce only an ens'. I deny this also. 'To pronounce' is to affirm or deny something. The object of a pronouncement is not an ens, but the nexus, that is, the predication itself.

We can indeed pronounce that an ens is false or true, but in

---

[284] *NE*, vol. 2, 552.

[285] *Ibid.*, 1062–1064; 1112–1135.

[286] Cf. Plato in *Euthydemus, Cratylus, Sophist* and *Theaetetus*. He attributes the invention of this sophism to philosophers who preceded Protagoras, although this famous sophist made great use of it.

this case it is the pronouncement, a subjective operation of the spirit, which is false, not the ens.

1491. As far as I know, philosophers have neither felt the force of this most important distinction, nor sufficiently known and described the nature of subjective cognition resulting from a pronouncement, judgment or word of the spirit.

What then is the nature of this way of knowledge?

It does not consist in the spirit's acquisition of a new object, as I said above, but is 'the power the spirit has to dispose itself in a certain mode relative to the object before it.' In one mode the spirit affirms, in another it denies, although the object, 'the essence of what is seen in the idea' (as I have said), remains the same. There is neither affirmation nor denial in the object; only the spirit affirms or denies. Essence, whether we affirm or deny anything of it, remains the same. For example, I deny that there is a pear or a fig in the garden. The essence (my mental *object*) of the pear or fig remains what it was before my denial. My spirit has simply denied that the essence is realised in the garden. The same is true if I affirm the presence of the pear; its essence would remain unaltered.

1492. What effect does this act produce in the spirit, and what do we call this effect or disposition? I have called it 'persuasion'. This kind of knowledge can be called 'knowledge by persuasion' or 'knowledge by predication'. The ancients sometimes confused *persuasion* with *opinion*, but the two differ greatly: opinion can be joined either to a firm or to a weak, vacillating persuasion.

1493. I will now suggest solutions to possible difficulties. The *object* intuited and grasped directly by the spirit is one thing; the subsequent *predication* made by the spirit is another. The spirit does not err in its intuition and apprehension,[287] but can err in its predication, which may conform or deviate from the object.

Here difficulties easily arise, which could be presented in the following way: 'If I predicate something of the object, the predicate itself must be an object. In this case, the term of my knowledge by predication is an object, a new object.'

I reply. The term of knowledge by predication is not an object of any kind; it is the union of subject and predicate, not the

[287] *NE*, vol. 3, 1247–1278.

subject and predicate in themselves. I know this union in the object through the predication made by my spirit.

It may then be objected that the object of knowledge by predication is the *union* itself of subject and predicate. This knowledge therefore has an object of its own, a new object supplied by the spirit.

This reasoning reveals one of those common illusions which are very difficult to avoid. I always try to identify them because they prevent the mind from philosophising accurately. The illusion is this.

The *relationship* between predicate and subject can be considered solely as possible (intuitable). Considered as such, the relationship is an object, which is known by intuition, not by *predication*. For example, when I say, 'This body is cold', I predicate coldness of the body and am persuaded that the body is cold. But before affirming that the body is cold, I can conceive the relationship between the coldness and the body without affirming the relationship. In this case I intuit the relationship simply as possible. At the same time I can also intuit a relationship between the body and heat. But I still do not affirm either relationship. By having the intuition of these possible relationships, my spirit possesses the object, which it can either affirm or deny. When my spirit actually affirms or denies the object, it is already in possession of the object. Consequently my affirmation or denial does not concern *possession* of the object; they simply provide my spirit with the persuasion that one of the two relationships intuited as possible is; when my spirit pronounces that the relationship is, it is persuaded.

1494. 'But what does this "is" signify, pronounced about one or other of the two possible, contradictory relationships?' 'Is' has two significations: either the act of ideal being or the act of real being. If the affirmation remains within the sphere of possibility, which is the case of logical or mathematical affirmations (for example, 'The consequence IS contained in the principle', or 'The sum of the three angles of a triangle IS equal to two right angles'), the copulative IS simply signifies ideal being. If the affirmation enters the sphere of reality, as in the case of physical affirmation (for example, 'This metal IS gold', 'The sun IS a body'), the copulative IS signifies a reality pertaining to a real subject. The subject can also be an ens abstracted from its forms, with the predicate as its real form; for example, 'This ens subsists', where *subsistence*, that is, reality, is taken as the predicate of the essence of the ens.

If the copulative IS, which is always pronounced in the predication, signifies ideal being, the process is as follows. *Ideal ens* is the object. If this object were not present to the mind, the spirit could predicate nothing about it. But the object is present to the mind, and the mind intuits it in its totality according to the ontological laws I have described. But in addition to the intuitive faculty in the spirit, a faculty of *abstraction* is also present. This abstraction is carried out by means of limitation and concentration of attention. Abstraction does not destroy the object but divides it up and distinguishes its elements. This action, because *subjective*, does not affect the object, which remains intact in itself present to the mind. The mind now possesses not only the total object through intuition, but also the object divided into its elements through abstraction. This *abstraction*, a kind of analysis or dismantling, is the origin of *predication*, a kind of synthesis joining the separated elements. When I say *analysis* and *synthesis*, I am talking about the form of the spirit's act and not strictly speaking about the result of the two processes. In fact we can divide the form of a synthesis when we deny a predicate to a subject instead of affirming it. But because our discussion here concerns subjective actions, we must note their form, not their result. If the *predication* is false as a result of a union between an element of the object and an element not pertaining to the object, the spirit pronounces an *absurdity* (in the world of ideas, of course), which is only a putative object. The spirit pronounces an absurdity because, when it affirms an ideal predicate of an ideal subject, as in this case, the affirmation concerns *possibility*; to pronounce as possible what is impossible is simply to pronounce an absurdity. The predication of possibility means therefore to *acknowledge* what is *known*, to affirm the intuition of what is intuited. But in the case of pure acknowledgement, that is, knowing *in another way* something already known, no new object is presented to our mind; we merely change the *mode* with which our spirit seeks to know the same object. This different mode, which cannot pertain to the object, pertains to the subject, and is simply a new disposition assumed by the spirit relative to the object, a disposition called *subjective* or *persuasive cognition*. When this cognition conforms to the object, it is true; when it does not conform, it is false.

1495. If the copulative IS signifies real being, as in the examples I have given, the same thing applies, except that the elements of predication are not given by abstraction. Hence if the judgment is false, it is not necessarily absurd. For example, when I say, 'This metal is gold', although it is brass, I pronounce a non-absurd falsehood; the metal can in fact be conceived as gold. Similarly, when I say, 'The phoenix subsists', I say something false, but not impossible.

Here the elements of judgment are given partly by feeling, at least on the part of the *predicate*, which is something real. 'Real' means 'what happens in feeling', which is subjective and totally outside the object of the mind. The spirit, which is subject, performs an act by which it unites the feeling-predicate (real) with the subject under discussion. This subject may itself be real, or perhaps essential being abstracted from its forms. But the union of identity produces nothing new in the object; it takes place totally in the subject that accomplishes it and of which it is a new disposition, a disposition which constitutes *subjective cognition*.

1496. In fact I have already distinguished between the subject's *fundamental union* with the object (effected through intuition) and the more intimate *union* that the subject effects with its object. This second union pertaining, as I said, to operative or *practical reason*, does not produce a new object but a new degree and mode of union. It does produce however a new *cognition*, true or false, relative to the object.

1497. Reality is certainly added in this case, but reality is not a new object; it is a predicate, an appurtenance of the previous perceived object. If this previous object were the essence of bread intuited in the idea of bread, then when I say 'The bread subsists', I simply add reality to the object already known (ideal bread). The reality is a subjective feeling, not an object. Consequently, although the subject of the proposition is truly an object, the predicate is not; on the contrary, it is rather a term of affirmation, a subjective term, present in the feeling of bread. The proposition is equivalent to: 'The bread, an object of my mind, has a mode of being outside my mind, and this mode of being is sensible to me in one way or another.' Note carefully: if 'sensible being' is understood as an object of the mind and not as a feeling, it is something possible, but devoid of affirmation; it is not what we are discussing. If the two terms of the proposition, 1. the bread, 2. the subsistence, are considered as possible, they are objects, and in this case subsistence is no longer subsistence but the *idea of subsistence*. We have returned to the ideal order but not yet pronounced any connection between these objects, although when we do, our pronouncement does not add another object. As long as we intuit the connection as possible, we neither pronounce nor affirm it. When we affirm it, it becomes a persuasion, a subjective cognition.

In the ideal essence therefore of an ens, reality is already contained as ideal. But properly speaking this is *reality* for the human spirit only when the spirit affirms it. The spirit affirms the intuited object and does so because it feels the object. This affirmation is purely a new mode by which the spirit unites the object to itself.

CHAPTER 24

Corollary on the classification of human cognitions

1498. I must now deal with an important corollary resulting from what has been said.

The two activities of the rational principle, one aroused solely by the object and the other proper to the subject, result in two kinds of human cognition, *objective* and *subjective*.

Objective cognition, governed totally by the ontological laws I have described, corresponds to the first activity aroused by the object in the rational principle. Subjective cognition, originated by predication and governed by psychological laws, corresponds to the second activity proper to the subject.

1499. The term of the first kind of activity is the intuited object (that which is possible). An example is the proposition, 'Knowledge is about necessary things'.[288]

---

[288] The ancient dictum, 'All knowledge is through form' (St. Thomas, *S. T.*, I, q.12, art. 1, ad 2), pertains also to this knowledge. Consequently 'the infinite,

The term of the second kind is *persuasion*, or a certain state of the spirit relative to the object, by which the spirit, the subject, is united to the object in another way, and thus increases its cognition. The proposition 'Knowledge is about necessary things' cannot be included in it because subjective cognition can refer to contingent things. Anything real can be contingent; indeed every contingent thing is real, although not every real thing is contingent.

1500. The distinction is sufficient to destroy idealistic pantheism which, beginning from the false principle 'All knowledge is objective', induces that all knowledge concerns necessary things which in turn are reduced to God. It lays down that God is the universal, direct object of knowledge and, because every entity is an object of knowledge, soon concludes that every entity is God. The error in this reasoning lies in the principle. As I said, the statement that all knowledge is objective is false, just as it is false to say that all knowledge is 'about necessary things'. There is a mode of knowledge relative to contingent things, that is, a subjective knowledge obtained by predication.

1501. This distinction between knowledge through intuition and knowledge through *affirmation* gives a solid basis for *philosophical method*. It excludes the error of those who claim that 1. all human knowledge is reduced to *facts*, 2. human beings do not know the reasons for things, and consequently 3. only positive, not speculative sciences have real value.

The word 'facts' can of course be understood in many ways. In its most obvious sense, it means the term of knowledge acquired through *affirmation*. But this is not the only knowledge possessed by human beings. On the contrary, before we know through affirmation, we know through intuition, that is, through the ideal object. We can therefore refer the cognitions acquired by our *affirmations* (known facts) to cognitions acquired through *intuition*, and find the relationships between them. These relationships contain the *reasons for the facts*, and

considered through form relative to imperfect matter, is in itself unknown' (*ibid.*). However I say more generally that every *subsistence* (except the divine subsistence) is *per se* unknowable. Hence the *idea* (objective knowledge) must precede every cognition which predicates (subjective knowledge).

these reasons become a third genus of cognitions. Not even Scottish philosophy is immune from this error.[289]

If however we give a very extensive but inaccurate sense to the word 'fact', we must distinguish between 1. real facts, 2. ideal facts, and 3. the relationships between these two, that is, the reasons explaining real facts. Only in this inaccurate sense can we say that all human cognitions are reduced to having facts as their matter.

CHAPTER 25

Summary

1502. The four psychological laws I have explained and distinguished from the ontological laws can be summarised as follows:

The rational subject acts according to two negative and two positive laws.

The negative laws are the first and third psychological laws. They say that 1. The object does not arouse any other activity in the subject than that by which the subject rests in the object through intuition; and 2. the object does not provide the subject with self-consciousness which begins only with the subject's second acts.

1503. The positive laws are the second and fourth psychological laws. These state: 1. granted that the rational principle has been moved to second acts through cosmological stimuli, it can concentrate and limit its attention on any of the elements of the object or of the objects (if there are many), or on one or other relationship between the objects, and thus become conscious also of intuiting the object; and 2. granted such movement, the rational principle can intuit its subjective modifications in the object, and form concepts. In this way it acquires subjective cognition or cognition by predication, and with this cognition acknowledges the object itself.

[289] Cf. Stewart, *Éléments de Philosophie de l'Esprit humain*, vol. 1, c. 1, sect. 2, where he describes Reid's system.

CHAPTER 26

The cosmological laws proper to the rational principle in general — Two species of cosmological laws, 'laws of motion' and laws which determine the rational principle's 'quality of movement'

1504. In expounding the psychological laws proper to the rational principle, I had to intermingle them with that which the world administers to the spirit because the movement of second acts is given to the spirit only by the action of the world.

We have to distinguish, therefore, between laws governing the movement of an already constituted rational principle, which I shall call *laws of motion*, and laws determining the *mode* governing that movement, which we can call *laws of quality of movement*.

1505. The *laws of motion* are cosmological, that is, imposed on the spirit by the action of contingent entities.

The laws of *quality of movement* are in part cosmological and in part psychological.

1506. We can, therefore, reduce all cosmological laws to two supreme laws, one of which I shall call the *law of motion*, because it expresses the dependence of acts of the spirit on the stimulating action of the world; the other I shall call the *law of aesthetic harmony*, because it expresses the quality and mode proper to the movement of the spirit and of second acts. This movement has been determined by the harmony in the world pre-established by the Creator so that a corresponding harmony might enter the spirit as it develops its activity.

CHAPTER 27

The cosmological law of motion

Article 1
The two parts of the law of motion

1507. In Fichte's sensism (his idealism is nothing more than sensism) the spirit posits itself together with the act with which it posits the world. At one and the same time, the spirit affirms MYSELF and NOT-MYSELF as co-relative and contrary elements, which limit and distinguish one another. According to me, the spirit is not constituted in this way, but works through the following acts:

1. It intuits the object, being in general, without affirming it, without affirming itself, without having any consciousness of itself or its act; it lives and is in being;

2. Contemporaneously, the spirit perceives a fundamental feeling and has, as a consequence, a *fundamental perception* which is *apprehension* without *express affirmation*. However, it neither perceives itself as *perceiving*, nor has consciousness of itself. Nevertheless it knows its own feeling, the term of its feeling and the principle of feeling without any act of the spirit dividing this principle from the term in which it lies.

Consciousness, and MYSELF, come much later, as I have explained.

The term of the fundamental feeling is not, therefore, perceived in the enunciation of a NOT-MYSELF, which is a relationship with and denial of MYSELF. It is perceived simply as something extended, without any comparison with MYSELF, which as yet is not even revealed. MYSELF, as we know, is not the sentient but the rational principle which, with conscious reflection, perceives the feeling it has acquired, that is, perceived. Nevertheless, there is in the feeling some duality, badly expressed indeed by Fichte with the words MYSELF and NOT-MYSELF. This duality should have been expressed with words signifying the correlative concepts of *principle* and *term*.

1508. But the change arising in feeling is the condition of the motion which the rational principle receives for its second acts. Because this change happens naturally through the action of the agents which compose the world, the spirit is said to be subject to this law of dependence on the world for its development (a cosmological law).

This law is reduced, therefore, to what I have already indicated: *what is real* is the term arousing *attention*, which is the *radical force of subjective knowledge*; what is real actuates and concentrates attention.[290] If what is real is removed from the

[290] This law, therefore, possesses a negative element which states: 'The

soul, no cognitive act is possible except the soul's first act of intuition, without any subjective attention, without any concentration proper to subjective attention. It can be said, therefore, that in such a state the subject as subject has no actual cognition of its own.

1509. But two things have to be considered in this law:

1. The reason why the rational principle, overcoming its inertia, passes to its second acts: 'What is real, the term of the rational principle, is that which arouses *attention* and draws it to acts of subjective knowledge.'

2. The reason why these second acts of the rational principle are lively, enduring and satisfying: 'If acts of the rational principle find a real term, they are stable and lively. Otherwise, they are weak and tiring, and soon cease.'

Let us consider both parts of this law.

Article 2
The first part of the cosmological law of motion: what is real
as term of the rational principle is that which arouses
the attention of the principle and leads it to acts of
subjective knowledge

1510. This law is obvious from experience. The following comments on it will be of some assistance.

1. Not everything real stimulates the rational principle to the same degree of attention nor posits in it an equal quantity of action. Some real things attract attention exclusively to themselves. This attention comes to rest in perception. Other real things initiate *reasoning*.

1511. 2. Real things which, in addition to perception, initiate *reasoning*, are our *needs*. The rational principle instinctively endeavours to satisfy them in every way possible. One of these

rational principle is not moved to its second acts without some stimulus from what is real'. In this negative aspect, it is a psychological law corresponding to the ontological laws. It has also a positive element which states: 'What is real arouses attention, maintains it in act and focuses it.' In this respect, it is a cosmological law of the human spirit because it expresses the activity of the spirit corresponding to the real term, the world.

ways is the power of reasoning. *Need*, then, is not a simple feeling, but results from many simple feelings grouped together in a certain order. This, properly speaking, explains why motion also evolves in multiple acts.

1512. 3. Again, real things, when connected in virtue of animal laws and instincts, stimulate reasoning and an action which extends beyond perception. As a consequence, granted one image, more and more images are aroused; granted a feeling, other feelings are connected with it, according to the tenor of these laws.

1513. 4. When thought has conceived and proposed an *end* to the will, a free decision gives rise to thinking about means. Thus activity is extended, although this cognitive activity needs continual help from new, real things in order to follow through with thought and action.

1514. 5. Finally, not everything real which excites lively perception, is sufficient to produce *consciousness*, that is, to move us to reflect on ourselves. We are brought to this principally by social language and our needs. In fact, in society, names and personal pronouns stimulate reflection to consider person. The need to do this soon arises, as we see in the case of children. When some wrong has been done to a child, he begins to defend his own right and to judge between himself and the companion who has offended him. He begins to reflect on his own person and on the person of others.

6. Finally feelings, granted they last for some time, help to maintain thought in act. This forms the second part of the law which I shall now explain.

Article 3
The second part of the law of motion: attention and thought
are kept lively through the stability of what is real

1515. No one accustomed to observe human activity will deny this fact.

Here, however, an interesting investigation presents itself.

We have seen 1. that movement is not continuous, but comes about through instantaneous changes from state to state, each of which lasts for a brief period; 2. that certain extrasubjective movements in our fibre precede or correspond to stimulated feelings. However, feeling is one thing; the change from one feeling to another is something else. The latter can be done in an instant; the former must have some duration. *Stimulated feeling*, therefore, is always a more or less enduring state. But if *stimulated feeling* is an enduring state and stimulated along with *non-lasting changes* (movement of fibres), we must conclude that the instantaneous *changes* present in movement are not feelings and cannot be the full cause of feelings. The fullness of this cause must come from the enduring sentient principle.

1516. In the second place, and as confirmation, we have a *non-stimulated feeling* which has for its term not movement but what is extended, that is, several extended things which rub against one another.[291]

1517. In the third place, we notice that movements which arise in the extended element are not felt in their individual, instantaneous changes because 1. the change *is* instantaneous and feeling does not last longer than its term. Feeling, therefore, would be of zero duration if it had these changes as its terms. Consequently, it would not be feeling. 2. If this were how things happened, we would never have a constant feeling, but in every feeling would have to feel incessant change. Every feeling would be a complex of many successive feelings between which there would be intervals without feeling. This is totally opposed to what we know from experience. Nor could we object that such multiplicity and intervals could be present in every feeling without our adverting to them. If this were the case, we should notice far more easily the enduring intervals between one feeling and another than the non-lasting feelings. All the feelings taken together would last less than a single interval, just as zero duration is less than any minimum duration, however small. Moreover, we do not advert to certain things which happen in us because we are occupied and distracted by other sensible things which attract and hold our rational attention. In our present case, we should be able to advert to the cessation of feeling that should last. Indeed, such feeling would be more apt to draw and hold our attention than feelings with zero duration. But we still have to establish that 'everything which we feel, and

---

[291] *AMS*, 318–322.

all passages from one feeling to another, are *per se* capable of being adverted to', and that lack of advertence is, for the reason given, only accidental. Finally, non-advertence to what is present is one thing; advertence to what is not present is another. The former may occur because we are subject to distraction, but this is obviously inapplicable to the latter. Advertence to the duration of our feelings is inexplicable if there is no duration. Indeed, we must say: 'We advert to this; everyone adverts to this: therefore, it is.' If it were not, we could not advert to it.

1518. We have to conclude, therefore, with the following beautiful and important proposition which throws great light on the nature of animal feeling: 'Sensations and other stimulated feelings do not have as their term movements of our fibre, that is, any change of place or state in the parts which make up the extended felt element. Their term is the extended felt element itself. The movement of the parts of the extended felt element, together with their reciprocal pressure and irritation, ensures that the extended element is felt in another way, and with greater liveliness.'[292]

1519. One thing, then, proves another. The fact of duration of stimulated feeling proves the impossibility of continuous movement as its term. Continuous movement, which has no lasting state or place, cannot be the term of feeling. We have to say, therefore, that the changes taking place in the movement of the fibres can (in their own way) *excite* feeling, but cannot of themselves alone be its term. We also have to say that stimulated feeling *lasts*, although the stimulus (the change in the fibre) which serves to excite, does not.

---

[292] It may be objected that our argument runs as follows: 'The extra-subjective body is extended because the subjective term of feeling is extended (*NE*, vol. 2, 846–870). Why not argue in the same way, that because stimulated feeling is lasting, movement is continuous and hence lasting?' The two cases cannot in fact be compared. The second contains an absurdity not present in the first. Again, in the first argument we know the term of feeling and we argue from it to its proximate cause, that is, from the extension of the term to the extension of the proximate cause (although the remote cause, the corporeal principle, may be or rather must be simple). In the second argument, we argue from the duration of feeling to the duration of its term. Granted, therefore, that its term must endure, feeling cannot consist in instantaneous changes which have zero duration.

If the Creator had not arranged for sensations to have some prolonged duration, they would not have served their purpose, nor would the observations and experiments of natural scientists be possible.

1520. We now use the second part of the laws of motion to explain certain facts. There is no doubt that the rational principle, once drawn to its second acts, acquires free movement, that is, movement which can be directed according to the ends proposed by the will. Nevertheless, if this rational movement (moved originally by a real term, by a need, etc.) does not find a real term as its aim, it cannot form long-lasting, easy and lively acts.

1521. The facts explained by this law are principally the following. It explains

I. Why the mind cannot think subjectively without sensations or phantasms.[293]

1522. II. Why incorporeal substances cannot easily be conceived in their purity if nothing corporeal is mixed with them. The reason is this. In the order of nature, we perceive only our soul as an incorporeal substance and moreover perceive it through feeling which is in our soul as in its principle. But our very own feeling has as its term a purely extended element, or a corporeal extended element. It is true that the intuiting principle is the first act of feeling itself, but for this very reason it has no consciousness; although it is something real, it is not a *real term* (and only a *real-term* attracts attention). In the natural order, we have no other real term except our body. The attention of the rational principle is, therefore, drawn by corporeal feeling. Only later, by means of *free reflection*, does it consider the *intuiting principle* which it cannot know through any lively, concentrated conception because it does not find anything real in the intuiting principle to serve as a stimulating term. Because we have in us no perception of any incorporeal substance except our own, which is not suitable as a term for stimulating our attention except in so far as it is united with our body, we are inclined to conceive and imagine other substances as possessing

---

[293] St. Thomas acknowledged this law to such an extent that although he attributes a certain fullness of infused knowledge to the first human being, he nevertheless teaches that the first man needed phantasms in order to *ponder*.

the same nature as the term of our substance, that is, corporeal nature.

1523. III. Why abstractions need natural or artificial signs if we are to think them and reason about them.

1524. IV. Why spiritual substances and abstracts are always indicated in more ancient languages by words drawn from corporeal sources. Thus *anima, animus* (from ἄνενος), *spiritus* (πνεῦμα) are all words first signifying wind or corporeal air, and then taken to mean incorporeal substance. Again, abstract moral good did not have a word of its own but was called sometimes *virtue*, which means power,[294] sometimes *honestas* which means beauty, sometimes *mos*, which means custom. The word *obligatio* is also taken from a sensible bond and taken to mean 'force of law'.

1525. The same can be said about every spiritual substance and abstract except for the verb *to be* which was never expressed metaphorically. This fact alone is already an obvious witness furnished by common sense in favour of the philosophical system I have proposed. It shows that *being* cannot be confused with other abstractions because it is the immediate object always present to the mind.[295]

1526. V. Why languages are tools suitable for synthetical and analytical thought. Their synthetical quality is seen through the imposition of words in cases where a name is used to bind together a group of ideas or memories. When thought, which is bound through an ontological law to *unity*, has to retain several concepts or thoughts, it attempts to group them. One of the ways it uses to achieve this is to attach concepts to a single *word*. This is something real that serves to hold our attention and memory alert and alive — otherwise attention and memory would vanish; they would not exist without the presence of some *real* bond amid the plurality of things to join and unite these things. This explains our instinct for marking places where something has happened. We want to impress the matter in our memory through a *word* reminding us of it. The happening and the place have no natural, essential connection, and we find a single *mark* which commemorates both. Our rational

---

[294] Cf. *Storia comparativa de' sistemi morali*, c. 5, art. 7.

[295] Cf. Leibniz, *Nouveaux essais sur l'entendement humain*, bk 3, c. 1, §5.

instinct aims not only at passing on those memories to future generations, but of preserving their presence here and now.

This was very obvious amongst the first human beings whose language was still impoverished and who, as a result, had greater need to impose such names. Thus Agar called a well the 'well of the seer' because the angel of the Lord had appeared there.[296] In the same way, Abraham called the mountain of sacrifice 'the Lord sees';[297] Jacob called the place where he had the vision of the ladder Bethel, that is, 'house of God'[298] and gave the name *Mahanaim* to a place where he had experienced another vision of angels. The name was, as it were, a spontaneous expression of his feeling, shown by the instinctive way in which he pronounced it: 'These are the encampments of God'; *mahanaim* means 'encampment'.[299] The wells dug by the patriarchs were named according to the events occasioning the opening of the wells and according to the feeling which animated the patriarchs at that moment.[300] The fact of the imposition of names on places connected with very important events is very frequent throughout the whole of Genesis.

The same rational instinct explains why people were moved to name stars in memory of heroes or events whose memory (when they ceased to be or act as something real) they wished to recall after their passing. By using the stars in this way, memory was bound to two real things: 1. to a star which was always vividly and visibly present above and could not be ruined by time, as earthly monuments were; 2. to a name, which was heard, and consigned to the society formed by succeeding generations. As Giuseppe Bianchi wrote so wisely:

> It is clear that the heavenly and earthly globes were the oldest books of profane literature. The earthly globe preserves in its various names of provinces and seas a

[296] *Gen* 16: 14. — Agar also called 'the seer' the angel who had appeared to her, or rather God represented by the angel. She named him from his *action*, or manifestation.

[297] *Gen* 22: 14.

[298] *Gen* 28: 19.

[299] *Gen* 32: 1.

[300] *Gen* 26.

faithful catalogue of the different nations which inhabited it and of the many princes who ruled it. The heavenly globe, set out in very ancient images which precede Homer and Hesiodus, is a clear monument to undertakings and leaders, to arts and artificers, transmitted for the knowledge of future generations.[301]

1527. Every word we utter is, practically speaking, a synthesis; it is very rare for a word to stand for a single concept. We see this in synonyms which converge on a principal concept, but arouse so many others that it is very difficult, except for acute observers such as Tommaseo, to be mindful of them all. Nevertheless, people in general feel this effect and are unanimous in noticing the lack of propriety in the use of words, although they may not be able to express what is lacking and, in endeavouring to describe it, may sometimes err, just as they may not always write it correctly. Words, therefore, serve amongst other things to give *unity* to a certain plurality of concepts. This *plurality* is not something real; it needs a real sign if it is to be retained and designated.

1528. Everything which is not a *real entity acting* upon us needs *real signs* if we are to maintain and concentrate our attention upon it. Entities of this kind of real being are *a*) incorporeal substances, *b*) abstracts, *c*) multiples, *d*) real things which belong to the past (such as historical facts which no longer *act* upon us), *e*) real things which are absent and which, in the same way, do not act upon us, and so on.

1529. Proof of what we have said about real but absent things is found in our desire to possess *portraits* and *souvenirs*, which remind us vividly of beloved persons or things which cannot be continually present to us.

1530. *Incorporeal substances* can also be considered as absent in so far as they do not act immediately upon us as real things do. Hence our propensity and need for images and symbols which represent these substances for our veneration. This explains all external worship. Iconoclasts, therefore, acted contrary to the laws of human nature, despite the subtlety of their vain arguments.

1531. As every word is a *synthesis*, so every proposition and

---

[301] *Istoria Universale*, Introd., c. 3.

every discourse is an *analysis*. From what has been said (that is, plurality is not something real), we can see that for analysis and especially abstraction our thought needs signs and in particular words, which are the most suitable and natural signs. Analysis simply divides what is one into what is many. By the very fact of leading us to *plurality*, analysis needs signs to bind our attention to concentrate on the individual parts and, at the same time, embrace them without forgetting that they are parts of a single whole. Language which is, at one and the same time, a synthetical and analytical tool is of great assistance here.

1532. As a result of the discovery of language, therefore;

1. We satisfy a need proper to thought. We discover language not only to communicate our thoughts to others, but to determine, direct, retain and concentrate our own thought.

2. We satisfy also the need to communicate our thought to our fellows by furnishing them with the same easy means of thinking, that is, of directing and concentrating their own attention. In other words, we use the same means to help them as to help ourselves.

Here we have to admire the wisdom of the Creator who has not left this discovery of language to free, thought-out activity on the part of the human mind. He has put in us an instinct for language, as we shall show when we speak of the kind of *psychological* laws of thought which correspond to cosmological laws. Moreover, the Creator himself positively communicated the first elements of language to mankind.

1533. VI. The law also explains the laws of memory which provide certain facts that cannot be easily explained:

1. The first difficulty lies in explaining how thoughts are preserved in us without our thinking of them. — Does this happen simply because we no longer pay attention to them, just as we do not see a picture unless we turn to look at it, although it is always present? This does not explain the fact fully. If cognitions dormant within us could be explained solely by our lack of advertence to them, we could remember them whenever we wanted, just as we can look at a picture whenever we like. But we cannot remember many things which we have forgotten, or we remember them only with difficulty. We have to say rather that in this case attention is not activated and held by anything real, that is, by an image or other feeling. Consequently,

our attention does not know where to turn, where to fix itself, in order to find the information or cognition which it is searching for in the soul. When images and feelings, to which the desired information or cognition is bound, cease to exist, the information is immersed in uniform being in general where it remains hidden (the ancients called this 'potential' or 'virtual knowing'). It is not lost forever though, but emerges every time the force of attention succeeds in grasping an image or real feeling to which the information is joined in the instinct of attention itself. The information clothes itself, as it were, with this real thing or, more properly speaking, is indicated by it. The cognitions which are totally lost and of which there is no memory can be called *unmarked cognitions*. Consequently, they are not distinct in ideal being.

1534. 2. The second difficulty relative to facts about memory is that some cognition or information presents itself to the memory irrespective of or even against our will, and thus sometimes fuels what we call distractions, temptations, and so on. The explanation is the same as before: granted the principle that information and cognitions in us call and hold our attention whenever they are marked, that is, connected with something real such as images, feelings, external bodies, etc., and granted, on the other hand, that the real things to which they are connected present themselves to us irrespective or even against our will — for example, things which depend on the movement of animality and the animal potencies — it is clear that a great deal of obliterated information must return of its own accord to thought and attract our cogitative attention according to the laws of instinct and of habits. Sometimes this information even forces itself upon us when it has greater power to attract and hold our attention than our will has to keep it at bay. Daily experience shows the power and independence of our imagination and animal feelings. This is a great humiliation for us, whose dwelling place is the rational principle. This principle, which is ourselves, is often so unmanned that despite every reason urging it to precede and command, it follows instead like an enchained slave and obeys willy-nilly.

1535. 3. The third question is this: why is some information recalled easily and other information with difficulty? We have seen that the presence of *real feelings*, which characterise information, does not depend totally upon us. This will help us to overcome our present difficulty also. Our animal movements and feelings are neither entirely submissive to nor entirely exempt from the influence of the rational principle, which can to a great extent act upon our animal feelings, although not as much as it likes. Sometimes the rational principle has no difficulty in influencing the feelings it has; sometimes this is difficult and sometimes totally impossible.

1536. We could then ask about the law which increases or diminishes this ease or difficulty of action. If we restrict ourselves to what concerns memory alone, I say: 1. Anyone who thinks has always before him some real things (by 'real things' I mean images and feelings). 2. Real, present things are connected more or less, with real, absent things. 3. The bond is either a *sign*, or even an *organic* bond. Thus one sensible movement is the continuation or direct effect of other movements, or a bond which receives its relationship with feeling through *instinct* and *habit*, and so on. But if the rational principle is to be capable of arousing and reducing to act the feelings it seeks, these feelings must have 1. some connection with those actually present to the rational principle, 2. some more or less suitable connection, stimulating spontaneous passage, and enabling the rational principle to succeed more or less easily in restoring to their pristine state the animal movements and connected feelings which it searches for as signs of the information it needs to remember.

CHAPTER 28

The cosmological law of harmony governing the activity of the rational principle. — How this law is mingled with and distinguished from the psychological laws

Article 1
The law of harmony to which the rational soul is subject is cosmological in so far as it proceeds from
the intrinsic order of animality

1537. By cosmological law governing the activity of the

rational principle, I understand the law imposed upon this principle by the action of created things, by the world or, as Fichte would say, by the NON-EGO (Fichte's concept of the world excludes the rational principle and places it in contrast with the world although EGO forms part of the world. This is another error of Fichte's system).[302] Nevertheless, because the intellective soul has in the idea a mirror both of the real world and of itself, it is not absurd to look at this soul from two points of view: as known and as knowing, as part of the world and as opposed to the world. Thus, the nature of the world, including the soul, the term of knowing, is the source of the cosmological laws according to which the rational principle (soul) operates. And the nature of the soul (rational principle) is the source of the corresponding psychological laws.

1538. At this point, we ask if animality pertains to the knowing soul to which it administers direct matter. This question must be solved before we begin to speak about the law of harmony. We need to know if this law, in so far as it is a cosmic law, has to be derived not only from the order proper to exterior things but also from the order intrinsic to animality. In other words, does it form part of the world considered in contraposition to the rational principle?

My answer is this. Animality as such does not pertain to the knowing soul. Soul signifies principle. Animality, relative to the soul, is simply term in so far as it forms part of the fundamental perception. The harmony, therefore, which the rational principle finds in its term, and in which it shares, comes to it not only from the harmony present in external things different from animal feelings, but also from the harmony present in animality itself.

1539. Ancient thinkers of the Italic school knew about the existence of the law of harmony in the operations of the rational principle, but took it more as a *uniquely psychological* law than

---

[302] When Fichte put the *ego* in contraposition to nature, to the world, he took the first step towards the philosophical divinisation of man. His successors went even further. From the opposition between the world and *self* they wrongly deduced that the *ego* is different from the world; it is outside nature. Here we have an example of that overweening pride which makes us speak about things as their judge, and forget that we are one of them.

as a law which, in part at least, is *cosmological*. They did this because they were unable to conceive of a purely intellective soul. Moreover, they did not understand the nature of the rational soul, but began their philosophical investigation from what is most obvious to us, that is, from matter and sense. They fixed their attention on the sensitive soul and reduced every activity, even intellectual activity, to this soul as a principle. Relative to the sensitive soul, they did not succeed in distinguishing *principle*, which alone merits the name 'soul', from *term*, which is the extended, materiated element. Consequently, they considered as proper to the soul that which also comes to it from its term. Moreover, because order is felt vividly at the sensible level of harmonious sounds, they called all order and harmony *music*. They generalised the meaning of this word, which initially had been used to indicate the pleasure found in suitable sounds by the ear,[303] according to laws for the invention of words, laws which we have explained.

1540. Thus music was first located in the soul of the world, then in other souls, which by taking something from the soul of the world, were constituted and individuated. We can see this from a place in Macrobius who brought together the ancient teachings. He says that we ought not to wonder that music had such power over human beings as it did over beasts (note how he refers to the sensitive soul):

> As we said, the causes of music, with which the soul is interwoven, are present to the soul of the world which provides life (he is speaking of life, not reason) for all living things (he is speaking of living beings in general, not of reasoning beings in particular). This explains the origin and life of human beings, beasts, and birds, and of the monsters of the sea. Rightly, therefore, all that lives is captivated by love of music. The heavenly soul, by which everything is animated, originates from music.[304]

1541. This ancient mistake is overcome once we know that the harmony secretly directing both rational and sentient principle comes to the sentient principle from its term; it does not

[303] Cf. *Predicazione*, Milan, 1843, p. 362
[304] *In Somn. Scip.*, bk. 2, c. 4.

reside in the principle itself. The ancients, in attributing the origin of harmony to the soul alone, which is principle, were even led, or at least many were, to affirm that the nature of the soul consists in harmony itself.[305]

Article 2
The law of harmony according to which the sensitive soul operates is mostly psychological

1542. Animality, therefore, is not the rational principle, relative to which it stands as term; it pertains to the *world* and is in contraposition to the rational soul which then shares in its harmony.

If, however, we speak of the sensitive soul which is the direct principle of feeling, we can ask whether the harmony found in animality springs from the soul, that is, from the *sensitive principle*, or from the extended element which is the soul's *term*. If the ancients had put the question in this way, they would not have made such a serious error in attributing the origin of harmony to the soul alone because harmony does indeed come from the nature of the sensitive soul, at least in part. But they confused the sensitive with the rational soul, and spoke about the former as if it were the latter. I intend, however, to explain the origin of the law of harmony relative to the rational soul and to show how, in this respect, the law is cosmological precisely because the sensitive soul, which is principle relative to the extended element, that is, to its own term, is term relative to the rational principle which perceives the sentient element in what is felt. The sensitive soul therefore, itself pertains to the world in contraposition to the rational principle.

1543. Let us see how this soul is in part the source of the harmony found in animality, although we shall have to speak more at length about this same subject very soon.

First, the *continuous extended element* acquires unity from the simplicity of the sensitive principle and, together with unity, its nature as something continuous.[306]

---

[305] Cf. the book *Delle sentenze dei Filosofi intorno alla natura dell'anima*.

[306] The sensiferous element also possesses continuous extension (*NE*, vol. 2, 858–860). But where does it get it? In my opinion, it comes from the

Second, we have seen how the unity of time lies in the simplicity of the sensitive principle.

Now the harmony of animality is shown in the felt extension and in time; the *multiplicity* necessary for harmony arises in the felt extension; *number* arises in time.

1544. Indeed, multiplicity and number would not exist unless there were a simple ens to which and in which several unities were present. If each unity as such is present to itself, it cannot be present to other unities because each unity as such finishes in itself and cannot exceed the confines of its own being. The sensitive principle, on the other hand, can receive multiple, contemporaneous and successive feelings. As a result, multiplicity, number and succession of multiple things is found in it alone (and in the rational principle, but at a higher level and in a different way).

1545. Harmony, therefore, results from *unity* and *plurality*. Unity, posited by the soul, is a *psychological* element; plurality, provided for the sensitive soul by its term, is the *cosmological* element. Hence harmony in the sphere of animal feeling is a kind of union with nature, and as it were a generative embrace between soul and world.

1546. Unity, however, is properly speaking the form of what is beautiful, as St. Augustine says.[307] We can conclude, therefore,

---

corporeal principle which by that very fact is shown as necessarily simple because it has a continuous extended element as the term of its action. Just as we argue to the simplicity of the sentient principle from the extended term of its *passion*, so we must argue legitimately to the simplicity of the corporeal principle from the extended term of its *action*.

[307] But since we say that everything is IN SO FAR AS IT ENDURES (note in passing that the holy Doctor recognises duration as a condition of an ens) unity is the form of all beauty, etc.' (*Ep*, 18: 2). St. Augustine says that what is beautiful is present in the rational principle alone. In other words, he maintains that objectivity is essential to beauty. Consequently, he proceeds to seek the eternal law of beauty (*De Vera Relig.*, c. 30–33; *De Musica*, bk. 6, c. 13 — *Ep*. 18: 2). I am in complete agreement about this with the great master. I distinguish *harmony*, the harmonic convergence of several things, *from what is beautiful*. Such harmonic convergence, found in animality, is grounded in the simplicity of the sensitive soul which embraces what is multiple. This sensible harmony is itself matter for the rational principle which contemplates it in the object. In this way, harmony acquires all that is necessary for beauty.

[1544–1546]

that the *formal part* of sensible harmony is psychological by nature, the *material part* is cosmological by nature.

Article 3
The distinction between the psychological and the cosmological in the law of harmony governing the sensitive soul

1547. But how can plurality in the felt element be reduced to unity? Where does this unity come from, and what is the role of the principle and term in forming it?

The term of corporeal feeling is a single, continuous, extended element. If this element were to divide into several continua, the sentient principles would be multiplied. We already have a unity of continuum.

1548. A continuum however has limits, and these constitute a kind of plurality. If we ask: 'What is the origin of the limits[308] which determine the size and form of a single continuum?', the answer is that the limits do not come from the sentient principle (which *per se* is indifferent to every extension and shape of its felt element); they come from external cosmic power. I have said that there is not only an extension (whose conditions or limits are *size* and *form*) but also an extrasubjective, sensiferous power,[309] whose principle must be unextended (the corporeal principle).

1549. In addition to the multiplicity of *size*, *form* and limits revealed later by acquired sensations, multiplicity of sensations is in animality itself. Another question therefore arises: 'What accounts for the variety of sensation in a single, continuous, extended element?'

1550. As I have explained, even the extended fundamental feeling itself is not totally uniform in quality, but contains differences and is, as it were, variegated. This seems to be necessary because of the different degrees of stimulated sensitivity in the different members of the body and sensory organs. However, in my opinion, the spirit does not advert to these differences

---

[308] Note, these limits do not occur in the fundamental *felt element*, that is, they are not felt in it but felt later through acquired surface sensations. Cf. *AMS*, 135–229.

[309] *NE*, vol. 2, 882–885.

because the fundamental feeling, as constituted, is virtually, if not totally, incapable of attracting and holding our intellective attention.[310] If one part is more sensitive than another or responds differently to stimulation, a different fundamental feeling must evidently exist in which every part is felt in its own way and in varying degree. The optic nerve, for example, has, it seems to me, a different fundamental feeling; I mean a feeling with a sensitivity totally different from the other feeling parts of the body, a feeling which is precisely that of *black*. To define *black* as purely the absence of colour is to confuse the cause of sight-sensations with the sensations themselves. Certainly, when all external stimuli are removed from the retina, black remains, the result of a total lack of light. But the stimulating body called 'light' is not the sensation it produces. Sensations of colour produced by the stimulus of light are partial sensations, that is, particular modifications of an already existing fundamental feeling which can be only the feeling of black.

We can convince ourselves of this if we go into some perfectly dark place, fix our attention on the feeling in our eyes and compare this feeling with another part of our body, for example with the neck. Careful attention to both sensations will convince us that the feeling of black is present in our eyes, as if they were covered by a black sheet. This is not the feeling in our neck. We cannot attribute this 'vision experience' to our remembrance of colour-sensations previously experienced but now absent, because our attention tells us that we are dealing strictly with a feeling actually present in our eyes, totally independent of every remembrance and mental reflection.

We can say something similar, it seems to me, about the acoustic nerve. The fundamental feeling proper to this nerve is the feeling of silence, so that silence (considered as feeling and prescinding from its external occasion, which is certainly negative) is something not entirely negative but positive, the foundation of all acoustic sensations.

Hence the variety present in the extended feeling must arise from the different tissue of the felt continuum: the continuum

---

[310] Another difficulty of proving this by experience is that the *extended feeling* may perhaps never totally lack *stimulated feeling* in us, because in human beings everything is in motion.

could have greater or smaller intervals, could result from molecules of different form; one molecule could press on another with greater force; particular molecules could vary in complexity; different kinds of composition could give rise to different organs.

1551. The multiplicity seen in the feeling of stimulation prompts a third question: 'What is the origin of the variety of the different parts of the stimulated feeling, a variety clearly visible and giving rise to the variety of shaped sensations that differ in character and intensity? Is the origin dependent on the soul or the world?'

We have seen that these variations stimulated in the felt element correspond to the movement of the molecules composing the felt element. This movement is determined partly by external stimuli and partly by the activity of the sensitive principle. Consequently its cause must be partly *cosmological* and partly *psychological*: cosmological in so far as it overcomes the *inertia* of the spirit; *psychological* in so far as it obeys the law of *spontaneity* with which the spirit is endowed.[311]

1552. But this movement is not itself sensation. In sensation we must distinguish 1. the *mode* of the sensation, that is, extension and the conditions (the limits of *size* and *form*) proper to the extended element; 2. the extrasubjective stimulatory (cosmological) cause of the sensation, that is, the *sensiferous* power, and the intestine movements in the felt extended element; and finally 3. pure *sensation*, which is either *quiescent* and primal or *stimulated*. Relative to the *extended mode* of sensation and of feelings, cosmological action certainly contributes to its constitution because the mode is the *term* both of such action and of the soul. Cosmological action is also present relative to the extrasubjective cause, that is, to the corporeal principle or sensiferous power. *Pure sensation* however is not cosmological action. It is proper to the sentient principle in such a way that it is the *act* proper to the principle and pertaining entirely to the principle's essential power; it is totally subjective and psychological.[312] Cosmological action is the cause which

---

[311] Cf. *AMS*, 439–483 for the two laws of inertia and spontaneity which govern the soul.

[312] *NE*, vol. 2, 878–905.

posits the act in being, and with it the sentient principle itself, the soul, and determines the act relative to its mode of extension. In the final analysis however the act of feeling is the act of the sentient principle, the sole subject of all sensations.

Consequently, pure sensation, although dependent on the external world for its term, is an act of the soul, not of the world.

1553. Pure sensation, which I call the 'feel' of a sensation (to give it a suitable name that separates it from extension), changes, but the extended element retains its size and form, as we see in the sensations of different sensory organs, and even in the same organ. Smell is not only of a totally different 'feel' from colour, but the 'feel' itself varies in each in quality and degree. Although the 'feel' of a sensation can vary in kind and degree according to the difference in the extended term and in the intestine movements in the term, we can easily see that the 'feel' (a positive quality of sensation) is neither extension nor movement, but always the varied act of the sentient principle alone. In the case of extension, for example, a sensation may vary in 'feel' but not in extension. Thus while the sensation both of the eye and of the touch can terminate in one and the same extension, the sensations differ greatly and have a very different 'feel'. In the case of movement, I have already shown that the 'feel' of the sensation, when stimulated by movements of the sensory organ, does not at all resemble these movements, which are multiple, while the 'feel' of the stimulated sensation is one. The movements are instantaneous (because every change is instantaneous), but the 'feel' of the sensation endures. If the case were otherwise, nothing would be felt. Hence the 'feel' of a sensation is due entirely to the sensitive soul (in the way that an act is due to its subject) and is therefore totally of a *psychological* nature.

We still need to know however how the 'feel' can vary with the variation of organs, their movements and the number of movements.

Article 4
Does the variation in the 'feel' of a sensation result from cosmological or psychological laws?

1554. Our investigation is rendered more difficult by the

intermingling of feelings with attention and rational activity
which in their own way divide what in feeling itself is united.
But we must not omit any difficulty.

The rational principle converts the sensiferous element into
an ens and detaches it from feeling. If the principle did not do
this, the sensiferous element would be nothing more than an
agent dwelling in the sentient element; it would not be an ens
but the action of an ens. In fact the rational principle changes the
sensiferous terms of sensitive perceptions into entia with the result that every sensory organ moves in its own world. Except
for extension, each of these worlds is totally divided from the
world proper to any other sensory and, in the case of the
particular 'feel' of a sensation, is totally unlike the others. If the
rational principle compares these different worlds and brings
them all together, it does so by *analogy*, and not by any real
similarity between them. The comparison cannot be made
through any similarity in the quality of their sensible 'feel', but
because they are the same in quantity, space, etc., that is, in
things which do not pertain to pure sensation. The sensitive
principle, by making use of the identity present in these conditions which do not constitute sensation, joins and harmonises
them through its simplicity. For example, when the eye guides
the hand to touch an object, the visual sensation (the extended
thing felt by the eye) is entirely different from the extended
thing touched by the hand. The visual sensation does for the
hand what a good map does for a traveller, who is using the map
to guide his way. We are not easily aware of this because of the
very notable difference between the map and the visual sensation. The map is perceived as a very small space compared to the
space the traveller will cover. The visual sensation seems to
present the object as an area equal to that felt by the hand. In
reality however this is not the case because the sensation of the
optic universe actually extends no further than the extension of
the retina which contains the optic universe (when the retina is
perceived by touch). The difference is this: when I see the map, I
simultaneously see everything outside it, all the space beyond
its edges, the immense space of the plains, the mountains and
the sky, and I can imagine even more space beyond what I see.
The map, compared with all these spaces, appears very small
indeed, and in this very small area the plains, mountains, seas

[1554]

and sky, seen by my eye, are all indicated and distinct. Then as I journey on my way, my eye sees the same things twice: what I see as very small on the map I see as very large in nature. One organ (my eye) sees the little and the large representations in such a way that I can use the same sensory to compare different parts of my sensation.

The case however is totally different when our spirit, instead of comparing the size of the different parts of a sensation of the same sensory, compares the sensation of one sensory, the eye, for example, with the sensation of another sensory, the touch, let us say. Here two universes are compared, not parts of the same universe; the seen universe is compared with the touched universe. The total sensation of the eye, which I call the 'visual mirror', contains the whole optic universe, that is, everything seen by the eye in one glance (and in several glances by the retentive faculty and imagination). In this optic universe there is a hand that touches and an object touched. Both are present with their dimensions so that if the touched object is smaller than the hand, it appears smaller in the visual mirror; if larger, it appears larger. Furthermore, the hand and the touched extension retain their own dimensions relative to all the surrounding objects visible in the visual mirror. All these dimensions can be transferred by the eye to the rational principle which is now able to say how much bigger than the hand is the column which the hand is touching, how much larger is the temple than the column, and how much bigger than the temple is the nearby hill, etc. Hence, whenever a body touches the whole of my hand, my rational principle, guided by my eye, can say 'The extension of the body is that of the sensation of the whole of my hand'. All these proportions are indicated in the colours felt on my retina, just like a map. But my eye cannot see anything outside all this, outside this map, that is, outside its visual mirror. Because the map is its universe, it cannot compare the map with anything greater, nor find anything greater because it cannot see anything else. The visual mirror therefore is as large as the visual universe because there are no universes other than that of the mirror. Hence, when my hand and foot are directed by my soul aided by my eye, then my hand and the extended thing it wants to grasp, my foot and the path it wants to follow, and the surrounding spaces, are all drawings in the visual

[1554]

universe (the optic mirror). These drawings are the principle of the regulated movements made by my hand or foot at the command of the soul; they are signs which occupy a very small part of the retina and correspond in a very precise way to the dimensions of my hand, foot, etc. Because these signs contain the principle of the movements of the hand and foot, the soul can, by their means alone, move the hand to the object it wants and turn its steps in the desired direction.

Note however that the path, object, hand and foot are not in the eye. The hand and foot cannot be moved unless they communicate with the brain by means of the sensory or motor nerves. The optic sensory representing the hand and foot must also terminate in the brain. Furthermore the animal principle must unify in itself the active feeling of the motor nerves together with the hand and foot seen by the optic sensory (a passive feeling). The movements themselves of the hand and foot must begin from tiny movements of the brain by the soul's command. These tiny movements are then propagated to the nerves and muscles by the law of spontaneity. Consequently, if we say that the visual sensation occupies a very tiny space in the brain, we can also say that the soul, directed or even stimulated by this sensation, can stimulate a tiny movement in the brain. This results in the movement of the hand and foot, which are both intimately united with the soul in subjective feeling. We now see how a sensation, which occupies a very tiny space (in the optic sensory) as a passive feeling, initiates its corresponding active feeling in another tiny space (in the roots of the motor nerves). The movements begin in this very tiny space, and then 'through the law that the animal tends to preserve and increase pleasant movements' increase to the point where they move the hand and foot in the direction determined by the visual sensation. All of which simply demonstrates the wonderful harmony posited by the Creator in the composition of animals.

1555. How then do we become aware that the visual universe within the limits of the extension of the retina is so tiny relative to the real universe?

The awareness cannot result from the comparison between sizes given by touch and the eye. Sizes given by touch always conform to those given by the eye, and vice versa; one is the measure of the other. A comparison between them can quickly reveal how much they correspond with each other, but never tell us if one sensation is absolutely more extensive than the other. For example, although my eye sees a statuette at the same time as I draw my hand over it, we cannot induce anything from the simultaneity of these two sensations except that the extension of the object seen by my eye produces a sensation of a corresponding extension in my hand. Because the sensation of one is the measure of the sensation of the other, the measurements must always agree and coincide with each other; they are proportionate, not absolute.

How then do we become aware that the *visual* sensation of an extension occupies less space than the *touch* sensation of the same extension? To solve the question, we need to find the ratio between the space occupied by the sensation of one sensory and the space occupied by the corresponding sensation of the other sensory. But no proportion is possible between the two sensories because neither of them furnishes a *common measure* suitable for measuring the two specifically different sense-experiences. The optic sensory encompasses nothing of the touch sensory, and vice versa. Every sensory is limited to its own world, and when the animal or rational principle compares them, it finds only equality. This comparison is made solely by analogy; proportion is not compared with proportion, nor proportion with proportion. We have to say therefore that the measure of the size of the optic sensation is the sensation itself, and the measure of the size of the touch sensation is the touch sensation itself, as I will now explain.

The retina has two relationships with us, as a sensory and as an external, felt term. As an act of the sensory the retina is the visual mirror itself, the visual universe, and outside this visual universe, that is, outside the retina, there is no visual feeling. Consequently the soul, which sees by means of this organ, cannot compare the mirror supplied by the organ with anything else, because it does not see anything outside the organ. Moreover, even though it feels only the organ, we cannot say that it sees the organ, because the word 'see' refers to terms separate and distinct from the organ. The soul's attention is directed to these terms without stopping at what is directly felt, that is, at the retina which indicates and presents them. Thus while the retina is felt subjectively, the soul does not restrict its attention to this alone. Instead, its attention proceeds to the different colours on the retina and, in virtue of the rational principle, takes these colours as external objects, that is, entia. As long as the soul feels the retina subjectively in this way, that is, as a sensory in act, it cannot compare the space of the retina with any other space because the total possible space given to the soul to contemplate, all the space of the visual universe, is the retina itself, which alone exists for the soul. The onlooker's head, where the eye and retina are, does not exist, nor does his body, where the head, etc., are. If all these things do exist, they exist in the retina, not outside it.

But let us consider the retina in its other relationship with us, not as a sensory but as an external felt term. The opposition between the two relationships becomes apparent when we look at someone else's retina. In this situation, our eye acts as a sensory; our soul feels internally, subjectively, the other's retina. On the other hand, the other's retina relative to us does not act as a sensory but as an external term felt by us, seen by us. In this relationship, the other's retina does not present anything; it is presented in our retina where it occupies a tiny space. It becomes a small part of our visual mirror and universe, an extension much smaller than the eye which I see. The other's retina becomes even smaller than his head or body, and much, much smaller than the whole internal visual universe I feel in my retina which, felt subjectively, is as large as the space of my visual universe. The other's retina, which I feel extrasubjectively, is only a very small part of that universe. The same is true for the person whose retina I am looking at. His retina, a sensory in act, is the whole visual space, of which my retina is a tiny part.

I can also look at my retina in a mirror. In this case the same retina acquires the two relationships relative to me: my retina is subjectively felt and as such is the visual universe; it is also seen, that is, felt extrasubjectively, in which case it is a very tiny bit of the space of the same universe. But I also know that my retina which I feel subjectively as a sensory act and the retina which I see, that is, feel extrasubjectively as an external term, are identical. I note that if I cover my retina which I see as an external object, vision ceases, that is, the retina ceases to be a sensory in act; if I want to measure the size of objects by touch, I find that my retina is one of them. In this case a comparison between the sensations of touch tells me that my retina occupies a very small part of space in the touch-universe. I experience the touched retina acting as a sensory, because when I cover it with my hand, I notice that it ceases to see.

1556. These facts confirm what I said earlier, namely, that continuous space is in the sentient principle, and that we measure the size of external objects only by applying to them the space we have in ourselves, that is, the space in which our own feeling terminates. Hence bodies receive different measurements according to the different ways in which they shape themselves in subjective, fundamental space.

1557. Strictly speaking, bodies as seen do not touch the eye but are sketched upon it by the light they vibrate. Hence the perception of the eyes is a perception of signs corresponding to bodies, but not of bodies themselves. Nevertheless the size of these signs, despite their smallness, seems to equal the size of bodies perceived by touch, because, as I said, both kinds of feeling do not have a measure common to their respective sizes. What they have *in common* is the equal proportion of their parts, a proportion which is compared only by the rational principle.

1558. Our investigation must now turn to the space occupied by optical sensations and see how it appears separate from the total space of the fundamental feeling (if it did not appear separate, we would have a common measure). Furthermore, the little space of the retina (the site of the felt element) would indicate only a small part of the total space of the fundamental feeling, not a separate world.

There are several reasons for this separation:

1. Space (term of the fundamental feeling) is not measured in the feeling itself, but only later, by external, shaped, surface sensations pertaining to particular organs. Limits are not part of the fundamental feeling; no lines or shapes of any kind exist in the continuity of the fundamental feeling. Limits are the surface sensations themselves and pertain to the feeling stimulated in particular organs. Hence, if a surface sensation establishes a limit confined to a surface feeling, the extension of this sensation is precisely what is felt. It cannot be compared with the total extension of the fundamental feeling, because the total extension is not felt in that way. In fact no such extension exists

for us as a result of our use of organs which impose limits and consequently fixed measures. The little space of the retina which we feel when light has stimulated feeling is felt in total isolation from the remaining surface-space of the human body. The stimulation is present only in the little space, not in the remaining space.

1559. 2. Furthermore, even if the surrounding parts, when stimulated by their own stimuli at the time the retina were stimulated by colour, also gave a surface sensation, it would not follow that we felt those sensations in a single, continuous surface. There is an interval and separation between the optic nerve and the surrounding nerves which, when stimulated, make us feel. The surface sensation would therefore have some lacunae which would break it up into several sensations each of which would measure itself without measuring the other sensations because 1. none would be part of a greater surface sensation and 2. no measurement is possible unless the parts to be measured have a relationship with the whole.

1560. 3. Again, granted that the 'feel' of sensations varies greatly, and that the 'feel' of light is extremely vivid and distinct, the retina would attract attention to itself and present a surface different from an adjacent surface.

1561. 4. Finally, as a result principally of the interference of the rational principle, our attention does not stop at the subjective sensation of the retina nor at the extrasubjective sensation. It goes directly to the external objects presented in the visual mirror, believing that it perceives them directly. Thus, the possibility of comparing the retina's surface sensation with the total surface of the human body ceases: we ignore the former and give our attention to the objects whose signs are presented by it.

1562. The second and third reasons deserve further consideration. We must remember that the different organisation of the sensitive parts of the human body makes different parts susceptible to very different kinds of stimulation. There are, therefore, sensations whose 'feel' is very different. This is the case with each kind of sensation pertaining to the five organs. Their 'feel' is in no way similar. No one could find any similarity between colour, smell, taste, etc. This explains why the organs are different sensories. But nature has gone further and separated them in such a way that the sensations of one sensory are not continuous with the sensations of the others, that is, the sensations of one sensory occupy a small space discontinuous with the sensations of another. Such lack of continuity means that there is no single space in which these sensations appear, and through which we can see the part of space occupied by each. Thus, the extremity of the acoustic nerve, which receives the impression of the oscillating air, occupies a place totally different from that occupied by the extremity of the optic nerve, which receives the impression of light. The same applies to the other special sensories. Moreover we cannot claim that these nerves or sensories are continuous with parts pertaining to the sense of touch, because each nerve or sensory is protected and enveloped by parts lacking feeling. Even if they had feeling, either they would not all be stimulated at the same time or the stimulation would produce such a weak sensation that it would not be noticed against the very vivid sensation of the adjacent sensory; the space occupied by the sensation of this sensory would still be isolated and not a part of the total surface space of the human body.

1563. Discontinuity is also present in the small spaces stimulated in the same sensory. When we consider how the ear clearly hears different sounds coming from different points, for example the sounds of the various instruments of an orchestra, we have to presume that the sound waves strike and stimulate different parts of our acoustic nerve. Under this aspect we should perhaps investigate the different, little-known mechanisms making up the ear to see if one of their purposes is to keep sounds apart so that the sound waves stimulate the nerve in different parts.[313] Physicists rightly explain that what they call 'the principle of superimposition of little movements' prevents

[313] To explain how several sounds are simultaneously perceived without being confused, some physicists have supposed that the different parts of the acoustic nerve are attuned to unison with different tones. According to this law, only that part oscillates which corresponds to its tone. I think this is an inadequate explanation of the phenomenon in question because:

1. Contemporary sounds that have the same tone remain as distinct as those that have a different tone.

2. Not only are tones distinct but also their intensity, their different timbre, the direction from which they come, etc. All these things are not explained by the law of attunement to unison.

sound-waves from being confused with each other. But this does not explain the phenomenon of distinct sensations taking place not in the air-waves but in the sensory. Let us suppose that sound-waves bunch together and come to a point in the way that light refracts and bends in a lens, and that by doing so they stimulate different points of the acoustic membrane. Clearly, only those points struck by the sound-waves are stimulated, not the whole membrane. Only one wave is produced from a single point of the oscillating, sonorous body. A few rays of this wave land on the ear and end at a single point. Light is different. Every point of a luminous body is a centre from which light is emitted. Hence although the entire retina is stimulated, stimulation varies as the points of bodies which reflect light onto the retina vary. This renders the visual sensation capable of presenting in itself bodies whose proportions, planes and perspectives are drawn with extreme accuracy. In the case of the ear, however, the process is totally different. The ear receives isolated sounds because only that part of the membrane is struck on which the soniferous ray falls. The various small spaces in the membrane which remain unstimulated are therefore devoid of sound sensation.[314]

1564. My explanation of the variation in the 'feel' of stimulated sensations would not be perfect, unless I said something about the relationship between that 'feel' and the extrasubjective, oscillatory movements of molecules which make up the nervous fibres.

First, we must bear in mind that the *efficient cause* of sensations is the activity of the sensitive principle, not the movements

---

[314] Not even smell and taste can present the forms of external bodies, because they are not emitted from all the points of the odiferous and soniferous bodies in conformity with the same law and in right proportion to the sizes and forms of the bodies. However it is not absurd to imagine an animal in which, by disposition of the Creator, a sensation of touch is equal to the sensation of sound, smell and taste, and used to distinguish bodies as accurately and precisely as sight in human beings and animals. Such an animal (which certainly belongs to another world, to another order of things) would be so different from present animals that our imagination would have difficulty in picturing the difference. The sound, smell and taste of this animal would present bodies as accurately and precisely as sight, as if they were seen clearly by the nose or ear.

of the molecules of the fibres, which are only the *excitatory cause*. In an animate body these movements are accompanied by sensation, but not in an inanimate body; the stimulus would be present but not the stimulated and actuated cause.

Second, the term of both *stimulated feeling* and *feeling at rest* is always an *extended element*. Movements stimulated in the felt extended term do not sever the extension and make it discontinuous. There is simply a displacement of molecules which, without ceasing to be continuous with each other, move about and, so to speak, rub against each other's surfaces with varying pressure.

Granted this, the following is clear:

1. The stimulatory movement effects no change in the continuum-extended element. Any change in this element is solely in its limits, which are insensible. However, the movement changes the mode of feeling, which it renders more vivid and different. The continuous extended element is felt by the soul, but the more vivid, different mode gives the sensation another 'feel'. As I said, the direct term of feeling is not motion but the extended element moved intestinely. Hence the movement of the molecules cannot be felt in each particular sensation; only the extended element is felt. The movement does not enter into the sentient principle, which is the constant cause of the unity of the felt element, that is, of its continuity. In other words, the law of sensitive (animal) activity is such that the activity produces a *continuous* feeling. No sensible movement takes place in the continuum, however, because movement cannot be felt unless the continuum is divided. In other words, while the limits of the moved parts must be known and distinguished, the distinction of the parts together with their limits is abolished in the continuum.

1565. 2. Consequently, several movements which are close in time, in the same sensory organ, produce only one sensation, not several. In fact, all they can do is change the 'feel' of sensation by the quantity of oscillations communicated to the sensory organ during the short time the sensation is formed. We see this in musical notes. They are sensations of a specifically different 'feel', and differ according to the number of oscillations of the sonorous body.[315] This number produces a correspondingly

[315] The proportion between the number of oscillations of the seven notes,

equal number of vibrations, that is, oscillations in the elastic molecules of the sensory organ struck by the vibrations.

1566. If we suppose that 24 oscillations of a sonorous body produce the note *doh*, then 27 oscillations will produce the note *re*. The reason is the special nature of the constitution of the acoustic sensory, and more particularly, the nature of the sensitive principle producing the sensation. It is therefore a partly psychological, partly cosmological reason.

This reason must also explain the difference of three oscillations between the first three notes (always on the basis that *doh* is produced by 24 oscillations). But between *mi* and *fa* there is only a difference of two oscillations, in which case the ear itself discerns that the interval between these two notes is smaller than that between the others. In the same way we can explain the last three notes, where there is a difference of four oscillations: the ear discerns only the tonic interval between *so, la* and *ti* as equal to that which it discerns between *doh, re* and *mi*.[316]

1567. We can therefore summarise the psychological element in animal feelings, that is, the elements which the soul with its own activity contributes to the harmony in feeling, by saying that these elements are: 1. unity of space, 2. unity of succession, 3. unity of multiplicity and therefore the form of harmony seen in animality, and 4. the 'feel' of feeling.

---

beginning from *doh*, is $\frac{1}{1}$ $\frac{9}{8}$ $\frac{5}{4}$ $\frac{4}{3}$ $\frac{3}{2}$ $\frac{5}{3}$ $\frac{18}{8}$ or, expressed in whole numbers, 24 27 30 32 40 45.

[316] It is said that a perfect, experienced ear can distinguish up to 43 notes in an octave. If these were distributed equally between the 48 oscillations supposed in the octave of *doh*, the distance between them would be $\frac{5}{43}$ oscillation. This shows that the difference of one oscillation could not be distinguished. But if the 24 oscillations we have allotted to *doh* are increased by one, we have *doh diesis*, which is very easily distinguished. This further proves that in the last notes of the gamma, the difference of one oscillation is imperceptible, that is, the difference in the number of their oscillations cannot be noted unless the difference is greater than $1\frac{5}{43}$, precisely because only 43 notes are distinguished in the whole octave. At the beginning of the scale, a difference of a single oscillation is sensible, and the three last *diesis* have a difference of oscillations of $1\frac{1}{2}$, $1\frac{2}{3}$, $1\frac{7}{8}$. If we allot *doh* another quantity of oscillations, the result is the same: the difference between the distance of the first three tones and the distance of the three last is *per se* insensible.

[1566–1567]

CHAPTER 29

Continuation of the cosmological law of harmony. How it is formed in animality

1568. We need to investigate more thoroughly the origin of harmony in animality. Although I have indicated its elements and their psychological or cosmological origin, I have still not explained the origin and formation of harmony.

Time and space are as it were the seat of multiplicity in animal feeling, a multiplicity to which the soul gives unity. But there would be no harmony unless there were enjoyment, which must be sought in feeling's 'feel'. This, however, is still not sufficient to complete the concept of sensible harmony. Although every individual feeling has its own 'feel', harmony is the result of several feelings. Even the enjoyable unity of these different feelings comes from the soul. If harmony is to be present therefore, the soul must give its own unity not only to space, which is continuity, and to time, which is duration, but also to multiplicity of feelings. In fact the soul gives unity to this multiplicity, whether the feelings, which arise deep in a calm, fundamental feeling, are of different or of the same 'feel'.[317] But, in order to produce harmony it must do even more: the kind of unity it must give to several feelings (it always and necessarily gives some unity to feelings, of which it is the identical subject), must be an *enjoyable unity*. This is the kind of unity I wish to explain and distinguish from the unity always present as a result of the identity of the sentient subject.

1569. To explain the nature and origin of this pleasurable unity, we must turn to the universal (ontological or cosmological) laws governing the action and passion of every substance. These laws, applicable also to the sensitive and rational principle, are the following.

---

[317] Feelings that have the same 'feel' are distinguished from each other only by 1. the different space which is their term in the calm-fundamental feeling, 2. the different time, when they are successive, and 3. the different intensity or degree.

Article 1
The fitting action of entia — The first law

1570. The first law states: 'An ens loves the act it has begun, and is distressed if it encounters some impediment which cuts its action short. On the other hand, it experiences enjoyment if the whole act can be unfolded in accordance with its free movement.'

1571. I say 'An ens loves the act which it has begun' because it could not be distressed by an act it had not started. It would simply lack the enjoyment which pertains essentially to every act of a sensitive ens.

1572. I say 'if the whole act can be completed in accordance with its free movement' because, when an ens is about to begin an act, its motion is limited in kind and degree by its own virtuality. The act has a natural conclusion where its motion comes to rest.

1573. The explanation I gave about pain comes under this law, when the law is applied to the sensitive principle. The animal principle, intent on positing its fundamental feeling as fully as possible (vital instinct), is distressed if it is impeded from doing so totally; this distress is pain.

Article 2
The fitting action of entia — The second law

1574. The second law is: 'The act begun by an ens is sometimes multiple through succession, that is, results from a series of links which can be considered as a single act through the unity of the ens unfolding its activity in several communicating potencies. In this case the ens seeks to complete the whole series of links right up to the last; it is distressed if its progress is cut short.'

1575. The action of the rational principle, to which the sensitive principle is connected and subordinate, is an example of this law. The action is composed of three links: 1. judgment, 2. affections, 3. external movements. Sometimes however there are four links: 1. judgment, 2. affections, 3. decrees of the will, 4. external acts. The activity of the principle does not normally stop at pure judgment but, seconding the judgment (first link), conceives some affection (second link) for the thing judged good or bad, etc. Nor does it stop here; either it activates decrees of the will followed by the external actions, or affections instinctively produce corresponding movements in the body (third link). Among corporeal movements are vocal sounds, which explains why we are inclined to follow up a vivid feeling with a sound, a natural completion of our sensitive activity drawn into movement.

1576. These sounds, intimately bound as ultimate effects with thought and affection, become natural, external signs by which people who have the same experiences can know what we are thinking and feeling interiorly. But before sounds fulfil this office, they are the spontaneous, natural completion of the human, sensitive, rational act seeking completion and wanting to go as far as it can. We see this principally when we are moved interiorly by some marvellous feeling: we emit a great sound or expression which strictly speaking has no tie with our thought or feeling except as its final expression. For example, in anger we can utter blasphemy or an imprecation against something totally different from what causes our anger, or we may proffer some obscene word or make a meaningless sound, such as babai, *papae, capperi*. More commonly however we use the name of God to relieve our feelings, that is, we name the greatest thing we can find. Thus in Hebrew 'God' is added as a superlative to all words, for example, 'mountain of God', 'prince of God', etc. meaning the highest mountain, the great prince, etc.[318] The Arabs and all oriental peoples follow the same usage,[319] as does Euripides.[320] We also have an explanation for the origin of swearing and of exclamations instinctively emitted; for example, the Latins used words like *Pol, Edepol, Jupiter*, etc. A positive law was needed to forbid people taking such an august name in vain, and to restrain human instinct, which could hardly desist from emitting such exclamations. Similarly, in English we make use of whatever is great; we say, 'By heavens!', 'By Jove!', 'My

[318] Gen 23: 6; Ps 35: 7; Ps 67: 16; Song 8: 6; Is 28 [27]: 2; Jn 3: 3.

[319] Cf. Schultens, *Not. ad Haririi consess.*, 4, n. 76.

[320] Eurip., *Orest.*, 5: 1172.

[1576]

God!', etc. Swearing by someone's head or by a creature almost divinises the thing, and was forbidden for this very reason.

This release of feeling terminating in a word pertains, it must be noted, to the rational principle, and is continued by the sensitive principle. Hence, whatever word or expression is used, the speaker always intends to say something, not simply to make a noise; he intends to say and indicate something exceedingly great, even when the word *per se* has no meaning. It is a new word invented precisely to terminate the act of the thought which cannot remain shut in but wants to become sensible, to be bound to a reality which makes it more vivid and more consistent with the person who has the thought. As we have seen, this office is usually fulfilled by imagined or, generally speaking, sensible *realities* expressing internal thoughts. This need to terminate, in a real external act, the act begun in our thought is so great that even when taking God's name in vain is forbidden by divine law, the best human beings still feel the need to do so and, almost to deceive themselves, substitute similar words. Some people, for example, have substituted 'My giddy aunt!' for 'Good God!', and Italian Capuchins came out with the innocent exclamation 'Buzzards!' to express their amazement.

1577. Human instinct seeks to complete the act which is begun in thought, passes to affection, sometimes moves our will to decisions, and terminates in the external act, where we find some expression to emphasise it more vividly. This extremely powerful instinct suffers considerably when so opposed and crippled that it cannot complete its act. It explains many facts of human action.

The law I have mentioned is precisely the reason why people who have suffered some great catastrophe scream and howl, injure and harm themselves, tear their clothing, soil themselves with ashes and mud, beat their forehead, pull out their hair, roll about on the ground, bite and cut themselves, and even commit suicide. It is indeed one of the causes of suicide, as shown by those Indian widows who burn themselves to death on the funeral pyre of their husband.[321] Perhaps people who harm

---

[321] It is well-known how difficult it has been for the English to abolish this custom in India, where the sublime act is repeated from time to time.

[1577]

themselves, that is, add more suffering to themselves, are seeking relief from the pain they already suffer. The cause of such incredible cruelty to oneself is the internal act of great sorrow which cannot however be contained and restricted to the first stage. It must pursue its way, be carried out in all its natural extension, increased, finalised, signified and allowed to raise a kind of eternal monument in the wounded person. The hurt we do to ourselves in these conditions is easier to tolerate than restraining our instinct by containing the act of sorrow which begins in thought and finishes in the body as a result of the unity of the animal-intellective subject. This dynamic bond binds together our various potencies, so that the movement of one passes and continues into another. Thus, when people experience great joy, they express their joy externally: they make themselves look good, dress up, dine and wine and converse expansively; and we should not think that they do these things simply to be able to enjoy them better. Instinct plays a large part in making the act of interior joy pass through all its natural cycle, as it were, releasing and exhausting its activity.

1578. What Seneca says is true: 'Small and trouble-free cares are talked about; tremendous cares stupefy.' This stupor is explained by the same law, partly because vehement animal passion upsets the organs which then lose all virtue to further the spirit's movement, and partly because the intensity of the internal act compensates for its extension. Instinct, by increasing the intensity of the act, as it were feeds on and finds satisfaction in its desire and effort to perfect the act of internal sorrow. Consequently, the sorrowing person, unable to find strength to

Similarly ancient legislators had to enact very strict laws to forbid certain acts of cruelty in which people scourged themselves with serious consequences. The Twelve Tables prohibited women from cutting their cheeks: *Mulieres genas ne radunto*. 'In this place,' Festus explains, "cut" means "cut with their nails"'. Plutarch, in his life of Solon, narrates that Epimenides put a stop to the excessive cruelties which the Athenians practised on themselves at funerals. The Hebrews were forbidden to slash their limbs and tear themselves with their nails (Lev 19: 28) or shave their beards (Lev 19: 27), a sign of sorrow among the Egyptians. Nevertheless we see in the books of the prophets that the people could not totally abstain from practising such customs (Jer 41; Ezek 5; Gen 50).

[1578]

develop the act and communicate it to his external potencies, becomes interiorly hard and unfeeling.

1579. Solitude is loved and sought by those who are deeply afflicted; they can never stop thinking about what causes their sorrow, nor speak of anything except their catastrophe; they have to dissect it, reflect on it in all its minute details, and those who claim to diminish this sorrow become intolerable. All this is the result of the same law, of the same instinct which, using all the activity available to it, strives to complete and perfect the act of sorrow already begun. The act does not remain simply as a seed, but develops a body and grows to fullest maturity.

The same law must also be seen as the cause why tears bring relief to an unhappy person, for whom perhaps nothing is more welcome than weeping. Here the act is finally exhausted. If there were no weeping the incomplete act would remain full of power and bent on coming to fruition.

1580. The same law must also explain the origin of sacrifices to the divinity and particularly of human sacrifices (whose role was subsequently replaced by immolation to God of things very dear to human beings). The feeling of profound humility, of a Lord supreme over all things, and particularly of our need to acknowledge the guilt of our sin before that most powerful and infinite sovereign, requires more than a sterile, cold act of pure thought. It has to be expressed in a very real act which penetrates and dominates the whole of the human being, an act which is naturally infinite because it corresponds to the concept of an infinite ens. The only way a human being can perform this act perfectly is by self-destruction and, more imperfectly, by destruction of his possessions. Strictly speaking the essence of sacrifice, whether the sacrifice is a holocaust or sin-offering, requires the human being himself as the victim; other sacrifices are only a surrogate for the perfect sacrifice. In fact in a holocaust, the act of feeling begins from the thought that 'in comparison with the Creator, the creature is nothing; only the Creator is an ens.' The feeling of nothingness can be expressed sensibly and, so to speak, monumentally, only by destruction. In sacrifice for sin on the other hand the act of feeling begins from another thought: 'The creature who has offended the Creator must not exist'. The thought of undue existence receives its final actuation only by making non-existence real, that is, by destruction. Finally, sacrifice is also an expression of a supreme love. Because there is no act in which love is more intense and operative than in suffering for the loved one, the great lover seeks this act as the ultimate loving effort given him to accomplish. He is invited to this above all when the desperate sorrow for the lost loved one gives him resolve and launches him into cruel acts. Thus, at the death of Patroclus, Achilles' soldiers shaved their heads and covered his body with their hair. The same applies to the cruelties found among all ancient peoples in their burial rites or in their feasts for the dead [*App.*, no. 15].

Article 3
The fitting action of entia — The third law

1581. The third law of harmony, that is, of the fitting action of entia is: 'A simple or multiple act, carried out through several communicating potencies, does not always cease suddenly, but regresses according to a certain law by which it passes through different ordered states in successive series. This gradual passage, right up to the total extinction of the act, is natural and hence pleasant for the subject of the act. When the gradual passage is impeded however, the subject is under stress.'

1582. In *Anthropology*, I demonstrated this law with an example of imagined colours and sounds.[322] I will make some further observations about these.

Fresnel and Arago's theory about the wave system to explain the phenomena of light was considered very probable. But they limited their studies to laws governing the action of luminous waves of fluid which, they supposed, was diffused through all nature. This however is not sufficient to explain vision. Vision arises in the visual sensory and not in the ether, whose only function can be that of stimulator. The psychologist must therefore avail himself of their efforts in order to know or suggest the way in which the visual sensory might operate when luminous sensations arise in the soul. I think that this difficult question would be considerably illuminated if the findings or conjectures of those two enlightened physicists concerning what happens in

[322] *AMS*, 443–454.

the above-mentioned fluid outside the sensory were applied to the sensory itself.

1583. According to this concept the optic nerve would be a bundle of nerve-filaments. The bundle would be filled with an extremely elastic substance (or perhaps fluid) whose molecules received the impression of the ethereal waves and vibrated longitudinally like the string of a violin. The size, speed, number and different contrasts of these vibrations would explain the phenomena of vision.

First of all, different colours would be the result of different numbers of vibrations made by the molecules in the nerve-filament. This number would correspond to the number of ethereal vibrations. We can accept as demonstrated that the number of ethereal vibrations varies according to different colours, for example, those of yellow light are more numerous than those of light which stimulates red.

1584. The speed and size of the waves is in proportion to their number. Their diversity of speed, size and number must mean therefore that similar vibrations take place in the molecules of the nerve substance and, by producing different stimulations, result in different colours. This explains how each nerve-filament is capable of giving the sensation of all the colours by means of the different stimulation it receives from different luminous rays.[323]

1585. Furthermore, vibrations propagated along the nerve-filament would be reflected and turned back on themselves when they reached the extremity, in conformity with some law. Their return would explain how imagined and complementary colours, whose image we have,[324] remain when the external sensation ceases. In fact, a vibration which breaks against an obstacle before completion produces a reflex vibration whose velocity must differ from the first according to a complementary law.

1586. This would enable us to understand why complementary, accidental colours oppose and cancel each other, that is, produce black instead of white. If a complementary, reflex vibration returns in the nerve-filament, while the eye is

---

[323] *AMS*, 104.

[324] Cf. the theory I have put forward about *phantasy* in *AMS*, 350–366.

impressed by the same colour, a vibration must be produced in the opposite direction, leaving the pupil at rest. Let us consider an experiment known to physicists.

Suppose that two small, coloured squares, one violet and the other orange, each with a black spot in the centre, are placed on a black background. If we look alternately at each spot for a second and then close our eyes, we will seem to see three squares, one yellow (which is the complementary colour of violet), the other blue (the complementary of orange), and the third (in the middle) green, the result of the composition of yellow and blue. On the other hand, if the two squares themselves are complementary colours, for example violet and yellow, or orange and blue, the middle square is no longer visible, that is, it becomes black.

The explanation of these phenomena seems to be the following:

1. When we look successively at the two coloured squares, our optic axes have different directions. The squares therefore strike the retina in different spaces so that each eye has the impression of two squares, in all four impressions. But two of these impressions, one of one square, the other of the other square, strike the same space in each retina, because the optic axis of one eye has the same alignment on one colour as the optic axis of the other eye has on the other colour. As a result the impressions of two colours strike the same space of the retina of both eyes. Nevertheless, as long as both eyes are fixed on the squares, they see only two squares, either because the impressions have no time to combine, or because the spontaneity of the soul does not co-operate in producing images in the phantasy, or because the attention is turned solely to looking at the two squares without interest in anything else.

This is not the case with the imaginary colours that follow. The impressions on the three different spaces in the two retinas must result in three series of longitudinal vibrations in the nerve-filaments. The two spaces impressed by a single colour must each produce the complementary colour as an imagined or reflex colour, because the reflex vibration must complement the stalled vibration. The space between, impressed contemporaneously by the two colours, must produce reflex vibrations complementary to the individual colours. These reflex vibrations

[1586]

are not confused because they vary in size and speed. Now, since a nerve-filament can produce only one sensation at a time proportioned to the number of its molecules, the result must be a colour composed of the two complementary colours. But if the two colours of the squares are themselves complementary, it is clear that the vibration caused by one of the colours must, while on its way from the outside to the inside, meet the perfectly equal reflex vibration of the other colour moving in an opposite direction from the inside to the outside. In this way the two series of vibrations cancel each other: the two series moving outwards destroy alternately the other two reflected series which are returning.

1587. The same hypothesis would also explain why a colour, before ceasing in the eye, leaves behind other colours, for example white becomes yellow, then red, indigo, blue and finally green, when it disappears. If we consider that the molecular vibration which reflects from the external extremity of the nerve-filament is complementary to the colour impressed on the retina, we can conceive that the reflex, complementary vibration breaks once more as soon as it reaches the extremity of the nerve-filament. It must then return from the outside to the inside with a different speed. This outward and inward movement of ever-changing waves must result in different, imaginary colours until excitation entirely ceases or the vibration becomes so small that it is insufficient to produce a distinct colour.[325]

[325] It may perhaps be objected that nerve-filaments must vary in length in different-sized people, and hence the same phenomena are not verified in all human beings, as in fact is the case. I reply: the wisdom of the Creator was able to make the number of vertebrae, teeth and, generally speaking, bones, muscles, etc. the same in every human being. We can therefore suppose that with the same wisdom he made the number of elastic molecules in each filament of the optic nerve the same for us all. The vibrations must therefore be the same for a given number of molecules. That the molecules could vary in size, etc., would cause no difficulty. Nor can we say that optic sensations are perfectly equal in all of us; we can only say they are analogous. Indeed, to know whether the sensations in several human beings are totally and in every respect equal, we would need to compare them. This we cannot do because we have no awareness of others' sensations, only of our own. Moreover some diversity must evidently exist, if we note that when people see the same colours, they do not all have the same feelings; their feelings can vary at least in intensity.

[1587]

1588. Similar reasoning could be used to explain the laws of mechanics according to which the acoustic nerve is stimulated by sound. I think it also very probable that the sensations of all the other sensories arise from similar vibrations and obey analogous laws.

1589. Now, if every subject enjoys its act (first law) so that any impediment to the progress of the act or any disturbance which forces the subject to cut short one act and undertake another is distressful, then the sensitive soul must welcome 1. vibrations of sensory molecules which produce a greater feeling in the soul, 2. vibrations which develop harmoniously without clashing, and finally, 3. vibrations which work together to increase stimulation as much as possible. This explains the pleasure we receive when some colours and sounds harmonise, and our various levels of displeasure with other colours and sounds. As I said in *Anthropology*, natural and spontaneous vibrations must produce pleasing colours and sounds. This is true also for imaginary and complementary colours and sounds, that is, those to which the mechanics of the nervous system are spontaneously determined. Because these are pleasant, the external impression simply associates itself with the sensitive spontaneity, which it helps by alleviating the effort contributed by the sentient principle's activity. On the other hand, the sentient principle is distressed and suffers discord and disharmony when it experiences 1. contrary excitations, or 2. excitations which are confused and mutually obstructive, so that it cannot complete the sensitive acts it has begun, or when new excitations force it to change to different acts and abandon the first.

1590. I will use this theory to explain harmony and consonance of sounds.

First, if several sounds began from the same point and at the same time, they would produce only one sensation corresponding to the vibrations of the nerve-filament they stimulated. This is proved by Savart's experiment. He made a ratchet turn in such a way that the teeth struck a rigid piece of paper. When the wheel turned slowly, the strikes made by the teeth against the paper could be distinguished because of the a noticeable interval of time between them. But if the wheel's movement were greatly accelerated, only one continuous sound was heard, whose sharpness increased with the speed of rotation, resulting in a vibration of higher frequency. The explanation is that the individual strikes succeeded one another with the smallest interval of time, that is, smaller than the interval necessary for causing a sensation. Several acoustic sensations cannot harmonise unless the air vibrations strike the ear at the same time or begin from different points, in which case they act on a different nerve-filament.

1591. Harmony is possible both between successive sounds, provided they are separated by a very short interval, and between simultaneous sounds coming from different points, for example, from the different instruments of an orchestra. The harmony of successive sounds, such as those of an individual singer or instrument, must stimulate sensation in the same nerve-filaments, but there can be no pleasure unless the soul, which receives the different sounds, makes them simultaneous through its own nature which is immune from time. It is the soul which feels only a single feeling resulting from several successive sounds. This is a feeling of melody, another proof of the simplicity and identity of the sensitive principle at different times. In fact, the act of the fundamental feeling has a constant duration; successive sounds are simply modifications of this identical feeling. In this feeling successive sounds are compared and posit the pleasant harmony called 'melody'. Once again, we see how the unity of harmony is entirely psychological in origin.

1592. But according to the law I have enunciated, this pleasure arises in the essentially sensitive soul because two or more successive sounds are natural and spontaneous to it. The soul easily exercises its activity on them and produces sensitive acts without being cut short or obstructed, or forced to change them before they are completed. The reason is that 1. pleasure always arises in the soul from each of its acts, because feeling is always pleasant for it — this is not harmony but ordinary pleasure which suffers when individual acts are cut short — and 2. pleasure arises in the soul from several acts, provided one act helps rather than disturbs another — this is the pleasure of consonance or harmony.

1593. In fact the soul takes pleasure whenever it carries out its act with the greatest possible ease and least possible fatigue. This happens when it is not forced to change its act.

Consequently the *regularity* of its acts is pleasing because regularity does not require change in the kind of action it is doing, but preserves the rhythm or form of its the action without additions and alterations.

1594. This explains why harmonic sounds consonant with each other are produced by a number of vibrations whose mutual relationship can be indicated by whole numbers, 1, 2, 3, etc. without fractions. As a result the size of the vibrations corresponds to those numbers, so that two or three or four, etc. vibrations of one sound are exactly equal to one vibration of another sound. Similarly, the velocity of the vibrations of one sound are precisely double or triple or quadruple that of another, with no remainder. Vibrations distributed in this way 1. are never confused or impeded, 2. have easily perceptible relationships, which 3. are always the same, so that the rhythm is of a constant measure. Hence the soul, which must co-operate with its activity in the production of these sensations, immediately finds the law for producing them. In other words, its action is regular. This regular form produces *habit* which makes the soul's action spontaneous and extremely easy. If we want to know which sounds harmonise best, it is sufficient to note the sounds produced by ethereal vibrations whose relationships are expressed by whole numbers. The octave, for example, corresponds to these numbers; its vibrations are 1 to 2. The harmony of a fifth has vibrations of 2 to 3; that of a fourth, vibrations of 3 to 4;[326] and that of a third, 4 to 5. The number of vibrations of the consonances called 'perfect' (*fa-la-doh*, *doh-mi-so* and *so-ti-re*) is always 4, 5 and 6.

1595. We see therefore that divine wisdom ordered external, corporeal things so that their laws might help the soul in its acts. We know for example that a vibrating cord not only vibrates as a whole, but also in halves and in quarters, etc. As a result, other sounds and harmonising sounds are felt together with the sound of the whole cord.[327]

1596. The same explanation applies to consonances which

---

[326] Professor Toscani assures me he has observed that babies begin by making a unisonal sound, after which their next baby noise jumps a fourth.

[327] Cf. *AMS*, 434 for the correspondence between the external world and the soul.

[1594–1596]

arise from simultaneous sounds coming from different points. Although we suppose that discordant sensations are received by different nerve-filaments to prevent their being confused, the soul's spontaneity nevertheless co-operates in producing them. If therefore the number of vibrations is not correctly and exactly interrelated, the soul is always obliged to act irregularly and to vary the rhythm of its action. This confirms and seals what I said, namely, that the unity of harmony is psychological in origin, although the spontaneity of the soul may be stimulated either regularly or irregularly by external stimuli which change its term.

1597. Finally the reason why the regular beat of time is pleasant is found in the same law governing the soul's action.

Article 4
Conclusion to the cosmological law of harmony

1598. From all this we can conclude:

1. The corporeal world, thanks to the wonderful order it has received from creative wisdom, can bestow order and harmony on feeling and on the rational principle.

2. This order lies not only in things external to us but in our own organisation (to which I will return later) and in the exquisite composition of our sensories, all of which are designed and arranged with such art and mastery of proportion that they correspond wonderfully to and accord with the proportions of the external, material world.

3. The sensitive principle itself accepts this wonderful order in the external world and in its term (the sensories), while with its own activity it posits *form*. The external world, which *per se* would not have the nature of order, proportion and harmony but only of separate, disjointed entities and actions, receives all these things from the sensitive principle through the unity created by the principle itself in that appropriate multiplicity. This last formal part of harmony, although not of *rational* origin, is nevertheless *psychological* in origin because it comes from the soul as sensitive.

[1597–1598]

CHAPTER 30

The psychological laws of the rational principle which correspond to the cosmological laws in general

1599. The action of the rational principle results from a combination of its activity with the lucidity of the object and the stimulus provided by the world. The former combination, we note, contains an element of ontological origin, an element of cosmological origin and an element of psychological origin. Determining which part is of psychological origin and which part of some other origin is difficult because every rational action has two terms, the object and the extrasubjective world, which are the cause of the action. No full discussion of the soul's ontological and cosmological laws therefore could take place without mention of the psychological laws. However, to avoid repetition in the necessary discussion about psychological laws which relate to the cosmic term, I will either omit what has been said or mention it briefly for the sake of continuity in reasoning.

The psychological laws corresponding to the cosmological laws divide into those governing speculative reason and those governing practical reason. I begin with the former.

CHAPTER 31

The psychological laws of speculative reason which correspond to the cosmological laws — The law of subjective analysis

1600. Speculative reason, determined in its action by its terms and needs, sometimes concentrates its attention and divides into several parts objects or terms of cognition which in themselves are undivided. Afterwards, wishing to have full information about things, it must re-assemble what it has divided. Finally, speculative reason, if not given the real object of its meditation by means of perception, argues from analogy. Hence three subjective laws: *analysis*, *synthesis* and *analogy*.

1601. Different sensories receive different impressions and stimulations from the same bodies. These stimuli, that is, the resultant stimulated sensations, enable perception of the agent body; they are its *representation*; relative to the soul they are *vicarious signs of the real thing* that has produced and occasioned them.[328] Because these sensations are simply modifications of the fundamental feeling, we can say that there is innate in us *something which represents* the whole external, material world: our internal world represents the external world; the *subject* represents to itself all that is *extrasubjective* and connected with it in reality.

1602. Since every corporeal ens is represented by several sensations, the rational principle is led or invited by this seemingly sensory prism to divide bodies into several aspects or natures. This provides the first occasion for *subjective analysis*.

1603. The rational principle not only uses these *natural signs to guide its attention to extrasubjective entities and their activi*ties, but soon invents *analogous, man-made signs*, that is, languages, as we have seen, which have a marvellously analytical virtue, and result from the needs of the rational principle.

Human *needs*, which are *groups of active and passive feelings*, are not always related to entia in their totality, or to their substance, or to the perceptions which divide entia according to their effects in our different sensories. Very often human needs are satisfied by certain determined actions and the accidental aptitudes of entia which, because of our lack of interest in anything else, alone attract our attention. This gives us new occasions for further division of the known objects; we consider them under certain particular relationships which they have with us, not in themselves or in their individual being.

1604. By means of the ontological law of cognition, we transform these accidents and multiple relationships into entia, which is a kind of subjective synthesis. We reduce the appurtenances of entia to abstract entia, contemplate them as essences

[328] In this sense we can truly say that 'the form of the intellect is the likeness of the thing understood' (St. Thomas, *S.T.*, I, q. 95, art. 1, ad 1). These *sensible likenesses* of bodies need to be conceived by the mind through the idea. On the other hand, the idea is the direct intuition of the essence of some thing. This ideal essence is not the likeness of the thing, but its essence. Cf. *NE*, vol. 2.

existing in themselves and give them a name. Properly speaking, these names can only be *signs of signs* because they indicate sensible signs which are themselves signs of entia.[329]

1605. Speculative reason on the other hand, when it concentrates its attention, spontaneously divides entia according to

1. their particular *actions and passions*;
2. their *relationships*.

The various *actions and passions* we experience and observe in entia are rooted in the intrinsic multiplicity of the activity and passivity of entia, and in the intrinsic multiplicity of the human subject who receives these actions from the entia and, by his action upon the entia, produces these passions in them.

1606. The *relationships* divide in various ways. Some are *essential* and constitute entia, for example, the continuum in the case of bodies; others are *accidental*, for example, a given colour which is a relationship with the optic sensory. Other relationships, called *dialectic relationships*, are not in entia as accidents but are produced by the mind which compares what is one with what is multiple. These are extrinsic relationships which posit nothing substantial or accidental in an ens, but exist between one ens and another in the mind which unites and compares them. Examples are: the distance between one body and another, likenesses, etc.

1607. This is the origin of *mental entia*, which must be carefully distinguished from *ideal entia*, the object of the mind's intuition, the essences of things. *Mental entia* are *partial views by the mind* which do not encompass some whole ens or essence. The mind limits itself to some element or to a relationship of an element, and posits this element or relationship as if it were an

---

[329] I have already noted that *names* can have three functions:

1. They can stimulate the mind to think of a real thing without stopping at its abstract quality. This is the case of proper nouns applied to several individual things. They indicate *nominal abstracts*. They do not represent any *ideal essence* to the soul but lead the mind from one individual to another through the relationship of nominal identity.

2. They can stimulate the mind to think of a specific or generic essence. This is the function of abstract nouns, for example, whiteness, etc.

3. They can stimulate the mind to think of a *real thing* or an *ideal essence* through which the real thing is thought. This is the function of common nouns.

ens. Guided by the principle of cognition and by what I have called the faculty of *invention* or *intellectual creation*, the mind reasons about this element or relationship as if it were an ens.

The mind can even change what is negative into a positive ens. For example, the mind changes limitation and nothingness into entia although, as I said, these are only *mental views*. In fact, the limitation of an ens is simply the mind's denial that the essence of an ens contains some entity, which the ens does not in fact contain. The act of *denial* pertains to what I have called the faculty of *judgment* and of *affirmation*. The resulting cognition is therefore subjective, not objective. *Nothing* is simply the negation of an ens; it is an ens with the addition of the mental act which removes the ens, a cognition given to the mind by its own act relative to the object (ens).

1608. If ancient thinkers had carefully noted this distinction between objective knowledge, given by the object, and subjective knowledge, given by an act of the subject himself, they would not have disputed so hotly whether the human spirit can think of a non-ens.[330] Parmenides, who denied this possibility,[331] spoke of non-ens in an objective sense; a non-ens understood absolutely and simply is certainly not an object of the mind. Plato and Aristotle, who showed that even a non-ens is known in some way, spoke as people applying dialectic (which they did). In other words, they spoke subjectively: 'nothing' is known, not because it is an object, but because the mind imagines for itself an object which is solely a negative relationship that it finds among entia, an ens that is denied by the mind.

1609. These thinkers therefore disputed whether generable things (as they called things and forms which begin to be — I would call them transient acts) arose from an *ens* or *non-ens*. The principal systems are four.

Some thinkers could not conceive how anything could come from a non-ens, or how an *ens* could produce anything outside itself which was not already present. They denied that anything began, and admitted only an eternal, immutable ens.[332]

---

[330] Plato, *Soph.*, pp. 243–244 (Bipont. edition).

[331] vv. 39–40, Karsten.

[332] Xenophanes' argument is well-known: cf. Arist., *De Xenophane,*

Others could not deny that some things begin nor could they conceive how an ens, if it already existed, could generate, that is, produce what is not. Consequently they said that everything came from non-ens and that all things were corruptible and unstable.[333]

Others again considered that some entity lay midway between ens simply understood and non-ens (nothing), and that the principles of things had to be found in this middle entity. Aristotle's system distinguished between an ens as *simply ens* and as *ens according to power* or else as *ens in act* and *ens in potency*.[334] In this way he flattered himself that he had defeated the Eleatics and solved the difficult question they had proposed.

Finally the Platonists did not appeal, like Aristotle, to something between ens and non-ens in order to explain the beginning of entia. Instead, they tried to show that the beginning, even of all contingent things, can be found in *ens* by distinguishing between *ens as such* and *perfect ens* in which lay the complex of all entia. This, I think, is Plato's own view. Otherwise he would not have censured Parmenides for having divided the all from the all.[335]

1610. The difference of opinion between these thinkers was in part due to their confusing *object ens* with *abstract ens*, *mental ens* and *absolute ens*. In other words they relied on a false distinction between different kinds of human knowledge.

1611. The first group of thinkers fixed their attention on *abstract ens* which is not totally *object ens*. *Abstract ens* is that concept of an ens, which positively excludes every possible determination and completion in an ens; *ideal ens* is that to which every real ens and therefore every entity is conformed. The formation of an *abstract ens* is a subjective action of the mind; an *ideal ens* is the result of natural intuition, although

---

Zenone et Gorgia; Phys., 1: 8; *De Coelo,* 3: 1. Chalcideus reports the same argument: 'If something becomes, it must become either out of what already was, or out of what is not; both are impossible' (*In Tim.,* p. 283).

[333] Sext. Empiricus says that Xeniades of Corinth considered all things to be in flux and generated from non-ens (*Adv. Math.,* 8: 53, 388, 399; *Pyrrhon. Hypot.,* 2.:18). Cf. Aristotle, *Phys.,* 1: 9.

[334] *Phys.,* 1: 8; *De Coelo,* 3: 1.

[335] *Soph.,* p. 259.

reflection discovers it afterwards by abstraction, that is, by removing the particular modes and determinations which limit the ens.

1612. The second group began from a *mental ens*, which is non-ens, because the negation of ens is a purely subjective action of the mind. Although the mind is not mistaken *per se*, the negation occasions error when these philosophers, and ourselves, convert non-ens into a true ens which can be the beginning or efficient cause of things.

1613. The third group (Aristotle and his followers) began with ens in potency as a kind of matter for ens in act. Thus they began purely from a mind-ens. The concept was suggested by Aristotle's experience which showed that certain things developed, as it were, from a seed and acquired a more explicit existence. Generally speaking, the concept was suggested to him when he saw that perceptible things were *limited*. This concept of limited-entia is composed of an objective and subjective element. As entia (knowledge of object), they are objects but, as limited, are known as a result of a mental vision which, as I said, denies them certain entities (knowledge of affirmation). Aristotle took this concept composed of ens and limitation and increased the limitation to such an extent that he failed to see its inevitable consequence, the disappearance of ens. He therefore retained ens by giving it an infinite limitation, and thus made it his ens in potency or first matter. In fact it was nothing more than the non-ens of Xeniades but Aristotle, always striving for novelty, denied this and called it 'ens in potency'.

1614. If he had not left this pure potency on its own but seen it in God, he would have come to the fourth system, that of the Platonists, whose sole mistake lay in the accessories and development of their system.

1615. The function of philosophy (and hence, strictly speaking, of dialectics) is to distinguish *mental ens* (an action of the mind) from true, objective or objectivisable ens. Reasoning about the former as if it were the latter is the sole cause of error, into which it is easy to fall. The mind, influenced by the words or signs to which it attaches its concepts (positive acts), not only changes its negations into positive entia, but sometimes does the opposite by giving a negative form to what is positive. Furthermore, the positive and negative elements are changed at will by the forms with which they are clothed. Thus, through its forms, what was negative is now made positive. Then it takes once more a negative form, then another positive form. In this way, it makes a composite of its mental concepts, one within another, by means of the innumerable forms with which it wishes to clothe them. We see this procedure clearly in algebra where any negative or positive sign is used for any negative or positive quantity. We deny the negation and then we deny the denied negation and so on. For example, a positive quantity can be indicated with two negative signs, $-(-A)$, and a negative quantity with a positive sign, $+(-A)$. Again, any signs can be used about any quantity without its ceasing to be what it was, without the quantity ever ceasing to be either positive or negative. The same is true of speech: if I say, 'Nothing is lacking to God', I express the greatest affirmation under the form of a double negation because this proposition equals the other proposition of positive form, 'God has everything'.

1616. The first function of dialectics, if it wishes to conclude a discussion, is to remove, one by one, all the layers with which the mind, principally by speech, has enveloped the proposition under discussion. When the proposition has been reduced to its pristine state, we must note whether its primitive form is a negative or affirmative. In this way, we simplify our reasoning and sweep away the sophisms that have been constructed by the subjective action of our understanding.

1617. This process also allows us to see very clearly whether what is predicated of anything is an accident of the thing itself or simply a mental relationship. For example, Plato and Aristotle accused Parmenides of contradiction for saying that ens, although *one*, is *eternal*, and thus placing in ens a plurality of substance and accident.[336] Parmenides could have replied: 'Yes, the *form* of my predication, "ens is eternal", splits ens in two, ens-being and eternal being. The division however lies solely in the form of the subjective conception and expression of the thing; eternity is simply an external relationship, conceived by the mind, which negates time, that is, cessation. The division places nothing more in objective ens than ens itself. In fact, the true value of the predicate is to prevent the prediction of

[336] Plato, *Soph*; Aristotle, *Phys*.

[1616–1617]

multiplicity about ens; the predicate is nothing more than a negation of multiplicity and accident.'

1618. Such is the task therefore to which dialects must apply itself. It must distinguish the different *forms* with which the mind continually clothes a concept or opinion, and in this way restore the concept to its simple, primal state.

CHAPTER 32

Continuation — The law of subjective synthesis

1619. Different sensories break up an ens. Strictly speaking, this is *cosmological analysis*, which the term (the world) supplies to the rational principle. Analysis becomes *psychological* when the rational principle divides what is not divided, either in sense or by passive and active feelings (sensible needs).

1620. There is also a cosmological synthesis, corresponding to cosmological analysis. It consists in the rational principle's unification of different, sensible representations of the same ens supplied by the different sensories. The principle is aware that it is dealing with only one ens, an ens represented in different ways by various effects of its action in the different sensories. I call this synthesis 'cosmological' because it is the world, the term of feeling, which furnishes the bond between all the different sensations and perceptions of a body. The bond is the identity of the space occupied by a body acting in different ways.[337] Consequently the difference between sensations is due to their different feel, not to the different space they occupy. Different parts of space, considered in isolation, are indiscernible; one part resembles another when the limits and situation of each part in total space are indistinguishable. No sensory can distinguish the situation and limits of its own space; as I said, they are not sensible to the sensory itself. Hence the rational principle does not receive from any single sensory its knowledge of the situation or limits of the sensory's total space. Each sensory supplies the rational principle with the situation and parts

[337] Cf. *NE*, vol. 2, [941–960].

relative to the totality of its own space alone, not with the situation and limits of this totality. But because the situation, the limits and the proportional distribution of these parts in the different sensories are identical, the space itself also seems identical, as we saw relative to the space occupied by the sensations of touch and sight, the two senses which present space with a more accurate outline of its various parts. This explains why we do not multiply bodies according to the number of our sensories. Rather we multiply the representations of bodies, and refer all these representations to a single ens which we say is tactile, coloured, saporific, sonorous, etc. This is cosmological synthesis.

1621. This fact gave rise to the distinction between *substance* and *accidents*. We call 'substance' the single ens to which we relate all the effects received in our sensories. We consider these effects as accidents of that ens. But because the effects represent the ens to us, we do not separate the representation from what is represented. If we were to divest what is represented totally from its representation, it would disappear. It is true, of course, that the effects produced by a body in our sensories differ according to the variety of our sensories. Hence an acting *body* produces one action only on the sensitive principle and another, nothing more, on the principle's term (the animate body). Indeed the only difference between these two actions results perhaps solely from the different nature of the sensitive principle, and of its term in which the operation takes place.

1622. This explanation of the origin of the concept of *substance* also explains the origin of both *full* and *abstract species*. Full species is the species or concept of an ens invested with all its accidents. Abstract species is the species of the ens stripped of its accidents, and left simply with the bond and unity to which all representative accidents are related. *Abstract species*, as I said, is the concept enabling us to know 'the act through which an ens subsists'.[338] However, I did not determine the nature of this act. I can now do so.

We know entia positively through the effects produced by their actions in our sensories, and more generally in our feeling. Feeling itself sometimes supplies a basis by means of which the

---

[338] Cf. *NE*, vol. 2, [646–659].

rational principle becomes aware that a group of effects must be attributed to one ens alone, as in the case of the concept of bodies. This concept is formed through feeling, which gives the perception of a force diffused in a single space, although in the same space there are sensations of a different 'feel'.[339] We conclude that a single force or agent, which becomes the *abstract species*, produces the multiple effects. Abstraction of this species is the task of the rational principle because the sensories supply only the force or agent invested with effects of varying nature, but always effects. If, in the case of bodies, we experience another group of effects which do not have the same bond, do not possess the unity provided by feeling, and do not relate to the same identical space, we immediately form another ens from this second group and have another species. This is the origin of the *multiplicity of entia*.

1623. But a group of sensible effects can differ only in reality. In this case, and because of their similarity in every other respect, these effects are known through the same idea or species. Their multiplicity therefore is a multiplicity of individuals; it is not a multiplicity of species, nor diversity of abstract or full species. Many individuals can correspond to the full species in the order of reality, while each individual can contain substance and accidents, both of which are multiplied by different *reality*.

When I said therefore that abstract species divide according to the different act of being, I meant according to the act of ideal, not real being. The diversity of acts of real being multiply only real individuals, to which only one abstract species corresponds. In other words, the act of being in the order of ideality remains one and identical. Consequently the abstract species is purely one, just as the ideal substance of many, equal individuals is also purely one.

1624. I said that the abstract species remains the same when

[339] The *identity of space* I am discussing is not absolute but relative to the group of effects. A body moved to different places is said to be identical because in every place where it is present the group of its sensible effects remains united, and always relates to one and the same space. The diversity of the place in which a body is found does not therefore enter into the specific idea of body.

the different groups of sensible effects which make an ens known differ relative to their reality alone. But would there not be a contradiction if, in different groups of sensible effects corresponding to one and the same species, we saw some variations, over and above the difference in reality, without a change in the abstract species? A pear, for example, can differ from other pears in size, colour, etc., and from itself at different times. Nevertheless all pears are known through the same abstract species of pear. The explanation is that the group of sensible effects representing a single ens must be taken in its totality. Thus, if the same pear has different aspects and is perceived at different times, these aspects or sensible effects, although successive, pertain to the same group and can be said to belong to the variations found in various individual pears.

1625. What therefore is the principle which multiplies individuals? — Their different *reality*.

1626. What is the principle that multiplies entia? — A finite ens is constituted by the unity of the group of its sensible effects. This unity binds these effects together in such way that they show all the effects of the same agent. Relative to a body, this unity is rooted in the identity of space; relative to the soul, in the identity of feeling, etc. Hence the multiplicity of entia is given in the feeling we have of them when a single principle or cause of a certain number of sensible effects is felt in the feeling. We feel we cannot in any way attribute to this principle or cause other sensible effects arising from some other principle or single cause which is also felt. I call this principle or cause of a given group of effects 'the sensible basis of an ens', and maintain that entia multiply in keeping with the multiplication of their sensible bases.

1627. What is the principle that multiplies full species? — Because species lack the reality of an ens, the multiplicity arising from difference of reality is also lacking. A different, *real*, *sensible basis* multiplies entia, but if this multiplication takes place by means of reality, a single species corresponds to many sensible bases whose difference arises solely from their different reality. But the sensible bases, clothed with the group of their effects, are given by feeling, and the full species corresponds to such sensible bases. Not all sensible effects, however, attributed to the same basis, can be contemporary; one excludes the other;

for example a red body cannot be a yellow body. What the full species makes known to our spirit is the sensible basis clothed with all its contemporary or co-possible, sensible effects. Granted therefore the same sensible basis clothed with various sensible effects, full species multiply.

1628. What is the principle that multiplies abstract species? — The abstract species makes known the sensible basis of an ens. These species differ when they make known different bases, prescinding of course from their reality and from consideration of any sensible, accidental effects.

1629. Diversity of species therefore proceeds from the ontological relationship between real and ideal modes of being, whose interaction is determined by no other higher principle than the intrinsic order of being.

1630. I have posited different sensible bases as the principle of multiplication of entia. But the human spirit, with its faculty of invention, presupposes these bases, even when they do not exist, and so creates for itself *mental beings*. The careful classification of the different kinds of these beings pertains to dialectics.

The spirit sometimes does this when it takes an accident, a sensible effect, and considers it as if it were the sensible basis of an ens. It does this easily, particularly when the sensible effects are so ordered that one effect necessarily precedes another. Let us suppose that our spirit changes the colour (a purely sensible effect) of an ens. It will indicate the size, form and movement, etc. of the colour, considering the colour as an ens, as the subject of all these qualities. Similarly our spirit changes every abstract into an ens whose species can be multiplied without multiplication of the ens to which they relate. It does this in virtue of its power to limit its mental gaze and concentrate its attention.

1631. There is one creation or invention of the human mind which is so spontaneous and necessary to human nature, and hence common to the human race, that it certainly deserves the philosopher's attention. I refer to the concept of matter. The relationship of matter with the sensitive principle, whose term it is, is so essential to matter that it cannot be conceived for what it is without the principle. Nevertheless, the spirit does detach it, and in this detached state arbitrarily considers it as a being *per se*. But matter separated from feeling can no longer be conceived as an ens; it is simply the rudiment of an ens, of an ens *in via* which has not yet attained its full being. What kind of species, therefore, is this concept of matter? Full or abstract, or something else?

Clearly it cannot be a full species because we prescind from its sensible effects. Nor can it be an abstract species, which also relates to a sensible basis. Its concept therefore can be classified only in the class of (ideal) genera, that is, ideas which do not represent an ens but something pertaining to an ens. The word 'matter' therefore signifies no species of entia but only that of which many species of entia are composed. It can be considered under two aspects: 1. as the matter of which corporeal entia are composed relative to form (in this case it is something entirely passive to or receptive of form and, as synthesism demands, cannot be without form); or 2. as relative to our concept, that is, as present in the act in which our concept is formed (in this case it is what I have called 'the sensiferous element'). If, in conformity with the teaching given above about the origin of the multiplicity of beings, we now wish to define the sensiferous element or matter under this aspect, we would do so as follows. The abstract species in the ideal order corresponds to the *sensible basis*; whenever many *abstract species* correspond to many sensible bases, we say that the sensible bases differ from each other specifically as well as individually. If then I take many sensible bases of different species and form an abstract of them, prescinding from their specific differences, I have formed their genus which is precisely the concept of sensiferous matter. The concept of matter is therefore generic (ideal).

1632. However, when abstraction has removed the species determined by the group of sensible effects from the *generic, sensible basis*, we are left with a *sensible, formless basis*. It is clear, therefore

1. that the *abstract species* makes known the *form* of entia,[340] taking the word 'form' in the ancient sense of 'that which makes an ens be what it is';

2. that the concept of matter excludes that of form and therefore of species.

---

[340] In Latin, *forma* corresponds to the Greek εἶδος, which means precisely *species, visum.*

1633. We can now ask whether the individual is comprised in the abstract species or the full species. I have already deduced the multiplicity of individuals from reality. But to say that the multiplicity of individuals (real individuals) is not comprised in the *species* is one thing; it is another to say that the individual (specific individual) is not comprised in it. In my opinion, therefore two things have to be said. First, the *multiplicity* of individuals is contained neither in the full nor the abstract species. Consequently, we could never know the number of real individuals of this species (at least in the case of the species of contingent beings known to us), if the species alone were present to our mind. Second, I also maintain that the *specific individual* is contained in the species. In other words, every species makes known an individual ens whose realisation can be repeated many times without any change in the species. In fact the *form* of entia, their complete form, is simply their individuality as known in the species. I call this *specific individuality*.

1634. We can now see the distinction between the concept of *nature* and of *individual*. Nature means both an ens without form (for example, matter) and an ens with form. In this second case, it corresponds to the abstract species and expresses not the multiplicity of real individuals but the individual as found in the abstract species. It applies to each individual, not to all. When we say, 'Human nature subsists in many individuals', we do not mean that human nature is divided into many individuals, but that the whole of human nature subsists in each individual. It would be incorrect to say that human nature is divided into many individuals.

1635. The *form* of entia therefore constitutes their *specific* or *ideal individuality*. If through abstraction we break the individual down into parts and distinguish *nature* and *individuality*, we understand nature as *an ens without form*, and *individuality* as its form, its completion, the last act that perfects and specifies it.[341]

1636. Natures without *individuality* are formless; they are incomplete entia. Individuality is therefore an essential characteristic of an ens.

1637. *Matter*, therefore, is an ens without form and in this

---

[341] In intellective beings, *individuality* is called *person* Cf. *AMS*, 832–837.

sense a non-ens. Consequently the opinion of ancient thinkers that things were produced from non-ens[342] is not without truth if interpreted in reference to material things and a material cause.

Aristotelians maintained that this ens-without-form, an incomplete ens, can receive a form and be individualised. Indeed the whole Aristotelian teaching about forms is drawn from the forms with which matter is considered to be clothed. This may well be the case; I do not wish to oppose the teaching but explain it in a reasonable way. I want to see how much *absolute knowledge* and how much *subjective knowledge* is present in these forms conceived by the human mind (that is, how much the rational subject himself contributes when he acquires concepts). The concept of *matter* is the 'generic concept of different sensible bases', that is, it is known only by what sense has provided and on which mental abstraction has carried out its operation. But everything that sense presents to the mind is the term of sense. Animal sense, which we are discussing, presents to the mind a (sensiferous) force diffused in extension. Sometimes extension presents it as shapeless, as in the fundamental feeling and in the particular sensories when the extension is understood in its totality. At other times, animal sense presents the force as shaped. This is the case with parts of the extension presented by certain sensories, for example, touch, sight, etc. Nobody claims that the shapeless extension presented by the fundamental feeling or by particular sensories is individuated; this kind of extension is supplied only by the concept of *nature* or of *indefinite space*. But in the case of the sensories we say that the parts shaped by their term are individuated. It is to these parts we owe the concept of particular bodies. As we have seen, particular bodies are unified by means of their *sensible basis*, a determined part of space in which certain sensations become representative of the body itself, of the space itself, through the very unity of the space.

1638. I also said that although the sensible bases clothed with their groups of sensations are many, the *abstract species* by which they are known is only one. Thus, their multiplication takes place in the order of reality and not in that of ideality; individuals of the human species are many, but the concept of

---

[342] Aristotle, *Phys.*, 1: 9.

human being is only one. The multiplicity of individuals is
known not through the concept of the human being, which is
only one, but through the different, real, sensible bases which
are many. Their plurality is known therefore with the help of
sense (a potency communicating with real being).

In the case of material entia, subsistence or reality is material.
In every *sensible basis* some matter (force diffused in extension)
is perceived, clothed and determined by a group of sensations.
It is this group which informs us that we are dealing with some
particular matter, not another. But this group of sensations can
be broken up by abstraction as we reject some and keep others
present to our spirit. Now, each group of sensations contains
1. a sensiferous force, 2. a shaped extension, and 3. sensations
of different 'feel', or of the same 'feel' but different in quality.
Through the virtue of abstraction we can separate these three
elements which form a body from every point of view and form
many ideal, *generic concepts*.

1639. In fact we can limit our attention to:

1. The sensiferous force alone, in which case we have the
concept of formless *matter*.

2. Extension, which gives us the concept of *mathematical
bodies*.

3. The sensations of different 'feel', or a genus of sensations.
This is the concept of accident, or of a genus of accidents.

4. Two of the elements (force and extension), which give us
the concept of body in general.

5. The shaped extension and the 'feel' of the sensations.
Here we have a concept, limited by some extension, of shaped
accidents.

6. Lastly, the force and the sensations of different quality
pertaining to some other sensible basis. This gives us the concept of the different kinds *of matter*, for example, water, air, fire,
wood, etc.

1640. All these concepts are generic, not specific. They do not
make an individual known because none of them makes known
a complete form. The first excludes any form whatsoever; the
others posit *imperfect forms*, which are parts of some form. We
see therefore that there are some genera which make matter
known, and others which, while making a part of the form
known, do not attain individuality.

[1639–1640]

1641. Now, because on the one hand the concept of *matter* excludes the individual and thus has no limit (form alone limits what is limitable), and on the other the subsistence of material things *is material*, we understand why *matter* (according to the concept under discussion) can be divided into parts but not multiplied; the concept remains the same under all forms. If matter were multiplied, it would receive limitations and no longer be matter. The multiplication of individuals therefore comes from the *form* in so far as this makes them subsistent, that is, from the *reality* of the form, not from matter, as the ancients thought.[343]

1642. What we have said about formless matter must also be said about the *genera of matter* (the sixth concept given above). Water does not *multiply* into many drops — the whole substance of water is present in each drop, expressed by the word 'water'. It is divided into *parts*, because the part of water in one drop is not in another drop. Thus *matter* which is either totally formless or has form only generically, acts in an opposite way to *soul*, which can be *multiplied* but *not divided*.

The *form* of bodies therefore, the complete form corresponding to the species, is formed by a whole *group* of representative sensations referred to the *sensible basis* and hence to the ens; this form individuates a body. Is this individuation perfect; is there an absolute individual in a body? Or do we use subjective knowledge to think the individual in the body because we are obliged by an ontological law to give to every object of our thought the form of ens, and therefore give individuality without which an ens cannot be? I have discussed this question elsewhere. I said that bodies, although without individuality in themselves, take their real individuality from the spirit whose term they are. Divided from the spirit, they are incomplete entia and can be called 'non-entia', which distinguishes them from *nothing*.[344] They do not subsist detached from their principle, but are part of an ens and as such

---

[343] *AMS*, 782–788 [*App.*, no. 16].

[344] The word 'non-ens' is, I think, very valuable. My definition, 'that which is on the way to being an ens but is not at present' (abstract concept), provides a useful tool for a reasonable interpretation of many otherwise absurd opinions of ancient philosophers.

correspond to a mental, abstract concept. Hence, the spirit, when it considers bodies as individuals, does so through the law *of subjective synthesis.*

1643. We can view bodies united to the spirit in two ways: either according to what we know about them through our feeling-experience or according to reasoning, which has at least conjectural value. In the first case, our knowledge is expressed by all the words invented to indicate corporeal things. In the second, bodies are considered as effects of a simple agent foreign to us, called 'corporeal principle'. In this case, there are no words to properly express our reasonings. Furthermore, if this *corporeal principle* does in fact act in our spirit, bringing into effect the sensible basis and the sensations clothing the basis, bodies receive some other individuality dependent upon their proximate cause. Moreover, because everything we can say about this kind of individuality can be said about the individuality of bodies as terms of our spirit, I will speak about the latter.

1644. This *individuality* attributed to bodies is twofold: either we consider the corporeal elements which we take as extended and continuous, or bodies themselves composed of these elements. The only individuality possessed by the corporeal elements comes to them 1. from the continuity of the extended element they occupy and 2. from the sensible difference of this occupied, extended element. *Individuality* whose foundation is the *continuum* is not true individuality because it does not give proper unity to an ens; in the continuum every assignable space is outside the other spaces, with which it cannot form one and the same being. It is clear therefore that the continuum can have only the unity it receives from the sentient principle, to which in fact it is totally present and by which it is constituted. The rational principle therefore effects a subjective synthesis by attributing to the elements the individuality proper only to the *sentient principle.*

1645. Composite bodies are either unorganised or organised. Unorganised bodies are composed of elements which are even less susceptible of unity and individuality. Nevertheless the rational principle attributes unity and individuality to them because of the ontological law it must follow in thinking of things, and because of the psychological law of subjective synthesis. It is helped in this by the composite of attracting forces which pertains to the constitution of the external world. Thanks to this constitution, every body with a centre of gravity seems to have a single force determining it in one direction or position. But because this force or cause of motion does not of itself alone constitute an ens, it is an abstraction. Consequently the individuality granted to a body through the concentration of its forces is merely abstract, not specific individuality.

1646. Does organisation provide a better basis for the individuality of bodies? The organisation must either be 1. considered as an effect of brute, insensitive forces, in which case its unity is still an abstraction (the resulting individuality is abstract, and attributed by the rational principle to the body when the principle conceives it through the law of subjective synthesis); or 2. be formed and dominated by a sensitive principle which, with its perfect unity and simplicity, is seen as the true foundation of the individual. In this second case, however, the individual is no longer a body but a composite of (sentient) principle and (felt) term, a composite which is truly one and indivisible.

1647. From this we can deduce a rule for knowing the nature of a specific idea: it is that idea which makes us know an ens, an individuated ens. To do this, it has to make known the *sensible basis of the ens*, or something that performs this function, such as a subject or a proximate cause. In a word, the function must be a point of union for the group of qualities which determine the ens. Either the qualities clothe the ens, in which case we have the full, specific idea, or they are abstracted, leaving only the relationship between them and the *basis* of the ens, in which case we have the abstract, specific idea.

1648. I then described another synthesis carried out by the rational principle under the influence of the different feelings of the sentient principle where many different sensations representing different entia take place. For example, various sensations cause a feeling of joy or sadness, etc., in the soul. These feelings become as it were a bond which mentally binds together the actions of very different entia, and is another source of the genera which the human spirit composes.

1649. Again, the human spirit, when acting freely, makes all kinds of syntheses. It arbitrarily joins together any kind of complex of things which it then considers as a unity. This notably reduces its reasoning, as we see in algebra: for example, in the calculation of analytical functions, a function of one or more letters represents at one glance all the infinite ways in which the letter and letters can be bound together or with other quantities. The letters themselves are already an arbitrary synthesis of as many units as we desire, joined in any way according to the need of the calculation. To perform these syntheses as one wishes, the rational principle uses signs, one of which can represent many different things, as we choose and according to what has been agreed. Here we have *complex ideas*, one of which is sufficient to make known any group of other ideas, the last of which is the *idea of the whole*.

1650. But the idea of the whole is not arbitrary. Its foundation is partly in the unity of universal being, outside of which nothing is, as Parmenides observed.[345] We cannot say, however, that it is founded in the same way in the organism of the universe because we could think of *the whole* even if the universe were not organated or assembled as it is, like a kind of great, single being. On the other hand, the universe, properly speaking, is only the *relative* not the *absolute whole*.

CHAPTER 33

Continuation — The law of subjective analogy

1651. We form ideas of entia, whether specific or generic, according to the limited mode in which we communicate with them through feeling. Our action is limited by certain laws, which are partly cosmological, arising from the *term* of our feeling, and partly psychological, arising from the soul which follows its nature in responding to the terms presented to it. The terms of feeling do not of course present entia to our sense but signs which represent them to our rational principle. These signs are actions and effects whose disposition and characteristics come from the nature of the recipient, the soul, and are the real *efficient cause*; the agents different from the soul are merely

---

[345] Vv. 95–96, Karsten.

excitatory causes. Hence only our intellect, not our natural feeling, is in direct communication with *entia* in themselves. Because our understanding, whose only proper object is an *ens*, cannot know *entia* except by their representative signs, it is dependent solely on signs for the extent of its knowledge. Our mind, therefore, is limited in its knowledge because of the limited matter presented to it, on which it must exercise its rational operations. This limitation however does not prevent it from acquiring many, absolutely true cognitions about *entia*,[346] a fact which gives the lie to the philosophy which asserts (I say 'asserts' because it gives no proof at all of its opinions) that 'the order of human knowledge corresponds exactly to the order of *entia*'. Such a claim transforms the human being into God, a paradox contradicted by all the most serious philosophical schools. I shall waste no time refuting it; instead, I will explain the law of subjective analogy.

1652. This law is another limitation added to the act of human knowledge. If the knowledge of things of which we have sensible perception contains so much that is limited and subjective, the understanding will be even more restricted when it tries to argue and reason about things supplied neither by feeling nor perception.

Analogy concerns precisely those *entia* with which our feeling has no direct communication and from which we receive no action, modification or effect. What can we know about such *entia*?

1653. I divided all human cognitions into two great classes, *intuition* and *predication*.

Pure *intuition* enables us to know only universal being.

Predication normally begins from the sensible perception of a subsistent *ens*. Once we possess this perception, we know its *form* in its *species* (universal being limited by the sensible effect connected with it), and its *subsistence* in *affirmation*. We then analyse the form or matter, and come to know their abstracts and parts. Next we synthesise, and finally, by comparing many beings, we determine different kinds of relationships.

1654. But without *perception*, we lack the basis for the whole process. What can replace this basis?

[346] *Rinnovamento*, bk. 3, c. 47 [bk. 4, c. 5].

[1652–1654]

1. Words or other signs which have no representative virtue of the ens in question.

2. Ontological relationships between perceived entia and the unperceived ens about which we seek information.

Entia which do not fall under human perception are of two kinds: 1. Those whose non-perception is accidental. An example is of people born blind or kept from light or colour throughout their life. 2. Those which are totally unperceived because alien to or distant from our sensories or natural feeling. Pure spirits are examples of this.

Objects of the first kind have ontological relationships only by means of words. They are contingent beings incapable of being revealed by the intuition of necessary, universal being. The only means of knowing them is by *non-representative signs*. An example are the words used by someone talking to a blind person about colours. The words do not represent colours for him in any way whatsoever. Their total affect is to make the blind person understand what colours have in common with sounds and other feelings, or with some sensible entia perceived by the blind person. This common element is so small that it constitutes only an *analogy*, not a *likeness*.

1655. What then is *analogy*? Which area of knowledge does it concern? — Analogy is founded in *proportion*, not in *feeling*. In fact, there are often equal proportions between specifically different entia: largeness, smallness, simple composition, multiple composition, greater and lesser multiplicity or numbers, etc. constitute properties relative to entia not as *perceived and felt*, but as entia or a given kind of entia, for example, contingent beings. These characteristics, or generic and ontological properties, do not establish a likeness between entia, but only what we call *analogy*.

1656. Non-representative signs of such entia give therefore some *analogical* knowledge, by which we simultaneously acquire knowledge of their subsistence, but not of their *positive form*. In place of this form, we acquire some *determinations* which are sufficient to prevent our confusing this ens with other entia. These determinations can be called a vicarious, *analogical form* of the positive form.

1657. The same must be said about angels, who are also contingent beings. However, because they are complete entia, not accidents like colours, we can receive their *effects* but not their direct, representative effects, that is, effects felt in our feeling by the direct action of an ens, action which represents the ens for us. The effects of the angels upon us are indirect and external; from them we argue to the angels' subsistence and to some of their endowments and potencies. Even here, we generally refer the effects to potencies similar to those of which we have positive knowledge, except that we can conceive the angelic potencies with greater efficacy if the effects do not differ in species but only in magnitude from those we observe in nature. Nevertheless we could not be certain of the accuracy of this likeness because we know that sometimes there are causes, called *equivocal* by the ancients, which maintain only a virtual, eminent likeness with their effect. In this case the concept of such a cause or potency could be only *analogous* to the causes or potencies we know positively.

1658. However, the cognition of infinite, absolute being, that is, of God, comes to us from three sources:

1. From revelation which, if we prescind from the internal light of grace, gives us only an *analogous cognition*, communicated by words, that is, by non-representative signs.

2. From effects, that is, from creation, etc. These also give us an *analogous* cognition because we do not see how creation operates. Only ontological reasoning tells us that the cause is equivocal relative to its effect, and supereminent.

3. From *ontological* reasoning. This again gives us an *analogical* cognition of God. However, it shows us 1. that such a cognition is purely analogical and consequently totally insufficient to give us positive knowledge of the supreme Being, and 2. that we cannot have positive knowledge of God in either of the two ways in which we have positive knowledge of the entia we know. In other words, we cannot know 1. his essence by means of the species, nor 2. his subsistence by means of feeling and affirmation. There must however be a third way of vision or intellective apprehension, which has no example in nature but is such that we perceive the subsistence in the idea itself.

1659. We must therefore distinguish two actions of our mind relative to the supreme Being: that by which we form some analogical cognition and that by which we know that such a cognition is inadequate and imperfect, although it is the highest and truest knowledge we can naturally have of God. Let me explain this *analogical* cognition better.

1660. First, we must establish that God in not intuited naturally by human beings. To say otherwise is 1. to fall into an error contrary to revelation, which tells us that God is he 'whom no man sees or can see';[347] 2. to oppose theological science which teaches that we do not know *what* God is but simply *that* he is, and that we do not know even this without some *demonstration*;[348] and 3. to oppose both common sense and philosophy. In order to explain human cognitions, philosophy requires human beings to know 'what being is', and thus have the intuition of 'being', but nothing more, not the intuition of the first being. St. Thomas, the greatest Italian philosopher and theologian, writes, 'that TRUTH IN GENERAL is known to us *per se*, but it is not known to us *per se* that THERE IS A FIRST TRUTH.'[349] He acknowledges that there would be no intellective power or potency unless it contained within itself some *likeness of God*,[350] which is not God but *being in general*. We can fittingly say that being in general is like God, not in the way that two real entia are alike, but in the way that a real ens and the ideal essence which makes it known are alike. The realisation of an essence can be said to be like the essence, although we should more accurately say that an ideal essence is the likeness of the realised ens which, therefore, is known through and in the ideal essence.[351]

1661. Having excluded the error that the natural object of

---

[347] 1 Tim 6: 16; Jn 1: 18; 1 Jn 4: 12.

[348] 'The proposition, "God is, in so far as he is in himself", is known *per se* because the predicate is the same as the subject; God is his own being. — But because we do not know what God is, the proposition is not known *per se* [but must be shown through things better known] relative to ourselves and less known relative to their nature, that is, through effects' (St. Thomas, *S.T.*, I, q. 2, art 1; *Theod.*, 55–60, 75–78).

[349] St. Thomas, *S.T.*, I, q. 2, art. 1, ad 3.

[350] Because the intellective virtue of the creature is not the essence of God, it must be some shared likeness of him who is the first intellect. Hence the intellectual virtue of the creature is called an intelligible light, derived as it were from the first light' (St. Thomas, *S.T.*, I, q. 12, art. 2). Here we must distinguish between the objective light of the intellect and its subjective potency which is enlightened by that light.

[351] *NE*, vol. 3, 1180–1189.

[1660–1661]

intuition is God, we must see what kind of cognition we can naturally obtain of this being superior to nature.

Being in general, as intuited by the soul, makes us know nothing real; with it alone we would not even know that any reality existed. Moreover, because it is a most simple, uniform light, nothing can be distinguished in it, not even elementary ideas. In fact all ideas, except that of being, can always be reduced to relationships between real things and ideal being, to relationships of relationships, and to abstracts of these relationships, obtained by means of different views of the spirit. Consequently we do not naturally possess the first principles of reasoning, which are applied ideas, but form them through relating real beings to being in general.

Supreme ideas and the supreme principles themselves therefore retain something of the same limitation as the real entia from which they were originally obtained through the action of our spirit. Real entia are those we perceive with our feeling and are, above all, corporeal entia. Only being in general is without any limitation whatever; it alone endows us with the faculty of knowing the limitation of our own ideas and of not falling into the error of believing that our limited, relative knowledge is unlimited and absolute. This guarantees for us the possession of truth

1662. I will take a few examples of the most general ideas which then become the guiding principles of reasoning.

1. *Essence* and *subsistence*. — Because all the things we perceive are contingent, they do not have their *subsistence* in their *essence*; they can be thought, but may still not subsist. Every time we think of *essence* and say the word, we do so without including subsistence; we posit essence without subsistence. This is the only concept we have of the essence of anything, the only language in which to express it. When, for example, we think of God, who does not come under our perception, we apply to him our limited concepts of *essence* and of *subsistence*, and reason about him by analogy with these known entities. Having no word to express the identity of *essence* and *subsistence* (the only word suitable for expressing the supreme Ens), we are forced to apply separately to him two imperfect phrases *divine essence* and *divine subsistence*, as if they were two things; nor can we attribute to the divine essence what

applies to the divine subsistence, and vice versa, without error, although these are one single thing in God. Hence theologians wisely observe that we can indeed truthfully say: 'God, (subsistence, subsistent person) generates God (another subsistent person)', but not: 'Godhead (essence) generates Godhead (another essence)'. This second statement would mean positing many gods, whereas the first posits only many persons because the noun *God*, understood as subsistence, receives the value of person. It is true that ontological reasoning (carried out later by comparing with ens in general the reasoning we produce with the aid of derived ideas) corrects our limited thinking and reveals the imperfection of our language. But we have no substitute. It protects us, therefore, from error but does not supply us with other ideas and other words suitable for accurate reasoning about the divinity. We are in fact always obliged to take the following tortuous course and: 1. reason about God with imperfect and analogical ideas taken from contingent natures, the only ideas we have; and 2. then acknowledge that our language is imperfect, limited, inadequate and incapable of being changed into a perfect, unlimited language on a par with such a wonderful subject.[352]

1663. 2. *Generic essence, abstract specific essence* and *full specific essence* (individuated, formed). — Although these distinctions are not found in God, the ideas with which we reason (and we have no others) always pertain to one or other of these three modes. Even the words with which we reason indicate the same three modes of ideas. Thus in reasoning about God, we can use only these words and ideas, which are totally inadequate and discordant with divine being.

[352] 'Although in reality God is the same as the Godhead, THE MODE OF MEANING is not the same for both. Because the name "God" means DIVINE ESSENCE IN ITS POSSESSOR, it can, according to this mode of its meaning, be naturally taken as person. — Hence things proper to persons can be predicated of this name "God"; we can say, for example, that God is generated or generates. — But the word, "ESSENCE" cannot, according to the mode of its meaning, be taken as person, because it means ESSENCE AS ABSTRACT FORM. — Consequently things proper to persons which distinguish them from each other cannot be attributed to essence. This would mean a distinction in the divine essence, just as there is a distinction in the *supposita*' (St. Thomas, *S.T.*, I, q. 39, art. 5).

Wisdom, goodness, power, etc. are generic ideas expressing the abstract perfections of entia: 'Godhead' is an abstract, specific idea. 'God', as a common name, is a full, individuated, specific essence; as a proper name, it is subsistent person. We use these ideas to reason about the supreme being and apply to him words which express the ideas. Strictly speaking, however, there is in God neither generic essence nor abstract or full, specific essence; God is a subsistent, extremely simple being without division of any kind. It is we who unfailingly suppose division by applying to him ideas drawn from contingent entia where we find the real distinctions made known by distinct, separate ideas. They are the only ideas and means of knowledge we have in this life and we are compelled to use them to know God, whom we do truly come to know in some way. We are helped by ontological reasoning, which tells us 1. that each separate perfection outside God is, in God, God himself;[353] 2. the Godhead we conceive as an abstract form is

---

[353] St. Thomas, following the traces of ecclesiastical tradition, wisely says: 'We must first consider that our understanding of anything is indicated by its name, just as our understanding of a stone is indicated by its name. Names are signs of intellectual conceptions so that our understanding of every single thing, indicated by a name, is the intellectual conception indicated by the name. — However our intellect, which cannot comprehend God nor IN OUR PRESENT STATE SEE HIM IN HIS ESSENCE, knows him from created things; the different perfections of the conduct of creatures, such as wisdom, will and so forth, imperfectly represent divine perfection. — In the same way our intellect, RECEIVING ITS KNOWLEDGE FROM CREATED THINGS, BECOMES LIKE THE ONE DIVINE ESSENCE BY MEANS OF DIFFERENT CONCEPTIONS, ALTHOUGH IMPERFECTLY. Thus goodness, wisdom, power and anything else we predicate of God DIFFER IN OUR UNDERSTANDING BECAUSE WE CONCEIVE THEM DIFFERENTLY. Nevertheless they are the same thing in reality because the divine essence, which our intellect represents BY DIFFERENT CONCEPTS just as different things represent divine essence in different forms, is one and the same thing. This is indeed the proper way of understanding what we were first considering. Because every perfection is most truly in God, and a true understanding of wisdom differs from that of goodness, our understanding of them in God must differ, although in him they are in a real, simple mode, and are consequently the same thing' (Opusc. 9, *De articulis CVIII sumptis ex opere Petri de Tarantasia*). We note here that the phrase, 'our understanding of them in God', means 'according to the different conceptions of our intellect', as St. Thomas, who posits no *real distinction* of any kind in God himself, later explains.

the subsistent God himself;[354] and finally 3. 'God', normally understood as a common noun and applied to many beings (although incorrectly), does not express a *species* but simply a real subsistent being. However our reasoning, which tells us that this must be the case relative to the supreme being, does not explain how this is so, that is, it reveals neither subsistent perfection nor subsistent abstract species nor subsistent full species. It tells us what God is not (there is no division in genus, species and subsistence), but does not tell us what 'that subsistence is which includes in its simplicity all that is in the species and genus'. It neither shows nor makes us perceive or think a subsistence of this kind, just as the definition of colour does not make a blind person think of colour. It reveals the terms but not their *connection*, in which the divine being consists.

1664. These are common principles accepted by theologians and by the most famous philosophers. Being immutable, these principles show that a system which teaches the following is as contrary to philosophical argument as it is to Catholic faith:

1. The order of our conceptions is perfectly equal to the order of things. This is not true of divine things nor of anything of which we have no perception.

2. God is the object of the natural intuition of the human mind. If this were so, the human mind could have conceptions adequate to supreme being.

These two principles are in themselves very serious errors, and very serious in their consequences, one of which is pantheism.

1665. I conclude:

1. A subjective law of our rational principle obliges us to reason about God, and things which do not fall under our perception, by *analogy* with the things we do perceive.

---

[354] Again St. Thomas wisely observes: 'We cannot speak about simple things except according to the mode of composites FROM WHICH WE OBTAIN OUR KNOWLEDGE. When we speak of God therefore, we use concrete nouns to indicate his subsistence, because only composites subsist for us. We use abstract nouns to indicate his simplicity. 'Godhead' or 'life', or similar words about God, must relate to THE DIFFERENCE IN THE WAY OUR INTELLECT RECEIVES THEM, not to any difference in reality' (St. Thomas, *S.T.*, I, q. 3, art. 3, ad 1).

[1664–1665]

2. This reasoning results in a negative, limited knowledge which is nevertheless true, not false.

3. To obtain this knowledge, which is the only kind we can have of these things, we must accept our ideas, our means of knowledge, as they are, without confusing or arbitrarily changing them. Similarly we must use current words for what they mean, in conformity with the important teaching of scholasticism that 'the truth of statements depends not only on what is meant but also on how it is meant.'[355]

4. Finally, ontological reasoning informs us of the limitation and imperfection of our knowledge and thus protects us from error. No error is committed by anyone with limited, imperfect knowledge if he knows that his knowledge is such and does not accept it as positive and perfect. Only reasoning of this kind is perfectly in conformity with absolute truth, so that the order of entia corresponds to what such reasoning posits in our mind. This reasoning, although it seems of little consequence, is, I repeat, sufficient to avoid error because we can use our other imperfect cognitions to advantage without falling into any error.

CHAPTER 34

Psychological laws corresponding to the cosmological laws directing practical reason — The psychological law of spontaneity

1666. We have reduced to two the cosmological laws imposed on the rational principle by the nature and order of the world: the law of *motion* and the law of *harmony*. In the same way, we can reduce to two the psychological laws corresponding to the cosmological. As we said, the activity of the rational principle is influenced partly by its excitatory term and partly by the activity itself of the excited principle which, having been put in motion, operates according to its law of spontaneity and, having received harmonious elements from the world, once

---

[355] St. Thomas, *S.T.*, I, q. 39, arts. 4 and 5.

more contributes something of its own vigour in rendering its own activity harmonic. The operating principle also enjoys this activity in so far as it manifests in the principle a law of harmony that completes and informs the harmony of the world. I call this harmony 'psychic' to distinguish it from the quasi-harmonic matter it receives from what is different from itself.

1667. We have to speak therefore about the law of spontaneity but without describing its nature, which we have already examined.[356] We shall deal instead with the special characteristics and accidents which it shows in its acts, but which are rather difficult to observe. The most important of these accidents are the two brought about in us as a result of the hidden action of spontaneity: our lack of consciousness about our spontaneity and exclusive interest in the term of our rational attention, a term of which we easily become conscious.

Article 1
Human life: direct and reflective

1668. I shall complete here what I said previously about consciousness. We saw that ideal being alone, intuited by our mind, does not provide us with any consciousness of itself. For that, some real stimulus or term is necessary.[357] This is the first, but not the only condition. The other was posited when we noticed that the formation of consciousness requires the human principle to draw rational attention to itself when it experiences some need. The need is 'the instinct requiring us to complete an action already begun.' Nor can we say that we ought to be moved immediately to form some self-awareness because we find self-awareness pleasing. The privation of a natural pleasure is not a need, nor does the pleasure become a need as long as we have not experienced it.

[356] *AMS*, 439–483.

[357] St. Thomas says more or less the same when he affirms that 'the intellect understands itself and other things' (*S. T.*, I, q. 77, art. 1). In other words, the intellective principle is not known *per se*, but needs to acquire cognition of itself (that is, consciousness), just as it needs to acquire awareness of other things.

1669. Note:

1. that consciousness does not pertain to the science of *intuition*, but to that of *predication*;

2. that rational activity has two levels. First, we rejoice in truth (although we have no consciousness); second, we rejoice in the *possession of truth* (when we are conscious of possessing it). What we say about enjoyment must also be said about knowledge. At the first level, we know truth; at the second, we know that we know truth (we are conscious of knowing it). And what we say about truth must also be said about all good and all evil. At the first level, we enjoy good and suffer evil; at the second level, we enjoy the enjoyment of our own good and suffer the suffering of our own evil. These two levels constitute two very different human states which are distinguished only with difficulty. The philosopher, a reflective, conscious person, easily captivated by reflection, does not acknowledge what is present in his prior feeling but has not passed into his consciousness.

1670. It follows that there are two principles of action within us. With one, we tend to unite ourselves to our term and enjoy it; with the other, we tend to know and enjoy our union with the term, that is, to be conscious of our own enjoyment.

The first of these two principles of action and levels of activity constitutes our *direct life*; the second our *life of reflection*.

1671. The person who lives a life of reflection remains at the second level of activity where he acts with and becomes identified with the second active principle because 'The human being in act is the principle which operates.' When we act with the first principle, we are actually the direct principle; when we act with the second principle, we are actually the reflective principle. We are always the principle which acts.[358] If, then, in the operation of a life of reflection we are the *reflective principle*, it is not to be wondered that we deny our prior state and believe that everything in us is furnished with consciousness. Certainly, the reflective principle cannot know that human state on which reflection has not yet taken place. It denies, therefore, what does not enter its sphere, what is not reflective.

1672. Only as a reflective principle do we deal with our

---

[358] Cf. *AMS*, 419–425.

fellows and speak comprehensively. Social life is, for the most part, a life of reflection. It is clear, therefore, that without such a manner of life in the world, people would never associate; human interrelationship would be impossible. This indicates the excellence of reflective over *direct life.*

1673. Nevertheless, we must not believe that the good proper to reflective life is better than the good of direct life. The latter is fundamental good, good itself; reflective life is only another way of enjoying the good furnished by direct life. Reflective life is, therefore, at a higher level, more enlightening, more attractive, but not more noble or more precious than direct, primitive life.

1674. On the other hand, we must not imagine that reflective life is constantly on the increase or reaches out to all that is good in the direct life (the same is true, *mutatis mutandis*, of evil). While living a reflective and social life, we carry out many actions pertaining solely to direct life, actions of which we are unconscious and about which we say nothing. These actions begin in us, pursue their course and are completed in profound silence. Nevertheless, they are of immense importance to human subsistence and happiness. The two active principles operate in each other's presence; we are sometimes one, sometimes another of these principles. But the first principle acts as it were quietly and in the background; the second is loquacious, and disports itself openly, manifestly.

1675. This teaching, and this alone, explains many human facts, one of which is the pleasure we take in sleep. There is no doubt that when we have been awake for a long time, or are tired as a result of activity, we feel the need for sleep, and experience great delight in abandoning ourselves to it. I have come across people for whom the pleasure of sound sleep is amongst the greatest joys of life. But what is sleep except an animal function in which we lose consciousness of ourselves, at least to a great extent, and no longer act with free reflection? Nevertheless, we find pleasure both in the passage from wakefulness to sleep (during which we lose consciousness), and in sleep itself (during which consciousness has been lost). We cannot say in any way that the delight of sleep consists in *foreseeing* the advantage that we will get from sleep. The pleasure we have in sleep consists rather in losing all foresight which is proper to

[1673–1675]

wakefulness. Nor can we say that our delight springs from feeling our animal forces strengthened after sleep. The delightful state that follows on sleep is a pleasure pertaining to wakefulness; it is not the pleasure of sleep, which has already ceased. When we desire to lose consciousness of self by passing from a state of wakefulness to sleep, the pleasure of our *direct life* prevails over the pleasure of our *reflective life*. We want this second life to cease for a moment so that we may enjoy the first more fully. In other words, there is a kind of balance between the two lives. The pleasure and need of one is balanced with the pleasure and need of the other. Sometimes one prevails, sometimes the other. The two lives alternate unceasingly; wakefulness and sleep alternate unceasingly.

1676. One immediate question comes to the fore. Who desires the passage from wakefulness to sleep, and the state itself of sleep: the one who actually consists in the *reflective principle*, or the other who actually consists in the *direct principle*? — A simple experiment will show us that the one desirous of sleep is the direct, not the reflective principle. Let us imagine that as we go to sleep we think about what is going to happen, about the cessation of our reflective principle, about the sensation of the very thought with which we observe our increasing drowsiness. We will feel a certain sense of revulsion. I have carried out this experiment several times, and it appeared to me that I feared the approach of sleep as a kind of death. The revulsion was felt by the reflective principle which foresaw the annihilation of its activity. The pleasure of sleep, therefore, does not pertain to the reflective but the direct principle. The former re-acts against sleep; the latter enjoys it. This proves that those who live a reflective life do not totally abandon the direct life. They enjoy one life in part, and the other in part, although in different ways, one unknown to the other.

Article 2
The limitation of the radical power of the soul
sometimes suppresses, sometimes limits reflection

1677. Direct and reflective life are actualities arising from the essence of the rational soul. They pertain to the order of second acts. They do not constitute the first act, the essence, the radical power of the soul, which is a limited ens with a resultant limited radical power.

The soul is limited not because it cannot increase indefinitely as a result of increase in its terms (in this respect its receptivity is unlimited), but because it is limited to the degree of intensity with which it can adhere to and bind itself to the terms given it. If its virtue is totally employed in one actuality, it diminishes relative to another. In our present case, the radical activity of the soul could be totally used up in the actuality of direct life and leave nothing for reflective life. Here consciousness would cease precisely because the act of reflection would cease.

1678. Indeed, reflection could remain impeded and suppressed not only by the overpowering actuality of direct life, but even by a single act of this life, as Dante said:

> Sometimes we see, here below,
> A face that shows
> The soul absorbed in love alone.[359]

Our philosopher-poet notices that when the activity of the soul is absorbed by some term proper to it, the possibility of reflection and consciousness ceases. This is true, he sees, not only when the soul acts, but even afterwards. So, although no longer absorbed, it has no memory of what has happened; actual memory is itself an act of reflection on what has occurred. If there is no reflection when the act took place, there can be no reflection later, except some obscure reflection on the vestiges of the act which remain habitually in the soul. So, Dante says:

> It's not my tongue that's tied.
> My mind's o'ercome, to heaven's bliss
> Unable to return without a guide.
> But how much I could say
> About that point whose sheer remembrance
> Makes other longings fade![360]

1679. But in the present life the radical, total virtue of the soul, limited as it is, does not pour itself out in some actuality for any

---

[359] *Par* 18: 22–24.
[360] *Par* 18: 10–15.

great length of time. It tires of the intensity of its act, despite the great pleasure it finds there, and assisted by corporeal stimuli *spontaneously* returns to reflective life. Here, too, there is a certain alternating between direct and reflective life.

1680. Moreover, this radical power does not pour itself out totally in a single act, but in two, three or even more acts, in a complex of acts. But the acts in which it does pour itself out, whether many or few, leave it incapable of further acts of reflection if its power has been truly poured out. Reflection is thus restricted to the sphere left free by the actuality of direct life.

1681. Again, I want to emphasise that it is the spontaneous action of the soul which, more than anything else, takes charge of the proportion between the dominion of direct life and that of reflective life in us. We have to admit, therefore, that we *enjoy* both lives, as I said before, and that we sometimes prefer the delight we have in the direct life to our delight in the life of reflection. We even want the reflective life to give way to direct life because spontaneity always follows the greatest delight.

We have shown this with our example of desire for sleep, a phenomenon pertaining to animal life and fundamental rational perception. It is clear, however, that we could say the same about examples drawn from purely rational activity. Take ecstasy, for instance. Everyone knows that there is nothing more delightful for human beings than this degree of intense contemplation and fulfilled love. Indeed, it is delight at its highest peak, although it necessarily brings with it the suppression of reflective acts and consciousness. Despite our lack of awareness, we can desire nothing more satisfying than this kind of sleep in which intellect and spirit are absorbed in the object of ecstatic contemplation. Here we are transported into quasi-oblivion, into a most delightful death formed of extremely full, vital life. Yes! The delight proper to a life of reflection is not the greatest, and even in this present life we can enjoy the object-good much, much more than our consciousness of such enjoyment. We can give priority to the enjoyment of a greater share in the object even at the cost of sacrificing consciousness of our enjoyment.

Article 3
Human life can never be entirely reflective; it remains
partly direct

1682. Finally, we must note that even the adult, who cannot entirely live a direct life (unlike the child who has not come to the age of reflection), is also unable to live an exclusively reflective life for either a long or short period.

1683. This becomes clear if we consider that the act of reflection is reflective relative to its object. In other words, the act is reflective if its object is something not only felt, but already thought. This act is not called 'reflective' relative to itself, therefore, as though it were such relative to itself. The reflective act is not its own object; it requires another, further act of reflection if it is to become an object. But granted that any series of reflections must be limited, the final reflection has no further reflection by which it is known. Thus, remaining as it were unknown and without consciousness, it pertains to direct life. The actuality of human life can never be totally poured out in reflection alone. Something remains in us on which we have not reflected, something therefore still unknown.

Article 4
When we reason, reflection is concerned with the last link in
rational activity, not on previous links: this explains
hidden reasoning

1684. We now have to note a fact of the greatest importance in explaining the various phenomena of reflective life: this faculty usually attends only to the last link in any rational activity. This link is the term of attention; it is the end which the reflective life seeks and longs to attain, the object of its accumulated psychological virtue. Consequently, preceding links, over which mental activity passes lightly without pausing, neither attract nor hold reflective attention. These links, which we make, lie hidden from us; free attention is needed if we are to become aware of them. This free attention, with which we desire to know the progress of all the steps relevant to the activity of our spirit, enables every step to become a final term of our attention. Generally speaking, however, people ignore this and press on like travellers totally occupied with their destination and unmindful of the way they take to it.

1685. This fact first explains the hidden reasoning often carried out by us mentally, but unconsciously. Thus, although people come to extremely lucid conclusions which presuppose lengthy reasoning, and do this with extreme rapidity, they cannot explain the fact to themselves or others. Indeed, they do not even know that they have done it; they are totally unaware of it. All their attention rests in their conclusion, which alone has some weight with them. They would think a joke, something stupid, a laughable waste of time, to retrace their steps over their intellectual operations. There is no doubt whatsoever that philosophical attention to familiar, social conversation of ordinary people shows how little they express what passes contemporaneously through their minds. All conversation is made up of thought-out conclusions; every word expresses a thought dependent on many preceding thoughts. Nevertheless, no attention is paid to these thoughts; they are not even remembered.

Take a taxi driver, for example. As soon as he sees you, he offers his services and addresses you as 'Bishop' or 'Monsignor', although he has never met you. Yet that title, which came so easily to him, was undoubtedly the result of the following lengthy reasoning, carried out in a flash but totally without awareness:

'By showing respect and making someone think I esteem him, I gain his favour;

'This makes it easier for him to accept my offer of service;

'If he employs me, I gain a day's work and pay, which is what I need;

'"Bishop" or "Monsignor" flatters him; I can use it to show my esteem for him and gain his favour;

'This kind of address is therefore a good way of obtaining the money I am looking for;

'I shall use it, therefore, to this person, whom I see for the first time. It's no skin off my nose.'

Article 5
Continuation — Synthetical reasoning

1686. Nevertheless, we need to note that the reasoning with which we swiftly reach conclusions which we need to know and communicate in our ordinary social life does not always proceed in such a way that all its propositions and mediate links remain distinct. Often the mind finds shortcuts and abbreviations of its own. Arithmeticians, for example, invent summary rules to enable them to complete a calculation. One step, or a few, brings them to a point which would otherwise require considerable work. I have noticed this often in peasants who count on their fingers with considerable ingenuity. Such a summary way of reasoning can be called *synthetical reasoning*; we use it every day in the ordinary affairs of life.

1687. I have already mentioned the *mediate rules* used to guide our ordinary judgments.[361] These *rules* shorten and facilitate our reasoning. Once formed and established, they are constantly applied without any further thought about their proof. We never turn back to examine the series of reasoning which produced them. *Faith* takes the place of reasoning.

1688. A few common examples will be helpful. Experts calculate at a glance how many sacks of mulberry leaves a tree will provide. Their mistakes, if any, are minimal. But how can they calculate so quickly and securely, at a glance, the quantity of leaves? They would never finish if they took some unit as their rule, even if they were clear in their minds about the volume corresponding to a unit of weight or a sack of leaves. A unit, therefore, does not serve as their rule. Other volumes have been assigned mentally as their standard. They note the volume corresponding to ten or twenty, fifty or a hundred weights or sacks and immediately apply to the tree whatever imaginary measure is necessary. One or other of such equations determines the quantity for them.

The same occurs whenever a person professes to measure a quantity visually. An architect will measure by eye the front of a house and perhaps come within a foot of its length; the wine

[361] *Teodicea*, 14.

expert will tell you how many gallons there are in a cask as soon as he sees it. The same is true of many other things.

1689. But it is certain that people who can measure quantities visually cannot explain even to themselves how they do it. Nor will they be able to explain their conclusions, or say what rules or measures they use. In fact, the different measures impressed on their imagination are not what they are seeking. These standards are simply means to an end, that is, to the final link where their attention comes to rest. This is what they want to know reflectively and consciously. The rest is unimportant.

1690. We should also note that these *mediate rules* summarising reasoning have to be drawn from experience, or from preceding reasoning, unless they come from some authority.

Article 6
Continuation — Prudence in wise people depends on synthetical reasoning

1691. The level of aptitude for forming a great number of these secure *mediate rules* which are then ready for various needs makes some people wiser than others.

1692. Here we must note how often certain people seem to reason better in theory without always finding in practice what is more expedient for their end. The advice they give, for example, is well thought-out, but fails when put to the test. Others, who have no idea how to support their opinions in the same reasoned way, hit the target so well that they seem to possess a sixth sense enabling them to do exactly what circumstances require.

A learned doctor does not always provide the best cure for his patients; an eloquent, subtle lawyer often loses a case for his client with his display of learning; a theologian, who has perhaps spent his life in teaching moral science, may well fail to cure spiritual illness in souls. Experts in economy have often lost everything through imprudent speculation; others, who did not seem particularly intelligent, have become extremely rich. But the exquisite sense of prudence of which we are speaking is particularly obvious where we least expect it, that is, in managers, business people and those concerned with social governance.

1693. Thought proper to theoreticians and splendid thinkers is characterised by *analytical reasoning*; thought in prudent, sagacious workers is characterised by *synthetical reasoning*.

1694. The effort to omit nothing, to desire to be conscious of every step in one's reasoning, to want to be persuaded that nothing is omitted from the analysis of the object in view: all this is proper to *analytical reasoning*. But many of the parts which have been scrutinised and analysed with such attention are totally useless for concluding business, for a choice of counsel, for discovering some necessary expedient. They are out of place, because we are looking for what has to be done *here and now*. We do not want to know what parts make up an object present to the mind. The person who reasons analytically often strays into matters which are alien to his aim; the great number of things he has in mind weigh him down and make a solution more difficult. His rag-bag of considerations even makes him lose sight of factual circumstances necessary for drawing some useful conclusion. He may well be capable of providing a splendid account of the whole series of his thought, but his conclusions, based on the causes we have mentioned, are either imperfect or insufficient; they are either deficient or superfluous.

1695. A prudent person, on the contrary, is much more direct. Using synthetical reasoning, he measures and compares whole with whole, not parts with parts. The secret of his efficient prudence lies in separating the *whole* about which he has to decide from all irrelevancies, and applying to it the exact, appropriate mediate rule.

Consequently, the prudent, operative wisdom of which we are speaking consists in two talents: 1. that of forming many *mediate rules* applicable to contingencies in life and governance; 2. in penetrating intellectually and unhesitatingly to the heart of the matter, to the precise group of contingent circumstances. Once this group of connected circumstances is known, it is easy enough to find — in the arsenal of an experienced, wise mind — the formula or rule with which to measure immediately appropriate action and proffer right judgment and prudent deliberation about it.

[1693–1695]

1696. This explains why *prudence* always appears greater in the old than in the young, other things being equal. Analytical reasoning appears less vigorous in older people who have either found it less useful or necessary, or have abbreviated it little by little into synthetical rules. Older people have also had more time to accumulate mediate rules and to train their attention to concentrate on the *whole* of a question by separating it from accessory and useless circumstances that sometimes muddy it. This *whole* can then be easily subjected to suitable rules.

1697. It is true, therefore, that hidden, shortened and unconscious reasoning is responsible for a great deal of what goes on in the minds of prudent, practical people. In fact, we commonly say that their deliberations depend on a *practical sense* rather than thought. Synthetical reasoning does indeed resemble sense as it moves readily, surely and obscurely to its final conclusions.

Article 7
The operations of the rational principle are sometimes aroused and directed by a hidden principle

1698. The law, 'reflection falls on the last link of our rational activity, not on preceding links', has another consequence which may be stated as follows: 'Principles which arouse and direct our rational operations remain hidden from us unless we freely make them terms of our attention.' It is clear that these principles are not, of their nature, the last link in the chain of rational operations, but the first.

1699. To know ourselves therefore, we need to return freely upon ourselves and investigate the secrets of our own heart. This is often an extremely difficult task and almost impossible to carry out completely. Hence, the great value of the ancient saying: 'Know yourself.'

1700. The first principles of human activity are animal instinct, in so far as it resides in fundamental perception, and being in general, intuited by us. Animal instinct is a *principle of movement*; the idea of being is a *directive rule*. In our ordinary state, we act in accord with these first principles, but without paying them any attention, and without knowing that we are moved and directed by them. This kind of knowledge is not of great importance to us; what is important is to reach our aim.

But *animal instinct* develops by clothing itself in habits proper to different passions, and thus as it were multiplying itself.

The rational principle, in so far as it perceives animal instinct, accompanies it throughout its development. However, with another act the very same principle refers everything to being and sees that being itself, the supreme norm of good and evil, disapproves, forbids, approves or commands in these operations. We find ourselves, therefore, at a fork. The rational principle either holds to what *being* prescribes, or abandons itself blindly to instinct, or forms a conspiracy with instinct. Vice is the effect of the last two steps.

1701. But the rational principle does not stop there; it also classifies good and evil into different genera. 'Mediate rules' are formed, each of which shows and makes immediately known to the rational principle an entire class of good and bad things. The principle chooses between the genera of what is good, and the genera of what is evil. This choice means that the principle embraces 'some of these mediate rules' as directives for its activity. Other rules are rejected.

1702. This choice between *mediate rules* which discerns between good and evil, is in practice the foundation of the *desires* and *general aversions* to which we give our assent. Just as we have certain general rules in our mind, so we have certain general desires and aversions in our heart. These desires habitually and freely arouse our appetite for an entire class of good things, or at least for things thought to be good; our aversions habitually and freely cause us to reject an entire class of evil things, or at least of things thought to be evil. Thus, our spirit finds itself habitually determined towards and against certain things in general, although these determinations can be changed at every moment by free intervention on our part. As long as such freely consented habits remain in us, they constitute a number of secret principles of action which, given appropriate circumstances, readily determine us to a given action, as though it had already been deliberated.[362]

[362] *CS*, 76–105; *AMS*, 745–763.

1703. I maintain that these *principles* of human activity, these freely consented general desires, remain secretly within us until we make them the object of our research. At this point, they become final rather than first or mediate links of our rational activity. We give them our attention and become conscious of them. (There are, of course, principles and desires which are not freely consented to. These should properly speaking be called innate or acquired inclinations. In addition, there are other desires and principles to which we consent imperfectly, with different levels or modes of consent, and with different tacit conditions.)

1704. We must also note that moral characteristics vary according to the quality of these principles and habitual rules, which are secretly taken as directives of our activity. These very different characteristics have profound origins and present a hard task to philosophical investigation.

Article 8
The hidden part of our rational activity provides occasion for error and immorality

1705. We have, therefore, two kinds of *cognitions*: those hidden from us, others *clear, luminous, reflective*. The first kind does not normally interest us. We find no need to be conscious of them; we use them as a means without paying attention to them.

This is another extremely important fact which, in addition, shows how essentially reasoning beings such as ourselves can err; it also shows how vice has its place in essentially moral beings such as ourselves.[363] This fact clearly demonstrates that it depends upon ourselves to take an interest in and to pay attention to certain cognitions which need to be made clear and luminous to us. It also shows that we leave other cognitions in the shade, in an inferior condition to those which we choose as our end and in which consequently our activity rests.

1706. Sometimes, for example, the person making mistakes is the principle living a reflective life. But self-deception or perverse actions should not surprise us if the information which

---

[363] Cf. *Teodicea*, 396–410.

could save a person from error, the rules which could protect him from vice, are left as it were buried in the silent night of direct life and not brought to the light of reflective life. We must not wonder at the errors and waywardness of a reflective principle which has, as its sole guide, cognition leading to error and favouring vice.

Article 9
How in the human mind a secret, spontaneous operation is carried out which orders our cognitions without any realisation or free co-operation on our part

1707. Here, I must mention a fact which I have experienced myself on many occasions. Others, too, will have experienced it if they are accustomed to consider what takes place in their spirit.

I refer to that slow work which the mind carries out of its own accord and through which information and teaching, deposited in the treasure of our memory without our realising it, is gradually sorted out and correctly ordered. It happens many times that people who devote themselves to study, and especially to philosophical speculation, think about some subject for a long time and then find themselves exhausted and unsatisfied with the result of their effort. A day or two passes without their giving any further deliberate attention to the subject. Nevertheless, the mind has adjusted itself of its own accord, and ideas appear with such order that difficulties vanish and the solution of the problem takes place spontaneously and clearly.

This, it is true, must have happened in part even during initial meditation. The imagination works, grows tired and muddies the purity of reasoning by intruding importunate, unstable phantasy. When peace has been found, the work of strict reason remains untarnished.

1708. This must also explain how the memory, having studied something at night without grasping it before falling asleep, is fresh in the morning. Once the imagination has been calmed and comforted by sleep, the memory offers a faithful impression of what it has received the evening before when tiredness or some disturbance rendered it incapable of working.

1709. It is, of course, a good rule to allow our deliberations to rest and mature for a time in the mind. Prudent people do this. These thoughts then improve of their own accord without our expressly thinking of them. The rapidly formed opinion improves with time, even though we give it no attention; with all probability it will succeed not only because it is re-examined, but because it matures of its own accord through hidden activity by direct, intellective life, unmarked by consciousness.

1710. For this work to continue, we need the secret spring which, through dedication and habitual desire, moves a person to find the truth. This characteristic should be present in the scholar who seeks a solution to some question, and in the prudent person who is habitually concerned about the business with which he is engaged.

Article 10
Continuation — Other unconscious mental activity

1711. There is another mental task operating in our minds without reflection or consciousness. This work is confused in part with the first.

There are certain concepts, certain thoughts, which as it were attract one another, show some affinity to one another, and are associated in various ways.[364] This affinity and association is carried out or completed in our understanding without our realisation. The following are the ways in which this happens.

1712. First, human thought finds a bond which naturally reduces these concepts to unity in the *idea of being*, the supreme principle of all cognition. This super-eminent being is the hidden regulator of the human mind, which is always turned to the idea of being. Without realising it (or realising it only perfunctorily), the mind through this habitual operation sees many convergences between the things it knows. This work is therefore a continual return, made by thought, from multiplicity to the unity of being.

1713. Again, we have to consider that different thoughts in the human mind produce a sensible effect in us, who are

[364] Cf. *Preface* to the *Opusculi filosofici*, Milan, 1836.

[1709–1713]

essentially feeling. Thoughts which are *per se* different some-times move us to a single sensible effect, a special feeling of the same nature. But because feelings easily become instinctive principles of operation, these identical or similar feelings dispose us equally towards the manner of thoughts which gave rise to them.

1714. This fact is supported by the presence in us of *general desires and affections* which are already formed, as I have said. They are like musical strings which respond in the same way whether we touch them with a feather or a piece of metal or anything else. Such affections aroused by different concepts or thoughts become a guide to the attention of the mind and the thinking activity which takes a spontaneous direction and often works unknown to ourselves, who do not reflect upon this fact as it runs its course in us.

Article 11
Granted a suitable occasion, things hidden in the spirit sometimes manifest themselves with great impetus and clarity

1715. *General affections* in the human spirit use and direct thoughts to their own advantage by associating them in groups and recalling even their distant memory. For instance, we see ourselves reaching today some thought or determination with strict affinity to a year-old thought or deliberation, although we cannot remember it. This previous, now forgotten thought causes our present thought because it left the spirit disposed and ready to tend towards it. Given the slightest occasion, the spirit then produces this thought.

1716. Even more notable, however, is the way in which *habit-ual, general affections*, which rely upon the *mediate rules* we have discussed, sometimes develop of their own accord. They are like a seed moving underground. Reaching a high level of intensity, they gradually reinforce the persuasion which serves as their foundation. Nevertheless, they remain hidden in the spirit unless some stimulus draws our reflective attention to attend to them. In this case, they sometimes explode in full, tumultuous light. This is perhaps the hidden cause which explains the sudden manifestation of heroes who find themselves in circumstances consonant with their internal hidden disposition.[365] It is also the cause of upheavals brought about by political revolutions.

1717. This also explains many other facts found in humanity. A poet or a writer gains great notoriety in an age or in a nation when he becomes the faithful and talented interpreter of those feelings and great persuasions which each individual unknowingly carries in himself, without being able to express them, because he has never thought about them. Great jubilation and applause greets the person who knows how to draw universal attention and reflection to those secret, but powerful persuasions, and is able to provide suitable formulas for furnishing such persuasions with reflective, splendid existence. These formulas can make persuasions noble and beautiful, like hidden treasure. People possess these persuasions without realising how fine they are, and are grateful to the genius who first expresses what all would have wanted to say if only they had known how. They willingly consent and adhere to such a person.

1718. This also explains the sudden, furious reaction of any apparently calm, tranquil people, at times of sedition. They seemed tranquil because they were unaware of the affections causing pressure within; they were tranquil because their reflective life hid the ferment of passion deep within direct life. The turbulence of passion had not yet spilled forth into reflective life.

A person acting as reflective principle is at peace because the person as direct principle, which is burning within, does not manifest himself outwardly, although interiorly he prepares the outburst. It is true that in the case of sedition another principle helps to change people's nature. Each individual feels the force of all; each feels that he possesses the power of the mass-force of which he is a part; each senses the fervour which increases persuasion as a result of the new unanimity of an assembled multitude. All of this produces enthusiasm and pride, together with a stimulus to dominion, and the abuse of force. But this

[365] Cf. what I have said about the dominion possessed by thought over people whose zealous activity gains them acceptance as heroes. *AMS*, 697–703.

cause alone would be insufficient unless there were already in the spirit uniform, internal, hidden and long-prepared dispositions, together with opinions and general affections harmonising and conspiring in everyone to produce that immediate, powerful outburst which, capturing and disturbing reason, easily turns to exultation and cruel anger. Without this condition, sedition does not take place. The people disperse either before assembling or after if curiosity alone has brought them together.

1719. The same can be said about national revolutions. The sole reason for their success is the hidden disposition present in the minds and spirits of the masses. If this disposition is present, raising a flag is sufficient to reveal what all are thinking. No revolution attains its end unless such a hidden disposition has been accumulated in the spirit. In the same way, all failed revolutions, despite the heroic valour and magnanimous sacrifice of certain individuals, come to nothing simply because the excited reflection does not find arms sufficient to produce success in the direct life of the people, which is the arsenal of force.

Article 12
Why we pass beyond an image to the ens it represents

1720. The psychological law, 'Attention is centred only on the last link of rational activity; reflection is present only where attention halts (although not always even here); and consciousness is acquired only of things on which we reflect', is an extremely precious tool for explaining other innumerable, mysterious phenomena present in the human spirit. One important example is found partly in the celebrated controversy about the worship of images.

There is no doubt, as every proficient observer can see, that when a person makes use of an image, his thought never halts at the image but moves on to the ens represented by the image.

The image serves only as an aid to phantasy; it directs thought immediately to the absent object, where it halts. This depends on the cosmological law of motion which says: 'What is real, that is, the term of the rational principle, arouses the attention and draws it to subjective acts of knowledge.'

1721. No one is going to say, for example, that a girl who is delighted with a portrait of her fiancé and kisses it repeatedly has the portrait itself as the object of her love. What she really wants is to bestow those acts of affection on the person represented by the portrait. Nobody in his right mind would say that she is in love with the piece of paper or inanimate canvas, or the slab of cold marble or bronze, which reminds her of her beloved. If this were the case, and the portrait were the true object of her affections, the presence of the portrait would be sufficient. The absence of the beloved would not distress her; she would not anxiously count the minutes to his return. Her good would lie in the portrait; she would want nothing more.

Again, if the portrait were the object of her love, many portraits of the same person would entail many objects of love. If you were to question her about that, she would insist that she had only one love, and would be unfaithful if she shared him with others. Nevertheless, you have to agree that sometimes she pours her heart out to one portrait and sometimes to another. How can she insist that she has only one love, and that one is sufficient? Because it is absolutely clear that she does not halt at the multiple images but rests in the true object portrayed by them all.

Again, different portraits are not equally representative of her husband-to-be. One shows only his face; another, the entire person. Nevertheless, each of them arouses in her heart acts of the same love. Indeed, these acts arise not only in the presence of a portrait but even when a letter arrives. She kisses it in the same way, and holds it tight; she does the same with any little present, any little sign of her lover, or with anything which represents for her the sole object of her love. She does not care if the portrait is not entirely accurate; it is sufficient for it to remind her of the object in whom she hopes to find her future happiness. It would be madness, therefore, to believe that the thoughts of a girl in love end and halt in such a portrait or sign. The term of her thoughts is found only beyond the portrait. This is the final link of her rational activity; this is where her attention and reflection rest. The portrait is only a mediate link through which her thought passes rapidly without stopping.

[1721]

1722. Nevertheless, we have to note here that in its different perceptions the rational principle does nothing more than develop, specify and actuate *fundamental perception*. This fundamental perception, and consequently all acquired perceptions, have in themselves something corporeal-sensible and something intellective. The rational principle, uniting animality and intellect, makes these elements a single term, that is, the term of perception. Hence, when the object is not perceived *per se*, but by way of image and vicarious sign, the rational principle by the very law of perception composes the term of perception from 1. the sensible, vicarious sign in place of the sensible-action of the ens, and 2. the intellective element. It thus individuates in some way the sensible sign with the ens itself which is in the intellective concept. Consequently, the intellective object, although the true, real object, is so intimately associated with the *sign* that it appears to form a single thing with it. The intellect, therefore, sees and contemplates an object in the sign in a way totally like that in which it sees an ens in sensations. The sensations, as we know, are not the ens thought by the understanding. Nevertheless, the sensations, in the act of perception, clothe and determine an ens. The same happens when a person or other ens is perceived through an image.

1723. If we are clear about this, we will not be surprised that nations prior to Christ or unenlightened by Christ fell into idolatry by joining and confusing the sign with the thing signified. Their intellectual force was weak, their imagination and sensuality extremely strong, and their intellective development never very far removed from perception. Their idolatry, however, did not consist in adoring rocks, stones and animals as such, but in joining to these as individuals certain superior, divine powers which were the true intellective object of their worship. Later, they changed the nature of natural and artificial beings into divinities, thus deifying the creature. They would never have adored statues or other material entia unless they had mentally united something divine to them. Ancient idolatry, therefore, consisted not simply in adoring the sign or image (this is impossible for human beings, as we have said, because they cannot fix their attention on an intermediate link of their rational activity such as an image or sign), but in changing the sign and image into an object with their imagination. They associated and individuated the divine object with material forms through an error in thought. Thus, they adored these material forms, persuaded that they were the divine object or its visible part. This error of ancient peoples was facilitated and brought about when they beheld the matter of the universe full of extremely strong powers which, although not inert matter itself, were presumed to be hidden within it. This kind of reasoning, which I used to discover the necessity of the corporeal principle, is correct — although the ancients were mistaken in deifying it. Hence the adoration of a jinn, of angels and of that worship which is described by holy Scripture; 'All the gods of the gentiles are demons.' Lamennais mistakenly claimed to have shown that the gentiles were not true idolaters because they referred their worship to divine force and power without restricting it to their idols.

1724. We also have to distinguish between the image intended to draw our attention to an absent but sensible object already perceived by us. An example is the case of the engaged girl who sees her future husband in the portrait she has before her. Another example is the image or sign intended to draw our attention to some invisible, spiritual object, such as the divinity. In the first case, there is no cause for confusing the sign with what is signified because the sensible, signed thing is itself known immediately and can be imagined as it is in itself; it is easy to see that it differs from the sign. The same could be said if we had perceived not the identical thing, but other individuals of its species. Thus we do not confuse a man's portrait with the man himself although we may never have seen him.

In dealing with invisible things, however, when our thought is drawn towards them by a sensible sign we would like to pinpoint them in themselves. To do this, we would need to find something sensible in them. This need depends upon the law of motion already described, that is, 'our attention is aroused and held by what is real, namely, the term of our rational principle.' But because our attention cannot be fixed on what is invisible (except with extreme difficulty and in virtue of free thought) without attributing some sensible vesture to it, the uneducated attribute to it the form which they see in the sign. Thus, the likeness of the idol easily becomes the form attributed to the god who is adored. Those nations which furnished the likenesses of gods with human form fell into *anthropomorphism* as well as idolatry.

1725. We need to remember however that amongst ancient peoples the understanding operated spontaneously. Free thought was either not developed or developed at a very low level. If we keep this in mind, we will understand clearly why God forbade the Hebrews to depict the divinity with pictures and statues. It would have been very easy, if not inevitable, for minds still in a childlike state to fall into the two errors whose natural origin we have indicated, that is, idolatry and anthropomorphism. On the other hand, the following fact shows clearly that free thought can avoid such errors or at least recognise them as errors (one is equivalent to the other). In that ever memorable 6th century before Christ, when Italian genius began its philosophical journey, one of the first truths to become clear was the falsity of human forms and customs attributed by the masses to the gods. Pythagoras and Xenophanes thought in this way.[366] We have, for instance, the following verses of Xenophanes:

> If oxen and lions had hands
> And knew how to paint or sculpt,
> They would, like man, depict
> The figures of gods in their own likeness.
> Horses would choose horses, and cows choose cows.

Again:

> God is one,
> Greater than all gods and mortals
> To whom he bears no resemblance in body or in mind.[367]

---

[366] Diogenes Laertius, *Proem.*, Segm. 15, lists Xenophanes in the school of Pythagoras.

[367] Clem. Alex., *Strom.*, 7, p. 711 — Euseb., *Praep. Evang.* 14, p. 757 — Theodoret, *Graec. Affect.*, Serm. 3, p. 49 — Cicero repeats this thought of Xenophanes as follows: 'Do you think there is any beast on land or sea that does not take the greatest delight in beasts of its own kind? — So why are you surprised if in the same way nature prescribes that man should think nothing more beautiful than man, if we think that this explains why we make gods similar to man? (*This refers to Greeks and Romans, not to other nations whose gods bore the likeness of beasts or inanimate things*) Do you think that if beasts had REASON, they would not have attributed it in a special way to

Psychological laws corresponding to the cosmological laws directing practical reason — the psychological law of harmony

1726. Divine wisdom has placed order in the world. This order, however, is not in and for the world in isolation from the spirit. It is order in the spirit and for the spirit in which the exterior world receives the substantial completion through which it passes from non-ens to ens. Order in the world isolated from the spirit is not order, but the beginning of order which is then found in the world existing in the spirit. The cosmological law of harmony, therefore, must be followed by the psychological law which completes it. These are two parts of the same law, two relationships in which the same law is considered.[368]

This connection pertaining to the *synthesism* of nature made it imperative for me, when speaking about the cosmological law of harmony, to deal in part with the question 'What does the soul contribute of its own in positing harmony?' There, however, I restricted myself to the sensitive soul which, in relationship to the rational principle, pertains to the world, that is, to the term of the rational principle, because the animal feeling and its felt element are truly the natural term of human intelligence.

Here we have to continue our investigation of what is posited in the constitution of harmony by the soul in so far as it is

---

any of their kind?' (*De Nat. Deor.*, I, 27). Simon Karsten notes very acutely that Xenophanes says, 'If beasts had hands,' while Cicero says: 'If they had reason.' This indicates a different age of philosophy. At Xenophanes' time, philosophers had still not considered carefully the force of reason through which man is superior to brutes. *Philosophorum Graecor. veterum reliquiae*, vol. 1, P. 1, p. 43 (Amsterdam, 1830).

[368] This was already known by the wisest minds. Italy, my country, why not become a disciple of great intellects instead of wasting time in frivolous, superficial reading? Yet you dream of becoming once more mistress of the nations! — To understand how great thinkers realised that all harmony would perish if the sensitive and intellective spirit were taken from the world, it is sufficient to open the *Harmonice Mundi* of John Kepler (Lincii Austriae, 1619) and read bk. 4.

rational. This will enable me to complete in some way the question I have proposed. However, we cannot deal with rational harmony without examining certain things about the animal harmony mixed with it. This discussion is always new, and contains inexhaustible richness.

Article 1
Law of regularity

1727. It is a fact that everything tends to operate with regularity and that the rational principle delights in regularity. We now have to investigate the origin of this law and tendency.

Regularity can be considered in the operation carried out (subjective regularity) and in the object contemplated (objective regularity).

1728. What is the origin of this subjective regularity, of this tendency and of the pleasure we feel in operating with regularity? Pleasure and tendency are common to both the sensitive and the rational principle. Indeed, it is an extremely general law, proper to all agents which pass from potency to act and hence have transient acts in themselves. What kind of origin, what kind of causes explain this law?

1729. Three causes combine in every agent to produce delight in the regularity of its operations;

1. The natural order proper to the constitution of every agent.

2. The law which determines the mode of spontaneous operation.

3. The unity of the agent.

We must consider each of these separately.

§1. *Regularity of operation proceeding from the natural order constituting the agent*

1730. Every simple ens has an intrinsic order without which it would not be an ens. Moreover, every agent in nature composed of several elements is united and organated in a wonderful order by the wisdom of the Creator. Now, because order resides in the nature of the agent, it must also be present in its potencies and acts. It follows that the operation of every agent must be ordered by nature.

1731. The concept of *natural regularity of operation* in entia must be drawn from this truth. In other words, when asking: 'What does the regularity of their operation consist in?', we cannot impose an arbitrary regularity on the agents but rely on the order in which these agents are constituted by nature. For example, apparent regularity is found in gardens laid out in the French manner where plants are pruned and cruelly cut back in the shape of pyramids, columns, vases, statues. This is not regularity, but barbarous destruction of their natural, true regularity. What we say about plants can equally be said about the education of human beings who have their own *natural regularity* which must be protected and developed as a result of wise education and good governance. Capriciousness in education is equivalent to denaturing human beings.

1732. *Natural regularity* is not therefore comprised in a single formula applicable to all entia; regularity varies according to the nature of each.

§2. Regularity of operation resulting from the mode of spontaneity

1733. Spontaneity in the operation proper to entia depends upon the following law: having received an impulse, spontaneity seconds and continues the movement along the path marked out by the impulse.[369] Such constancy of direction is by nature a font of *regularity* because it causes movements to go ahead without digressing to left or right. If, however, during spontaneous movement in one direction, another impulse is applied which forces spontaneity to interrupt its course and proceed in another direction, the agent is upset because prevented from completing the operation to which it had already spontaneously directed itself. On the other hand, pleasure is found if spontaneous operations are not disturbed or broken off halfway. Pleasure is to be found, therefore, in that regularity

[369] *AMS*, 443–451.

of movement which consists in continued motion until an ens reaches its natural rest.

1734. I have already indicated the *law of inertia* as the reason why spontaneity does not change course of itself. This law affects spontaneity because inertia consists in the tendency towards rest, which is the contrary of labour, and towards repose, which is the contrary of movement. No agent, as we saw, is moved unless it aims at reaching a *state* in which it can rest. Similarly, no agent moves from rest unless it is disturbed by a foreign influence putting it into motion. Once forced to move, it continues in order to find eventually a better state of quiet, or at least a condition of uniform or immanent activity. Spontaneity, therefore, does not start, but continues movement. This law governs not only animality, but all agents, even rational agents, although allowance must be made for free will.

1735. The law of *habit* also depends on the law of spontaneity. Habit consists in the developed sense of ease which is felt by a sensitive or rational agent when repeating operations rather than carrying out altogether new operations. Actions which have already been done do not totally cease in the agent, but leave certain traces which serve as a path marked out for repetition of the operation. This explains our instinct for taking the way already clearly marked out for us; it is easier to do this than to open or find a completely different way. The entire operation, which had apparently ceased, remains slightly actuated in the operating principle. An outline remains as a virtual operation which is actuated at every new, slight impulse. Acting through habit, therefore, means continuing a preceding operation which has only partly ceased.

Consequently, we find 1. *purely spontaneous regularity* and 2. *habitual regularity*.

§3. *Regularity of activity proceeding from the unity of the agent*

1736. But explanation of habit remains incomplete as long as we do not have recourse to the unity of the operating subject. The very closest attention must be given to this unity which, as we have already seen, explains in a wonderful way the facts of the spirit that Aristotle attributed to what he called 'common sense'. Animality is composed of an extended, multiple term and a simple principle in which what is extended and multiple resides, and from which it receives unity. The principle, as we saw, is present equally in all the assignable parts of the continuum which forms its term. It can operate according to the laws of its own spontaneity in all or many of these parts simultaneously, and produce in them several contemporaneous movements. These movements must, therefore, receive a twofold order: one from the organisation possessed by the parts of the extended term, the other from the unity of the principle which moves these parts and from the laws of spontaneity of the principle which, precisely because it is single, maintains the same law in all the parts of the continuum embraced by its action. If the parts of the animal body are disposed with regularity, and the principle moving them is single, regular movements must necessarily take place.

§4. *Continuation — Regularity proceeding from laws of the imagination*

1737. This, however, is not sufficient. The law of imagination, wonderfully ordered by the Creator, also contributes to this regularity. This law states: 'The world is indicated in miniature in the brain in the way that it is indicated in the optic sensory by light-bearing impressions. The world indicated in the brain (the sensory of the imagination) has such a correspondence with the human body that the vestiges of the world found in the tiny aureoles of the brain (which considered subjectively are images) become the principles and roots of opportune movements. This happens because the sensitive principle needs only to act in the extreme, tiniest parts of the brain to produce the movements it desires. These movements, then, are propagated to the bodily members.'

This does not happen in exactly the same way as a pianist plays simply by touching the keys of his instrument, or as the captain of the ship, seated on the bridge, can with a tiny lever move and govern at will a ship's huge rudder. These likenesses are approximate, but do not match completely. Movement produced by the pianist immediately on the keys, and that produced by the captain on the rudder, is propagated to the strings of the instrument and to the rudder by means of an entirely mechanical movement. The sensitive principle, however, accepts from the image only the stimulus and direction needed to carry out immediately the act which moves the members of the whole sensible body to the need felt in its appetite.

For example, a starving animal experiences some disquiet which serves as the start of a principle of movement towards the satisfaction of its appetite. But if the animal imagines itself going to the place where it has satisfied its hunger and found food, the complex image of its state in that place, of the satisfaction it received there, and of the path which led it there, is an association of several images fused into one, into a single feeling. This is sufficient to arouse a quantity of motor forces in the animal and to determine accurately the direction of movement which brings it swiftly to the actual place corresponding to the imaginary one. This depends on the correspondence of the images with the real entia that caused the sensations, and this again on the sensible confrontation between *sensation* and *image*, which are proportionate to one another. Proportion in turn is present because space, that is, unlimited extension, is present to the animal feeling and exists in it, as I have said. At the same time, the limits which shape this space are equally marked by external sensation and by image, two modes of one feeling. The movements which cause the animal to stride to the place where it has already fed are active feelings which it carries out to perfect, through *sensation*, the satisfaction which is already present in the *image*. Thus the animal passes from an imaginary state (unsatisfying) to a state of sensation (satisfying). The movements propelling the legs are a series of active feelings which bind these two states, that is, of feelings which, starting from the imaginary state of satisfaction, reach a state of felt and fully enjoyed satisfaction. This series of active feelings and consequent movements is outlined in the sensory, and reproduced as a result of that outline. If, on the contrary, these active feelings and consequent movements had not been experienced, they could arise as a kind of attempt to escape a troublesome state of disquiet. But in this case the animal disengages itself

[1737]

from disquiet only with difficulty. The desired satisfaction is not easy to find.[370]

1738. Here we have to remember that what was said about the brain, which is solely 'the sensory of the imagination', not of thought, must also be said of every other sensory which contains some force of retention. Animal feelings do not consist solely in images, but are multiple and extremely varied.[371] However, in order to simplify the argument, I shall speak only of movements which begin and are directed as a result of images.

1739. From what has been said about the way in which animals move to reach the place where they have satisfied their hunger, we can conclude:

1. that *imagination* or retention *of the satisfying state* now lacking to the animal is the principle determining its movement;

2. that its movement is aimed at seeking the *imagined satisfying state*, that is, in passing from the state of *imagined satisfaction to the state of felt* and enjoyed *satisfaction*;

3. that these two states are divided by a more or less long series of other states through which the animal must pass in order to obtain its desired state of *felt satisfaction*;

4. that the animal, when moved to this passage, attempts to pass through a *series of states*, beginning with its state of *imagined satisfaction*, through which it is led finally to a state of *felt satisfaction*;

5. that the intermediate states are the successive states in which the animal is found during its movements towards satisfaction — for example the movements with which it sets out to reach its feeding place;

6. that if the series of intermediate states was not experienced by the animal nor, consequently, marked in its encephalous sensory, the animal is forced to use various attempts to reach it, as the wolf does when, after moving in different directions, it finally turns in the direction where it has scented the sheep;

7. that when a series of states has been disposed successively, the succession itself, although apparently unsuitable for being marked in the brain as succession, remains there in virtue of the unity and identity of the sensitive principle. It is this unity

[370] *AMS*, 439–440.
[371] *AMS*, bk. 2.

and identity which enables the principle to be present to the multiplicity of successive series as it is present to the multiplicity of assignable parts in an extended element. The law of habit also plays its part here; the principle has the power to retrace the steps in the succession. It does this with one, single, principal act as it extends its simple activity immediately to the entire succession. And I think that further help is provided for the principle by the docility of its organism in which several movements are so linked together that some must follow almost necessarily upon others. This has to be the case with entia which dream of running or flying.

We have therefore to uphold three distinct parts in the chain of operations according to which animal instinct progresses: 1. the state from which the animal starts, that is, a state of *imagined*, presented, awaited *satisfaction*; 2. the state which the animal reaches by its own movements and efforts, which is a state of *felt*, complete, total *satisfaction*; 3. the intermediate states through which the animal passes in order to move from the first to the second state.

1740. The intermediate states through which the animal passes to fulfil the satisfaction in its phantasy or, in general, in the internal sensory, vary in number. This variation depends upon the distance between the state at which the animal starts and the state which it aims to reach. Let us imagine that none of these intermediate states exists. Here, the case of fulfilled or increased satisfaction would follow very soon after the state of imaginary satisfaction. This is precisely what occurs in the animal when it tends to increase some sensible satisfaction or pleasure simply by actuating its sensories more intently for the sake of feeling more vivid pleasure and delight in that which it has already begun to feel slightly.

Here, too, relative to this fact of immediate passage from an initial state of satisfaction to one of complete satisfaction, we have to generalise what was said about *imagination* and apply it to every species of internal *feeling*. *Imagination* is only a way of feeling; it is feeling in the brain where the optic sensations which take the form of the image are principally reproduced. There are, however, many other sensories and each animal feeling, whatever sensory it pertains to, is a source of instinct. Whenever an animal begins to feel a pleasurable sensation, it

[1740]

endeavours to complete it, using all its powers to bring the sensation to the greatest degree of intensity beyond which its effort is limited by its fatigue.

1741. Here again we are face to face with *formative energy* through which living elements are composed into seeds and animals. Seeds develop into animals, and animals grow, develop, mature, corrupt and die. But in every aggregate put together by formative energy, there is a single principle of action and a union made up of feelings disposed in an extended term. From this we easily understand that formative energy can be considered under two aspects: 1. from the point of view of the single principle underlying its efficacy; 2. from the point of view of the felt term, with its harmoniously connected sensations, which stands as the *norm* directing the principle in its operation. This term, considered as sensuous instinct, can conveniently be represented almost as a living *stamp*, operating on its own. It should, I think, be called *plastic force*.

1742. Whether this sensory called imagination contributes in more perfect animals with a brain to some conformation, to certain accidents, to certain dispositions of the foetus, is a question beyond my knowledge. But I think it possible to say: 1. that not only the mother's imagination but her entire maternal feeling, together with the feeling connected with the elements making up the foetus, and the composed foetus itself, contribute to the foetus' formation and disposition; 2. that because imagination is a part of maternal feeling, it is likely that it has some more or less mediate influence on the foetus. In fact, imagination certainly influences the whole animal being of the mother, which remains modified by the passions to which imagination gives rise and strength.[372]

1743. But to complete this discussion, we still have to investigate the principle which moves imagination. — We have to

---

[372] Consequently, it is not possible to accept, according to me, the thesis upheld by ancient doctors, that 'the phantasy directs formative energy by way of example through species' (Cf. Fyens, *Quaest.* 15). One proof that formative energy does not act merely through the species of the phantasy, over which such species have only the slightest influence, is the fact that the operation of formative energy is highly separate from consciousness. If this energy operated through species, it would not be difficult to reflect upon it and come to some awareness of it.

consider that every image is composed of several parts, with straight and curved outlines, with colours of varying tint and even with different movements that make the image rather like a horse in motion. Parts, tints and movements are not there by chance; they fit one another. But what wonderful painter has been able to arouse so many tiny movements in the encephalic sensory, movements so mutually proportioned that the image is perfect? One movement more, or one less, would have ruined everything.

Careful consideration shows that this wonderful work is proper to nature itself. The sensory is *per se* suitable for rendering not only those internal images, but their parts and even certain unrepresentative colours. But what is the single principle determining the sensory to the complex of sensations which renders the image so complete and beautiful? Note that this is done not successively as though tint were added to tint and brush-stroke to brush-stroke by a painter, but by positing the image in act immediately and totally without mistakes and in a single instant. Take, for example, what nature does to colour flowers and insects. Harmonious colours are all posited simultaneously, and the delightful picture appears totally formed and whole; not one leaf or one wing has been painted without its matching completely the leaf or wing which is its counterpart. To explain this fact of order and perfect regularity of the image which appears entire in a single instant, we have recourse to three principles: 1. to the operator, the efficient cause, which is simple. This cause is the sensitive principle (although other excitatory causes may contribute), present simultaneously to the whole of the primitive sensation which the image reproduces; 2. to habit which renders the act already performed several times more easy to posit. The beginnings of the primitive act, that is, of the sensation, remain although the sensation has ceased. The soul can, therefore, determine itself to perform an act which it has already experienced; 3. but because the images which are present in a dream or even during wakefulness are not the exact reproduction of sensations already experienced, we have to appeal to a third principle: 'The animal always does that which is easier and more pleasurable.' This principle has to be used relative to all the conditions in which the animal's sensitive and instinctive principle is found.

[1743]

But the simple, single, sensitive principle, when moved to produce images in itself, is set in motion by a multitude of internal stimuli. These are principally the bodily humours which by their regular or irregular movement, excite both the internal sensory of the imagination to its acts, and the single principle from which arises the vital action of the sensory. This principle, therefore, allows itself to be aroused to action by the concurrence of this multitude of stimuli. Its spontaneity is determined according to the complex action easiest and most pleasurable for the principle, which does not resist any urge from any stimulus unless led to do so by some greater, more urgent stimulus. At the same time, its singleness and simplicity, aided also by habit, makes the sensitive principle necessarily and spontaneously posit order amongst all the tiny images or parts of images provoked by the stimuli in its sensory. This must happen because the principle could not simultaneously produce all these images in a single act without first synthesising and ordering them to unity. If this were not the case, the principle would find it extremely troublesome to leave them scattered, or to suppress them by resisting the stimuli which arouse them. Moreover, the harmonious union between these images is more pleasing and more delightful for the principle which has no difficulty in finding the harmony immediately because it is determined by nature itself, that is, by the law of what is easiest and most pleasurable. The principle, therefore, posits its ruling, organising activity in this event, and thus obtains a scene of images which, although partly different from sensations already experienced, are well ordered — like a story, for example — and bound together. The dominant activity of the sensible principle on the images which are about to be excited has a very great part to play here.

The act, therefore, with which the image is re-presented is single, although it extends to many simultaneous movements in the various fibres of the brain. These movements have to reproduce the image. This comes about because the sensitive soul can, with a single act, carry out several effects to which it is contemporaneously present in its simplicity. Every group of different effects is in fact a single, different act. Moreover, if spontaneity obeys habit, the sensitive soul is determined, at least in part, to reproduce more easily the images of which it has sensations.

Habit is, as it were, a continuation and strengthening of a preceding act which has not entirely ceased.

1744. There is, therefore, in the animal a single principle governing all its instinctive operations. This principle is 'the tendency to reach the already initiated state of satisfaction.' This principle, which must provide an extraordinary regularity to the animal's operation, is at odds with everything irregular, that is, with everything opposed to the regularity following on the unity in its multiple nature.

§5. *Regularity arising from the rational principle*

1745. Having found such regularity in animal operations, it is even more certain that this regularity must be present in the operations of the rational principle. However, the term of the rational principle is the *object*. We must, therefore, deal with objective regularity.

Why is the mind happy to contemplate what it finds set out with regularity?

1746. The first reason, which shows how it is more pleasing to contemplate several things when they are regularly disposed, lies in the way that many things, disposed with regularity, are more easily conceived and embraced by thought. But we always prefer what is easier, according to the law of spontaneity which governs every agent. Indeed, to be disposed in a regular way means to be disposed in order which, in turn, means to be disposed according to a single rule in which the mind sees what the entire disposition is and must be. For example, imagine that a series of numbers is disposed in arithmetic or geometric proportion in the mind. The person who knows the first number of this series and the difference between the first and the second, or the result of the first divided by the second, needs no other number in order to know how all successive numbers will be distributed. The simple information he has enables him to describe, of his own accord, those series, however long they may be. Hence in the *rule* of distribution (that is, difference for the arithmetic series and proportion for the geometric), which is the final and extremely simple rule, the intelligence embraces in summary all the multitude of things in so far as they are regularly disposed. Indeed, the intelligence embraces any multiplicity it is prepared to imagine as disposed in a similar way. People with some mathematical knowledge know very well how curves are indicated by means of algebraic equations which simply present the *rule* according to which all points assignable in a curve are disposed. In other words, the rule indicates the order taken by determined points in their positions relative to one another. It is true that the algebraic equation does not offer the form of the curve to the imagination, but it does provide the intelligence with the key to the curve. It teaches the intelligence how to describe the curve whenever it wishes to do so, either on paper or in its own imagination. Such simplified, abbreviated knowledge is extremely delightful to the mind which uses it to obtain and know far more than anything it could conclude from some sense-perception limited to a number of individuals. Consequently, the intellective *rule* enables us to know the pluralities of things in *species*, not in *individuals*. Such specific knowledge embraces very much more than knowledge of the individual.

1747. This is another reason why intelligence loves regularity in the multiple object of its contemplation. It loves regularity not only because regularity enables the mind to think of multiplicity in an *easier* way, but also because it enables it *to think further*. Again, regularity enables the mind to think in such a way that it can reproduce multiplicities for itself at its pleasure. It is true that an irregular multiplicity can be changed by the mind into a *species* through contemplation separated from sensible perception, but this is extremely tiring, especially if the irregular multiplicity is large. Moreover, this kind of multiplicity cannot be increased by the mind without a rule according to which such increase is possible, as happens in series. Consequently, multiplicity always remains limited.

1748. At this point, we can indicate a *third reason* why the rational principle finds regularity delightful. Regularity does in fact make the principle capable of operating. Consequently, when the principle is in possession of a *rule* which orders and disposes the multiplicity of things in a given way, the *rule* becomes the principle and norm of its operation relative both to *reasoning* and to every other way of *acting*.

[1747–1748]

Let us go back to Descartes' immortal discovery. He reduced curves to algebraic formulae. As we saw, expressing a curve in an algebraic formula simply means expressing it in a *rule* according to which the points assignable in the curve are distributed. Now everyone knows that the possession of these formulae is of immense assistance to science in determining the many beautiful properties of curves which would otherwise remain unknown. But mathematicians determined these properties only by founding their reasoning on the *rule* which enabled them to discover the disposition of points assignable in various curves. They then expressed these dispositions in formulae or equations. Granted knowledge of the *formula* which expresses the regularity of curves, the formula then becomes an immense source of new mental cognitions. Knowing the *rule* according to which regularity is formed in a multiplicity of things is an extremely fruitful principle of ever new cognitions, all virtually contained in that principle.

1749. Note that these cognitions, which are discovered when the reason begins with information about the *rule* which orders the relationships between several things, not only provide delight for the mind but, in addition, practical applications. This is well-known to those who are aware of the extent to which much mechanics and hydrodynamics have benefited by the discovery of *rules* which set out in summary fashion the regularity of different straight and curved lines and of their various systems. Human beings, therefore, must be led to love regularity in things for this reason also: that in regularity, once its rule has been discovered, we have a principle which: 1. opens the way to obtaining new cognitions; 2. and increases our powers of action in the exterior world to a new, incredible degree.

1750. We must add a *fourth*, more subtle reason why the regularity of things contemplated by the mind and expressed in a brief *rule* helps us to order *ourselves*, and thus become better, morally speaking. We actually like reproducing in ourselves the order that we are accustomed to contemplate mentally. We even do this instinctively because the rational principle does not lack its own instinct. The order of cognitions present in the human mind is the instinctive principle of well-ordered operations.

1751. But the *fifth reason* for the rational principle's

inclination towards regularities explains and completes all the preceding reasons. This reason springs from the principle of cognition: 'The object of thought is an ens'. Now an ens is one by essence. Hence in the contemplation of an ens the intelligence rises to the degree that it begins to notice unity in the multiplicity of things. What is the unity of multiple things? It means considering them in universal being and referring them to being, their supreme container. But because its own term is *good* the intelligence aspires to see all things in universal being where they are found united. Hence the principal reason why intelligence loves what it knows through principles rather than through consequences is that principles not only extend infinitely further than a multitude of consequences deduced from them and thus possess greater light, but because consequences are resplendently unified within principles. And knowing multiple things in the *rule* which gives them regular distribution means knowing them through principles. It is true that knowledge of things through principles, taken on its own, is simply initial, virtual cognition. From this point of view, knowledge through principles is knowledge at a lesser level than knowledge through consequences. However, consequences known without principles provide only perceptive cognition which is extremely imperfect because limited in an extraordinary manner relative to the extension of its light. In the same way, the knowledge of pure principles without any distinct reference to consequences is abstract knowledge. It, too, is imperfect, not relative to the extension of its light which is infinite, but relative to the intensity of the light, and as a result of defective communication with reality. But when principles and consequences are known at the same time, and consequences are known in principles (as for instance in the case of a multitude of things in which we are aware of the *rule* according to which they are distributed and disposed), then we have perfect knowledge which entirely satisfies the intelligence, and endlessly arouses and increases human activity.

1752. These are the reasons why the rational principle loves to contemplate things regularly disposed.

But this *regularity* can be extremely varied. The *rule* determining regularity can vary infinitely, and the classification of these different rules through demonstration of their properties would be an immense work to be undertaken by anyone wishing to write a treatise on Callology. Here I will have to content myself with distinguishing these rules into two great genera:

1. The genus of those *rules* which distribute entia in an exterior order, according to their position (symmetry) and their number (proportion) — Co-ordination.

2. The genus of those rules which distribute entia according to the convergence between interior and exterior, principle and term (organism), end and means, principles and consequences, cause and effect, etc. — Subordination.

1753. The first genus of regularity is *easier* to know because it appears even in things perceived with our senses.

The second is more *difficult*. The difficulty arises because such regularity often appears absent where the first genus is not seen. Nevertheless, it is present and is indeed more noble and excellent. In this respect, defective vision allows a gardener to believe he renders a tree more regular by shaping it as a cross. In forcing this shape on the tree he seems to impose the first genus of regularity. In fact, he destroys the regularity proper to the nature of the tree, a regularity of the second genus unknown to the uneducated gardener and his master.

Article 2
Continuation — Does the sensitive principle enjoy the numerical proportion present in its movements?

1754. It will help us considerably if we distinguish accurately the kind of species and nature of harmony which the sensitive principle can enjoy from that which only the rational principle enjoys. Let us consider for a moment the opinion of Leibniz who defined music as 'an arithmetic of the soul.'

Does the sensitive soul truly enjoy numbers and their proportion? Does it enjoy the symmetry present in parts? Does it enjoy proportional movements?

This opinion entails several distinctions and reflections.

1755. First, it is certain that everything enjoyed by the sensitive principle is *subjective*; all enjoyment is a modification of the sensitive principle. The intellective, rational principle, on the other hand, enjoys the *object*; it enjoys what it knows as present in the object, not as present in itself; it enjoys good which it considers outside itself and without reference to itself.

1756. Nevertheless, the sensitive principle also has an extended, multiple term characterised by symmetry, number in movement, and (between movements) proportion in number and time. But does it enjoy all these things?

What we have said excludes objective enjoyment, which pertains only to the intellective and rational principle, from these different kinds of orders. This exclusion means that the sensitive principle cannot enjoy symmetry and proportion considered as good and beautiful in themselves, independently of the subject. The rational principle, however, which considers symmetry and proportion objectively as good independently of itself, esteems and praises them even if they are accidentally harmful to itself. This principle esteems and praises symmetry and proportion solely for the excellence it sees in them itself. If the effects of symmetry and proportion are painful for the subject, he will make a contrary judgment about the effects; he will judge them as evil (and in these effects there is already some disorder). But while he makes this judgment about the effects, his preceding judgment about the cause, that is, about symmetry and proportion, will remain intact. The beauty and good admired in symmetry and proportion by the subject are unchangeable and eternal, like being itself.

All this is outside the possibilities of the sensitive principle which can neither know nor consequently appreciate symmetry and proportion in themselves, but can only feel and enjoy their effects if these are good for it. The effects of symmetry and of proportion found in the term of feeling are not symmetry and proportion themselves, although the effect (the feeling produced) is analogous and corresponds to them. It could even be said that this effect has symmetry and proportion in itself. The sensitive principle, therefore, does not enjoy symmetry and proportion as such.

1757. But if sensible enjoyment possesses symmetry and proportion, the sensitive principle surely enjoys them?

This is not the case. When something is enjoyed, that which is enjoyed is one thing; enjoyment itself is another. To say that enjoyment enjoys itself is tautologous; the affirmation duplicates what is simple. Enjoyment does not enjoy itself; the human being simply enjoys through it. If, therefore, enjoyment itself, contemplated by the mind, contains some order similar to that of symmetry and proportion, it does not follow that the sensitive principle enjoys these dispositions. Rather, we have to say that enjoyment is a kind of living, enjoying symmetry and proportion. It is not the things that possess symmetry and proportion which enjoy the order they have in themselves; symmetry and proportion are enjoyed by the person who contemplates them and notices them. Hence, the rational principle, which finds symmetry and proportion in the intimate constitution of animal enjoyment, enjoys the order present in the enjoyment. Enjoyment itself is only an extremely simple fact, ignorant of self and its own nature. Constituted by the symmetry and proportion in its term, enjoyment is an effect of these harmonic dispositions; it is not enjoyment of them.

1758. The following, therefore, are very different questions: Does the sensitive principle enjoy symmetry and proportion? Does the sensitive principle enjoy, as an effect, that which the symmetry and proportion proper to its term produce in it?

The first question must be answered negatively. This is confirmed when we note that the sensitive principle, if it were suitable for enjoying symmetry and proportion, should enjoy all symmetry and proportion present in its term in the same way as the rational principle, which contemplates such order in its object. But there is no doubt that the sensitive principle, which experiences enjoyment as a consequence of certain symmetries and proportions taken by its term, does not enjoy other symmetries and proportions which do not have the pleasurable effect aimed at by the sensible principle. The sensitive principle does not enjoy the essence or reason for symmetry, but the effect which symmetry sometimes, but not always, produces in it.

1759. Confusing these two very distinct questions caused great men, such as Plato and Leibniz, to posit in the sensitive soul a certain hidden, mysterious reasoning power enabling it to exercise some kind of expertise in exquisite arithmetic and sublime geometry. Such a sublime error is possible only to those rare geniuses who have succeeded in uncovering symmetry and proportions innate in the felt term. However, they did not have

[1758–1759]

the same success in distinguishing the pleasurable feeling which is the effect of symmetry and proportion. Consequently, they attributed to feeling itself the enjoyment of the cause constituting feeling. But feeling does not even know this cause; it enjoys its symmetrical, proportional term, but not symmetry and proportion themselves.

1760. It is not difficult for great minds to be deceived at this point. The sensitive soul does seem to perform the same operations as the arithmetician although, in fact, it does nothing of the kind.

Take, for instance, the way in which the sensitive soul seems to add two quantities. Imagine that we are crossing a lake in a small boat while another small boat passes us in the opposite direction. Our eye, which looks at the boat as it passes, seems to add the speed of the two boats with extreme accuracy; the apparent movement of the other boat registers a speed equal precisely to the speed of both.

The sensitive soul also appears to subtract. Imagine that while we are slowly crossing the lake, another boat going in the same direction overtakes us at two or three times our speed. Our eye, as it looks at the other boat, sees its speed as precisely the difference between its speed and ours. No calculation could be more exact than the precision with which our eye notices the difference.

Let us see how the sensitive soul seems to multiply or divide. We can shorten our investigation by examining a fact according to which the sensitive soul seems to carry out both operations together, and sets up a true geometric proportion in order to reach its conclusion. Imagine that our boat is moving in a straight line across the lake. From the boat, we see two mountain peaks, one further away than the other. What is the speed of the movement by which these two peaks seem to approach or distance themselves from one another? Some calculation has to be made to indicate the distance between the two peaks, and the distance of the nearer one from the boat. Only the person who can calculate will be able to say that the apparent movement of the two peaks results from an equation expressing a geometric proportion. But the eye has unhesitatingly solved the problem without measuring anything. It sees the relative movement of the two peaks proceed with the speed, neither more nor less, found in the calculation. The difference is that the mathematician's result can be mistaken, while the result seen in nature by the eye is never mistaken.

Do we have to say, therefore, that sense does in fact calculate, and calculate the speed with greater accuracy than the mind of geometricians. This would be crazy; it would transform sense into a mind more perspicacious than the mind itself. It is not sense that finds these results, but nature, which first produces them and then offers them to sense. Nature, as we said, is ordered in this way although it neither feels nor knows its own order. The movement given to sight follows its own laws, and is seen in accordance with those laws. We should not be surprised, therefore, that sense has such quantities as its terms, with their relevant dispositions and proportions, and that the mathematician who wishes to know the disposition and order of these things needs to undertake extremely complicated calculations.

1761. It is clear, therefore, that order in matter and in the movements of matter entails the presence of order in the sensory organs, which are composed of matter. Again, there is no doubt that the sensitive principle tends to possess as its term both a determined organism, and one which is more suitable than another because it enables the sensitive principle to develop great sensitive activity. It is not surprising, therefore, that the sensitive principle itself tends to have some movements rather than others in its sensory organs. These movements, moreover, are regulated according to certain proportions of size and time.

1762. We also need to consider that the direction and communication of movement receives its form from the configuration and composition of a body itself. For example, a body of a certain shape which receives an impulse to movement carries out different movements dependent on the point and direction in which the motor force is applied. This same force, applied to a body of another shape, produces another kind of movement. But the sensory organs themselves possess a certain regular configuration suitable for the sensitive principle. Their movements, therefore, if suitable for them, must share in the same regularity and consequently possess a certain order.

1763. Again, it is natural that one of the elements in this order is the proportion between the various times in which the different movements, impressed at these times, come about. The communication of movement obeys the law of time. The same movement impressed on two bodies, one of which is double the size of the other, takes double the time to pass through the whole of the body and communicate itself to all the molecules. Hence, time is proportioned to the proportion of the mass. If the density of the body is equal, and the volume double, communication of movement from molecule to molecule will take place relative to the volume. What is said about simple communication of movement by way of impulse must also be said equally, or similarly, of movement through affinity or attraction, through waves or vibrations, and of simple and composite movement resulting from a single force or several forces, and so on. Granted the law: 'The sensitive principle finds pleasure in completing its acts, in not being disturbed half-way and made to begin new acts', it is clear that the movements which it seeks in its term must be proportioned in time. They must not be jammed upon one another, or interspersed and confused, but distinct and ordered so that their regular pauses leave time for the sensitive principle to complete its actions and develop all that is actually taking place in it without turning back. The sensitive principle, therefore, does not take pleasure in this order *per se*, but for the sake of developing leisurely the activity which it always wants to finish and complete. The principle would suffer if this activity were impeded.

1764. When sensations such as sight and sound are produced, one extremely simple sensation, white or red, alarmire or feffaute, corresponds to a given number and rhythm of vibrations. This is a clear proof that the number of vibrations and their proportions has no part in the feeling, which arises as a single effect of multiple, extrasubjective movements.

1765. It may be objected that greater light renders the eye insensible to lesser, or that in entering two equally red rooms the first seems more red than the second.[373] A sudden passage

---

[373] The harmonic colour following red in the optic sensory is greenish. Consequently, in the passage from the first to the second room, the prior sensation of red must degenerate in the eye to greenish. This is perhaps the reason why the red of the second room appears weaker.

[1764–1765]

from a high temperature to a much lower one gives a cold sensation. And in general where the same length of time contains a more marked passage between one state of stimulation and another, greater liveliness is found in sensation. In other words, it seems that sensation is produced not in proportion to the absolute action of the external stimulus, but in proportion to various, successive stimuli. — This does not prove that the sensory feels the proportion between the stimuli, but only that the effect of this proportion in certain circumstances is a more or less lively sensation. To complete its acts, the sensory needs to be stimulated with order and proportion, not by chance. Over-violent and disproportionate movements can produce a lesser or null feeling relative to lighter, suitably proportioned movements.

Article 3
The different rules applied by the rational principle to regular multiplicity uncovered in the multiplicity proper to various kinds of simultaneous regularities

1766. The rational principle, therefore, enjoys symmetrical, proportional *regularity*, that is, *order*, which is essentially objective; the rational principle alone discovers and contemplates more or less distinctly the single, simple *rule* which determines regularity.

Another observation confirms this. A given multitude of things can be considered from different points of view by the intelligence. Consequently, it presents different regularities, different symmetries, without any change in the real distribution of these things. If different regularities exist within the same distribution of things, this regularity comes about as a result of different mental reflections; it is not proper to things materially considered, nor to any feeling of them.

What are these different mental aspects? How are things distributed regularly in different ways? This certainly comes about because the mind sees that the very distribution of things can be determined in this way by different *rules*. The mind, by applying different *rules* (using as it were, different paths), comes to distribute those things in the very same order. Let us take a chessboard as our example.

Everyone knows that a chessboard is a square surface divided into sixty-four lesser squares. The distribution of these squares is very simple, and follows a single pattern. But the mind can consider the small squares placed and united in various ways; the aspect they present looked at in one way is very different from that presented from another point of view. If I consider these squares united along their sides, I have a different pattern from that which is present if I look at them united at their corners. I can also form a shape from several of them. This shape, constantly repeated, embraces the whole of the chessboard, and gives me a new pattern. Let us consider for a moment the movement of different chess pieces. I limit myself to three for the sake of brevity: the rook, the bishop and the knight. The rook's movement goes from one end of the board to the other along a row in which the squares are united at their sides. If I now take an entire row of eight squares, I can define the chessboard as 'a board made up of eight rows of equal squares united at their sides'. This is a *rule* which determines one symmetric distribution. I now take the bishops, which move diagonally along rows of squares joined at their corners. These rows of squares, touching at their corners, give me the same chessboard which I can now define as 'a square composed of sixteen rows of chess squares joined diagonally at their corners.' If I fix my eye on the sixteen rows making up the board, I now seem to have a pattern totally different from the first. Now take the knight's move. It is made up of three squares, one of which is in an oblique direction. I now focus my eye on the shape resulting from these three squares, and then consider them repeated in such a way that they fill the whole chessboard which I can now define as 'a square divided into twenty-one shapes each of which has the shape of two small squares in one direction and one oblique, plus one other small square.' If I consider the chessboard as an aggregate of such shapes, it now appears with a totally different pattern from that seen previously. In other words the same, real chessboard becomes a plane possessing different symmetries according to different relationships between its shapes, resulting from different mental points of view which come to indicate different *rules* used by the mind to determine symmetry. These

[1766]

rules or principles enable symmetry to be conceived in its reason, in its rule, in a way suitable for the intelligence.

1767. This shows clearly that the *regularity* contemplated by the mind is posited by the mind itself which, however, would be unable to posit it if the multiplicity forming the object of its contemplation did not have certain relationships and correspondences with what is *ideal*, where the rules of things are present. Once again, we see a *synthesis* between what is *real* and what is *ideal*.

1768. This also explains why beasts do not give any sign of appreciating what is beautiful, even musical harmony, although they do react to some kind of melody as, for instance, in the case of snakes which do not savour what is beautiful but what pleases the senses.

Article 4
Harmony in succession

1769. Multiplicity is *contemporaneous* or *successive*. Consequently the harmony which can be found in multiplicity is also *contemporaneous* as a result of the order possessed by the simultaneous presence of several things. This order is manifested in the symmetry of which we have spoken, in the order that parts have relative to the whole, in harmonic sensations, and so on. On the other hand, harmony is successive if it results from the order and convergence which preceding and successive terms of a series of facts have with one another.

We have already dealt with successive harmony when we spoke about the sensitive soul. Our example was the imaginary colours and sounds which spontaneously succeed one another in the optic and acoustic sensories. Let us consider these examples now in the rational principle itself, which is the whole man.

1770. The five reasons given above show why the rational principle takes pleasure whenever it contemplates order.

The rational principle can consider this order both in something different from itself and in its own proper feeling. The order that a person contemplates in his own feeling constitutes what I call *aesthetic beauty*. One's own feeling is ordered when it is pleasurable. Consequently a*esthetic beauty* is simultaneously beautiful and pleasurable for the senses. But beauty, considered in things outside one's own feeling, is *beautiful* without being *pleasurable* to the senses themselves, without being aesthetic. This does not mean that the sight of something beautiful is not pleasant, but that the pleasure of pure beauty is wholly intellective. Properly speaking, it is contemplation of what is beautiful that pleases, rather than the object which is contemplated, the beautiful thing itself. If, however, we speak of order in our own feeling, there is present, in addition to the intellective pleasure in contemplation itself, the pleasure which constitutes the nature of what is contemplated, that is, the *pleasing feeling*. In this case, *pleasure* itself is the *rule* for knowing whether feeling is well-ordered (I am speaking about true, natural, prevailing pleasure). However, authors dealing with what is beautiful have not made these distinctions between *aesthetic beauty* and *what is beautiful in general,* and between *pleasurable beauty* and what is *simply pleasurable.* They have almost always confused *what is pleasurable* with *what is beautiful,* and restricted the science of callology to the narrow limits of aesthetics.

1771. We need to recall that every animal sensory is so ordered that on stimulation it is immediately determined and moved to a given series of successive movements, not to others. This is partly the result of the laws of the matter composing it and the laws of the communication of motion, partly the result of the organism and partly the result of the relationships of matter and organisation with the activity of the sentient principle. If, however, another series were to interrupt and disturb the first series, sensitive nature would find this unfitting and upsetting. It follows that the spontaneity of the sentient principle, which always tends to the state and act of greatest pleasure, assists and promotes the first series of movements while refusing to further the second series. Thus, if a violin string is plucked, it gives isochronic oscillations which diminish in extension and speed in a constant proportion. If the string were animated or were a sensory organ, it would tend to complete all its oscillations until it came to rest. It would resist the forces which wished to interrupt or alter the isochronism, that is, the activity which is more easy and natural to the string.[374]

We now need to consider that the animal, although it has a single, constitutive, sentient principle, possesses many sensories. These are very many in the human being, the most perfect animal of all, who possesses as many species of sensations as he has organs and sensitive apparatus. Each one of our human sensories has a series of successive movements which are connatural and pleasing to it, that is, has a series of sensations through which sensation passes before being totally extinguished.

Moreover, exterior stimuli are pleasant if they correspond to such oscillation in the sensory organ and help it pass through the ordered series of sensations with a fixed rhythm, rendering them more lively. Otherwise, they are troublesome, annoying and, in varying degrees, even painful.

1772. Amongst other circumstances determining the natural succession of sensations proper to a sensory organ, we find frustration and tiredness. These arise when sensations have not posited those pauses which, in giving rest to the organ, refresh and strengthen it. The need for rest depends on the same law that prescribes rhythm. This law determines the pauses between sensations, the duration and the intensity of these pauses, and so on.

1773. But, you may say, if the sensories are many and each has its own rhythm proper to the series of pleasing sensations, why do different sensories, operating simultaneously, not come into collision? — We certainly have to suppose that the wise author of human nature has first of all harmonised the sensories in the wonderful organism he has created. Besides, over and above all the rest, stands the single, sensitive principle which dominates and harmonises all the sensories. The prevalent taste of this sensitive principle is that which determines the true *pleasure*

---

[374] The law of isochronism of the oscillations in a violin string corresponds perfectly to the law which demonstrates that the cycloid is the line of most rapid descent. This observation will provide considerable light for readers familiar with physics and mathematics. They will recognise that isochronism of forces is one of those cases in which nature is clearly seen to be regulated by the sublime law of the least means. Cf. *Teodicea*, 495–503.

that we enjoy as human beings. This also explains why the contemporaneous and successive operation of various sensories receives a supreme *rule* determining the duration of their operation, their pauses, their proportions, their intensities, and so on.

1774. Finally, there is in human beings, besides *animal feeling*, an *intellective feeling* and a *moral feeling*. These two extremely noble feelings possess their own natural harmony in their operations and pleasures. On the one hand, the *intellective feeling*, which must prevail because it belongs to a more sublime order, modifies with its own harmony the animal harmony in us, which it unites with itself. Similarly, *moral feeling* modifies and tempers with its own proper harmony the animal, intellective harmony which it unites with itself and makes use of. The result is a single harmony, possessing an extremely high degree of unity.

1775. Consequently, the following harmonies, which fuse into a single harmony, are preordained and pre-established in the human being:

1. The harmony of naturally successive acts in the singular sensories.

2. The harmony between sensories as a result of the unity of the sensitive principle. This accounts for animal harmony.

3. Animal harmony dominated, ruled and informed by the intellective principle. This accounts for animal-intellective harmony.

4. Animal-intellective harmony, ruled, informed and completed by the moral principle. This truly confers total harmony to the human being — human harmony.

1776. This entire complex of harmonic activities possesses, predetermined by nature, a certain succession of acts disposed in various ways.

Human beings have an *instinct* for this succession, an instinct which is indeed truly human, but does not always act at full strength on account of some defect or weakness and vice in us. The result is *disharmony*. But these disharmonies, which indicate weakness and vice in our great human instinct, do not indicate total cessation of the instinct. It operates, and the partial harmonic instincts operate with it. This complex of activities determines the successive dispositions, propensities and aversions which we experience during our life on earth. It

[1774–1776]

also accounts for the same tendencies in nations, and in the way centuries evolve.

1777. Let us apply some of these principles to explain certain phenomena. Why do we have continual changes in fashion? Are these changes the arbitrary effect of capriciousness amongst vain people, or perhaps the result of decisions made by entrepreneurs? This is what we normally think; when a cause lies hidden because it is too deep, too difficult to find, we attribute the result to some accident. But if we consider this extraordinary fact called 'fashion', manifested at various levels in nations which have reached a certain degree of civilisation, we will easily see that mere *arbitrariness* on the part of those who introduce a new style of dress and ornament is insufficient to exact such docile obedience that a nation appears unanimous and totally at one in accepting the new fashion. It is even less possible to ensure that everyone's taste is conformed and changed daily in submission to the entrepreneurs, who do not form but speculate upon universal taste. On the other hand, if we question fashionable people of both sexes, they are quite definite that the fashions are the most beautiful. What was previously most beautiful, but has been in vogue for some time, soon becomes displeasing; it irritates, it seems out of place. In other words, we have to believe that every appearance of the *latest fashion* provides them with an agreeable feeling, and that the preceding fashion now seems out of date. But there is an explanation of this apparently frivolous phenomenon which in fact is worthy of philosophical attention (although the explanation certainly cannot be used to justify the light-headedness found in the followers of the changeable, inexorable goddess of fashion which, we notice, is more lively and more pronounced in capital cities).

First, we have to accept that a presupposition to the reign of fashion is a developed and actuated sense of the complex of sensual pleasures which fashion itself presents in ever varied ways, a complex resulting from infinite, extremely subtle elements — ethereal essences as it were — and forming something 'unknown and indistinct', as Dante would put it. This sense lies dormant in crude or still youthful, strict societies. But given that it and its consequent instinct have been aroused, actuated and refined, I have no doubt that the flow of fashions, daily created and destroyed, is determined by the *law of successive harmony*. As a result of this law, the instinct for fashion arising from innumerable feelings and particular instincts has a profound need for certain new forms from which (and not from others) it gains pleasure. This wonderful law secretly directs the varied duration of fashions and their quality. It also contains the natural reason why one kind of cut follows another, why one colour follows another, why one type of dress follows another, etc. Again, it explains why the new fashion pleases, and the previous one does not. The pleasure taken in one fashion or usage should not be attributed to its form and quality in isolation, but to its suitable place in a whole succession of feelings.

Another argument leading to the same conclusion can be drawn from the fact that a fashion which seemed beautiful to various nations during its brief dominion sometimes appears very distasteful to a foreigner coming from a distance who remains uninfluenced by the whole circle of fashions which had previously developed.

A secret law, therefore, determines the course of fashions and frivolous customs with a certain kind of fatality. Harmony, pre-established by the nature of feeling, produces these fashions one after another. Where sense is more delicate and lively, as in capital cities, it enunciates readily and exactly what suits it. This affirmation is generally accepted as a kind of interpretation of common taste which satisfies the public who previously had been unable to provide shape and existence for their indistinct desire. There is no doubt that the universal, docile acceptance of new fashion results from innumerable small feelings, as we said, pertaining to different sensories and faculties, each of which possesses a succession of acts preferable to every other. Every faculty is a sensory and, considered as such, is subject to the same law.

1778. This also explains why the course of fashions and social behaviour varies in different nations. Different circumstances, which dispose the *sense of fashion* in different ways, determine it along an equally fatal course.

1779. Yet another point which adds emphasis to our argument. Careful consideration shows that the *law of successive harmony* of which we are speaking has an extremely extended dominion, an incredible extension, even to other things. It is capable of exercising immense influence in determining various customs of peoples, the course of their opinions, and even of historical events.

Taste in arts and literature is also dependent on the law of harmonic succession. Even ideas lose and acquire splendour at different times as a result of hidden, but unavoidable laws. This explains why it would be impossible for the severe virtue of such people as Cincinnatus, Curius and Fabricius to be practised in Rome at the time of Horace and Ovid. Latter-day Rome had lost its feeling for these things, although admiration for them still remained high. But this is explained by the contemplation of unchangeable truth and beauty, which does not have succession as sensible pleasure does.

Many other facts are subject to this law. Why do certain universal tastes reveal themselves irresistibly in one period or another? What is the explanation of certain characteristic opinions, certain characteristic ways of acting? These phenomena are fully explained if we add the law of spontaneity of direct life to the law of *successive harmony* which secretly guides the whole human being. Apparent leaps then disappear; leaps are only the sudden manifestation in reflection and consciousness of work which has already gone on within human beings without reflection and consciousness. — It is sufficient, I think, to have indicated this vast field of meditation. Philosophers who come after us, with more time and ability than ourselves, will perhaps be able to cultivate it usefully.

[1779]

Appendix

1. (792).

As far as I can see, ancient philosophers did not distinguish between general, indeterminate *extension* which pertains to first matter, and determined extension or extended quantity which does not. This is how St. Thomas explains one of Plato's teachings: 'Quantity and quality, the first accidents to flow from substance, are co-related to the two essential principles of substance, that is, form and matter. QUANTITY CORRESPONDS TO MATTER, which explains why Plato posited "great" and "small" amongst the differences pertaining to matter, and quality to form' (*In IV Sent.*, d. 12, q. 1, art. 1, ad 1). It is fairly easy to understand why St. Thomas says that these entities are accidents consequent upon substance, rather than essential to its constitution, if we remember that the concept or *essence* of substance is one thing, its *realisation* another. *Quantity*, which is determined extension, does not form part of the *essence* of substance, and in particular of matter, until it is *realised* with the quantity determined by the will of the Creator. Determined extension or quantity is, therefore, dependent on the extent of the *realisation* of matter. This also explains the truth of the statement: 'Measured quantity, although not depending on sensible matter for its explanation, does depend on it for its being. Hence, in predication and in subjection, it takes up the mode of substance and accident. We say, therefore, that a line has quantity because *etc.*' (*ibid.*, ad 2). 'For its explanation' means 'according to its concept, according to its essence', because quantity can be thought in abstraction from sensible matter, or rather sensible matter can be thought without quantity — the idea of matter does not contain any determinate quantity of this matter. But 'for its being', that is, according to its realisation, it does depend upon sensible matter because quantity is a mode of matter. The opposite is said of *matter* in its concept, where no quantity is assigned. When matter is realised, however, it must receive a certain quantity according to the decision of whoever realises it. I conclude that *extensive quantity* does not come forth either from matter, or from the form of bodies, but from their *reality* which, in turn, comes from the will of the Creator.

2. (797).

St. Thomas says more or less the same. 'You must know that corporeal substance has what makes it the subject of accidents because of its matter WHOSE FIRST CHARACTERISTIC IS TO BE PRESENT IN SOMETHING ELSE AS SUBJECT TO IT' (hence matter is also the subject of substantial form). 'but the first disposition of matter is QUANTITY' (note that determined quantity does not pertain to matter, but is a disposition coming from elsewhere; indetermined quantity, that is, quantity in potency to determination, is essential to the concept of matter) 'because the division or lack of division in matter depends on gether with unity and multitude which are its first consequences. Dispositions of the whole of matter, but not particular dispositions, are another consequence of this' (indetermined *continuous quantity* and the unity of the continuum is an essential constitutive of matter. This is not the case with *discrete quantity*, that is, with multiplicity, which is essential only in potency in so far as the continuum can always be thought as divided into further continua). 'Hence all other accidents are founded in substance THROUGH QUANTITY WHICH IS NATURALLY PRIOR TO THEM. Quantity, therefore, does not include sensible matter in its concept, although it does include intelligible matter, as we find in *VII Metaphysicorum*.' *Sensible matter* means matter in potency to sensible qualities; *intelligible matter* means matter conceived abstractly without reference to sensible qualities. It affirms that the definition of *quantity* presupposes matter as its subject; it does not affirm that we need think of this matter as subject of such qualities which are thought of after the abstract quantity. Indeed, quantity itself, when determined, is the subject of such qualities. This enables us to confute Descartes' error. For him, the substance of bodies lies in extension, a mistake already made by several Scholastics: 'Some have erred, and were led to believe that dimensions were the substance of material things because they saw nothing sensible remaining after the removal of the qualities except quantity which, however, according to its being, depends on substance in the same way as other accidents' (*In IV Sententiarum*, d. 12, q. 1, art. 1).

3. (fn. 36).

The confusion between the concept of *matter* and that of *reality* proved an obstacle to perfecting the theory of the human intellect which abstracts from the *reality of matter*, but not from *matter*. If this had been seen, unequivocal language would have been used to separate *ideal*, which pertains to the intellect, from *real*, which pertains to sense. The Scholastics maintained: 'Everything is understood to the extent that it is abstracted from matter. The forms present in matter are individual forms, which are not apprehended by the intellect as such' (St. Thomas, *S.T.*, I, q. 50, art. 2). This affirmation is true if we understand *matter* as *reality*, *subsistence*, but not if we are speaking about *matter*. In fact, it is not matter alone, but form also that is realised. Moreover, the intellect does not even apprehend the realised form (he means the individual forms which, as he says, the intellect does not apprehend). It is false to say that realised forms are not apprehended because they are united to matter; lack of apprehension occurs solely because they are realised, are subsistent. On the other hand, both *matter* and *form* are apprehended by the intellect as long as they are *ideal*, not *real*. Form and matter, for example, are present in the concept of human being, and the intellect certainly intuits that concept. Some Scholastics denied this, however, and claimed that the species, or idea, embraces *form* alone. In saying this, they are in harmony with the teaching which takes *matter* for *reality*, and makes matter the principle of individuation. But this is truly absurd and these Scholastics tried to avoid the absurdity by making a distinction between common or intelligible matter, and particular matter. This implies the recognition of the *reality of matter* on the one hand, and on the other the *essence* or idea of matter. They should, therefore, have kept the word 'matter' to express 'essence'. This would have contributed to the perfection of philosophical language. The obstacle was their reverence for Aristotle. Instead, they added confusion to confusion by giving 'matter' two meanings, one of which expressed the essence of matter, the other the realisation of the essence of matter. This led to equivocation in their teaching, and generated subtle and interminable questions. As St. Thomas says: 'According to some, the species of the natural thing (the idea) is the form alone; matter is a part of the species.' This is what they should have said if they understood matter as the principle of individuation. 'But according to this, matter would not be found in the definitions of natural things.' St. Thomas clearly recognises the absurdity. 'So we have to say instead that matter is twofold, namely, common (ideal matter) and signed or individual (real matter). It is common as flesh and bone, but individual as THIS (the pronoun indicates reality) flesh and THIS bone. The intellect abstracts, therefore, the species of the natural thing from the sensible, individual matter, not from the sensible common matter just as it abstracts the species of human being from *this* flesh and blood which do not pertain to the notion of species, but are parts of the individual, as we find in *VII Metaph.* (text 34–35), and so can be considered without them. But the species "human being" cannot be abstracted through the intellect from individual flesh and bone' (*S.T.*, I, 85, q. 1, art. 1, ad 2). Note that even here, by calling the second kind of matter *individual matter*, individuation is taken for granted although its cause is being sought.

4. (1048).

The word 'faith' (πίστις), which means *persuasion*, was used in different ways by the ancients. Parmenides divided human knowledge, or rather that about which human beings reason, into *truth* and *opinion*. Karsten, in his work *Philosophorum graecorum veterum praesertim qui ante Platonem floruerunt operum reliquiae* (Amsterdam, 1830), thinks that Parmenides attributes *faith* to *truth*, and *error* (ἀπατή) to *opinions*. Plato thinks the opposite, that is, he attributes faith to *opinion* (*Tim.*, p. 29; *Rep.*, 6, p. 511), and criticises Proclus for saying that Parmenides distinguishes *faith* from *certain knowledge* (*In Tim.*, p. 105). In my opinion however *faith*, understood as a synonym of *persuasion*, as the Greeks understood it, is something distinct from but not *contrary* to information. Indeed, I have often tried to distinguish accurately the *faculty of knowledge* from the *faculty of persuasion*. Parmenides, in the fragments we have of his work, speaks about *faith in the truth* (πίστις ἀληθής), which simply means the *persuasion* that comes from truth. Similarly he calls truth *a persuasive good* (ἀληθείης εὐπειθέος ἀτρεκὲς ἦτορ): its correlative is *persuasive evil*. He thus distinguishes good and true persuasion and its correlative non-good; Parmenides does not deny that *opinions* give persuasion, faith, but denies that they give good, truthful faith (ἠδέ βρότων δόξας τές οὐκ ἔνι πίστις ἀληθής). When Plato therefore attributes *faith* or *persuasion* to opinions and appearances, and contrasts it with truth (ὃ πρὸς γένεσις οὐσία τοῦτο προς πίστις ἀλήθεια, *Tim.* p. 29), he speaks of persuasion without qualification; he does not say, as Parmenides does, that it is good and true, but speaks about *persuasion* alone, considered in itself, separate from any other element and therefore an abstraction from truth. *Persuasion* without truth, because it is blind, certainly contrasts with truth. In this way Plato's affirmation is not as irreconcilable as it seems with that of Parmenides.

5. (1132).

We say that space is *immense*; we can also say that space is *infinite* in the sense that this word indicates a lack of possible limits. I mention Francesco Orioli as one Italian philosopher who recognises the infinity of space. He rightly notes that the *infinity* attributed to space has no relationship with the *infinity* which is proper to God alone. He says: 'We need to consider that the kind of *infinity* which, according to theology and philosophy, must be understood as exclusive to God is not an *infinity* unaccompanied by substantiality and consequently by all activity and potency; it is *operative infinity*, infinity in which the possibility of action is exercised or experienced. But the kind of *infinity* which we say is granted by nature to space (the same can and must be said of time, about which we shall speak later), is purely *extensive infinity*. It is, therefore, entirely proper to the first kind of infinity, and is not seen in anyway related to the second (the infinity of God is intensive and extensive at the same time). In a word, this infinity is dead, not alive — it is infinity of a species of nothing, lacking every potency for action and experience. This 'nothing' does not become anything except in correspondence with its content or with what is containable' (*Spighe e paglie, Opera periodica del Professore Francesco Orioli*, Corfù, Tipografia del Governo, 1844, vol. 1, quad. 1, lett. 2, *Elementi ultimi dell'Universo: Lo spazio*). The professor's words indicate an important truth. He says that the infinity of space is quite different from the infinity of God. But after that, as far as I can see, his words are rather inexact. I have to indicate these mistakes in order to avoid equivocation. 1. We cannot admit that God possesses an *exten*sive infinity, if we take this word *extensive* as the property of space. In God, there is no spatial extension; space is in God in the same way as all creatures are in God. 2. We cannot admit that space is a species of nothing. Nothing has no species, much less infinity. It cannot be objected that mathematicians distinguish several species of nothing; mathematical nothing is entirely different. It is the annihilation of something, brought about by means of some operation as, for example, when we subtract five from five and nothing remains. Space, on the contrary, does not arise as a result of a mental operation with which we take away what has first been posited. 3. We cannot say that space is unaccompanied by every activity and potency because it has the first act by which it exists, although it does not possess second acts. I think, therefore, that it can be called *ens*, but not *substance*. 4. Nor can we say that infinity proper to God is that alone in which there is some possibility of action, exercised or *experienced*. God is act, nothing else; in him there is neither passion nor experience.

6. (1184).

In considering the nature of the idea, we have shown that it is simple and eternal, and identically present to several intellects and to multiple acts of the intellect itself. Moreover, despite its being used and as it were bound by the spirit through perceptions to certain feelings, or certain acts, it remains intuited in itself. It is still free, and reusable. In other words, without ever multiplying itself, it is applied to itself by the spirit and to all the information that the spirit acquires through it. When all this has been clearly understood, or its factual truth has been recognised through contemplative observation, it is easy to reply to the objection that Plato puts in the mouth of Parmenides in the dialogue named after this great Italian philosopher. In the book, Socrates maintains that *species* are distinct from individual things and share in them; he insists that things are *many*, but species *one only*. Parmenides then made the following objection. He wanted to exclude multiplicity and reduce everything to unity in the following way: 'As far as I can see, your reason for thinking that each species is one is this. When you see, for example, several big things, you imagine that in contemplating all of them you have a single idea. Consequently, you imagine that bigness (size) is one.' Here, Parmenides hits upon the truth, because it is the unicity of the idea which unifies the species or essence of several equal individuals, who are nothing more than different realisations of the same idea. Parmenides then immediately objects that if this is so, species would have to be multiplied *ad infinitum*. He says, 'But if you consider in your spirit the biggest itself (size) in exactly the same way as other things which are big, don't you see the necessity of yet another big thing (another size) in which all these big things may be seen? — So it would seem. — In that case, we have another species of bigness, besides bigness itself and the things that share in it. And again, in all these things there is yet another bigness through which they are all big. In this case, each species will no longer be one, but rather infinite in number.' This difficulty is resolved if we consider that the idea of bigness is applied to itself without losing its identity and unity. This enables us to compare bigness and big things and, as it were, measure them. We do not need another idea of bigness. We can measure things with that bigness with which we conceive separately both bigness and big things. The objection, however, was very much to the point, and shows the acuteness of thought possessed by the ancients.

7. (1212).

Zeno's celebrated four arguments against the existence of motion are given by Aristotle in *Physics*, 6: 9. The first three arguments are against *continuous motion*, not properly speaking against motion. Two of them tend to demonstrate the impossibility of a movable thing's arriving at a term if it has to pass through infinite parts of space, and suppose space to be actually divisible into infinite small spaces. The third argument however supposes, as Aristotle himself observes, that time is actually divided into an infinite number of instants. He says that a moving body would be stationary at every instant, and would not move. Reduced to a better form, this argument could be put in the following way: 'A body must be in some place. But if it is in some place, it must be there for some time, however small this time may be. If it were not in a place for some time, it would not be in a place. It is essential to the existence of body that it remain stationary in some place. Therefore, it cannot be in continuous movement.' The fourth argument is not only against continuous movement, but against movement itself, whatever concept may be formed of it, and is used to show that motion would involve the following absurdity: 'Half a time is equal to a whole time.' This, however, is sophistry. The absurdity would arise from the fact that a body, in order to move on a stationary table, would have to use double the time to cross the table that another body of equal rapidity would use to cross another body as long as the table, if the table moves in the opposite direction and with a speed equal to the body which crosses it.

8. (1214).

I say here 'and not of the impetus', that is, of the endeavour to move, in order to avoid any question about the endeavour's being communicated through continuous communication, and not at frequent instants with small durations between them. However, if we did want to pose this question, it would not be difficult, I think, to find facts in nature which prove that even the endeavour to move requires time to communicate itself. Consequently, the communication of living force is intermittent. This is necessary if time is to be employed. If this communication were continuous, its changes would be instantaneous, but the sum even of an infinite number of instants gives nothing more than a single instant; no time, therefore, would be noticed in this communication. Note that when weights fall, the attracting force is increased in proportion to times and brief moments. This force is communicated, therefore, in time. We see the same thing in examples of minimal attraction. If you pick up a hair or handkerchief as soon as it falls to the ground, you will find that it has less dust on it than if you leave it on the ground for some time. This can only happen because time is needed to attract the dust which sticks to it. If, for instance, you leave your Spanish snuff in the snuff-box for a long time, it curls up, but so slowly that the movement goes unnoticed while you look at the snuff. Moreover, chemists know perfectly well that time is needed to obtain effects from affinities. Again, just as the endeavour to move needs time to communicate itself, so it needs time to be eliminated. A body shot into the air needs time to extinguish the movement which carries it up. Before falling, it halts for a tiny moment. The earth, for example, when it reaches its solstice, pauses and then takes up its reverse movement slowly, etc.

9. (1217).

If a wheel rotates quickly, the eye can no longer discern the spokes of the wheel. It fuses them together as though they were continued planes rather than slender spokes. This happens through the extremely rapid change of sensations which overtake another in the optic sensory. The fact is indubitable, and provides powerful confirmation of what I set out to prove. Granted high speed in the wheel, fusion is present in the sensory which receives impressions with too rapid a succession. We have to say that, if the wheel rotates less quickly so that the eye can distinguish its spokes, impressions follow one another less quickly with the result that each impression *endures* sufficiently long to be distinguished by the intuiting subject. But impressions follow one another in proportion to the quickness of the passage of the different states of the wheel they represent. If, therefore, impressions endure in the case of lower speed, it is necessary that successive states of the wheel also endure. Hence, the wheel does not run with continuous motion. Here we have already a *physical demonstration* that the motion of the wheel is not continuous as we normally believe.

But we can also prove from observation that fusion of the sensations is the result of the wheel's moving too quickly. The impressions made on the eye by the wheel follow one another with extreme speed so that a preceding sensation, which perhaps is not fully formed, is cancelled by a following sensation. In fact, if a wheel rotating swiftly in the dark is suddenly illuminated by a flash, the eye which receives the impression of the flash immediately distinguishes the spokes as if the wheel were stationary. The first impression has time to be formed into a sensation and be adverted to because there is no other impression. — Moreover, there is also an evident proof, from dreams, that the phenomenon of continuity of motion arises in feeling even when continuous motion is lacking in the external body. Movement is present in dreams. Sometimes we dream that we are running, or that we see other objects, persons or things, move swiftly with continuous motion. But outside ourselves no body corresponds to the representation of the phantasm; in other words, there is nothing moving outside us, either with continuous motion or any other kind. It may perhaps be objected that continuous movement is present in the molecules of our brain, the organ of phantasy, and that these lend themselves to the production of the scene of movement in our inner sensory. This, however, is impossible; the images do not arise in any way through movement on the part of molecules, but of molecules acting upon one another in such harmony that the image corresponds in all its parts to the corresponding movements of the group of molecules. We can see this in the coloured images of the eye which are aroused only if a fascia of rays disposed in different colours contemporaneously touches the retina. These rays are distributed according to the colours of the image which they arouse through the image in feeling. Hence, when we see a person running in a dream, we have to suppose that many images of the person follow one another granted that corresponding, harmonious movements follow one another in a band, as it were, of the brain. We can never suppose that the image itself runs through the brain. Nor can we suppose that the movements of the image aroused in the first tiny period of time run through the brain. In this case (if it were possible) we would not see the image run through the brain; the image would change into various bands of colour. The apparent motion, therefore, comes about through a number of ever-new, stationary images which succeed one another as a result of corresponding movements aroused in various tiny, tightly packed spaces of the brain. Each of these images lasts for the brief period necessary for its formation, for being distinguished and for memorisation.

10. (1228).

This is the source of the direct confutation of the pantheism of the School of Elea and, properly speaking, of Xenophanes, philosophers who fell into the error of pantheism because of their inability to uncover the mystery of transient acts. Xenophanes' starting point was *a nihilo nihil fit* [from nothing, nothing comes] (Aristotle, *bk. on Xenophanes, Zeno and Gorgia*). This meant: transient acts are in opposition to the principle of cause, and consequently are not. I reply: 'It is false that transient acts are in opposition to the principle of cause; these acts simply suppose a first cause which operates without the presence of transient acts. Now, because the transient acts have to remain distinct from the cause, it is necessary for them to be an effect of the operation of that cause, but not acts of which the cause is the subject. In other words, this cause, when operating immanently, creates immanent and transient acts outside itself.' The following quotation from Aristotle, if considered carefully, also shows that this is the logical origin of Eleatic pantheism. Aristotle wanted to indicate how philosophers, in their search for a material cause, were forced by the connection of ideas to pass to an investigation of efficient cause. He says: 'But moving in this direction, they were led and forced to go further by the subject itself. If all corruption especially, and all generation, proceeds from something, whether a single thing or several things, how does this happen and what is its cause? A given subject is unable to change itself. For example, neither wood nor bronze is a cause of changes in itself; wood does not make itself into a bed, nor does bronze make itself into a statue; the cause of the change is something different. Searching for this, however, means searching for another principle (*other than the material principle*). Like ourselves, these people are searching for the beginning of movement. Those, however, who first raised this question and posited a single subject were unaware of any difficulty. But some of those who set up the One, were overcome as it were by this question and said that the One is both immovable and nature in its entirety, not only according to generation and corruption (this is an ancient opinion to which all adhered) but indeed according to every transmutation. And this is proper to them' (*Metaph.* 1).

11. (1231).

Ancient philosophy found itself in great difficulty as a result of the poverty and imperfection of philosophical language. Tiedemann makes this observation about Greek philosophy in expounding Plato's *Parmenides*. I find the same obstacle present in all periods until our own time. A history of philosophy should bring together with great care examples of such obstacles to the free progress of philosophical thought. They arise from insufficient and ambiguous terms, one of the great sources of dissension and argument amongst philosophers, and a real obstacle to progress, as historians should indicate. However, we have no history of philosophy, nor will we have one soon, nor will the moment for one arise shortly if historians of philosophy, the mother and reason of all sciences, refuse to limit their investigation to narrow areas and provide accurate, partial accounts of Schools or nations. For the moment, I think it useful, whenever I have the opportunity, to indicate examples of the insufficiency of words used by the greatest philosophers, and of the inconstancy with which they use them.

The word *motion* pertains properly speaking to bodies, which pass from one place to another. Note, however, that little by little it receives a wider meaning in the *Psychology* left us by Aristotle where eventually it comes to mean generally every *transient act*.

1. Aristotle first distinguishes four species of motion: *passage*, *alteration*, *increase* and *decrease* (bk. 1, c. 1). Now, it is clear that *alteration*, *increase* and *decrease* are not properly speaking *motion*, but acts produced in a material substance by concurrence of multiple movements. Nevertheless, these so-called species of movement are confined to the body; they are movements, and effects of movements, in a material substance.

2. According to this concept of motion, Aristotle distinguishes *motion* from *sense* by maintaining that some of his predecessors had posited the essence of the soul in *motion*; some in *sense*; others in both (bk. 1, c. 1). A little later he says, rather incoherently, that 'all of them define the soul as three things: motion, sense and incorporeality.' He seems to mean by 'incorporeal', the intellect or idea. He finds motion also in sense. He says: 'But if the soul moves, someone will say that it is moved especially by sensible things,' and then, attacking Plato, adds that he (Plato) 'wants the soul of the universe to be what is called 'intellect', because this philosopher gives it circular motion. But the movement of the sensitive or appetitive soul is not circular.'

3. Next, not content with granting motion also to sense, Aristotle posits it about intellect. He says that 'the motion of the intellect is intellection.' Then, however, he removes motion from the intellect by saying that 'intellection is rather like a certain kind of quiet, a kind of state.' Again, in the following

chapter, he states that suffering, happiness and reasoning are *movements*, but maintains that the soul produces such movements without moving. It simply makes the heart and the body move, partly through the movement called 'passage', partly through the movement called 'alteration'. He says: 'This must not be understood as if motion were somehow in the soul. Sometimes, however, it comes to the soul, sometimes from the soul. For example, sense goes from these things (to the soul). Memory, then, comes out of it into those movements or states of quiet which are found in the instruments used by the senses.'

It may well be that when Aristotle speaks of some *movement* on the part of sense or reason, he uses the word metaphorically, but it cannot be denied that such use of metaphor often makes his reasoning laborious and uncertain.

In the third book of *Metaphysics* he uses the word with an even more extended meaning. He says that 'all actions are done through movement.' Plato, with the whole of ancient philosophy, attributes the same very broad meaning to the word *motion* (κίνησις) (cf. *Theaetetus*, and the whole of ancient philosophy).

12. (1368).

The ancients disputed whether Parmenides posited two kinds of things: *ens*, the object of truth (τὴν ἀλήθειαν) and non-ens, the opinions of the commonalty (τὰς δόξας). Alexander maintained that Parmenides rejected as pure fallacy non-ens and the opinions of the commonalty. Simplicius disagreed, maintaining he accepted both (Simplicius, *Phys.*, 1, f. 9). It is clear however that Parmenides 1. certainly spoke about the opinions of the commonalty, which he explained in the second part of his poem, but 2. at the same time rejected them as false, and accepted ens alone; indeed according to him, a single, unique and extremely simple ens existed which was all things at once. This is sustained by all the passages where Aristotle speaks about Parmenides, for example, *Metaph.*, 1: 6 and *De Gener. et Cor.*, 1: 8. In these two places Aristotle says that if Parmenides accepted sensible things, we must understand that he accepted them as an argument illustrating the false opinions of the commonalty, which is really a non-acceptance of them. I am surprised that the learned Karsten, referring to Aristotle's words, says that Parmenides 'neither accepted one truth nor disdained opinions. He did not exclude either, but granted each its place' (*Philosoph. Graecor. Veterum reliquiae*, vol. 1, p. 145, Amsterdam, 1830). Indeed Karsten, acknowledging the opinion that Aristotle had not interpreted Parmenides well or judged him equably, was forced to conclude that Aristotle's witness was not very great at this point. In his first book of *Physics*, Aristotle says that Parmenides' argument for proving the unity of ens does not pertain to physics, but nevertheless always supposes that Parmenides, in accepting *one ens*, wanted to establish a principle for explaining natural things. As Karsten himself acknowledges, this is clearly false because in fact Parmenides distinguished between the teaching about ens, which for him was the teaching of *truth*, and *opinions*, which refer to natural things and are, according to him, a false way. Karsten, opposing Aristotle, acutely notes, 'When he (Parmenides) considered the nature of ens, he was not looking for the principles of the world. He did not bring both arguments together; in one, he considered truth alone; the other he attributed to what opinion saw. But later thinkers, particularly the sceptics, emulated the Eleatics in many things, usurping and purloining their arguments for the purpose of refuting the tenets of the physicists, and overthrowing the whole nature of things. Many of these thinkers wrongly considered the physicists' opinion to be common among the Eleatics' (Sext. Emp., *Adv. Math.*, 10, 5.33; Fabricius, *ibid*, and *Ad Calcid.*, bk. 1). In some places Aristotle, clearly taking the one of Parmenides as the principle of natural things, censures him for it. In others (*Metaph.*, 1), he turns to the two principles of heat and cold, which Parmenides takes as *the opinion of the commonalty*, not as truth. According to him, Parmenides 'was compelled to follow appearances, and therefore thought that things were ONE ACCORDING TO REASONS and MANY ACCORDING TO SENSE'. If Aristotle had wanted to refute Parmenides fairly, he should have shown that 1. ONE ACCORDING TO REASON did not exist, and 2. the MANY ACCORDING TO SENSE did not sufficiently explain the principles of heat and cold, etc. Instead, in many places he exerts himself to show that the *one* does not explain natural things, which was precisely Parmenides' intention. Nevertheless I think Parmenides, as a disciple of Xenophanes, had in mind physical things, even if he does not say so, and that in conceiving his *one ens* he was speaking solely of the *universe*. Aristotle makes the following distinction between Xenophanes, Parmenides and Melissus:

> Parmenides seems to have been concerned with ONE PERTAINING TO CONCEPT (*unum secundum rationem*), and Melissus with ONE PERTAINING TO MATTER; hence Parmenides says that the one is finite, while Melissus says it is infinite. Xenophanes, although anterior to Melissus (we are told that Parmenides had been his pupil), posited the ONE without clearly explaining it and, it would seem, without describing its nature.
>
> *Metaph.*, 1.

But all this is conjecture on the part of Aristotle. Parmenides' arguments are certainly drawn from the CONCEPT OF ENS, but some expressions of his (and Melissus may have spoken more openly on the matter) show that he had in mind the immensity and continuity of space. Examples are: the attributes of *continuity*, *divisibility* and *immobility*, which he attributes to ens, and his description of it as one ens adhering to another (ἐὸν γὰρ ἐόντι πελάζει, cf. Karsten v. 80) and homogeneous in its parts:

> It is not divisible
> But totally like itself.
> Nor is one part like another.
> One part is not so prevalent,
> Nor another so weak
> That adherence is lost.
> The whole is full of ens.
>
> Vv. 77–79.

Parmenides' speculative mind may well have contemplated ens in the pure idea, and at the same time retained something of the *sensism* from which it was so difficult to be free. After all, philosophy was just beginning, and the nature of spirit had not yet been sufficiently considered. In fact the problem was so great that philosophy was never fully liberated from it, even by

Plato, as I could show — but not without prolonged discussion. But I will offer other arguments on the problem when I deal with it in other places. I will conclude this long observation by noting that Aristotle could perhaps be excused for using the *one* of Parmenides as the principle of things because, as I said, Parmenides spoke rationally about ens while keeping an eye indirectly on the material universe. It remains true however that Aristotle did not see the necessity for excluding the continuum and the continuously changeable, and that he was wrong in censuring Parmenides for saying that ens is continuous (συνεχὲς) and indivisible (ἀδιάιρετον) — according to Aristotle, only a mathematical point is indivisible (*Phys.*, 1, 3). Extension is certainly continuous and indivisible, although it possesses these qualities in the sentient principle, as I have shown.

13. (1368).

What is the precise line separating Parmenides' system from Plato's? Basing our judgment on the only extant fragments of Parmenides, we must say that he was content to establish a theory of *ens* in general without applying it to the various classes and categories of entia. The theory of ideas is still not present in Parmenides, and although he establishes that ens is the *truth* and that the truth is found by *reason* and not by sensible appearances, he does not give evidence of knowledge of the doctrine of ideas. On the other hand, if we consider the philosophical systems which his own opposed, that is, the Ionian systems, we see that his interest lay in physical, natural things, whose falseness, and principally their continuous flux, he strove to demonstrate. This explains the second part of his poem τὰ πρὸς δόξαν, where indeed he explains the doctrine of material nature as it appears to the senses. Parmenides had in mind only physical things in order to show that they were and put the truth in their place. This explains why Aristotle expounded Parmenides' teaching as if Parmenides wanted to indicate with his ens the principle of nature (*Phys.*, 1: 2; *Metaph.*, 1: 5). In fact Aristotle criticised Parmenides because, he said, Parmenides' system was not at all in keeping with nature. Thus Aristotle treated Parmenides, according to Bessarion, as he, that is, Aristotle had treated the Pythagoreans. Bessarion said: 'Aristotle applied to sensible things what the Pythagoreans had said about numbers and intelligible substances' (*In Calumn.*, 2, 4). The truth is that Parmenides was content to explain the general theory of ens without applying it, but simply contenting himself with the insufficiency of knowledge of physical things. Then came Plato. Although he supported Parmenides' general doctrine of *ens*, he added that it was true only for *ideal being*, but allowed that passing things ('generable', as he called them, because they have no permanence) do not endure: they could be considered as non-entia, and consequently as blind and *per se* unintelligible. This application to ideas of Parmenides' theory of ens was Plato's great contribution to the system of this sublime Italian philosopher. The Neoplatonists did Plato an injustice by attributing the addition to Parmenides himself.

14. (1461).

This fact of sense deceived the Aristotelians, who attributed a species of abstraction to sense. But St. Thomas uses it most aptly to demonstrate that *abstraction* does not pertain to the object but to a *psychological law*. He says: 'We can see a similarity of this in sense. Sight sees the colour of an apple without its odour. If we ask where is the colour seen without the odour, it is clear that the colour is seen only in the apple. The fact that it is perceived without the odour is partly due to vision in so far as the likeness of colour but not of odour is in vision. Similarly the humanity we understand is only in this or that human being, but the apprehension of humanity without its individual conditions, which is abstraction FOLLOWED BY THE CONSIDERATION OF UNIVERSALITY, concerns humanity as perceived by the intellect in which lies THE LIKENESS OF THE NATURE OF SPECIES, but not of individual principles' (*S.T.*, 1, q. 85, art. 2, ad 2). We must note several points here. An agent acting in two differently disposed patients produces two different passions. Hence the one and same body acting in different organs produces different passions. One organ cannot receive the action proper to another organ; for example, the organ of sight cannot receive the action of odour but only the action which causes colour; it is limited to colour and totally without odour or other sensations. This is still not what the Scholastics call *intentio universalitatis* [consideration of universality], because real odour is as particular to the organ of smell as colour is to the eye, and a body to any sensory. Sense therefore contains what is particular, which can be *partial* in the way, if we prefer, that the effect of smell is partial relative to all the other effects which a body can produce in the various sensories. There is nothing universal here. Sense contains something exclusive and negative: the sensation of colour excludes that of odour and the other sensations pertaining to the other senses. But *what is universal* does not have this characteristic of exclusivity and negativity; rather it is something that broadens out and encloses particular infinities in its possibility. Furthermore it cannot be partial because both a part and a whole can be universalised provided they are considered possible (ideal): an odour or sound can be universalised as a body can, even when endowed with all its sensible qualities without exception — the idea of a body is certainly universal. Hence, because the *consideration of universality* consists in what is possible, only the mind, not sense, can attain to this consideration. Sense does not feel *what is possible* but only what is real. *Universalisation* therefore and its sequel, *abstraction*, are operations of the mind, different operations which must not be confused. The mind can universalise only by adding what is *possible*, that is, the idea, to things perceived by sense. It cannot therefore extract this idea from sense; on the contrary, it adds it to things felt.

The Aristotelian illusion was caused by their failure to consider that sense, stripped of all that the understanding adds to it, feels only its modified self, and in this modification feels the direct (extrasubjective) modifier. The understanding however perceives an ens, an object, in opposition to itself as subject. Thus the modifications of sense receive a limit from the simple limitation of the sentient subject and of the action done in the subject. But the object, the ens, is that which is, and can be given only in its entirety to the understanding. Hence, when the understanding limits it by abstraction, it necessarily does so by limiting its attention but without ceasing to have the entire object before the mind. A particular sensory however has only its own passion, for example, odour; the other passions do not pertain to it. But the whole of ens pertains to the intellect, and subjective attention alone is limited by a special act so that a part of ens may be considered more vividly. If this were not the case, the human being would take the abstract as the entire ens.

15. (1580).

When the Egyptians mourned Adonis, they shaved their heads and slashed their bodies. They did the same in other instances of mourning (Herod., 2, c. 85). We know of similar practices among the Moabites (Is 15; Jer 48), the Babylonians (Is 7), the Assyrians (Strab. 16), the Persians (Herod., 9, c. 24) and the Scythians (Herod., 4, c. 71). On the death of Hephaestion, Alexander had all the manes and tails of the horses and mules docked (Plut., in *Alex*). On the death of Dido, Anna slashes herself: 'Her sister tears at her mouth with her nails, and beats her breasts with her fists' (Bk. 4, 673). Similar customs are found among barbarian nations in whom natural instinct is so active and dominant. Such acts, precisely because they are natural, instinctive effects of sorrowing love, are thought pleasing to the dead and therefore placatory. Pisastratus, the son of Nestor (Homer, *Odyssey*, 4) tells Menelaus that nothing better can be done to honour the dead than to shave his head and shed tears. Plutarch narrates how the cutting off of ears or nose, or the mutilation of oneself in some other way seemed to some barbarian peoples very pleasing to the dead (*De Consol. ad Apoll.*). Servius writes: 'Varro says that at burials and in mourning it was a custom to mutilate one's mouth so that satisfaction could be made to the dead by the flow of blood' (*4 Aeneid.*). In this last concept however another secret of human nature is concealed: why is the need to placate the dead presupposed? Why the presupposition that the dead long for blood?

16. (fn. 340).

The ancients, who were still without a formed *philosophical language*, expressed their thoughts about *individuation* (as about other difficult questions) in a rather confused way. They often confused *individual* with *subsistent*. Thus the Aristotelian affirmation that 'matter is the principle of individuation' meant, in their opinion, that matter made the individual *subsist*. But when they were discussing individuals lacking matter, they made an exception to their rule and said that in this case the *form* itself had to be subsistent. St. Thomas says: 'This kind of form, which is not acceptable in matter but is *per se* subsistent, is individuated by the very fact that it cannot be received in another' (*S.T.*, I, q. 3, art 2. ad 3). Consequently they could not conceive how form could individuate and not be subsistent. Again St. Thomas says, 'In these things which are not composed of matter and form and in which individuation is not present through individual matter, THE FORMS THEMSELVES MUST BE THE UNDERLYING SUBSISTENCES. Thus there is no difference in them between the underlying factor and nature' (*S.T.*, I, q. 3, art. 3). The truth therefore is that 1. only *form* individuates; 2. form is either *ideal* or *real*. As ideal, it is known in the species which, although it individuates ideal being and is the principle of individuation (of a specific individual), does not multiply an ens, nor is it the *principle of multiplication of individuals*. As real, form is the *principle of multiplication of individuals*. Moreover, the forms of matter, which need matter in order to subsist, do not receive from matter their aptitude for individuating or for multiplying individuals. Finally, 3. they confused *form* with *species* or idea, just as they confused matter with subsistence. They said that pure form 'is the intellect in act' (St. Thomas, *S.T.*, I, q. 66, art. 2), which is true however only of God, in whom the ideal form does not differ from the real form or subsistence, but not true of the angels, who are understood not through their subsistence but through an idea.

Index of Biblical References

Numbers in roman indicate paragraphs or, where stated, the appendix (app.); numbers in italic indicate footnotes. Bible references are from RSV (Common Bible) unless marked †. In these cases, where the author's use of Scripture is dependent solely upon the Vulgate, the Douai version is used.

Index of Persons

General Index

Numbers in roman indicate paragraphs or, where stated, the appendix (app.) and pages (pp.); numbers in italic indicate footnotes

the beautiful and, 1768
unitive affection in, 1076

Anthropomorphism
gods and, 1724

Appetence
common names and, 1463

Apprehension
affirmation, persuasion and,
1028–1029

Archetypes
faculty of, 1063

Aristotle
intellect according to, 1282–1292

Arts
successive harmony and, 1779

Assent
decision and, 1111

Astrolatry
origin of Ωεός and, *194*

Attention
consciousness and, 1480
free, 1684
intelligent subject and, *105*
limitation and concentration of,
1474–1478
need and, 1481
rational principle and, 1023–1024,
1032
sense-experiences and, 975
theoretical and practical reason and,
1408
two guides of, 1469
what is real and, 1724
words and, 1526

Attraction
motion and, 819, 1254, 1258, 1261

Authors
moral duty of, 932

Aversions
foundation of, 1702

Babies
abstraction and, 1314
brute-matter and, *20*

first sounds, *326*
particulars, universals and sense in,
1314
reflection and, 1314
words and, 1314

Beauty
aesthetic, 1770
contemplation and, 1062, 1414
harmony and, *307*
pleasure of, 1770
unity and, 1546

Being
abstractions and, 1525
act and, 874
active principle of real, 1026
contingent, 1046, 1344
corporeal entity and order of,
840–841
double perception of, *111*
entities and, 1175
good and, 1008
idea and, 1339
ideal and contingent, 1001
in itself, 1332, 1338
intellect and, 1006–1010
intuition of, 1338
mental beings, 1630
mode of, 741
moral, 952, 955, 1007
necessary, 1046
order of, 896, 906, 951, 1048, 1058,
1629
order within, 741–743
pure, 741, 895
reality and intuited, 889, 1001
soul and ideal and real, 954–955, 1001
substance and, 874
supreme norm, 1700
theoretical and practical reason and,
1057
three modes of, 895–396, 951; *51*
trine form, 1006
see also **Being in General, Human
Being(s), Ideal Being, Intelligent
Being, Sensitive Being**

Being in General
God and, 1660
human activity and, 1700
intelligibility and, 872
knowledge and, 1661
reality and 1661
simple and unchangeable, 892

being and, 741–743, 746
feeling and, 741
multiplicity and, 1059
subjective and moral-objective, 894
   see also **Moral Order, Rational**
      Order, Supernatural
      State/Order

Organ(s)
connection between, 998
sensitivity and, 998

Organisation
action of instincts and, 984, 988
individuality of bodies and, 1646
movement and, 982

Ownership
animal passion, 1081
human, 1081

Pain
action of ens as, 1573
feeling and, 1099
movements and, 1090

Panidealist
error of, 1311

Panpsychism
German philosophers and, 1286

Pantheism
destruction of, 1185, 1500
Eleatic, *app.* no. 10
two false principles and, 1664

Passions
affections and, 1071
animal, 1073–1089
instinct and, 1071–1072
rational, 1073–1089, 1091
sources of, 1089
sympathetic, 1089

Passivity
activity and, 947, 1021, 1066; *52*
receptivity and, 948, 974, 1066; *52,*
   163

Perception
acts of, 893
as feeling, 1024
concept acquired in, 1461–1462, 1468
duration of, 1154

elements of, 1460
extended felt element and, 1176
extension and, 779
feeling and, 1181
first act and, 1354
first, fundamental, 961, 1013,
   1022–1023, 1028, 1722
ideas and, 1459
infinite and, 1386–1395
intellective perception, 1021
intuition, reflection and, 1184
judgment and, 1149
knowledge of body and, 772, 775, 823
law of, 1306–1311, 1419
levels of, 1027–1032
limited ens and, 1421
matter and, 826, 840
natural sciences and, 1113
object and, 997
objective, 1386–1387
origin of language and, 1467
particularity of, 1463
real, contingent thing and, 1356
reflection and repeated, 1032
sensation and, *213*
substance and, 778, 842
   see also **Intellective Perception**

Personification
rational creation and, 1050, 1052

Person
individuality and, *341*
ontological condition of being, 876
peace and concord of just, 1440
principle of, 1060
struggle of malicious, 1440

Persuasion
affirmation, apprehension and, 1028,
   1030
concept and, 1306
faith and, *app.* no. 4
knowledge by, 1492
opinion and, 1492
spirit and, 1499

Phantasms
ens and, *51*
perception of the, 1467
spontaneous motion of, 1459
thought and, 1459–1460, 1521